Food Loss and Waste Policy

This book examines policy responses to food waste and loss, an issue of significant, global concern, with one-third of food produced for human consumption lost or wasted.

Investigating food waste and loss under an interdisciplinary lens, the contributors employ a variety of methodological approaches, including quantitative and qualitative techniques, drawing on in-depth case studies and action research. The volume is organised into four parts: Understanding Food Loss and Waste, International Programmes, National Policies, and Local Initiatives. The first part introduces the reader to the concept of food loss and waste, how it can be measured, its causes and consequences, and how it can be reduced. The second part is dedicated to international and cross-country case studies, with six chapters reviewing national policies implemented in France, Italy, Romania, Japan, China, and the United States. In Part Four, three chapters are dedicated to local food recovery and redistribution initiatives. By focusing on different territories and different levels of governance, the book provides a detailed evaluation of food loss and waste policies, the barriers and opportunities of implementing the policies, as well as the impact they are actually having. The chapters are both descriptive and evaluative and draw out lessons for designing, implementing, and reforming programmes.

This book will be of great interest to students and scholars working on food waste, food policy, sustainable food systems, agricultural production and supply chains, and public policy, as well as policymakers involved with developing and implementing programmes and policies to regulate and reduce food waste and loss.

Simone Busetti is a policy analyst and evaluator and is currently Associate Professor of Political Science and Public Policy Analysis at the University of Teramo, Italy. He has worked on local development, public administration reform, and food policy and served as a professional evaluator for several public administrations in Italy.

Noemi Pace is Associate Professor of Economics at the University of Teramo. She is also a research fellow at the UCL Centre for Global Health Economics, UK, and a research fellow in the Center for Economic and International Studies (CEIS) at the University of Tor Vergata, Italy.

Routledge Studies in Food, Society and the Environment

Food Loss and Waste Policy

From Theory to Practice

**Edited by Simone Busetti and
Noemi Pace**

Routledge
Taylor & Francis Group
LONDON AND NEW YORK

earthscan
from Routledge

Cover image: Getty

First published 2023
by Routledge
4 Park Square, Milton Park, Abingdon, Oxon OX14 4RN

and by Routledge
605 Third Avenue, New York, NY 10158

Routledge is an imprint of the Taylor & Francis Group, an informa business

British Library Cataloguing-in-Publication Data
A catalogue record for this book is available from the British Library

Library of Congress Cataloging-in-Publication Data
Names: Busetti, Simone, editor. | Pace, Noemi, editor.
Title: Food loss and waste policy : from theory to practice / Simone
    Busetti, Noemi Pace.
Description: New York, NY : Routledge, [2022] | Includes bibliographical
    references and index.
Identifiers: LCCN 2022017174 (print) | LCCN 2022017175 (ebook) |
    ISBN 9781032129419 (hardback) | ISBN 9781032129358 (paperback) |
    ISBN 9781003226932 (ebook)
Subjects: LCSH: Food waste. | Food industry and trade. | Food supply. |
    Food security.
Classification: LCC HD9000.5 .F6635 2022 (print) | LCC HD9000.5
    (ebook) | DDC 338.1/9—dc23/eng/20220718
LC record available at https://lccn.loc.gov/2022017174
LC ebook record available at https://lccn.loc.gov/2022017175

ISBN: 978-1-032-12941-9 (hbk)
ISBN: 978-1-032-12935-8 (pbk)
ISBN: 978-1-003-22693-2 (ebk)

DOI: 10.4324/9781003226932

Typeset in Bembo
by Apex CoVantage, LLC

Contents

Contributors

Ariel Ardura is Policy attorney based in Washington D.C. Her work primarily focuses on food systems and public health. She currently works as legislative counsel for the D.C. Council; she previously worked as Senior Fellow at the Harvard Law School Food Law and Policy Clinic.

Giulia Bartezzaghi is Program Manager of the Food Sustainability Lab and Director of the Food Sustainability Observatory at Politecnico di Milano, Department of Management, Economics and Industrial Engineering. Her research is focused on sustainability-oriented innovation and circular economy in the agri-food sector.

Omar Benammour is Social Protection Specialist at the Food and Agriculture Organization (FAO) of the UN, in the Inclusive Rural Transformation and Gender Equity division. Previously, he was Social Protection and Safety Nets Officer at the World Food Programme (WFP) and Regional School Feeding and Safety Nets Officer for West Africa.

Emily M. Broad Leib, JD, is Clinical Professor of Law at Harvard Law School, Founding Director of the Harvard Law School Food Law and Policy Clinic, and Deputy Director of the Harvard Law School Center for Health Law and Policy Innovation.

Simone Busetti is Policy analyst and Evaluator and is currently Associate Professor of Political Science and Public Policy Analysis at the University of Teramo. He has worked on local development, public administration reform, and food policy and served as a professional evaluator for several public administrations in Italy.

Romina Cavatassi is Lead economist in IFAD. She leads the Impact Assessment and Research, managed the Rural Development Report 2021, and led the Environment and Climate team. She holds a Ph.D. from Wageningen University, an M.Sc. from the LSE, and a master's degree in economics from the University of Bologna.

Clara Cicatiello is Assistant Professor of Agricultural Economics at University of Tuscia, Italy. Since 2020, she is the coordinator of the H2020 project

LOWINFOOD, focusing on implementation of innovations against food waste. She is Lecturer in food marketing and development economics and author of 31 Scopus-indexed articles, with over 500 citations.

Chen Liu, Ph.D., is Senior researcher at the Institute for Global Environmental Strategies (IGES). Before joining IGES, she worked as an associate professor in Nagoya University (2010–2014), Japan. She has worked on a wide range of environmental issues, including municipal solid waste, 3R policies, food production, consumption, and waste.

Claudia Colicchia is Associate Professor of Logistics and Supply Chain Management at Politecnico di Milano, Department of Management, Economics and Industrial Engineering, and Visiting Fellow in the Faculty of Business, Law and Politics, University of Hull, UK. She collaborates with the Food Sustainability Lab at Politecnico di Milano.

Fabrizio D'Angelo is Sustainability Project Officer at the European Economic and Social Committee (EESC) and at the European Committee of the Regions (CoR), where he is running a project on food waste monitoring and food donation. He is also a member of the EU Inter-institutional group on Green Public Procurement.

Anna R. Davies is Professor and Chair of Geography, Environment & Society at Trinity College Dublin, the University of Dublin. She is the principal investigator for multiple research projects, including the ERC research project, SHARECITY, which uses a collaborative and trans-disciplinary approach to assess the practice and sustainability potential of city-based food sharing economies.

Robert Delve is Lead global technical advisor, agronomy in IFAD, leading the team in providing technical support to the design, supervision, and implementation of projects. He holds a Ph.D. degree from the University of London. Before joining IFAD, he lived and worked in Africa for more than 25 years.

Daniele Eckert Matzembacher holds a Ph.D. degree in Management from Federal University of Rio Grande do Sul (UFRGS), Brazil. She has experience over ten years in the market, working in the public and private sectors in the management area, project coordination, and team management.

Paola Garrone is Full Professor of Business and Industrial Economics at Politecnico di Milano, Department of Management, Economics and Industrial Engineering. Paola is the School's deputy director for Sustainability, and a co-director of the Food Sustainability Lab. Her research focuses on food recovery and redistribution, sustainable agri-food start-ups and packaging innovation.

Giuseppe Maggio is Assistant Professor of Economics at the University of Palermo, and his research applies spatial models to answer questions in the field of agricultural economics, development, and human health. Giuseppe has served as a consultant for several international organisations, including the FAO, IFAD, and the World Bank.

Luciana Marques Vieira is Professor of Sustainable Operations Management at Fundacao Getulio Vargas/EAESP, Brazil. She holds a Ph.D. degree in Agricultural Economics from the University of Reading (UK). Her research interests are global value chains, multistakeholder initiatives and agri-food chains.

Alwynne McGeever is Postdoctoral researcher for the ERC funded research project SHARECITY. Her role raises awareness about SHARECITY's free sustainability impact assessment toolkit for food sharers, SHARE IT, working with food sharing groups to demonstrate their social, environmental, and economic impacts. Her research interests include sustainable development, consumption, and production.

Marco Melacini is Full Professor of Logistics Management and International Distribution at Politecnico di Milano, Department of Management, Economics and Industrial Engineering. He is the scientific responsible of the Food Sustainability Observatory at Politecnico di Milano. He is Scientific Advisor of the 'Neighbourhood Hubs Against Food Waste' project.

Marie Mourad, Ph.D., works as a food waste expert and consultant for non-profits and governmental agencies in France and the United States. Her Ph.D. in Sociology focused on public policies against food waste and new markets for surplus food in the two countries. Her work has been published internationally including in the *Journal of Cleaner Production* and the *Routledge Handbook of Food Waste*.

Noemi Pace is Associate Professor of Economics at the University of Teramo. She is also a research fellow at the UCL Centre for Global Health Economics and at the Center for Economic and International Studies (CEIS) at University of Tor Vergata.

Christian Reynolds is Senior Lecturer at the Centre for Food Policy, City University, London. Christian has worked on the issues of food loss and waste and sustainable diets in Australia, New Zealand, Indonesia, the United Kingdom, the United States, and Europe. Christian also researches sustainable cookery, food history, and the political power of food in international relations.

Andrea Rizzuni is Researcher and Ph.D. candidate at Politecnico di Milano, Department of Management, Economics and Industrial Engineering. He researches on cross-sector partnerships between business and non-profit organisations and at the Food Sustainability Lab, where his focus is mainly on collaborative networks for surplus food recovery and redistribution.

Daniella Salazar Herrera is a Fishery Officer (Social Protection) at the Food and Agriculture Organization (FAO) of the UN, in the Fisheries Division. In this role, she is supporting the coordination of the Social Protection for Fisheries and Aquaculture project (SocPro4Fish) and the related area of work. She holds an M.Phil. degree in Development Studies from the University of Cambridge.

Cristina Vasilescu is Policy Analyst and Evaluator, focusing on EU, Romanian, and Italian sustainable development policy from both a social and environmental perspective. In this field, she conducts research on agriculture and food, renewable energy, participatory processes for sustainable energy and institutional mechanisms and capacities for sustainable development.

Xiaohua Yu is Professor at the Department of Agricultural Economics and Rural Development at the University of Göttingen. His research interests cover agricultural economics, development economics, and behavioural economics. He serves as an associate editor for Agricultural Economics and China Economic Review.

Qiushi Yue is Programme Officer at the Food and Agriculture Organization (FAO) of the UN, in the Inclusive Rural Transformation and Gender Equity division. Previously, she worked with the UN system in China, including serving as a Donor Relations Officer with the World Food Programme (WFP) China.

Is this the era of food waste policy?

Simone Busetti and Noemi Pace

Scattered on the floor are grapes, leaves of vegetables, half a lemon, nuts, figs, and other edible food waste. It could be the score of some dumpster diving, but it is not. It is a decorative mosaic from the second century AD displayed in the Vatican Museums in Rome, a fine example of *asàrotos òikos*, or 'unswept floor'. Like the ancient Greeks before them, patricians and upper-class Romans used to decorate their dining rooms with hyperrealistic representations of the debris of a banquet; food waste was a symbol of the wealthy elite.

In the last 2,000 years, these decorations have gone out of fashion. We no longer showcase our garbage with pride, but food loss and waste (FLW) is an integral part of our lives. For an intuitive picture of the magnitude of the problem, start thinking of the last piece of food you wasted: an unopened package passed the expiry date, some spoiled fruit, leftovers from dinner, or the cooked food you diligently stored but then forgot. Now, consider that not only do these things happen in every household worldwide, but that the food you throw away has also survived a long journey along which other pieces of food just did not make it. Some remained in the field or were discarded for marketing standards, while others were just too abundant and were therefore destroyed to avoid price collapse. Some were rejected for passing the sell-by date. And still others were just a bit blemished or their packaging too damaged to be displayed to you; they were perfectly edible but never reached your table.

The latest estimates reveal that more than one-third of the food produced is lost or wasted. The Food and Agriculture Organization of the United Nation (FAO) estimated that 13.8% of food produced in 2016 was lost from farm up to, but excluding, the retail stage, with regional peaks reaching 20–21% (FAO 2019). In addition to losses, 17% of global food production is wasted in households, food services, and retail, amounting to about 931 million tonnes of food waste in 2019 alone (UNEP United Nations Environment Programme 2021). FLW has major consequences for environmental sustainability and food security. The FAO estimated that in 2013, FLW was the third largest contributor to GHG emissions after the United States and China, consumed an amount of blue water equivalent to the annual discharge of the Volga River (i.e. 250 km^3), and was produced occupying in vain about 30% of the world's agricultural land area (FAO 2013).

DOI: 10.4324/9781003226932-1

However, if there is an FLW crisis, it is not a crisis of attention. Interest in the topic began to rise in the aftermath of food price spikes between 2008 and 2011, when reducing waste and losses began to be reconsidered as a tool to increase food security (Rosegrant et al. 2018). More governments took action against FLW, and NGOs exposed the paradox of vast quantities of food surpluses failing to reach people in need (Lang and Heasman 2015). All major food institutions started to work on FLW, and in 2015, the problem obtained global institutionalisation. That year, the General Assembly of the United Nations adopted the 2030 Agenda for Sustainable Development. Among its 17 Sustainable Development Goals (SDGs), SDG 12 aims to ensure sustainable consumption and production patterns and sets a target (12.3) to halve per capita global FLW by 2030.

FLW is high on the public agenda. Since the 1990s, academic publications on the topic have constantly grown, with steep acceleration in the last 10–20 years (Chen et al. 2017; Zhang et al. 2018). The COVID-19 pandemic has further increased attention: food hardship has grown (Ziliak 2021), and the redistribution of surplus food to people in need has gained even more importance (Barker and Russell 2020). In March 2022, the latest Synthesis Report for the Food System Summit Dialogues of the United Nations reported that 72% of National Pathway Documents referenced 'ending food loss and waste' among their priority themes (United Nations 2022). Hundreds of government officials at all jurisdictional levels, international organisations, businesses, scholars from many disciplines, and citizens worldwide are thinking about reducing FLW. We have entered the era of food waste policy.

Indeed, greater centrality in public debate has meant that hundreds of putative solutions have been proposed. In the United States, ReFED reviewed 27 initiatives (ReFED 2016), later expanded into 42 potential solutions grouped around seven action areas (ReFED 2021). In the European Union, a Joint Research Centre report analysed 22 types of interventions (Caldeira, De Laurentiis, and Sala 2019), while the EU Platform on Food Losses and Food Waste (2019) presented 47 recommendations for prevention. As a last example, the World Resources Institute recently compiled a global agenda with 107 'To Dos', a list that was not intended to be exhaustive (Flanagan, Robertson, and Hanson 2019). More examples are reviewed by Christian Reynolds in Chapter 3.

Expanding on these inventories is not the ambition of this book, which takes precisely the opposite direction. Proposals of innovations constitute the fundamental first step towards policy change, but food waste policy is relatively recent, and the evidence accumulated about how it works is limited. There is a need for more analysis of its effectiveness and what is needed to make it (more) effective. Therefore, the first goal of this book is to conduct an in-depth analysis of a selection of programmes to contribute to the advancement of the evidence base, looking at their results and taking a practical stance towards detecting good ideas, obstacles, and possible advice for designers and implementers.

Its second goal is to frame FLW policy within the broader literature. When a new problem enters public debate, there is a tendency to overemphasise its special character and the distinctiveness of its features and purported solutions. Notwithstanding the obvious peculiarities, food waste policy is not a separate or special field and can profit from the knowledge accumulated in disciplines such as public administration, management, and public policy analysis. New problems are not exempt from old risks, and solutions can emerge thanks to ideas already developed in other sectors. The chapters in this volume present several examples of these circumstances regarding, for instance how the problem of FLW is framed, the likelihood of implementation gaps, and the presence of resistance and inter-administrative conflicts.

Research questions and case selection

The volume starts by addressing two research questions: What works to fight food waste and loss? And how do FLW policies work? The first concerns the impact of interventions, and it is not an easy one to answer. Beyond the difficulties in determining what impacts to measure, there is an overall paucity of data, and in several cases, this impairs a reliable assessment. Nonetheless, all the chapters in this book provide some measures of the effectiveness of the analysed interventions and—depending on the perspective they take—also shed light on the many ways in which effectiveness can be measured, such as reduction of FLW, environmental measures (e.g. efficiency in the use of resources), cost savings, increased food security, nutritional improvements, social impacts (e.g. sense of community), and even anti-corruption. This variety emphasises the multifaceted character of the problem of FLW and the various ways in which the problem and solutions are framed.

Because advancing learning is our main focus, the second question asks: How do interventions work? As mentioned, the book aims to offer an in-depth analysis of the practice of FLW policy—what happens when these tools are implemented on the ground: whether they work as expected, how target groups and beneficiaries react, what administrative and contextual conditions help or hinder effectiveness, and whether there are major gaps in or resistance to implementation.

The chapters intentionally focus on successful and promising interventions. The goal of the book is to discover patterns that can be useful to designers and implementers, and we start with the assumption that—although failures can certainly provide much information and stimulus to change—the conditions of success are present and detectable primarily in those cases that actually deliver positive results. National case studies in Chapters 7–12 provide comprehensive reviews of the interventions implemented in several countries and also present revealing examples of blind spots or cases of outright implementation gaps. Several chapters, especially those investigating local initiatives, highlight barriers and obstacles and suggest ways to overcome these hurdles through innovative interventions. All the chapters present good ideas and lessons for future policymaking.

Beyond looking for programmes and initiatives that have delivered positive results, we selected cases to increase the scope of evidence in terms of both geography and the type of intervention implemented. The chapters span several geographic areas—North and South America, Africa, Europe and Asia—while also differentiating in terms of the scale of the intervention, whether local, national, or supranational. In terms of the type of intervention, the case studies include examples of food redistribution, gleaning, valorisation, information campaigns, labels and certification, regulations, fiscal incentives, and administrative simplifications. Table 0.1 provides a summary of both the geography and the kinds of interventions covered by the book.

The content of the book

The volume is organised into four parts: Understanding FLW, International programmes, National policies, and Local initiatives. The first part comprises Chapters 1–3, which introduce the reader to the concept of FLW, how it can be measured, its causes and consequences, and how it can be reduced.

In Chapter 1, Clara Cicatiello introduces the book by briefly reviewing the definitions of FLW, as well as the rationale for and approaches to assessing FLW. She acknowledges how measurements and methods have greatly expanded in recent years, providing several examples of measurement in different contexts and at different stages of the food supply chain. However, reliability in measurements remains a challenge. After having presented the Food Loss Index and Food Waste Index and reviewed the EU methodology, the chapter analyses several methods of measurement in depth: direct measurement, waste compositional analysis, diaries, scanning, mass balance, food waste coefficients, proxy data, and surveys. The chapter also takes an applied approach, reviewing some of the methodological and practical challenges that practitioners face when using different methods at different stages of the food chain.

Noemi Pace investigates the causes and consequences of FLW in Chapter 2. She provides an extensive literature review that offers several insights into where FLW is produced and why. The chapter analyses micro-, meso-, and macro-level causes across the food supply chain. The impact of FLW is mainly analysed in terms of sustainability and food security. As for environmental consequences, it provides a thorough investigation of FLW's impacts on GHG emissions, depletion of blue water, and landfill disposal. Finally, the chapter provides an analysis of the complex interactions between FLW and food security, showing that positive outcomes following FLW reduction are not guaranteed.

In Chapter 3, Christian Reynolds provides a full overview of policy initiatives developed to tackle FLW, thus introducing the reader to the set of interventions analysed in the case studies. The chapter investigates the food waste hierarchy as a foundational framework for setting up policy actions and then reviews the possible interventions, distinguishing seven types of initiatives:

Table 0.1 Case studies: geographic area and interventions

Case studies	FLW interventions

Chapter 4
Ireland, Costa Rica,
  Alaska (US),
  Brazil
	– Social protection programmes
	– Food redistribution
	– Seafood bycatch redistribution
	– Incorporation of fish bycatch and by-products in school meals

Chapter 5
Indonesia,
  Mozambique,
  Rwanda, Timor-
  Leste, Lower
  Guinea and
  Faranah, Kenya
	– Investments and subsidies for new equipment
	– Infrastructures provision and maintenance
	– Training, capacity building and technical assistance
	– Networking of firms
	– Financial support schemes
	– Climate-smart post-harvest infrastructures
	– Improved access to markets

Chapter 6 European Union	– Regulation – Institutions – Monitoring, forecasting, prevention and redistribution
Chapter 7 France, California (US)	– Economic incentives – Campaigning – Obligation to follow the food waste hierarchy, sign a contract with food banks, sort food before donating – Measurement obligation for business and label for good performers – Food redistribution
Chapter 8 Italy	– Fiscal incentives and discounts on waste collection tax – Good Samaritan Law and donation of food past the best-before date – Software Logistics – Institutions – Data production and campaigns
Chapter 9 Romania	– Food waste law with liability exemption – Registry of food recovery organisations – Yearly plan on reduction by business – VAT exemptions – Food redistribution
Chapter 10 Japan	– Food recycling law and Food loss reduction promotion law – Valorisation – Campaigning and communication initiatives – Review of date marking and practices – Demand forecasting – Recovery and redistribution
Chapter 11 China	– Anti-corruption policy – Regulation against losses across the supply chain – Technological and infrastructural investments – Empty plate movement
Chapter 12 USA	– Good Samaritan Law

Chapter 13
Dublin (IE),
  London (GB),
  Barcelona (ES)
	– Food redistribution intermediary
	– Food service and cooked meals from surplus
	– Gleaning and transformation of gleaned food
	– Online platform for sustainability impact assessment

Chapter 14 Milan (IT)	– Neighbourhood Hubs Against Food Waste
Chapter 15 Sao Paulo (BR)	– Food redistribution intermediary – COVID-19 emergency food redistribution

public policy and regulation, taxes and fees, voluntary agreements, information provision, nudges, changes to standards, and others (including interventions in hospitality, surplus and donation, valorisation and animal feed, and technical and innovative actions). The chapter also discusses cross-cutting issues that impact FLW policy. It acknowledges the need for multiple initiatives to tackle FLW effectively, highlighting that strategies focusing only on reduction and prevention may not have long-term impacts. It also advocates for a broader food system approach, involving all actors in the food chain at all geographic levels. Finally, the chapter stresses paying attention to policy coherence by controlling for positive and negative spillover.

The second part is dedicated to international and cross-country case studies, which are reported in Chapters 4–6. In Chapter 4, Qiushi Yue, Daniella Salazar Herrera, and Omar Benammour discuss how social protection programmes can contribute to a sustainable and inclusive food system. The main proposal of the chapter is that embedding food aid initiatives—which are typically carried out by volunteers and NGOs—within wider social protection programmes can increase their precision, scale, and effectiveness. These kinds of synergies are investigated in four cases: Ireland, Costa Rica, Alaska, and Brazil. The case of Ireland allows for the assessment of the interaction between a supranational programme, the Fund for European Aid to the Most Deprived (FEAD), and its national implementation by the national ministerial administration and food recovery partner. The case of Costa Rica investigates the direct redistribution of food to people in need that was managed by the National Centre for Food Supply and Distribution. The cases of Alaska and Brazil allow us to explore the benefits of programmes for the redistribution of seafood bycatch, avoiding the waste of food and providing recipients quality proteins otherwise unavailable.

In Chapter 5, Romina Cavatassi, Robert Delve, and Giuseppe Maggio review seven interventions funded by the International Fund for Agricultural Development (IFAD). They show how the reduction of food loss, the increase in food security, and rural development are tightly linked. The seven cases in the chapter focus on three industries—fishing, crop production, and livestock—implemented in Indonesia, Mozambique, Rwanda, Timor-Leste, Lower Guinea and Faranah, and Kenya. The projects comprise investments in post-harvest equipment and infrastructures, processing and packaging facilities, market linkages, and training programmes. All the programmes provided relevant results in terms of preventing losses. Evidence from these initiatives allows the authors to draw five lessons regarding the impacts, design and implementation of projects that can reduce food loss, increase income, and ensure food security.

In Chapter 6, Fabrizio D'Angelo traces the history of efforts made by the European Union to tackle FLW. He acknowledges how, together with the SDGs, the first large study to estimate European food waste, the FUSIONS study, worked as a trigger for taking action to fight FLW. The chapter describes EU regulations (the Circular Economy package, the Green Deal, and the Farm to Fork Strategy) and the work of the EU Platform on Food Losses and Waste. The chapter ends with two case studies that analyse EU institutions not as regulators but as practitioners in the reduction of food waste. The case studies explore actions taken by the European Economic and Social Committee, the European Committee of the Regions and the Council of the European Union in reducing food waste on their premises. This 'inside look' allows us to evaluate how many actions can be implemented by the food service and how much effort is required for the successful implementation of a food waste reduction programme.

Part 3 of the book includes six chapters that review national policies implemented in France, Italy, Romania, Japan, China, and the United States. In Chapter 7, Marie Mourad provides an in-depth analysis of French policy, focusing on the 2016 reform. She debunks the idea of a tough French policy mandating a ban on food waste and shows how even apparently tough regulations may result in limited obligations and results. She analyses the obligation to respect the food waste hierarchy, the prohibition to destroy food voluntarily, the mandate to sign a contract with a food assistance organisation, and other regulations subsequent to the 2016 law. The findings indicate that the government capacity to control and enforce obligations is limited, transforming prescriptions into more voluntary measures. The chapter discusses several blind spots of current policymaking, especially regarding the dominance of donation over prevention, the quality of the food donated, the risk of donation dumping, and the unbalanced interests dominating food decision-making.

In Chapter 8, Simone Busetti investigates Italian food waste policy by tracing its evolution from the 1990s to the latest reforms in 2018. The analysis covers a wide array of tools, from incentives to software logistics and new institutions. The chapter shows how the subjects targeted by regulations and incentives may not respond as expected, thus limiting or neutralising the effect of the policy. This is shown in the case of the legal permission to donate food past the best-before date and for the municipal discounts on the waste collection tax. The chapter also stresses the importance of precisely targeting incentives and regulations to address not only the producers of waste, but also the decision-makers who can start prevention and recovery programmes. Finally, the analysis highlights the importance of producing policy-relevant data, discussing two cases related to overproduction in agriculture and consumers' behaviour.

In Chapter 9, Cristina Vasilescu analyses the recent implementation of the 2016 Food Waste Law in Romania. The law endured a tortuous process of amendment, suspension, and substitution that resulted in a completely new law being approved in 2018 and amended in 2020. The process transformed what was a set of compulsory measures into a set of mainly voluntary actions. The sole obligation left in the law mandates that businesses produce yearly plans for how to reduce food waste, a provision that lacks sufficient transparency requirements and enforcement mechanisms. One interesting tool, although insufficiently publicised by the government, is a registry of food banks that could be particularly important in a country in which food donation is new.

After analysing implementation at the local level, the chapter presents two in-depth case studies of organisations involved in food aid.

In Chapter 10, Chen Liu provides an overall investigation of a policy implemented in Japan, looking at actions undertaken by the national and local governments as well as initiatives promoted by businesses. The chapter shows the early commitment of Japan to fighting FLW and reviews regulations and practices for valorisation, recycling, and prevention. It also provides an analysis of several awareness campaigns, communication strategies, and other interventions to change consumer behaviour. Finally, the chapter presents two important initiatives undertaken by businesses regarding date marking. One regards changing the one-third rule, that is how the period from the date of manufacture to the best-before date is divided. This change drastically reduced the number of returned and unshipped products, simultaneously increasing efficiency in the supply chain. The other innovation regards switching from a best-before date to a best-before month, which has already been introduced by several companies.

In Chapter 11, Xiaohua Yu traces the evolution of FLW policies in China. Interestingly, attention to food waste as a policy problem started as part of an anti-corruption initiative prohibiting extravagance in public administration. FLW was subsequently framed as a problem of national food security. Given China's low self-sufficiency, the risk of the weaponisation of food made the government perceive FLW as another resource for increasing food availability. Notwithstanding the novelty of the policy, the chapter reviews several interventions taken at both the national and local levels, including the recent Empty Plate Movement, that is the obligation for consumers to eat all the food ordered in restaurants. The chapter also offers an analysis of the utility function of food waste.

In Chapter 12, Emily M. Broad Leib and Ariel Ardura provide a thorough examination of the 1996 Bill Emerson Good Samaritan Food Donation Act. The United States was the first country to implement such a law—an innovation that has been replicated and used as a model worldwide. The chapter investigates the results and limits of the liability protection offered by the law. One of the main points in the law is that by changing the structure of private law, it is extremely cost-effective: it does neither reduce government revenue nor require funds or enforcement costs. The bill resulted in an increase in donations and did not increase harm to beneficiaries of donated food. Concerning its limitations, the authors show that even after 25 years, there is still a lack of awareness and clarity about what the law prescribes. In appraising the benefits of the act, an important point is raised about how outdated protections can reduce innovation in food recovery and redistribution.

In Part 4, three chapters are dedicated to local food recovery and redistribution initiatives. In Chapter 13, Anna R. Davies and Alwynne McGeever open the section on local initiatives and present three cases of social innovation in Dublin, London, and Barcelona. They acknowledge how food recovery and redistribution can be a vibrant arena of social innovation and explore initiatives regarding food redistribution, cooking meals, and engaging in community projects, gleaning and awareness campaigns. They uncover several challenges to food recovery: unsupportive legislation, lack of resources, raising awareness about the availability of food aid, and development of trust with donors and farmers. Finally, the chapter acknowledges the lack of data and significant under-reporting of the social impacts of associations working with food aid. As a possible solution, the chapter presents the case of SHARE IT, a multi-dimensional online platform for sustainability impact assessment designed specifically for associations working in the urban food system, including a tool for sharing practices.

Chapter 14 consists of an analysis of the Milan Neighbourhood Hubs Against Food Waste by Giulia Bartezzaghi, Claudia Colicchia, Paola Garrone, Marco Melacini, Alessandro Perego, and Andrea Rizzuni. Conceived in 2016, the hubs allow for increased efficiency in recovery and redistribution by providing logistical support that allows for the recovery of small and heterogeneous volumes of surplus food, thus increasing the nutritional balance of the food mixes delivered to beneficiaries. The chapter reports the impacts of these hubs by showing how they allow to overcome several barriers to food recovery: short residual shelf life, discontinuity of demand for surplus food, poor fit with existing operational processes of donors, costs of additional tasks, lack of knowledge, and reputational risks. The governance of the hubs is also notable, as it directly involves the municipality, the authors' university, a food recovery organisation, donors, the business association, and the non-profit organisations receiving the food.

Chapter 15 by Luciana Marques Vieira and Daniele Eckert Matzembacher closes the book with an account of how the COVID-19 pandemic worked as a focusing event for policy change around food donation in Brazil. They provide in-depth evidence from two case studies of recovery initiatives implemented in Sao Paulo, one already consolidated and another started precisely in response to the pandemic. They highlight how recovery initiatives fill an 'institutional void' by substituting for public administrations and providing a fundamental public service. The analysis allows the authors to extrapolate macro-, meso-, and micro-level blind spots that suggest lessons to improve policy. Among the several insights offered by the chapter, the authors stress the importance of updating the technology of redistribution and making technology more accessible to recipients. They also show how the direct connection of farmers to low-income neighbourhoods allows them to provide food at low costs, which ensures fair remuneration to producers.

References

Barker, Margo, and Jean Russell. 2020. "Feeding the Food Insecure in Britain: Learning from the 2020 COVID-19 Crisis." *Food Security* 12 (4): 865–70. https://doi.org/10.1007/S12571-020-01080-5.

Caldeira, Carla, Valeria De Laurentiis, and Serenella Sala. 2019. "Assessment of Food Waste Prevention Actions." https://doi.org/10.2760/9773.

Chen, Haibin, Wei Jiang, Yu Yang, Yan Yang, and Xin Man. 2017. "State of the Art on Food Waste Research: A Bibliometrics Study from 1997 to 2014." *Journal of Cleaner Production* 140 (January): 840–46. https://doi.org/10.1016/J.JCLEPRO.2015.11.085.

FAO. 2013. "Food Wastage Footprint: Impacts on Natural Resources—Summary Report." www.fao.org/publications.

———. 2019, *The State of Food and Agriculture 2019. Moving Forward on Food Loss and Waste Reduction.* Rome.

Flanagan, Katie, Kai Robertson, and Craig Hanson. 2019. "Reducing Food Loss and Waste: Setting a Global Action Agenda." *World Resources Institute.* https://doi.org/10.46830/WRIRPT.18.00130.

Lang, Tim, and Michael Heasman. 2015. *Food Wars : The Global Battle for Mouths, Minds and Markets.* 2nd ed. Oxon: Routledge.

ReFED. 2016. "A Roadmap to Reduce U.S. Food Waste by 20 Percent." https://staging.refed.org/downloads/ReFED_Report_2016.pdf.

———. 2021. "Roadmap to 2030: Reducing U.S. Food Waste by 50% and the ReFED Insights Engine." https://refed.org/uploads/refed_roadmap2030-FINAL.pdf.

Rosegrant, Mark W., Eduardo Magalhaes, Rowena Valmonte-Santos, and Daniel Mason-D'Croz. 2018. "Returns to Investment in Reducing Postharvest Food Losses and Increasing Agricultural Productivity Growth." In *Prioritizing Development: A Cost Benefit Analysis of the United Nations' Sustainable Development Goals,* edited by Bjorn Lomborg, 322–36. Cambridge: Cambridge University Press.

UNEP United Nations Environment Programme. 2021. *Food Waste Index Report 2021.* Nairobi.

United Nations. 2022. "Food Systems Summit Dialogues. Member State Dialogues Synthesis—Report 4." https://summitdialogues.org/wp-content/uploads/2022/03/Member-State-Dialogue-Synthesis-Report-4-March-2022-EN.pdf.

Zhang, Min, Ming Gao, Siyuan Yue, Tianlong Zheng, Zhen Gao, Xiaoyu Ma, and Qunhui Wang. 2018. "Global Trends and Future Prospects of Food Waste Research: A Bibliometric Analysis." *Environmental Science and Pollution Research* 25 (25): 24600–10. https://doi.org/10.1007/S11356-018-2598-6/FIGURES/6.

Ziliak, James P. 2021. "Food Hardship During the COVID-19 Pandemic and Great Recession." *Applied Economic Perspectives and Policy* 43 (1): 132–52. https://doi.org/10.1002/AEPP.13099.

Part 1

Understanding food loss and waste

1 Assessing food loss and waste

Approaches, methodologies, and practices

Clara Cicatiello

Introduction

To design effective interventions against food loss and waste (FLW), policymakers and actors of the food systems need a detailed measurement of its extent along food supply chains. Evidence about the quantity and type of lost and wasted products is crucial to inform such interventions and assess their success. As simple as it may sound, it is definitely not. Indeed, there are several issues that must be addressed to make this measurement reliable, robust, and informative at the high-scale level.

First, the definitional framework is crucial. Several definitions of FLW have been used, with different boundaries in terms of resources' flows and stages of the supply chain included or excluded in/from the assessment.

Second, there are different methods to measure the quantity of FLW produced in different settings, but not all of them are reliable to the same extent; therefore, the choice of the quantification method is crucial to achieve a valid result.

Third, context-related drivers may be very important in shaping the results of FLW assessments, which means that it may not be very easy to generalise the results.

This chapter provides an overview of such issues by addressing some key elements of FLW definition, FLW quantification methods, and challenges to be tackled while planning an assessment. To frame this information in the right context, the chapter also includes some considerations about the rationale of food waste assessments and the targets of FLW reduction that are set at the global level.

The rationale for FLW assessment

The latest available data at the global level show that 8% of all food produced in the world is lost on the farm, 14% is lost between the farm gate and the retail sector, and 17% of the food available at consumer level (households, retailers, restaurants, and other food services) is wasted (FAO 2019; UNEP 2021). This represents a huge inefficiency of the food supply chains, entailing significant economic and environmental impacts, as well as hindering food security.

DOI: 10.4324/9781003226932-3

The economic impact of FLW is mainly related to the value of the food that is lost, which could be saved if this food waste was prevented. Several studies suggest that programmes against food waste typically have a very high economic return rate, with high economic benefits against little investment (Hanson and Mitchell 2017), especially when they are focused on prevention.

The environmental impact of FLW derives from the use of raw materials and natural resources to produce food that will never be consumed. Food production is responsible for 26% of global GHG emissions, mainly due to agricultural processes and livestock rearing. With the current FLW rates, this means that as much as 6% of the global GHG emissions are generated to produce food that is lost within the supply chain or during consumption (Poore and Nemecek 2018).

Food security is another aspect of FLW inefficiency. Indeed, in a world with a growing population, where we will soon have to feed a population of nine billion, FLW can affect the ability of food supply chains to deliver enough food to the people. Moreover, from an ethical perspective, it is a shame that billion tonnes of food are wasted while one in ten people is undernourished across the world (FAO 2019).

Reducing FLW is therefore a key challenge for the sustainability of current food systems. Binding targets have been set to achieve this reduction, requiring countries to demonstrate their progress towards these targets. It is in this context that properly measuring FLW becomes a key step in the fight against FLW. Indeed, despite the broad consensus on the importance of reducing FLW to make food systems more sustainable, considerable gaps in information about FLW assessment still exist.

Early studies on FLW provided an overview of the scale of the problem (Parfitt et al. 2010; Gustavsson et al. 2011), and had a very important role in spreading awareness about this issue. The number of studies reporting the amount of FLW at different stages of the food chain steeply increased after 2010, thus providing evidence of the amount of FLW generated in different settings. However, the approach of the studies has continued to be quite fragmented for several years, by providing studies that can hardly be scaled up or generalised, mostly focusing on case studies.

In the last years, after the global agreement on the Sustainable Development Goals of Agenda 2030, there has been more pressure in standardising the methods of FLW measurement across countries and stages of the food supply chain, with the aim to provide reliable input data for monitoring the progress towards the targets set for FLW reduction.

The next section shows the steps that have been taken at the global level, and in the European Union, in this regard.

FLW definition and its implementation

The definitional framework of FLW has undergone a wide discussion in the 2000s. Indeed, the boundaries of the definition are not always easy to be determined: while it is evident that we would all consider a mouldy tomato forgotten in the fridge a waste of food, what about a tomato that remains in the field because it is not harvested? Or a chicken bone that is discarded during processing? So, the first key question to address is: what is 'food'?

The World Resources Institute (2016) defines food as 'any substance—whether processed, semi-processed, or raw—that is intended for human consumption'. This definition of food includes drinks, as well as all ingredients that have been used in the processing or preparation of food. A very similar definition is provided by the EU regulation n. 178/2002, where 'food' means any substance or product, whether processed, partially processed, or unprocessed, intended to be, or reasonably expected to be ingested by humans. Inedible parts associated with food, but that are not intended to be consumed by humans, are usually excluded from the definition of 'food'.

The next question concerns the definition of waste, to understand when and how the food that is not consumed by humans becomes waste. This can be very tricky, because this definition can assume different shapes depending on the final destinations of non-consumed food. The EU project FUSIONS has provided a broad analysis of the possible destinations of non-consumed food, thus describing the theoretical framework for FLW definition. After this analysis, the following definition is suggested (FUSIONS 2014):

> Food waste is any food, and inedible parts of food, removed from the food supply chain to be recovered or disposed (including composted, crops ploughed in/not harvested, anaerobic digestion, bio-energy production, co-generation, incineration, disposal to sewer, landfill or discarded to sea).

One key point is that, while inedible parts of food are not considered a 'food' as such, they should be separately addressed in the definition but still considered as an object of measurement. WRI (2016) also suggests that inedible parts of food shall be kept into the accounting of FLW, but separately assessed as far as possible.

The definitional framework of FUSIONS considers food waste as the products removed from all stages of the supply chain. Instead, following the approach proposed by FAO (Gustavsson et al. 2011), it is now widely agreed that food removed from the upstream stages of the supply chain (farming and processing) should instead be referred to as 'food loss'. Under this approach, 'food waste' only refers to products removed from the supply chain at the stages of retail and final consumption. Such difference in the definition is meant to highlight the different influences of chain actors' behaviour in generating losses and waste.

In this chapter, we will adopt the same approach by referring to FLW when all the stages of the supply chain are concerned, but considering 'losses', those occurring at farming and processing, and 'waste', the food removed at retail, food services, and household levels.

FLW assessment as the starting point to reach global targets

In 2012, the member states of the United Nations came together in Rio de Janeiro to join the Conference for Sustainable Development. The purpose of this conference was to create a new agenda for sustainable development at the global level. At that time, the achievements of the eight Millennium Development Goals that guided countries from 2000 through 2015 in the fight against poverty and famine were discussed, and a more ambitious plan of development was agreed. The scope of this new agreement, which included a document entitled 'The future we want', was much wider and covered all aspects of sustainability: environmental challenges, social justice, and economic prosperity.

A long process of consultation and negotiation on a set of new SDGs started, leading to the delivery of the so-called Agenda 2030, in August 2015. Agenda 2030 states some basic principles for sustainable development, and it identifies a set of 17 SDGs, supported by 169 specific targets that should be reached by 2030. The Agenda 2030 was formally adopted on 25 September 2015, at a UN Summit attended by over 150 heads of state.

SDG n.12 is particularly relevant for the discussion presented in this book. It seeks to 'ensure sustainable consumption and production patterns'. It includes 8 + 3 targets; the third target under this SDG (Target 12.3) calls for 'By 2030, halve per capita global food waste at the retail and consumer levels and reduce food losses along production and supply chains, including post-harvest losses'. Indicators are also set to measure the progress of countries towards this target. They are:

(a) Food Loss Index
(b) Food Waste Index

The Food Loss Index measures the total losses of agricultural commodities in the upstream stages of the supply chain, from the production (at the farm level) up to (but not including) the retail level. The index focuses on the percentages of food removed from the supply chain, with respect to the total food produced. Considering that performing the evaluation on several groups of commodities, for each country, is very challenging, the calculation of the food loss index usually considers the top ten commodities by economic value within five commodity groups: (i) cereals and pulses; (ii) fruits and vegetables; (iii) roots, tubers, and oil-bearing crops; (iv) animal products; and (v) fish and fish products (FAO 2019). The calculation of the Food Loss Index entails some important limitations, especially that primary data on the production and loss of food commodities are very seldom available; therefore, the calculation is usually fed with estimates and modelled data. However, the rationale of the index is to monitor the rate of losses over time, in order to track progress against the SDG 12.3 target.

The Food Waste Index measures food waste at the subsequent stages of the supply chain, that is retail and consumption, including both at-home and out-of-home consumption. Contrarily to the Food Loss Index, which reports losses for each food category, the Food Waste Index measures total food waste. The Food Waste Index can be calculated with different accuracy, reflecting a

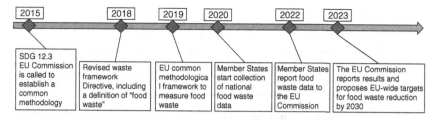

Figure 1.1 Steps in the construction of an FLW monitoring framework in the EU.

three-level approach (UNEP 2021): (i) calculation based on modelling and extrapolation; (ii) calculation based on direct measurement of food waste, without disaggregation; (iii) calculation based on direct measurement of food waste, disaggregated by destination, edible versus inedible food, food category.

The ambitious yet achievable target set by SDG 12.3 has pushed countries to set up FLW measurement strategies, to monitor and assess the progress towards the target.

One important example concerns the European Union, which has directly addressed this issue with an effort to define the methodological framework, the timeline, and the expected results of such assessment. The process of construction of an FLW monitoring framework that could support FLW assessment in the EU is described in Figure 1.1.

The process started in 2015 when the EU Commission was called to establish a common methodological framework for EU countries, to report progress towards SDG 12.3. Three years after, in 2018, the Waste Framework Directive 2008/98/EC underwent a very important update, namely:

- a specific definition of food waste was provided;
- an annual reporting obligation on food waste generation was established, as of reference year 2020.

The aim of such reporting is to monitor and assess the implementation of the food waste prevention measures in member states by measuring the levels of FLW at the different stages of the food supply chain. To support these assessments, a common methodological framework to develop FLW measurement at all stages of the supply chains was released in May 2019, and it entered into force in October of the same year. As a result of this process, member states were expected to deliver a baseline report of FLW quantities at the national level, referring to the year 2020, by June 2022. During the following year, the European Commission is expected to report EU-wide results and to use this baseline measurement to set a roadmap of targets that can lead to the achievement of the SDG 12.3 by 2030.

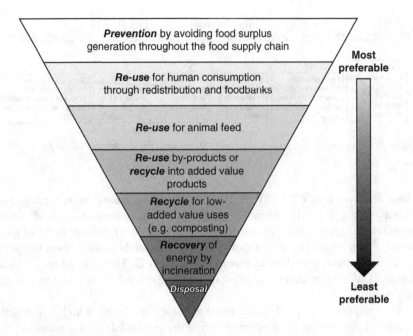

Figure 1.2 Food Waste Hierarchy.
Source: Editors' elaboration

The establishment of a common EU methodology has been a huge step to achieve a standardised and reliable assessment of FLW across countries, but it also serves to provide guidance to assess the success of actions against food waste at a small scale.

Actions against FLW are usually categorised in levels of priority, from source reduction (i.e. prevention) to recycling, recovery and disposal of, with the latter being, of course, the least preferred option. Such a hierarchy of priorities is widely agreed across the world, and it has been defined in a very similar way in North America—where the so-called 'food recovery hierarchy' is usually considered to this purpose (CEC 2019)—and in Europe—with the 'food waste hierarchy' represented in Figure 1.2.

This hierarchy of actions shows in a simple manner that solutions to prevent the generation of FLW at source should always be preferred; re-use of surplus food for human consumption via donations, or for animal feed is the second best. The other layers include options of food waste management that should only be considered when the priority actions are not possible. This is the case of recycling and revalorisation of FLW and energy recovery. Of course, disposal in landfills, incineration, or sewer without any energy recovery should be avoided as far as possible.

There is already a galaxy of these actions implemented to prevent and reduce FLW at all levels, from governmental actions to small initiatives at the local level. Many examples in this regard, set in Europe, are reported in the publication 'Assessment of food waste prevention actions' released by the EU Joint Research Centre (Caldeira, De Laurentiis, and Sala 2019).

Measuring the efficacy of these actions, by assessing the quantity of FLW that they allow to prevent or reduce, is a key element to assess their success. Other measures can also support this evaluation, for example the assessment of the environmental gains that can be achieved by implementing actions against food waste and/or of the socio-economic impact arising from the implementation of the solutions.

Methods to assess FLW

The management guru Peter Drucker once said: 'What gets measured gets managed'. This statement is particularly true in the case of FLW prevention and management, but it must be followed by a key question: 'How can FLW be measured?'.

There has been quite a history of measurement strategies and methods since the beginning of studies on FLW in the early 2000s. The UK no-profit agency WRAP was probably the first organisation to release a methodological report on how to measure food waste at households, in 2009. The World Resources Institute released a protocol to measure FLW all along the food supply chain in 2016. In the same year, the results of the EU project FUSIONS were released, providing the first assessment of FLW in EU-27 to date. More recently, reports with measures for the two indicators identified in SDG 12.3 have been published, namely for the food loss index (FAO 2019) and food waste index (UNEP 2021), including methodological details in dedicated sections. As already mentioned, a list of methods approved by the European Commission has been released in 2019; such a list provides an indication of the methods that are more suitable to assess FLW at each stage of the supply chain. In the same year, the Commission for Environmental Cooperation among Canada, Mexico, and the United States released a comprehensive practical guide on 'Why and How to Measure Food Loss and Waste' (CEC 2019), which provides a detailed description of the available methods to assess FLW, with their scope, strengths, and weaknesses. This guide also suggests that any FLW assessment effort should be planned along seven steps: the first six steps concern the definition of the rationale of the measurement exercise, the identification of the case, the definition of FLW to be used, the key performance indicators and impacts to be measured; all these steps support the decision of the method to be used, that represents the seventh step of the process.

In general, methods for FLW assessment can be divided into direct measurement and other methods.

Direct measurement consists of the use of a measuring device (e.g. a scale) to determine the mass of samples of food waste, directly or determined on the basis of volume. This method foresees that food waste is separated from other types of waste and weighted before disposal. Different fractions of food waste can be weighted separately (e.g. solids and liquids), provided that the weight of food waste is actually measured. It is possible also to determine the quantity of food waste by using volumetric measures, for example for liquids or other items that cannot be weighted. Direct measurement provides reliable, first-hand data on the quantity of food waste that is produced in a particular setting. However, it requires a huge effort in terms of hours and personnel to be performed on representative samples of food waste.

Other methods are intended to provide data that are as close as possible to direct measurement, while overcoming to any possible extent its limitations.

Waste compositional analysis can be considered a second best, as it determines the mass of food waste after disposal, by separating food waste from other fractions. This method is particularly relevant for FLW assessments conducted at food service and households. The results of waste compositional analyses are quite reliable, although a certain degree of uncertainty should be considered, as some food scraps or food products may not be easily sorted out from the other fractions. Another limitation is that liquid food waste (e.g. milk, beverages, oil) can hardly be measured with this method, as it may not be thrown out with other types of waste.

Diaries can also be used to assess FLW, especially at the consumption level. This method foresees that an individual, or a group of individuals, keeps a record of food waste information on a regular basis, for a limited period, by using print or electronic diaries or smartphone applications. Such record typically includes the mass of each food that is disposed of (weighted with a scale, or assessed with a volumetric measure) every day, along a study period. To provide reliable results, it is very important that the sample of respondents is randomly selected and adequately compensated for the effort. Indeed, fatigue is very common in diary studies, entailing that the accuracy of records decreases with days/weeks. Instead, a plus of this method is that several qualitative information can be collected along with the quantity of food that is wasted, for example the types of food, the reason behind wasting, as well as attitudes and behaviour towards food management and food shopping habitudes.

Scanning techniques for FLW measurement are widely used for specific settings where automatic recording of products is possible, typically at supermarkets and (to a lesser extent) restaurants. This technique foresees that the number of items that make up food waste is automatically recorded, for example via scanning the bar code of the products, and the result is used to determine the mass of the wasted products. This method is particularly useful to collect similar data for several months/years, with the aim to monitor the quantity of food waste over time.

Other methods for FLW measurement can be used when there is no direct access to food waste or when other methods are not feasible. **Mass balance** techniques foresee the calculation of the amount of food waste on the basis of the mass of inputs and outputs of food into and out of a defined system; mass balance measurement infers FLW levels by subtracting the outputs from the inputs, with the difference being considered the amount of FLW. This method relies very much on the statistics that are used to determine such inputs and outputs; therefore, the quality of the results strongly depends on the quality of the data feeding this method. **Food waste coefficients** are also sometimes used to assess the quantity of FLW, especially for food losses at the farm level or at the food industry; in this case, coefficients are established on the basis of sample data, and they are then applied to assess the quantity of food waste produced by a sector of the food industry or for an individual business operator. **Proxy data** from a similar geographic area, company, facility, and/or time can also be used when data from the specific case is not available or is not complete. Finally, **questionnaires** have largely been used in the past to assess the quantity of FLW at different stages of the supply chain; they are based on the respondents' self-assessment of the quantity of food waste produced, which can be highly biased due to social desirability and/or difficulty in estimating the quantity without actual measurement. For this reason, questionnaires should not be considered a reliable method when other techniques are feasible, especially at the retail and consumption stages of the supply chain. Instead, they can provide valuable insights about the reasons behind food waste, as well as attitudes and behaviours of food chain actors.

Challenges in FLW assessment

Given this methodological overview, it is quite clear that FLW assessment is a key step to support and monitor actions against food waste, as well as that such measurement has big challenges.

When FLW measurement involves households, the main challenges are the selection of a representative sample, allowing to generalise results. If waste compositional analysis is chosen as a method, the cost and effort required by the researchers are a huge challenge. Instead, if diaries are used, specific strategies to mitigate the respondents' fatigue must be planned. Another challenge is to include in the assessment the food drained as or with wastewaters; this fraction is not considered in most studies, but it can be remarkable (e.g. milk).

At restaurants and food services, representativeness is a big issue, not only because of the different types of business in this sector, but also for seasonal reasons that should be carefully considered. The use of direct measurement techniques, in these settings, besides being quite costly, might not be acceptable by the businesses involved due to organisational issues (e.g. not easy to spend time to weigh food waste during the service). The evidence provided by the bulk of research that has focused on the quantification of FLW in the food service sector also suggests that it is very important to separately assess the different types of food waste produced in these settings, namely preparation waste, serving waste, and plate waste (Eriksson et al. 2018).

The retail sector has long been the 'easiest' setting to perform food waste studies, which are strongly linked to the availability of the companies to share their data. Instead, there are few practical challenges because food waste data are usually stored as databases produced with daily scanning of wasted products. However, it should be mentioned that different studies (Eriksson, Strid, and Hansson 2012; Cicatiello and Franco 2020) have shown that about one-third of in-store retail food waste fails to be recorded with product scanning. This suggests that it would be wise to couple scanning techniques with direct measurement for short study periods, in order to assess the reliability of the data provided. Another issue is the need to standardise the results, by referring the quantity of food waste produced to the quantity of food delivered at the stores, or to the turnover, or to the sales area, in order to get results that can be more easily generalised.

Finally, at upstream stages of the supply chain—food industry and farming—lie the main challenges. Few studies exist at these settings. Direct measurement is very problematic, both for sampling issues and for the effort needed to collect the products. Most of these studies are very limited and cannot be easily generalised. Mass balance is currently the most used method, but efforts are being made to derive reliable food waste coefficients that can be scaled up and applied across farms and industries. Several challenges affect the calculation of these coefficients, especially homogeneity across countries/periods/seasons/businesses. Another issue is that food loss assessments require a clear definition of the boundaries of the study, because it should be clear at which point an item is considered 'food' and therefore included in the account of food losses.

While considering the methods that can be more suitable for specific cases of FLW assessment, it should be remarked that they all benefit from the involvement of food chain actors in the measurement effort and in the analysis of its results. Twenty years of intense research on FLW-related issues have shown that multi-actor approaches to measurement can improve the relevance of the results and—even more important—increase the sensitiveness of the food chain actors on the issue. FLW measurement is typically intended to support the identification of actions to prevent and reduce the generation of FLW; in turn, this can only be obtained if food chain actors are involved from the very beginning of the methodology setting, by sharing FLW indicators, methods and approach to reduction. Actors shall be involved in the discussion about the feasibility of the measurement, its frequency, and the sampling that is more appropriate to implement.

The establishment of continuous feedback loops during the measurement exercise is also very important to adapt the methodology to the different contexts and situations where the FLW measurement is implemented.

Conclusions

FLW measurement can be very challenging as it can be conducted at different stages of the food supply chain, rooted in different contexts. In the last twenty years, research and policy actions have pushed forward the knowledge about methods and tools to measure the quantity of FLW.

A wide range of accountable methodologies and indicators is currently available and serves as a base for FLW measurement exercises. This is very important to feed evidence-based policies against food waste, and to determine the extent to which they shall focus on preventing FLW generation and/or to promote circular approaches to FLW management.

Moreover, existing results from large-scale studies conducted at different stages of the food supply chain, and in different geographical contexts, are now available. This evidence should be used as a benchmark to compare results obtained in FLW assessment at any scale.

FLW measurement is a field of research that is expanding very fast, and new knowledge is continuously produced, but several research questions remain open and shall be addressed in the next future. Among these, the conduction of more reliable assessments of FLW at the upstream stages of the food supply chain—especially farming and, to a lesser extent, food processing—is certainly one of the big challenges ahead. Deepening the knowledge about the quantities of FLW in new geographical settings, especially in developing countries, is another open issue. To this respect, the latest report from UNEP (2021) suggests that the extent of food waste generated at consumption in these countries is much larger than expected, but the implementation of direct measurement is still limited, thus raising serious concerns over the quality of the results. At the same time, data on food waste at food service and retail in these countries are still insufficient to deliver reliable results.

References

Caldeira, C., V. De Laurentiis, and V. Sala. 2019. "Assessment of Food Waste Prevention Actions: Development of an Evaluation Framework to Assess the Performance of Food Waste Prevention Actions, EUR 29901 EN; Luxembourg (Luxembourg): Publications Office of the European Union." ISBN 978-92-76-12388-0. doi:10.2760/9773. JRC118276.

CEC. 2019. *Why and How to Measure Food Loss and Waste: A Practical Guide.* Montreal, Canada: Commission for Environmental Cooperation.

Cicatiello, C., and S. Franco. 2020. "Disclosure and Assessment of Unrecorded Food Waste at Retail Stores." *Journal of Retailing and Consumer Services* 52: 101932.

Eriksson, M., C. P. Osowski, J. Björkman, E. Hansson, C. Malefors, E. Eriksson, and R. Ghosh. 2018. "The Tree Structure—A General Framework for Food Waste Quantification in Food Services." *Resources, Conservation and Recycling* 130: 140–51.

Eriksson, M., I. Strid, and P. A. Hansson. 2012. "Food Losses in Six Swedish Retail Stores: Wastage of Fruit and Vegetables in Relation to Quantities Delivered." *Resources, Conservation and Recycling* 68: 14–20.

EU. 2019. "Delegated Decision n.1597 Establishing a Common EU Methodology to Measure Food Waste." https://eur-lex.europa.eu/eli/dec_del/2019/1597/oj.

FAO. 2019. *The State of Food and Agriculture 2019. Moving Forward on Food Loss and Waste Reduction.* Rome. Licence: CC BY-NC-SA 3.0 IGO.

FUSIONS. 2014. "FUSIONS Definitional Framework for Food Waste." www.eu-fusions.org.

Gustavsson, F., et al. 2011. *Global Food Losses and Food Waste.* Rome: FAO.

Hanson, C., and P. Mitchell. 2017. "The business case for reducing food loss and waste: A report on behalf of Champions 12.3." https://champions123.org/the-business-case-for-reducing-food-loss-and-waste/.

Parfitt, J., et al. 2010. "Food Waste Within Food Supply Chains: Quantification and Potential for Change to 2050." *Philosophical Transactions of the Royal Society B* 365 (1554): 3065–81.

Poore, J., and T. Nemecek. 2018. "Reducing Food's Environmental Impacts Through Producers and Consumers." *Science* 360 (6392): 987–92.

United Nations Environment Programme. 2021. *Food Waste Index Report 2021*. Nairobi: United Nations Environment Programme.

WRI. 2016. "Food Loss and Waste Accounting and Reporting Standard." ISBN 978-1-56973-892-4.

2 The policy problem

The causes and consequences of food loss and waste

Noemi Pace

Introduction

This chapter focuses on the causes (Section 'Causes of Food Loss and Waste') and on the consequences (Section 'The consequences of Food Loss and Waste') of food loss and waste (FLW).

Many causes of FLW have been identified. The circumstances under which food losses and waste occur are strongly dependent on the specific food and waste-related conditions in each country, each country having its own production, processing, distribution, and consumption practices. Disparities in the causes of FLW also depend on the income level of the country. Gustavsson et al. (2011) identified that the causes of food losses and waste in low-income countries are mainly related to financial, managerial, and technical limitations in harvesting techniques; storage and cooling facilities in difficult climatic conditions; and infrastructure, packaging, and marketing systems. The causes of food losses and waste in medium-/high-income countries mainly relate to consumer behaviour and a lack of coordination between actors in the supply chain (Chalak, Abou-Daher, and Abiad 2016). Farmer–buyer sales agreements in these countries are seen as contributing to quantities of farm crops being wasted, for example by the imposition of quality standards, which reject food items with imperfect shape or appearance. At the consumer level, medium-/high-income countries, insufficient purchase planning, and expiring 'best-before dates' were also identified as causing large amounts of waste, combined with the careless attitude of consumers who can afford to waste food. For these countries, Parfitt, Barthel, and Macnaughton (2010) identify the main drivers of food waste as quality standards, excessive management regulation, poor environmental conditions during display, and consumer behaviour.

The causes of FLW are also strictly interrelated with various stages on the Food Supply Chain (FSC; Parfitt, Barthel, and Macnaughton 2010; Gustavsson et al. 2011; Hodges, Buzby, and Bennett 2011; Canali et al. 2014). Canali et al. (2014) identify 105 drivers for the current causes of food waste and 133 future threats of increase of FLW. Of the current drivers, 28 drivers were related to technology, 38 to business management and economy, 23 to legislation, and 16 to consumer behaviour and lifestyles (Canali et al. 2014; Blakeney 2019).

DOI: 10.4324/9781003226932-4

As far as the consequences of FLW are concerned, the focus of the section 'The consequences of FLW' is on two main broad consequences, namely the consequences for the environment (greenhouse gas (GHG) emissions, the water footprint, and landfills) and the consequences for food security and nutrition.

Causes of FLW

The 2014 report of the High Panel of Experts classifies the causes of FLW at each stage of the food chain, which it described as the micro-level causes of FLW, as they result from the actions (or non-actions) of individual actors at each stage in response to external factors (HLPE 2014, 39).

In the next section, we discuss the micro-level causes of FLW at each stage of the FSC: pre-harvest, post-harvest, storage, transportation, wholesale and retail, hospitality sector, and household consumption. Subsequently, we present the meso-level and macro-level causes of FLW.

Micro-level causes of FLW

Pre-harvest factors

For pre-harvest factors, we refer to damage that can occur in the field prior to harvest, such as that caused by weeds, insect pests, and diseases, that is factors that indirectly lead to losses at later stages in the chain. The pre-harvest factors driving post-harvest FLW can be divided into the following (Blakeney 2019):

i)   The choice of crop varieties, which can have an important impact on the quality of produce (Kader 2005), for example the choice of incorrect varieties of cereals, such as maize, wheat, and sorghum, may render them vulnerable to fungal infections in moist climates and to the loss of harvestable seed in windy areas. Similar adverse impacts have been observed regarding fruit (de Jager and de Putter 1999; Galvis-Sánchez et al. 2004).

ii) Agronomic practices, including the management of fertilisers, soil additives, water management, and pest and disease management: Regarding fruit and vegetables, differences in agronomic practices have been identified as contributing to poor visual and nutritional results and the consequent rejection (Ferguson, Volz, and Woold 1999; Stanley et al. 2014; Magzawa et al. 2017). Harvesting at the wrong stage of maturity can compromise quality (Klahre et al. 1987) and vitamin content (Nagy 1980; Yang et al. 2011) and affect the suitability for transport and storage (Luton and Holland 1986; Florkowski et al. 2014). Poor water and nutrient management can contribute to poor product quality, resulting in a high level of rejection (Ambuko et al. 2013; Caleb et al. 2015). Poor fertilisation practices can affect the nutritional content of crops and fruit (Reitz and Koo 1960; Mann and Sandhu 1988; Toivonen, Zebarth, and Bowen 1994; Lee and Kader 2000).

iii) Climate and environment: Climatic and environmental factors have an obvious effect on yield, with climate change inflicting a series of agricultural stresses through increases in heat, salinity, and pest infestation (OECD 2010; Almas and Campbell 2012; Meldelsohn and Dinar 2012; Maharjan and Joshi 2013; Zolin and Rodrigues 2015; Das 2016).

iv) Market factors: These include the leaving of fruit and vegetables unharvested because of the failure to meet certain quality standards with regard to the appearance of produce dictated by processors, wholesalers, retailers, or consumers (Stuart 2009; Buzby et al. 2011; Aschemann-Witzel et al. 2015; de Hooge et al. 2017). A more recent pre-harvest market factor is the competition for crops from global food markets and subsequent increases in food prices (OECD 2005). Renzaho, Kamara, and Toole (2017) estimate that 40% of the US maize crop was diverted from global food markets to produce biofuels, accounting for 20–25% increases in the price of maize and 7–8% of soybean price increases between 2001 and 2017 (Zilberman et al. 2013).

Post-harvest factors

Losses of quantity and quality can occur at any stage of the postharvest chain (Grolleaud 2002). Post-harvest losses (PHLs) are difficult to estimate, especially in developing countries which lack reliable and up-to-date data. The causes of PHL are considerably different between perishable (fresh fruit and vegetables) and non-perishable (cereal grains) crops. A delay in harvesting can cause the loss of crops through bird, rodent, or insect attack. Alternatively, it might be caused by rotting and the development of moulds if the delay coincides with the rainy season (Lewis et al. 2005; Alakonya, Monda, and Ajanga 2008). The loss of perishable crops is common in both developed and developing countries, although developing countries, lacking appropriate harvest and post-harvest technologies for both grains, fruits and vegetables, are highly vulnerable to unfavourable weather conditions (Hailu and Derbew 2015). Grain losses in developed countries are much smaller than those in developing countries, although there is a lack of reliable data (Parfitt, Barthel, and Macnaughton 2010; Shafiee-Jood and Cai 2016).

Storage

Careless handling of produce during transport and storage will lead to damage reducing the value of the produce or causing it to be rejected.

Storage stability and shelf life depend on the quality of food resulting from cultivation practices and environmental influences. In developed countries, high-quality storage facilities and advanced post-harvest technologies, such as refrigeration and a controlled atmosphere, significantly extend the marketing period and shelf life of perishable foods. In developing countries, the lack of proper storage facilities is a major cause of PHLs due to the combined action of moulds, insects, rodents, and pests.

In the case of grains, pests and fungi are the major causes of deterioration at the storage phase. In West Africa, maize is an important part of the diets of both rural and urban populations in Nigeria, Ghana, Benin, and Burkina Faso. Losses due to post-harvest pests of maize in those countries are estimated to average between 20% and 30% after three months of storage (Boxall 2002).

Transportation

Transportation infrastructures are essential to reduce FLW. In developing countries, poor roads and a lack of suitable vehicles are responsible for the deterioration of perishable commodities during transport (Rolle 2006).

The transport of livestock, even in developed countries, causes FLW. Frimpong et al. (2012) estimate losses of livestock of 16% in Ghana due to death, injuries, or sickness.

Logistical factors can also have an impact on FLW. Shukla and Jharkharia (2013) and Negi and Anand (2015) show that where there is a long and fragmented supply chain of perishable produce, waste increases and the per-unit consumption price also increases.

Wholesale and retail

The environmental conditions within retail outlets can influence the quality, shelf life, and attractiveness of products to consumers (Blakeney 2019). FLW occurs in the retail stage in perishable commodities even in developed countries. Buzby, Wells, and Hyman (2014) estimate in-store food losses of 10% of the total food supply in the United States. In open-air markets in developing countries, traders' practice of sprinkling unclean water on vegetables and fruits results in unsafe foods, causing them to be rejected by buyers (HLPE 2014, 47).

Another significant cause of FLW at the retail stage is the miscalculation of consumer demand. In developed countries, food retailers apply the so-called rule of the one-third, requiring that processed foods must reach suppliers in up to one-third of their shelf life. Products that fail to arrive by the first third of their shelf life will be rejected by retailers, leading to the discarding of safe food (HLPE 2014, 47).

Hospitality sector

The hospitality sector includes for-profit establishments such as restaurants and not-for-profit establishments, such as canteens and cafeterias at school and hospitals. There is scarce evidence of FLW in this sector. Parfitt, Barthel, and Macnaughton (2010) studied the UK hospitality sector, and they estimate that up to 50% of the food was wasted and that 75% of this waste was avoidable.

Murphy et al. (2018) explore the hospitality FLW in relation to tourism. Block et al. (2016) and Juvan, Grun, and Dolnicar (2018) document that people on holiday tend towards excess and consume foods not available at home, particularly in buffets. Stenmark et al. (2016) estimate that hotels, restaurants, and the catering sector in the EU were responsible for about 14% of FLW.

Household consumption

In developed countries, consumers make a significant contribution to FLW. The European Commission (2010) estimates that food waste exceeds 40% for households, compared with 5% for retailers. Food waste in the United States was estimated to be 9% of annual expenditure on food per consumer (Buzby, Wells, and Hyman 2014) and 15% of expenditure on food and drink by UK consumers (Quested and Johnson 2009).

The causes of this waste in developed countries are largely behavioural and involve:

- Demanding the high-level appearance of food (de Hooge et al. 2017; Aschermann-Witzel et al. 2017)
- Poor planning (Aschermann-Witzel et al. 2017; Stancu, Haugaard, and Lahteenmaki 2016)
- Unawareness of the amount of food being wasted (Quested et al. 2013)
- Lack of the priority of minimising food waste (Graham-Rowe, Jessop, and Sparks 2014)

Buying less often and in greater quantities may increase waste. Purchasing in bulk to maximise value for money can result in waste from spoilage (Canali et al. 2014). The elimination of these behaviours will avoid or reduce the waste, but it will require a public education campaign.

Another important driver of FLW at the consumer stage of the food supply chain is the confusion about date labelling (Theotokis, Pramatari, and Tsiros 2012; van Boxstael et al. 2014). Among the options are 'Best by', 'Fresh by', Sell by', 'Use by', and 'Best if used by'. Several studies indicate that consumers tend to rely more on expiration dates than on a sensory evaluation of the safety of their food purchases (Tsiros and Heilman 2005; Newsome et al. 2014). Wilson et al. (2017) estimate that the 'Use by' date tends to generate the greatest amount of food waste.

Several studies have noted that consumers who purchase more frequently significantly limit their wastage of perishables (Setti et al. 2016) and that food waste is highest when consumers purchase mainly from supermarket chains, compared with purchases from smaller stores and farmers' markets (Yildirim et al. 2016).

Finally, household waste results from private decisions not subject to public scrutiny. Consequently, social censure does not play much of a role in discouraging wasteful behaviour (Blakeney 2019).

Meso-level causes of FLW

The High Level Panel of Experts points out that in evaluating the drivers of FLW, we should consider the meso-level causes of FLW, which include structural aspects of the food chain, such as the lack of support for investment and innovation, a lack of coordination among actors, and the general lack of adequate infrastructure (Blakeney 2019).

In developing countries, the small scale of food production and farming is a disincentive to investments, especially because of limited access to finance and credit. In rural areas, credit constraints are among the primary obstacles to investment in technologies to reduce FLW across the food supply chain (HLPE 2013). In addition, the lack of appropriate infrastructures for transportation and the storage of food such as cool and cold chambers, as well as an absence of effective processing and preservation techniques, causes a significant amount of FLW (Negi and Anand 2017). Negi and Anand (2015) estimate that a third of the losses of fruits and vegetables grown in India are attributed to gaps in the cold chain. Fonseca and Njie (2009) estimate similar losses for the same reason in Latin America and the Caribbean.

Macro-level causes of FLW

The 2014 report of the High Level Panel of Experts highlights the relevance of broader macro-level causes of FLW, arising from the policy and regulatory environments and systemic causes (HLPE 2014, 53).

As far as the policy and the regulatory environments are concerned, FLW can be affected by food labelling and packaging regulations. More generally, policies concerned with agricultural investment, agricultural development, transport, and storage infrastructure can also affect FLW (Blakeney 2019).

As far as the systemic causes of FLW are concerned, we need to distinguish between developing and developed countries. Developing countries are generally hampered by financial constraints in establishing a transport, storage, and marketing infrastructure and by a lack of managerial capacities. McCullough et al. (2008) suggest that the expansion of supermarkets in developing countries is another risk factor, given the difficulties of small producers in complying with the food standards imposed by supermarkets.

In developed countries, the increasingly low cost of food compared with other goods and services leads to poor food management practices, such as over-purchasing and the consequent waste. Moreover, as highlighted by Lundqvist et al. (2008), higher incomes induce a shift from starchy staples to perishable fruits and vegetables, which are associated with a higher level of waste.

The consequences of FLW

From a global perspective, the reduction of FLW improves both food security and environment; if less food gets lost, less needs to be produced to improve global food security, thus also reducing environmental impacts. Recently, FAO

(2019a) and Santeramo and Lamonaca (2021) summarise the current state of knowledge on FLW with a focus on food security and environmental concerns. This section focuses on the consequences of FLW in terms of impacts on the environment (Section 'Environmental Impacts of FLW') and impacts on food security and nutrition (Section 'Impacts of FLW on food security and nutrition').

Environmental impacts of FLW

The loss and waste of food has significant environmental impacts because FLW occurs in all phases of the food supply chain. Globally, the production of FLW has been estimated to account for 24% of total freshwater resources used in food production, 23% of global cropland, and 23% of global fertiliser use (Thyberg and Tonjes 2016). Thus, the reduction of FLW reduces the negative environmental consequences of FLW, which are presented in detail in the next sub-sections.

Greenhouse gas emission

FAO (2013) estimated that agriculture is associated with approximately 22% of all greenhouse gas (GHG) emissions. Besides the direct impact of agriculture on GHG emissions, there are also indirect impacts such as deforestation induced by agriculture, which is estimated to add between 6% and 17% of all GHG emissions. Wasted food represents a GHG cost that could otherwise have been avoided. UK National Statistics (2016) estimated that, in the United Kingdom, 3% of the total GHG emissions resulted from household food waste. In the United States, Venkat (2011) estimated that GHG emissions due to avoidable food waste amounted to 2%.

The consumption of energy used to produce lost and wasted food also has GHG implications. Cuéllar and Webber (2010) estimated that the energy embedded in wasted food represents approximately 2% of annual energy consumption in the United States. WRAP (2011) estimated that avoidable food waste led to the equivalent of 17 million tonnes of carbon dioxide in 2010. Buzby et al. (2011) estimated that the decomposition of food waste in the US landfills contributed to 34% of all human-related methane emissions in the world.

The wastage of fruits and vegetables across all regions contributes to a significant amount of GHG emissions because of the greater proportion of products that spoil (Blakeney 2019).

Water loss

Hoekstra et al. (2011) suggested the water footprint comprises three colour-coded components: (1) green water (water evaporated from soil moisture supplemented by rainfall); (2) blue water (water withdrawn from ground or surface water sources); and (3) grey water (the polluted volume of blue water returned after production). The discarding of food that does not meet the standards of wholesalers, retailers, and consumers represents an inefficient use of green and blue water resources. FLW accounts for 24% of total freshwater resources used in crop production (Kummu et al. 2012). In the United Kingdom, the water footprint of avoidable food waste amounts to 6% of the total water footprint per person.

Landfill

In both developed and developing countries, discarded food waste accounts for a significant percentage of municipal solid waste that is disposed of in a landfill. Ahamed et al. (2016) estimated that in the United States in 2012, food waste accounted for 21.1% of the municipal waste stream, and in China in 2010, it accounted for 51% of the municipal waste stream. In developing countries, one of the main environmental impacts of food waste relates to its final disposal in landfills. Adhikari, Barrington, and Martinez (2006) estimated that around 90% of FLW is disposed of by landfills. Landfills are the largest contributor to the generation of methane in developed countries. For instance, Abassi, Tauseef, and Abbasi (2012) estimated that in the United States, landfills account for 34% of all methane emissions.

Impacts of FLW on food security and nutrition

According to FAO (2019a), FLW has potential effects on food security and nutrition through changes in the four dimensions of food security: food availability, access, utilisation, and stability. However, the links between FLW reduction and food security are complex, and positive outcomes are not always certain. Reaching acceptable levels of food security and nutrition inevitably implies certain levels of FLW. Maintaining buffers to ensure food stability requires a certain amount of food to be lost or wasted (Kaaya, Kyamuhangire, and Kyamanywa 2006). At the same time, ensuring food safety involves discarding unsafe food, which then gets counted as lost or wasted, while higher quality diets tend to include more highly perishable foods. Location and point in the food supply chain matter for the food security and nutrition impact of reducing FLW. How the impacts on the different dimensions of food security play out and affect the food security of different population groups depends on where in the food supply chain the reduction in losses or waste takes place as well as on where nutritionally vulnerable and food-insecure people are located geographically.

A reduction in the amount of food wasted by consumers in high-income countries, for example does not necessarily mean there is more food available to poor households in distant, low-income countries. Subsistence farmers consume all or a considerable share of their own production. Thus, a reduction in losses of food sold commercially improves the availability of food beyond farming households (Kaaya, Kyamuhangire, and Kyamanywa 2006). For food-secure countries highly dependent on food imports, FLW reduction is seen as a strategy for safeguarding their food supply (FAO 2018).

Reducing on-farm losses—particularly for small-scale farmers in low-income countries—can allow farmers to improve their diets due to increased food availability and gain higher incomes if selling part of their produce. It can also lead to increased supply and lower prices further along the food supply chain and eventually for consumers. On the other hand, if a processor reduces losses, while this will also lead to increased supply and lower prices further down the food supply chain and eventually for consumers, it may result in farmers seeing reduced demand for their produce and thus lower income and worsening food security. Reducing consumers' food waste may improve their food availability and access, in addition to that of possible direct beneficiaries of food redistribution schemes, but farmers and other supply chain actors may be worse off as they are selling less and/or at lower prices (FAO 2019a).

Improving the availability of food is only a first step towards improving food security and nutrition. Any additional food resulting from loss or waste reduction must also be physically and economically accessible.

The reduction of FLW can have mixed results on the accessibility of food. Whether the net effect of loss or waste reductions on food accessibility is positive or negative depends on the price effects of the reductions, which are in turn determined by the location of the reductions. How these price effects influence the incomes of households depends, in turn, on their income sources (FAO 2019a).

A fall in prices from loss reductions improves consumer's access to food but it may diminish the food security status of commercial farming households, who receive a lower price for their output. The food security status of subsistence farmers, on the other hand, is improved by a reduction in on-farm losses, which boosts the amount of food available to farming households.

Avoiding qualitative food losses and waste throughout the food supply chain ensured that more nutritious and healthy foods become available for consumers. However, safe and healthy diets necessitate a certain level of FLW. Indeed, to ensure food safety, unsafe foods need to be discarded. Moreover, a nutritious and diversified diet includes highly perishable food products such as fruits, vegetables, and animal products, which are prone to spoilage.

A study based on an economy-wide modelling framework assesses the impact of reductions in FLW in the European Union (EU) on producers and consumers in sub-Saharan Africa. The study finds that a reduction in agricultural losses in the EU means that producers demand fewer inputs to produce more output. As a result, the supply of food in the EU increases, while food prices fall. The fall in food prices is partially transmitted to overseas markets, including sub-Saharan Africa, where consumers benefit from more affordable food imports. Meanwhile, the impact of reduced food losses in the EU on producers in sub-Saharan Africa is mixed. They benefit from the fall in the price of imported food to be used as an intermediate input, but are negatively affected by the competition from cheaper imports of final food products, forcing them to cut sales prices. Moreover, sub-Saharan Africa's exports to the EU have to compete there with lower priced domestically produced food. As a result of the increased competition in both domestic and foreign markets, farmers in sub-Saharan Africa produce less than before (Kumar and Kalita 2017). A similar study using the same modelling framework found that the long-distance impact on food security in sub-Saharan Africa of a reduction in the amount of food wasted by retailers and households in the EU is positive, but relatively small (COMCEC 2017).

The reduction in food losses through better on-farm storage can improve the food security status of farming households. Smallholders are often compelled to sell all their grain soon after the harvest because traditional storage facilities cannot guarantee protection against pests and pathogens. This may force them to buy grain for their own consumption later, at possibly higher prices. Case studies in Africa, Asia, and Latin America have demonstrated that the use of metal silos prevents grain storage losses and enhances household food security (Fonseca and Vergara 2015). One study found that in Kenya, farmers who used metal silos to store maize had 1.8 months more in adequate food provisioning than non-adopters, which ensured the stability of their food consumption throughout the year. Metal silos allowed farmers to limit their immediate sales to those necessary to meet urgent cash needs and to hold on to the bulk of their harvest for up to five months after production (Parfitt, Barthel, and Macnaughton 2010).

As far as the nexus between FLW and nutrition is concerned, nutrient loss due to quantitative and qualitative FLW may represent a missed opportunity to reduce malnutrition and micronutrient deficiencies (FAO 2019b).

A recent study based on FAO's 2011 FLW estimates found that while the supply of all digestible protein, fat, calories, amino acids, essential vitamins, and minerals exceeded average requirements, the large amounts of food lost throughout the food supply chain compound dietary inequalities within and between countries.

The results of the study further indicate that over 60% of total micronutrients, with the exception of vitamin B_{12}, are lost as a result of the loss and waste of highly perishable foods, including fruits, vegetables, and animal-based products. The study concludes that strategies focusing on improved storage and distribution management are likely to improve the availability of micronutrients more than that of macronutrients (EC 2010).

FAO recently piloted a method to estimate the percentage of children under five in Cameroon, India, and Kenya whose micronutrient requirements of vitamin A, iron, zinc, and vitamin C could theoretically be satisfied through reductions in food losses. The study shows that large amounts of nutrients are lost due to preventable PHLs. It demonstrates that reducing PHLs of selected crops could increase the availability of micronutrients, which could in turn improve nutrition (Lee, Tung, and Paratore 2019). The study is the first to estimate the connection between nutrient loss in the food supply chain and micronutrient deficiencies in children. However, its results should be interpreted with caution.

The study assumes that food loss decreases the intake of food and its nutrients by nutrient-deficient people and that micronutrient-deficient children would have access to the recovered nutrients. In reality, the lead cause of micronutrient deficiencies in children is not a lack of access to food, but rather infections, which reduce appetite and hamper the utilisation of nutrients (Fabi et al. 2018; FAO 2018).

The role of FLW reduction in lowering food insecurity also depends on the degree of food insecurity prevalent in different countries. A global measurement of the severity of food insecurity is available through the Food Insecurity Experience Scale (FIES), which measures limits in access to food, at the level of households or individuals, due to lack of resources. Respondents are asked eight direct yes/no questions about their experiences in accessing food over the previous 12 months (Bellamare et al. 2017).

On the basis of the responses, levels of food insecurity are assessed according to the following scale:

- severely food insecure: no food for a day or more;
- moderately food insecure: compromising on food quality and variety or reducing food quantity and skipping meals;
- mildly food insecure or food secure: potential uncertainty about the ability to obtain food.

The FIES provides useful insights into the degree of urgency of ensuring food access, including food quality considerations. Where severe food insecurity is high—as in low-income and lower middle-income countries—the scope for FLW reduction to contribute to reducing hunger through increased availability and access to food is potentially large. Interventions preventing avoidable food loss can ameliorate food shortages, particularly at local level in smallholder production as these areas are not well connected to markets and therefore trade is minimal (FAO 2019c). This could increase farmers' incomes and improve food access. If reductions in losses are large enough to affect prices, the urban food insecurity may also stand to benefit. Overall, a strategy aiming to reduce FLW is likely to be more effective in improving food security for the populations in these countries than in high-income countries, particularly by focusing on reducing losses at the farm level and early steps in the supply chain.

Conclusions

This chapter investigated the causes and consequences of FLW. As far as the causes of FLW are concerned, the chapter has analysed the micro-, meso-, and macro-level causes across the food supply chain, and for the micro-level causes, it analyses the drivers at each stage of the food-value supply chain, from the pre-harvest factors to consumer-related factors.

As far as the consequences of FLW are concerned, the chapter provided an investigation of the impacts of FLW on the environment (GHG emissions, depletion of blue water, and landfill disposal) and on food security and nutrition. On the first impacts, the chapter highlights that the loss and waste of food have significant environmental impacts because FLW occurs in all phases of the food supply chain. Globally, the production of FLW has been estimated to account for 24% of total freshwater resources used in food production, 23% of global cropland, and 23% of global fertiliser use. Moreover, wasted food represents a GHG cost that could otherwise have been avoided.

On the impacts of FLW on food security and nutrition, the chapter highlights that the nexus between FLW reduction and food security and nutrition is complex, and positive outcomes are not always certain. Reaching acceptable levels of food security and nutrition inevitably implies certain levels of FLW. Maintaining buffers to ensure food stability requires a certain amount of food to be lost or wasted. At the same time, ensuring food safety involves discarding unsafe food, which then gets counted as lost or wasted, while higher quality diets tend to include more highly perishable foods. In addition, the chapter highlighted how the location and point in the food supply chain matter for the food security and nutrition impact of reducing FLW. How the impacts on the different dimensions of food security play out and affect the food security of different population groups depends on where in the food supply chain the reduction in losses or waste takes place as well as on where nutritionally vulnerable and food-insecure people are located geographically.

References

Abassi, T., S. M. Tauseef, and S. A. Abbasi. 2012. "Anaerobic Digestion for Global Warming Control and Energy Generation—An Overview." *Renewable and Sustainable Energy Reviews* 16: 3228–42.

Adhikari, B. K., S. Barrington, and J. Martinez. 2006. "Predicted Growth of World Urban Food Waste and Methane Production." *Waste Management Research* 24 (5): 421–33.

Ahamed, A., K. Yin, B. H. J. Ng, F. Ren, V. W. C. Chang, and J. Y. Wang. 2016. "Life Cycle Assessment of the Present and Proposed Food Waste Management Technologies From Environmental and Economic Impact Perspectives." *Journal of Cleaner Production* 131: 607–14.

Alakonya, A. E., E. O. Monda, and S. Ajanga. 2008. "Effect of Delayed Harvesting on Maize Ear Rot in Western Kenya." *American-Eurasian Journal of Agriculture and Environment* 4 (3): 372–80.

Almas, R., and H. Campbell. 2012. *Rethinking Agricultural Policy Regimes: Food Security, Climate Change and the Future Resilience of Global Agriculture*. Bradford: Emerald Group Publishing.

Ambuko, J., Y. Sekozawa, S. Sugaya, and H. Gemma. 2013. "A Comparative Evaluation of Postharvest Quality Attributes of Two Banana (Musa Spp) Varieties as Affected by Preharvest Production Conditions." *Journal of Agricultural Science* 5 (3): 170–78.

Aschemann-Witzel, J., I. E. De Hooge, P. Amani, T. Bech-Larsen, and M. Oostindjer. 2015. "Consumer-Related Food Waste: Causes and Potential for Action." *Sustainability* 7: 6457–67.

Aschermann-Witzel, J., J. H. Jensen, M. H. Jensen, and V. Kulikovskja. 2017. "Consumer Behaviour Towards Price-Reduced Suboptimal Foods in the Supermarket and the Relation to Food Waste in Households." *Appetite* 116: 246–58.

Bellemare, M. F., M. Çakir, H. H. Peterson, L. Novak, and J. Rudi. 2017. "On the Measurement of Food Waste." *American Journal of Agricultural Economics* 99 (5): 1148–58.

Blakeney, M. 2019. *Food Loss and Food Waste: Causes and Solutions.* Northampton, MA: Edward Elgar Publishing, Inc.

Block, L. G., P. A. Keller, B. Vallen, S. Williamson, M. M. Birau, A. Grinstein, E. M. Moscato, R. W. Reczek, and A. H. Tangari. 2016. "The Squander Sequence: Understanding Food Waste at Each Stage of the Consumer Decision-Making Process." *Journal of Public Policy & Marketing* 35 (2): 292–304.

Boxall, J. P. 2002. "Storage Losses." In *Crops Post-Harvest: Science and Technology, Volume 1: Principles and Practice*, edited by P. Golob, G. Farrell, and J. E. Orchad, 143–69. Oxford: Blackwell Sciences, Ltd.

Buzby, J. C., J. Hyman, H. Stewart, and H. F. Wells. 2011. "The Value of Retail- and Consumer-Level Fruit and Vegetable Losses in the United States." *The Journal of Consumer Affairs* 45 (3): 492–515.

Buzby, J. C., H. F. Wells, and J. Hyman. 2014. "The Estimated Amount, Value and Calories of Postharvest Food Losses at the Retail and Consumer Levels in the United States." EIB-121, US Department of Agriculture, Economic Research Service.

Caleb, O. J., O. A. Fawole, R. R. Mphahlele, and U. L. Opara. 2015. "Impact of Preharvest and Postharvest Factors on Changes in Volatile Compounds of Pomegranate Fruit and Minimally Processed Arils—Review." *Scientia Horticulturae* 188: 106–14.

Canali, M., K. Östergren, P. Amani, L. Aramyan, S. Sijtsema, O. Korhonen, K. Silvennoinene, G. Moates, K. Waldron, and C. O'Connor. 2014. *Drivers of Current Food Waste Generation, Threats of Future Increase and Opportunities for Reduction.* Bologna: FUSIONS.

Chalak, A., C. Abou-Daher, and M. G. Abiad. 2016. "The Global Economic and Regulatory Determinants of Household Food Waste Generation: A Cross-Country Analysis." *Waste Management* 48: 418–22.

COMCEC Coordination Office. 2017. *Reducing Food Waste in the OIC Countries.* Ankara: Standing Committee for Economic and Commercial Cooperation of the Organization of Islamic Cooperation.

Cuéllar, A. D., and M. E. Webber. 2010. "Wasted Food, Wasted Energy: The Embedded Energy in Food Waste in the United States." *Environmental Science Technology* 44 (16): 6464–69.

Das, H. P. 2016. *Climate Change and Agriculture: Implication for Global Food Security.* London: CRC Press.

de Hooge, I. E., M. Oostindjer, J. Aschemann-Witzel, A. Normann, S. M. Loose, and V. L. Almli. 2017. "This Apple Is Too Ugly for Me! Consumer Preferences for Suboptimal Food Products in the Supermarket and at Home." *Food Quality and Preferences* 56: 80–92.

de Jager, A., and H. de Putter. 1999. "Preharvest Factors and Postharvest Quality Decline of Apples." *Acta Horticulturae* 485: 103–10.

EC (European Commission). 2010. *Preparatory Study on Food Waste Across EU 27 (Final Report).* Brussels: European Commission.

Fabi, C., A. English, M. Mingione, and G. Jona Lasinio. 2018. *SDG 12.3.1: Global Food Loss Index. Imputing Food Loss Percentages in the Absence of Data at the Global Level.* Rome: FAO.

FAO. 2013. *Food Wastage Footprint. Impacts on Natural Resources.* Rome: FAO.

———. 2018. *Methodological Proposal for Monitoring SDG Target 12.3. The Global Food Loss Index Design, Data Collection Methods and Challenges.* Rome: FAO Statistical Division.

———. 2019a. *The State of Food and Agriculture 2019. Moving Forward on Food Loss and Waste Reduction.* Rome: FAO.

———. 2019b. *Food Loss Index*. Online Statistical Working System for Loss Calculations. www.fao.org/food-loss-and-food-waste/flw-data.

———. 2019c. "Crop Market." In *Family Farming Knowledge Platform*. www.fao.org/family-farming/data-sources/dataportrait/crop-market/en/.

Ferguson, I., R. Volz, and A. Woold. 1999. "Factors Affecting Physiological Disorders of Fruit." *Postharvest Biology and Technology* 15: 255–62.

Florkowski, W. J., R. L. Shewfelt, B. Bruckner, and S. E. Prussia, eds. 2014. *Postharvest Handling, a Systems Approach*. 3rd ed. San Diego: Elsevier, Academic Press.

Fonseca, J. M., and D. N. Njie. 2009. *Addressing Food Losses Due to Non-Compliance with Quality and Safety Requirements in Export Markets: The Case of Fruits and Vegetables from the Latin America and the Caribbean Region*. Roma: FAO.

Fonseca, J. M., and N. Vergara. 2015. *Logistics in the Horticulture Supply Chain in Latin America and the Caribbean. Regional Report Based on Five Country Assessments and Findings from Regional Workshops*. Rome: FAO.

Frimpong, S., G. Gebresenbet, T. Bosona, E. Bobobee, E. Aklaku, and I. Hamdu. 2012. "Animal Supply and Logistics Activities of Abattoir Chain in Developing Countries: The Case of Kumasi Abattoir, Ghana." *Journal of Service Science and Management* 5: 20–27.

Galvis-Sánchez, A. C., S. C. F. Acilna, M. M. B. Morais, and F. X. Malcata. 2004. "Effects of Preharvest, Harvest and Post-Harvest Factors on the Quality of Pear (cv. 'Rocha') Stored Under Controlled Atmosphere Conditions." *Journal of Food Engineering* 64 (2): 161–72.

Graham-Rowe, E., D. C. Jessop, and P. Sparks. 2014. "Identifying Motivations and Barriers to Minimizing Household Food Waste." *Resources, Conservation and Recycling* 84: 15–23.

Grolleaud, M. 2002. *Post-Harvest Losses: Discovering the Full Story. Overview of the Phenomenon of Losses During the Post-Harvest System*. Rome: FAO.

Gustavsson, J., C. Cederberg, U. Sonesson, R. van Otterdijk, and A. Meybeck. 2011. *Global Food Losses and Food Waste—Extent, Causes and Prevention*. Rome: FAO.

Hailu, G., and B. Derbew. 2015. "Extent, Causes and Reduction Strategies of Postharvest Losses of Fresh Fruits and Vegetables—A Review." *Journal of Biology, Agriculture and Healthcare* 5 (5): 49–64.

HLPE. 2013. "Investing in Smallholder Agriculture for Food Security." A Report by the High Level Panel of Experts on Food Security and Nutrition of the Committee on World Food Security, Rome.

———. 2014. "Food Losses and Waste in the Context of Sustainable Food Systems." A Report by the High Level Panel of Experts on Food Security and Nutrition of the Committee on World Food Security, Rome.

Hodges, R. J., J. C. Buzby, and B. Bennett. 2011. "Postharvest Losses and Waste in Developed and Less Developed Countries: Opportunities to Improve Resource Use." *Journal of Agricultural Science* 149: 37–45.

Hoekstra, A. Y., A. K. Chapagain, M. M. Aldaya, and M. M. Mekonnen. 2011. *The Water Footprint Assessment Manual: Setting the Global Standard*. London: Earthscan.

Kaaya, A., W. Kyamuhangire, and S. Kyamanywa. 2006. "Factors Affecting Aflatoxin Contamination of Harvested Maize in the Three Agroecological Zones of Uganda." *Journal of Applied Sciences* 6 (11): 2401–7.

Kader, A. A. 2005. "Increasing Food Availability by Reducing Postharvest Losses of Fresh Produce." *Acta Horticulturae* 682: 2169–76.

Klahre, J., W. Mellenthin, P. Chen, F. Valentine, E. Talley, R. Bartram, and T. Raese. 1987. "D'Anjou Harvest Maturity and Storage." *Postharvest Pomology Newsletter* 5 (2): 10–14.

Kumar, D., and P. Kalita. 2017. "Reducing Postharvest Losses During Storage of Grain Crops to Strengthen Food Security in Developing Countries." *Foods* 6 (1).

Kummu, M., H. de Moel, M. Porkka, S. Siebert, O. Varis, and P. J. Ward. 2012. "Lost Food, Wasted Resources: Global Food Supply Chain Losses and Their Impacts on Freshwater, Cropland, and Fertilizer Use." *Science of the Total Environment* 438: 477–89.

Juvan, E., B. Grun, and S. Dolnicar. 2018. "Biting Off More Than They Can Chew: Food Waste at Hotel Breakfast Buffets." *Journal of Travel Research* 57 (2): 232–42.

Lee, S. K., and A. A. Kader. 2000. "Pre-harvest and Postharvest Factors Influencing Vitamin C Content of Horticultural Crops." *Postharvest Biology and Technology* 20 (3): 207–20.

Lee, W. T. K., J. Y. A. Tung, and G. Paratore. 2019. *Evaluation of Micronutrient Losses From Postharvest Food Losses (PHL) in Kenya, Cameroon and India—Implications on Micronutrient Deficiencies in Children Under 5 Years of Age.* Rome: FAO.

Lewis, L., M. Onsongo, H. Njapau, H. Schurz-Rogers, G. Luber, S. J. Nyamongo, L. Baker, A. M. Dayiye, A. Misore, and D. R. Kevin. 2005. "Aflatoxin Contamination of Commercial Maize Products During an Out-Break of Acute Aflatoxicosis in Eastern and Central Kenya." *Environmental Health Perspective* 113 (12): 1763–67.

Lundqvist, J., C. de Fraiture, and D. Molden. 2008. *Saving Water: From Field to Fork—Curbing Losses and Wastage in the Food Chain. SIWI Policy Brief.* Stockholm: SIWI.

Luton, M. T., and D. A. Holland. 1986. "The Effects of Preharvest Factors on the Quality of Stored Conference Pears 1. Effects of Orchard Factors." *Journal of Horticultural Science* 61 (1): 23–32.

Magzawa, L. S., A. Mditshwa, S. Z. Tesfay, and U. L. Opara. 2017. "An Overview of Preharvest Factors Affecting Vitamin C Content of Citrus Fruit." *Scientia Horticulturae* 216: 12–21.

Maharjan, K. L., and N. P. Joshi. 2013. *Climate Change, Agriculture and Rural Livelihoods in Developing Countries.* Tokyo: Springer.

Mann, M. S., and A. S. Sandhu. 1988. "Effect of NPK Fertilization on Fruit Quality and Maturity of Kinnow Mandarin." *Punjab Horticultural Journal* 28: 14–21.

McCullough, E. B., P. L. Pingalil, and K. G. Stamoulis. 2008. *The Transformation of Agri-food Systems, Globalization, Supply Chains and Smallholder Farmers.* London: Routledge.

Meldelsohn, R., and A. Dinar. 2012. *Handbook on Climate Change and Agriculture.* Cheltenham: Edward Elgar Publishing.

Murphy, J., U. Gretzel, J. Pesonen, A. L. Elorinne, and K. Silvennoinen. 2018. "Household Food Waste, Tourism, and Social Media: A Research Agenda." *Information and Communication Technologies in Tourism*: 228–39.

Nagy, S. 1980. "Vitamin C Contents of Citrus Fruit and Their Products: A Review." *Journal of Agriculture and Food Chemistry* 28 (1): 8–18.

National Statistics. 2016. *Final UK Greenhouse Gas Emissions National Statistics: 1990–2013.* London: UK Government, Department of Energy and Climate Change.

Negi, S., and N. Anand. 2015. "Issues and Challenges in the Supply Chain of Fruits and Vegetables Sector in India: A Review." *International Journal of Managing Value and Supply Chains* 6 (2): 47–62.

———. 2017. "Post-Harvest Losses and Wastage in Indian Fresh Agro Supply Chain Industry: A Challenge." *The IUP Journal of Supply Chain Management* 14 (2): 7–23.

Newsome, R., C. G. Balestrini, M. D. Baum, J. Corby, W. Fisher, K. Goodburn, P. Labuza, G. Prince, H. S. Thesmar, and F. Yiannas. 2014. "Applications and Perceptions of Date Labeling of Food." *Comprehensive Reviews in Food Science and Food Safety* 13 (4): 745–69.

OECD. 2005. *Agricultural Market Impacts of Future Growth in the Production of Biofuels.* Paris: OECD.

————. 2010. *Climate Change and Agriculture Impacts, Adaptation and Mitigation.* Paris: OECD.

Parfitt, J., M. Barthel, and S. Macnaughton. 2010. "Food Waste Within Food Supply Chains Quantification and Potential for Change to 2050." *Philosophical Transactions of the Royal Society B* 365: 3065–81.

Quested, T., and H. Johnson. 2009. *Household Food and Drink Waste in the UK.* Banbury: WRAP.

Quested, T., E. Marsh, R. Swannell, and A. D. Parry. 2013. "Spaghetti Soup: The Complex World of Food Waste Behaviours." *Resources, Conservation and Recycling* 79: 43–51.

Reitz, G. J., and R. C. Koo. 1960. "Effect of Nitrogen and Potassium Fertilization on Yield Fruit Quality and Leaf Analysis of Valencia Oranges." *Proceeding of the Journal of the American Society for Horticultural Science* 75: 43–51.

Renzaho, A. M. N., J. K. Kamara, and M. Toole. 2017. "Biofuel Production and Its Impact on Food Security in Low- and Middle-Income Countries: Implications for the Post-2015 Sustainable Development Goals." *Renewable and Sustainable Energy Reviews* 78: 503–15.

Rolle, R., ed. 2006. *Improving Postharvest Management and Marketing in the Asia-Pacific Region: Issues and Challenges Trends in the Fruit and Vegetable Sector.* Rome: FAO, Asian Productivity Organization (APO).

Santeramo, F. G., and E. Lamonaca. 2021. "Food Loss—Food Waste—Food Security: A New Research Agenda." *Sustainability* 13: 4642.

Setti, M., L. Falasconi, M. Vittuari, S. Andrea, I. Cusano, and C. Griffith. 2016. "Italian Consumers' Income and Food Waste Behavior." *British Food Journal* 118 (7): 1731–46.

Shafiee-Jood, M., and X. Cai. 2016. "Reducing Food Loss and Waste to Enhance Food Security and Environmental Sustainability." *Environmental Science & Technology* 50 (16): 8432–43.

Shukla, M., and S. Jharkharia. 2013. "Agri-Fresh Produce Supply Chain Management: A State-of-the-Art Literature Review." *International Journal of Operations & Production Management* 33 (2): 114–58.

Stancu, V., P. Haugaard, and L. Lahteenmaki. 2016. "Determinants of Consumer Food Waste Behaviour: Two Routes to Food Waste." *Appetite* 96: 7–17.

Stanley, J., R. Marshall, S. Tustin, and A. Woolf. 2014. "Preharvest Factors Affect Apricot Fruit Quality." *Acta Horticulturae* 1058: 269–76.

Stenmark, A. C., C. Jense, T. Quested, and G. Moates. 2016. "Estimates of European Food Waste Levels." www.eufusions.org/phocadownload/Publications/Estimates%20of%20European%20food%20waste%20levels.pdf.

Stuart, T. 2009. *Waste: Uncovering the Global Food Scandal.* London: W. W. Norton Co.

Theotokis, A., K. Pramatari, and M. Tsiros. 2012. "Effects of Expiration Date-Based Pricing on Brand Image Perceptions." *Journal of Retailing* 88 (1): 72–87.

Thyberg, K. I., and D. J. Tonjes. 2016. "Drivers of Food Waste and Their Implications for Sustainable Policy Development." *Resources, Conservation and Recycling* 106: 110–23.

Toivonen, P. M. A., B. J. Zebarth, and P. A. Bowen. 1994. "Effect of Nitrogen Fertilization on Head Size, Vitamin C Content and Storage Life of Broccoli (*Brassica oleracea var. italica*)." *Canadian Journal of Plant Science* 74: 607–10.

Tsiros, M., and C. M. Heilman. 2005. "The Effect of Expiration Dates and Perceived Risk on Purchasing Behavior in Grocery Store Perishable Categories." *Journal of Marketing* 69 (2): 114–29.

van Boxstael, S., F. Devlieghere, D. Berkvens, A. Vermeulen, and M. Uyttandaele. 2014. "Understanding and Attitude Regarding the Shelf Life Labels and Dates on Pre-Packed Food Products by Belgian Consumers." *Food Control* 37: 85–92.

Venkat, K. 2011. "The Climate Change and Economic Impacts of Food Waste in the United States." *International Journal on Food System Dynamics* 2 (4): 431–46.

Wilson, N. L. W., B. J. Rickard, R. Saputo, and S. Ho. 2017. "Food Waste: The Role of Date Labels, Package Size, and Product Category." *Food Quality Preference* 55: 35–44.

WRAP. 2011. "New Estimates for Household Food and Drink Waste in the UK." A Report Presenting Updated Estimates of Food and Drink Waste from UK, Banbury, WRAP.

Yang, X. Y., J. X. Xie, F. F. Wang, J. Zhong, Y. Z. Liu, G. H. Li, and S. A. Peng. 2011. "Comparison of Ascorbate Metabolism in Fruits of Two Citrus Species with Obvious Difference in Ascorbate Content in Pulp." *Journal of Plant Physiology* 168 (18): 2196–2205.

Yildirim, H., R. Capone, A. Karanlik, F. Bottalico, P. Debs, and H. El Bilali. 2016. "Food Wastage in Turkey: An Exploratory Survey on Household Food Waste." *Journal of Food and Nutrition Research* 4 (8): 483–89.

Zilberman, D., G. Hochman, D. Rajagopal, S. Sexton, and G. Timilsina. 2013. "The Impact of Biofuels on Commodity Food Prices: Assessment of Findings." *American Journal of Agricultural Economics* 95 (2): 275–81.

Zolin, C. A., and A. R. Rodrigues. 2015. *Impact of Climate Change on Water Resources in Agriculture*. London: CRC Press.

3 Tackling food loss and waste

An overview of policy actions

Christian Reynolds

Introduction

Since the early 2000s, policy issues relating to food loss and waste (FLW) have risen up the social and political agenda (Smith 2020). Major drivers of this rise have been climate change and resource use. Estimates suggest that globally one-third of food never reaches a human stomach (IMechE 2013); this represents a massive waste of resources with four trillion megajoules of energy and 82 billion cubic metres of water are lost yearly from consumer FLW alone (Coudard et al. 2021). Likewise, global FLW is associated with 8–10% of global GHG emissions (Mbow et al. 2019). Indeed, the case for reducing FLW has been successfully made in terms of nutrition, environment, society, and economic development (World Bank 2020), leading to wide and diverse stakeholder engagement. This rise of FLW up the policy agenda has meant that policies with the aim of reduction/prevention, diversion, valorisation, and redistribution of FLW have begun to be developed at multiple levels of government, and across and within multiple geographies (e.g. see international programmes (Chapters 4 to 6), national programmes (Chapters 7 to 12), and local programmes (Chapters 13 to 15). One of the most prominent policy goals adopted by many government (and non-government) actors is SDG 12.3—the ambition to halve edible food waste by 2030 (Lipinski et al. 2017).

Reports have now been published that propose multiple and varied FLW policy actions over a variety of time periods to meet or make progress towards SDG 12.3. The most recent reports include estimates of the tonnages reduced or diverted, and the environmental and economic impacts of each policy action (ReFED 2020; Sustainability Victoria 2020; FIAL 2021). Likewise, academic publications reviewing and establishing a peer-reviewed evidence base for the interventions available have been published (Stöckli, Niklaus, and Dorn 2018; De Laurentiis, Caldeira, and Sala 2020; Reynolds et al. 2019). However peer-reviewed documents illustrate the lack of evidence base that many of the policy actions currently have. Finally, curated policy databases have arisen concerning food banks (Harvard Law School Food Law and Policy Clinic and The Global

DOI: 10.4324/9781003226932-5

FoodBanking Network 2021) and local government policy actions (Reeve et al. 2020; University of Sydney 2020).

The previous two chapters have provided an introduction to how we currently define and measure FLW (Chapter 1), as well as the causes and consequences of FLW across the food chain (Chapter 2). This chapter provides an introduction to wider FLW policy concepts including the food waste hierarchy and the need for multiple policy aims in a food systems context; as well as the concept of policy coherence to enhance FLW policy implementation. This chapter then gives a wider review of policy actions and interventions that are available for tackling FLW. The overall intention of this chapter is to provide the reader with the wider 'menu' of policy actions that are available to address FLW and allow comparison with the actions that were chosen.

The FLW hierarchy—the key to understanding FLW policy development

Waste disposal hierarchies have been a key framework that has shaped the evolution of FLW policy (Smith 2020). Waste disposal hierarchies were introduced in 1970s to shift resource use and waste management policy from selecting linear discard based and land-fill solutions towards circular reuse/recycling-based solutions. Table 3.1 shows how different geographies and legal frameworks have slightly different versions of the FLW hierarchy—for a wider discussion, see Papargyropoulou et al. (2014). Overall, the majority of FLW hierarchies stipulate that actors should prioritise efforts (in order of most to least preferable) to reduce (or prevent) FLW, redistribute it (e.g. to the homeless or recycle

Table 3.1 Examples of previous FLW hierarchies in EU, the United Kingdom, and the United States

FLW hierarchies	Waste framework directive	WRAP food and material hierarchy	Food waste pyramid	Food recovery hierarchy
	EU (EC 2008)	UK (Downing, Priestley, and Carr 2015)	UK (ReFood 2013)	USA (USEPA 2015)
Highest priority	Prevention	Prevention	Reduce	Source reduction
	Preparation for reuse	Optimisation	Feed people in need	Feed people in need
	Recycling	Recycling	Feed livestock	Feed livestock
	Recovery	Recovery	Compost and renewable energy via AD	Industrial use compost
Lowest priority	Disposal	Disposal	Incineration or landfill	Incineration or landfill

it as animal feed), valorise,[1] compost, recover energy, and (finally) landfill the remainder. As discussed in Chapter 1, there are various definitions for FLW (e.g. edible vs. inedible), and the measurement definition used, along with the version of the FLW hierarchy used influences the policies that governments (and other actors) implement.

Giordano et al. (2020) provide analysis of how differing FLW hierarchies have led to different outcomes, illustrating how French and Italian laws and responses are different due to understandings of their FLW hierarchies.

The policy actions reviewed in this chapter have developed out of the FLW hierarchy aims. However, there are other policy issues that are interlinked with FLW and resource use beyond the FLW hierarchy. One such issue is the interpretation of over-consumption of food as a type of waste, for example over-consumption of food can be thought of as a misallocation of resources (food) that could be used to feed others, and (like FLW) this has negative health, environmental, economic, and social impacts (Schmidt and Matthies 2018; Parker, Umashankar, and Schleicher 2019; Clapp 2002; Horton et al. 2019; Toti, Di Mattia, and Serafini 2019; Smetana et al. 2021; Chalmers, Osei-Kwasi, and Reynolds 2019; Sundin et al. 2021). For now, this re-interpretation of FLW to include overconsumption of food is beyond this chapter's scope.

The need for a diverse, evidence-based FLW policy mix

Many FLW strategies are focused solely on the reduction/prevention of FLW. This is due to the use of the FLW hierarchy to develop policy actions, the definitions/scope of the FLW problem, and the drivers of FLW being (in part) consumption based. However, as highlighted by the Waste and Resource Action Programme (WRAP, a UK charity that works globally on FLW issues), a policy mix focused only on reduction/prevention does not have a long-term impact upon FLW generation (Parry et al. 2014). This is due to (1) population growth—meaning that per capita reductions reduce effectiveness over time and (2) the effectiveness of current reduction/prevention interventions varies and decreases over time. Instead, policy mixes need to be developed and implemented that are linked across all stages of the FLW hierarchy and the wider food system.

This need for diverse policy mix has been modelled in strategy documents (ReFED 2020; FIAL 2021), each having policy actions to divert, valorise, and redistribute FLW alongside reduction/prevention policy actions. Indeed, these other destinations on the FLW hierarchy have (in both referenced documents) a capacity to divert a much larger tonnage of FLW than reduction/prevention policy actions—even though reduction/prevention is preferred according to the FLW hierarchy.

The need for accurate measurement of FLW is also a priority in order to develop a comprehensive FLW policy mix. This is because accurate measurement of FLW enables targeting and refinement of policy actions to respond to the specifics of the situation and geography (Reynolds et al. 2020). There is no doubt that FLW measurement had increased in detail and scope over the last decade (World Resources Institute 2016; CEC 2019), and this has enabled the development of appropriate policy for each geographic situation. Indeed, there are now specific policies in many countries that mandate FLW measurement methodologies to quantify FLW at each stage of the food supply chain (for instance, EUROPEAN COMMISSION 2019).

The need for a food systems approach to FLW

Due to the complexity of causes and drivers of FLW (as outlined in Chapter 2), FLW solutions and policy need to be developed and implemented not only in a 'silo' by governments (be they municipal, local, and regional, national, international) but also by wider food system actors at each stage of the food chain. Within the food chain, actors who need to develop FLW policies include production (farmers), handling and storage (packinghouses, storage, transportation, and logistics), processing and packaging (processors, manufacturers, slaughterhouses, and packaging), distribution and market (wholesalers, retailers (formal and informal), consumption (households, restaurants), and waste management and valorisation. Policy also needs to be developed by and in partnership with financiers, innovators, the research community, and civil society (both grassroots community-led initiatives and wider special interest groups). Likewise, FLW needs policies that lead to action at all geographic levels, from municipal through global (Flanagan et al. 2019).

To enable food systemwide actions, FLW policy has begun to be co-developed using public-private partnerships and voluntary agreements (Boulding and Devine 2019). Even though there is evidence of an average 14 to one return on investment for FLW reduction (Champions 12.3 2017), the deployment of FLW policy actions without government assistance is slow and lacking focus without the use of voluntary agreements mechanisms.

This food system approach to FLW policy development is needed as different amounts of waste are generated at different stages in the food chain, depending on the types of foods, the production and consumption processes, and the geography in question. These differences in waste generation tonnage and location in the food system will also influence the types of policy actions deployed.

Policy coherence and wider FLW policy strategy

The use of a wider food systems approach also leads to a greater awareness of synergies and trade-offs between policy actions that can be taken. Both Roadmap to 2030 (ReFED 2020) and Australian National Food Waste Strategy (FIAL 2021) feature FLW policy actions that have potential synergies (e.g. when deployed simultaneously can lead to further enhanced FLW reduction in the wider food system, as well as wider positive social benefits). This can be seen in the selection of the final 23 interdependent actions within the

'Recommended scenario' published in the Australian National Food Waste Strategy (FIAL 2021).

One type of trade-off is the amount of FLW generated. Due to different policy actions, the amount of FLW generated can change in the intended sector, and across the wider system (World Bank 2020), for example a policy reducing on-farm FLW leads to increasing farm sales; some of these sales may then be wasted further down the supply chain, leading to increased household FLW. Alternatively, a policy focused on decreased household FLW may lead to reduced purchases, and so less food is sold by farmers. This may mean less is produced, and less wasted; or that the same amount of food is produced and is exported to other customers/countries. The exact trade-offs differ based on food type, geographic context etc. de Gorter et al. (2020) termed these wider FLW generation effects as indirect 'cascading effects'. In short, the cascading effects up and down the supply chain mean that in some cases, policy actions to reduce FLW will be reinforced while in other cases, partially offset. These cascading effects can be thought of as 'short-term' effects that occur as the food system adjusts to the policy, but are still important to consider.

FLW policy actions can also have wider unintentional positive and negative spill-over effects in different parts of the food system beyond tonnages of FLW generated. For example, in the case of the French Food Waste law (LOI n° 2016–138) though increasing donations from supermarkets, the law may have initially flooded an under-resourced food aid sector with too much food, leading to unintended disposal issues for the food aid sector—rather than the supermarkets (see Chapter 7, and Gore-Langton 2017; Mourad and Finn 2019).

This complexity of multiple policies interacting in the food system is linked to the term *policy coherence*. The concept of policy coherence is used to highlight and identify mutually reinforcing policies that create synergies towards achieving agreed objectives and to avoid (or minimise) negative outcomes in other policy areas (OECD 2016; Parsons and Hawkes 2019; OECD 2021; Thow et al. 2018). There are many food system policy areas that have direct and indirect impacts on FLW, and so policy actions in these areas also need consideration with regard to policy coherence. For instance, food system policies regarding nutrition, school food, public procurement, food safety, trading practices, waste management and bio-economy, animal welfare, transport, trade, and taxes have all been identified as linked FLW at the EU/nation-state level (FBR Supply Chain & Information Management et al. 2020). Likewise, at the local or municipal government level, the Australian Local Food System Policy Database (Reeve et al. 2020; University of Sydney 2020) places FLW alongside 33 other policy areas that are within a local/municipal domain. Each of these other policy areas could link with synergies and trade-offs to FLW policy actions. As policymakers and researchers, we need to think about FLW from a policy coherence perspective to ensure that FLW policies can be designed to improve one or multiple food system outcomes and does not undermine others.

Examples of where FLW policy actions intersect with wider policy coherence issues are (1) healthy sustainable diets (WRAP 2019a) and (2) green + digital technologies (UNEP DTU Partnership and United Nations Environment

Programme 2021). In the case of healthy sustainable diets, policy could enable greater amounts of FLW to be generated (e.g. shifting diets to healthy but high waste foods (e.g. salad greens). However, if FLW is considered during policy development, we could find policies that enable sustainable diets and further reduce FLW (e.g. changing diets towards healthy, longer shelf life, low waste foods, and frozen and canned vegetables).

Review of FLW policy actions

There have now been multiple FLW strategy documents that provide a review of available FLW policy actions. In the United States, 'A roadmap to reduce U.S. food waste by 20 percent' (ReFED 2016) provided 27 'solutions' (e.g. policy actions) while 'Roadmap to 2030' (ReFED 2020) provided 40 solutions. In Australia, 'The Path to Half' (Sustainability Victoria 2020) identified 25 solutions, while the Australian National Food Waste Strategy (FIAL 2021) identified a long list of 47 different interventions. In the EU, 'Halving food loss and waste in the EU by 2030' (Reynolds et al. 2020) highlighted three approaches to FLW reduction (measurement; valorisation, and voluntary agreements), 'Changing the rules of the game' (FBR Supply Chain & Information Management et al. 2020) identified 32 policy actions, 'Assessment of Food Waste Prevention Actions' (Caldeira, De Laurentiis, and Sala 2019) collated evidence from 91 actions, and 'Recommendations for Action in Food Waste Prevention' (EU Platform on Food Losses and Food Waste 2019) recommended 47 actions and suggested 12 possible additional actions. At a global level, 'Reducing Food Loss and Waste: Setting a Global Action Agenda' (Flanagan et al. 2019) provided a priority to-do list of 107 actions and identified ten specific interventions to scale and accelerate FLW reduction. This wide array of policy actions highlights the range, depth, detail, scope, and complexity that is possible in current FLW policy. The remainder of this section introduces some specific policy actions with these based upon the interventions as listed in the Australian National Food Waste Strategy (FIAL 2021).

Public policy and regulation

Infrastructure investment

Governments can invest in capital infrastructure, such as roads or ports. This can have a benefit of reducing transit times. There are multiple studies discussing this though limited quantification of impacts (Villarreal, Garcia, and Rosas 2009; Ishangulyyev, Kim, and Lee 2019; Jedermann et al. 2014; Stroecken 2017; Lipińska, Tomaszewska, and Kołożyn-Krajewska 2019).

Research funding and innovation grants

FLW can be identified as a strategic priority for public-funded research and innovation. In addition, the governments can set up additional funding scheme to reduce FLW. However, there is limited quantification of the return on investment for FLW research.

FLW measurement policy (as well as developing data infrastructure, analytics, and waste audits)

Implementing technologies and systems to better understand and measure the streams of waste produced in the food system is an important policy action (World Resources Institute 2016; CEC 2019).

Invest in cold storage and cold chain improvements

Effective storage, refrigeration, and stock management are critical for ensuring that shelf life is maximised and potential losses are avoided in the supply chain (Brodribb and McCann 2020). Food within the cold chain is likely to be of higher economic value, embodied environmental impact, and perishability (James and James 2010).

Encourage gleaning

Gleaning is the act of collecting leftover crops from farms after they have been commercially harvested. The gleaning of time-sensitive surplus unpicked crops from fields by local charities and organisations can prevent FLW but is constrained by labour/time factors. Academic modelling (Lee et al. 2017) estimated 0.08 tonne to 0.11 tonne per gleaner. Reports on USA gleaning effectiveness (County Health Rankings 2019; USDA 2019) estimate ~0.25 tonne per gleaner (23,286 gleaners rescuing 5,908 tonnes in 2019), while a Spanish gleaning organisation (Espigoladors 2018) gleaned at a rate of 0.17 tonnes per gleaner (~200 tonnes of food per year with ~1,148 gleaners).

Enable harvesting and sorting of all grades of crop at economic cost

A proportion of some crops are not picked as the economic value of second-grade product is not sufficient to cover the additional labour requirements. There is potential for this to be tackled through the development and use of technologies, for example picking and sorting machines. An additional system-wide solution would be processors and/or retailers agreeing to purchase the 'whole crop' and then having the responsibility for finding markets for all grades of produce.

Implement date labelling best practice

The development of uniform and understandable date labelling will allow for better communication of information to consumers and wider food systems actors (Wilson et al. 2017; Newsome et al. 2014; Turvey et al. 2021; Thompson et al. 2018). This will contribute to a reduction of FLW based on shelf life and storage. Additional sub-actions include removing best-before dates from items that do not require it by law; removing 'sell by and display by' dates; etc.

Improve manufacturing processes and technologies

There are many practices that reduce FLW in food and drink manufacturing: the introduction of new equipment and technology, changes to processes, and the adoption of continuous improvement initiatives.

Restricted residual waste capacity

The restriction of residual waste collection has been shown to encourage increased participation in recycling; for example, local authorities can impose a limited amount of waste, which can be collected every year through different mechanisms: special, authority-distributed residual waste bags; restricting the physical size of bins issued to households; and collecting residual waste less frequently. This may encourage food system actors who would not voluntarily participate in recycling to engage (due to not being able to fit plastics, glass, and food into their residual waste collection).

Separate food waste collection

The ability for all food system actors to separate out FLW is a fundamental criterion for many other FLW reduction practices. Rolling out specific FLW recycling and collection services is a crucial part of this provision.

Tackle unfair trading practices

Unfair Trading Practices (UTPs) have been identified by a number of reports (Piras et al. 2018; European Bank for Reconstruction and Development 2019; Sinclair Taylor, Parfitt, and Jarosz 2019; Messner, Johnson, and Richards 2021) as playing a significant role in increasing FLW at food manufacturing and agricultural stages—for example when suppliers are penalised for not delivering an agreed amount of product, there are significant incentives to over-produce food. UTPs can occur in food systems where market power is concentrated within a few large retailers interacting with a large number of suppliers. Perishable products (chilled foods, and fresh fruits and vegetables) supplied direct from primary producers to retailers are particularly at risk due to the time constraints (short shelf life) preventing the producer from finding alternate markets.

Taxes and fees

Low-interest financing

Low-interest finance and loans enable food system actors to invest in wider FLW policy actions. This is needed to allow an FLW policy ecosystem to develop. However, there is little data on impact and ROI of finance beyond the Champions 12.3 (Champions 12.3 2017) average 14-fold return on investment for investing in actions that reduce FLW.

Pay-as-you-throw (PAYT) taxes

Setting taxes for solid waste management can encourage reductions to avoid higher fees. In South Korea, there was a 2% recycling rate for FLW in 1995; however, the introduction of a PAYT tax led to a 95% recycling rate by 2019, as well as waste tonnage reductions (Sheldon 2020; Bloom 2019).

Tax credit schemes, VAT exemptions

Modification can be made to tax law to enabled value added tax (VAT) deductions for companies that made food donations to food banks. Other options may include tax reductions or credits for organisations to engage in FLW reduction, or invest in technology aiming at FLW reduction.

Ensuring energy policy does not promote FLW

Fiscal measures (such as subsidies and taxes) to increase renewable sources of energy through the use of technologies such as anaerobic digestion can incentivise the 'recycling' of FLW as energy ahead of the prevention or diversion of FLW (e.g. through re-distribution). Energy policy and fiscal measures must be designed to work in coherence with the FLW hierarchy to ensure that this outcome does not occur.

Voluntary agreements

Voluntary agreements are schemes through which public and private sector organisations make commitments to improve their environmental performance, without the need for legislation or sanctions. These agreements include an element of public reporting and target-setting as well as a forum for sharing best practice. Numerous voluntary agreements have been set up to tackle FLW, either covering a wide variety of sectors and stakeholders across the food chain (e.g. the Courtauld Commitment in the United Kingdom (WRAP 2019b, 2020a, 2020c), ForMat Project in Norway (Hanssen and Møller 2013) and Taskforce Circular Economy in Food in the Netherlands (Samen Tegen Voedselverspilling 2020)) or focusing on specific sectors (e.g. Dairy Roadmap (Dairy UK 2018) and the Hospitality and Food Service Agreement in the United Kingdom (WRAP 2020b)). Wider discussion of these can be found in Reynolds et al. (2020) and Boulding and Devine (2019).

Information provision

Employee and citizen engagement and behaviour change

Widespread adoption of best practice across the food system can reduce waste by informing and engaging staff and the wider citizenry in mitigation opportunities across supply and storage, preparation, serving and disposal, and in building confidence to make decisions. There is limited evidence of this intervention in the field. A REFRESH project pilot on employee engagement and behaviour change with the supermarket Penny (REFRESH 2020) found no evidence of effect at scale, but informal evidence that the piloted training and information provision was effective.

Consumer behaviour change campaigns

A large-scale consumer advocacy campaign (based on behavioural change theory) has been used in multiple contexts. These have been shown to reduce waste by between 5% and 15% (ReFED 2016; Reynolds et al. 2019).

Improved storage instructions

Providing better on-pack information to consumers on how to store and use products can lead to reduced consumer waste. However, this intervention only applies to part of household waste, ReFED (ReFED 2016) estimated that 20% consumer waste due to package size or design, with 5–10% of US consumers reacting to label changes and modifying their behaviour.

Nudging

Portioning nudges

There are a range of 'nudges' that can be applied to reduce FLW at home and in hospitals: providing smaller plates to influence portion size; providing the option for customers to select different size meals (e.g. regular or half portion); encouraging doggy bags etc. (Just and Swigert 2016; Milford, Øvrum, and Helgesen 2015; Jagau and Vyrastekova 2017).

Changes to standards

Changes to public procurement standards

Public procurement can be used as a lever to change the waste-related practices of schools, hospitals, prisons, the military, and other public sector canteens. The Champions 12.3 (Champions 12.3 2020) case studies provide evidence to show that FLW reduction is possible using procurement contracts that link and incentivise supply chain FLW reductions and effective ordering.

Relax product standards and specifications

Accepting food products that are cosmetically imperfect or that do not fit typical retail specifications is a method of reducing FLW. In the United States, it is estimated that 2.6% of US on-farm waste could be avoided through relaxing specific rules at the retail stage (ReFED 2016).

Increase residue tolerances in safety standards

In the majority of countries, there is a zero-tolerance approach to finding chemical residues in food product: if residues are detected the food must be disposed of for food safety reasons. However, advances in detection technologies can find traces of substances that may not be a risk to human health, and so this food could still be eaten if the residue tolerances in the standards were increased.

Extend allowable use-by dates

By extending use-by dates, a product has more chance to be sold and consumed. Møller et al. (2016) ran experiments for meat products, finding longer dates (increased durability) led to FLW reduction (8% to 2%, 11% to 3%, and 6% to 3%). WRAP's household simulation model (WRAP 2020d; Kandemir et al. 2020) shows 19% to 30% improvement for people who follow the guidance (e.g. ~30% of UK population) on milk waste, if date increased 1–3 days. This could be considered a change to food risk and public health standards.

Other policy actions

Hospitality policy

Menu planning

Designing menus with FLW prevention in mind, for example reducing the number of ingredients and repurposing food preparation trim and overproduction has been suggested as an industry led intervention by WRAP (WRAP 2016, 2020e) and the Nordic Council of Ministers (Nordic Council of Ministers et al. 2012).

Centralised and 'dark' commercial kitchens

Dark kitchens are virtual restaurants supplying food through web portals or mobile apps. Centralised and dark kitchens can reduce hospitality FLW through economies of scale in food preparation and storage.

Surplus and donation policy

Increase resale or donation of surplus food

Surplus food can be sold or donated to food aid organisation as a method to redistribute FLW. New information technology infrastructure can play a crucial part in operationalising this policy action (UNEP DTU Partnership and United Nations Environment Programme 2021). There are multiple financial and legal methods of increasing donation (KPMG 2020). Donation standardisation and Donation Tax Incentives are two such methods (ReFED 2016). Likewise, educating potential food donors on donation liability laws has been shown to increase the uptake of food rescue and donation.

Ensure product liability laws do not limit food donations

Companies who would like to donate surplus food may have concerns about the legal and reputational consequences from illness resulting from improper onward distribution of products. In the United States, a 'Good Samaritans Act' reduces the public liability risks to retailers and food companies that donate food to local communities and food redistribution charities (KPMG 2020; Harvard Law School Food Law and Policy Clinic and The Global FoodBanking Network 2021).

Improve re-distribution sector storage capacity and practices

One of the barriers to greater donation of surplus foods is the lack of capacity in local charitable sector to take surplus food in sufficient volumes safely. Improving and investing in surplus capacity as well as re-distribution practices helps with FLW diversion to food aid organisations.

Valorisation and animal feed policy

Increase diversion of FLW to animal feed

In many FLW hierarchies, food used for animal feed is not considered to be 'waste' and therefore feeding food to animals can be an attractive policy action. The REFRESH project had a work package on this intervention (Luyckx 2018; REFRESH 2019a, 2019b). Japan is a world leader in animal feed where 52% of waste from the food industry is now used as livestock feed, thanks to adequate policies and a certification system (Luyckx 2018).

Nutrient extraction from processing wastes

Bio-refining FLW to extract additional products is a common form of valorisation. There is limited quantification of scale in literature, but many use cases (Gedi et al. 2020).

Value-added processing and stabilisation of surplus food

Maximising the use of by-products and surplus production by creating new food products and brands from surplus raw ingredients (e.g. 'ugly fruit', soups). This new food is then stabilised through freezing, drying, or packaging technology to create longer shelf life value-added items with less waste. Multiple programmes have scaled and used this intervention (REFRESH 2018, 2019c; Lafon and Montoux 2015).

Fibre products from FLW

Using fibre in the manufacture of non-food products is another form of valorisation. A range of start-up, manufacturing textile products from fruit and vegetable waste are emerging globally.

Technical and innovative policy actions

Improving operational efficiency

This industry-focused policy action covers discounting; stock management; ordering process and replenishment sizes; maintenance of cold chain; on-shelf availability targets; etc. Forecasting food demand is a challenge to understand how much food needs to be produced, and how to address FLW due to product life issues within the food chain. Inaccurate forecasting can lead to overproduction and oversupply. A European Commission research project (Grant agreement ID: 867163) found that restaurants can reduce FLW by up to 50% by accurately predicting food demand (European Commission 2019). Other types of operational efficiency may include valorising in-store through production of foods on-site, for example bakery products, soups, pies, and salads using surplus/waste.

Processing technologies to extend shelf life

Implementing technological solutions to extend shelf life is another industry led policy action found in multiple reports and for multiple food types. WRAP's household simulation model (WRAP 2020d; Kandemir et al. 2020) has found consistent household FLW reductions based on shelf life extensions.

Optimise product and packaging to enable better portioning

Better combinations of packaging and portion size can lead to reductions in FLW. Specific interventions include offering additional size options and packaging design improvements, for example through smaller containers, pre-portioned serving.

Use anti-spoilage technologies in packaging

Better designed packaging and new technologies can prolong product freshness and slow down spoilage of perishable products.

Conclusions

This chapter has introduced a variety of policy actions that a government or other food system actor can deploy to reduce/prevent, divert, valorise, and redistribute of FLW. However, innovation is constantly occurring and new technology based policy actions are emerging (UNEP DTU Partnership and United Nations Environment Programme 2021). Likewise, as FLW is linked to many other food system areas, policy actions focused at diet, agriculture, safety, etc. may have impacts on FLW. No single policy action on its own will be sufficient to solve FLW (or even bring about a 50% reduction to meet SDG12.3), and so all policy actions need to be implemented in a wider food systems context and in a coherent manner for the best outcomes for FLW and wider food system.

Note

1 Valorise in this context means to 'Create *new food, new by-products for food and feed formulations, new high value added food and feed components or other novel products from wasted food*' (Gedi et al. 2020).

Bibliography

Bloom, Douglas. 2019. "South Korea Once Recycled 2% of Its Food Waste. Now It Recycles 95% | World Economic Forum." April 12. www.weforum.org/agenda/2019/04/south-korea-recycling-food-waste/.

Boulding, Andy, and Rachel Devine. 2019. "Evaluation of Framework for Action Pilots—Final Synthesis Report." REFRESH Deliverable 2.8. REFRESH.

Brodribb, Peter, and Michael McCann. 2020. *A Study of Waste in the Cold Food Chain and Opportunities for Improvements*. Australia: Department of Agriculture, Water and the Environment and Refrigerants Australia.

CEC. 2019. *Quantifying Food Loss and Waste and Its Impacts*. Montreal, Canada: Commission for Environmental Cooperation.

Chalmers, N., S. Stetkiewicz, P. Sudhakar, et al. 2019. "Impacts of Reducing UK Beef Consumption Using a Revised Sustainable Diets Framework." *Sustainability* 11 (23): 6863. doi:10.3390/su11236863.

Champions 12.3.2017. *The Business Case for Reducing Food Loss and Waste*. The Netherlands and USA: The Government of the Netherlands and World Resources Institute (WRI).

———. 2020. "10x20x30 | Champions 12.3." https://champions123.org/10-20-30.

Clapp, Jennifer. 2002. "The Distancing of Waste: Overconsumption in a Global Economy." In *Confronting Consumption*. Cambridge, MA: MIT Press.

Coudard, A., E. Corbin, J. de Koning, A. Tukker, and J. M. Mogollón. 2021. "Global Water and Energy Losses From Consumer Avoidable Food Waste." *Journal of Cleaner Production* (October): 129342. doi:10.1016/j.jclepro.2021.129342.

County Health Rankings. 2019. "Fruit & Vegetable Gleaning Initiatives." October 15. www.countyhealthrankings.org/take-action-to-improve-health/what-works-for-health/strategies/fruit-vegetable-gleaning-initiatives.

Dairy UK. 2018. "The Dairy Roadmap | Dairy UK." www.dairyuk.org/publications/the-dairy-roadmap/.

de Gorter, Harry, Dušan Drabik, David R. Just, Christian Reynolds, and Geeta Sethi. 2020. "Analyzing the Economics of Food Loss and Waste Reductions in a Food Supply Chain." *Food Policy* (August): 101953. doi:10.1016/j.foodpol.2020.101953.

De Laurentiis, Valeria, Carla Caldeira, and Serenella Sala. 2020. "No Time to Waste: Assessing the Performance of Food Waste Prevention Actions." *Resources, Conservation, and Recycling* 161 (October): 104946. doi:10.1016/j.resconrec.2020.104946.

Downing, E., S. Priestley, and W. Carr. 2015. *Food Waste: Briefing Paper*. London: House of Commons.

EC. 2008. *Waste Framework Directive (2008/98/EC)*. Brussels: European Commission.

Espigoladors. 2018. *Fundació Espigoladors Memoria de actividades 2018*. Barcelona, Spain: Espigoladors.

EU Platform on Food Losses and Food Waste. 2019. *Recommendations for Action in Food Waste Prevention*. Brussels: EU Platform on Food Losses and Food Waste.

European Bank for Reconstruction and Development. 2019. *Food Loss and Waste Sector Guidelines—Greece*. London: European Bank for Reconstruction and Development.

European Commission. 2019. *Commission Delegated Decision (EU) of 3.5.2019" Supplementing Directive 2008/98/EC of the European Parliament and of the Council as Regards a Common Methodology and Minimum Quality Requirements for the Uniform Measurement of Levels of Food Waste*, vol. C(2019)3211/F1. https://ec.europa.eu/transparency/regdoc/rep/3/2019/EN/C-2019-3211-F1-EN-MAIN-PART-1.PDF.

FBR Supply Chain & Information Management, FBR Consumer Science & Health, H. E. J. Bos-Brouwers, M. G. Kok, J. C. M. A. Snels, and A. A. van der Sluis. 2020. *Changing the Rules of the Game : Impact and Feasibility of Policy and Regulatory Measures on the Prevention and Reduction of Food Waste*. Wageningen: Wageningen Food & Biobased Research. doi:10.18174/529888.

FIAL. 2021. *The National Food Waste Strategy Feasibility Study—Final Report*. Australia: FIAL.

Flanagan, K., K. Robertson, C. Hanson, and A. J. Timmermans. 2019. *Reducing Food Loss and Waste: Setting a Global Action Agenda*. Washington, DC: World Resources Institute.

Gedi, Mohamed A., Vincenzo di Bari, Roger Ibbett, Randa Darwish, Ogueri Nwaiwu, Zainudin Umar, Deepa Agarwal, Richard Worrall, David Gray, and Tim Foster. 2020. "Upcycling and Valorisation of Food Waste." In *Routledge Handbook of Food Waste*, edited by Christian Reynolds, Tammara Soma, Charlotte Spring, and Jordon Lazell, 413–27. Routledge. doi:10.4324/9780429462795-31.

Giordano, Claudia, Luca Falasconi, Clara Cicatiello, and Barbara Pancino. 2020. "The Role of Food Waste Hierarchy in Addressing Policy and Research: A Comparative Analysis." *Journal of Cleaner Production* 252 (April): 119617. doi:10.1016/j.jclepro.2019.119617.

Gore-Langton, Louis. 2017. "France's Food Waste Ban: One Year on." *Food Navigator*, March 24. www.foodnavigator.com/Article/2017/03/24/France-s-food-waste-ban-One-year-on.

Hanssen, Ole Jørgen, and Hanne Møller. 2013. *Food Wastage in Norway 2013 Status and Trends 2009–13*. OR.32.13. Matvett AS/ForMat Project.

Harvard Law School Food Law and Policy Clinic and The Global FoodBanking Network. 2021. "The Global Food Donation Policy Atlas." https://atlas.foodbanking.org/atlas.html.

Horton, Peter, Richard Bruce, Christian Reynolds, and Gavin Milligan. 2019. "Food Chain Inefficiency (FCI): Accounting Conversion Efficiencies Across Entire Food Supply Chains to Re-define Food Loss and Waste." *Frontiers in Sustainable Food Systems* 3 (September). doi:10.3389/fsufs.2019.00079.

IMechE. 2013. *Global Food Waste Not, Want Not*. London: Institution of Mechanical Engineers.

Ishangulyyev, Rovshen, Sanghyo Kim, and Sang Hyeon Lee. 2019. "Understanding Food Loss and Waste-Why Are We Losing and Wasting Food?" *Foods* 8 (8). doi:10.3390/foods8080297.

Jagau, Henrik Luis, and Jana Vyrastekova. 2017. "Behavioral Approach to Food Waste: An Experiment." *British Food Journal* 119 (4): 882–94. doi:10.1108/BFJ-05-2016-0213.

James, S. J., and C. James. 2010. "The Food Cold-Chain and Climate Change." *Food Research International* 43 (7): 1944–1956. doi:10.1016/j.foodres.2010.02.001.

Jedermann, Reiner, Mike Nicometo, Ismail Uysal, and Walter Lang. 2014. "Reducing Food Losses by Intelligent Food Logistics." *Philosophical Transactions. Series A, Mathematical, Physical, and Engineering Sciences* 372 (2017): 20130302. doi:10.1098/rsta.2013.0302.

Just, David R., and Jeffrey M. Swigert. 2016. "The Role of Nudges in Reducing Food Waste." In *Food Security in a Food Abundant World: An Individual Country Perspective*, edited by Andrew Schmitz, P. Lynn Kennedy, and Troy G. Schmitz, vol. 16, 215–24. Frontiers of Economics and Globalization. Emerald Group Publishing Limited. doi:10.1108/S1574-871520150000016009.

Kandemir, Cansu, Christian Reynolds, Quested Tom, Karen Fisher, Rachel Devine, Estelle Herszenhorn, S. C. Lenny Koh, and David Evans. 2020. "Using Discrete Event Simulation to Explore Food Wasted in the Home." *Journal of Simulation* (November): 1–21. doi: 10.1080/17477778.2020.1829515.

KPMG. 2020. *A National Food Waste Tax Incentive—Boosting Food Relief Through Australia's Tax System.* Australia: KPMG.

Lafon, Marine, and Hortense Montoux. 2015. *Developing DISCO BÓCÓ WP4—Testing Social Innovation Feasibility Study Final Report.* The Netherlands: FUSIONS.

Lee, Deishin, Erkut Sönmez, Miguel I. Gómez, and Xiaoli Fan. 2017. "Combining Two Wrongs to Make Two Rights: Mitigating Food Insecurity and Food Waste Through Gleaning Operations." *Food policy* 68 (April): 40–52. doi:10.1016/j.foodpol.2016.12.004.

Lipińska, Milena, Marzena Tomaszewska, and Danuta Kołożyn-Krajewska. 2019. "Identifying Factors Associated With Food Losses During Transportation: Potentials for Social Purposes." *Sustainability* 11 (7): 2046. doi:10.3390/su11072046.

Lipinski, Brian, Austin Clowes, Liz Goodwin, Craig Hanson, Richard Swannell, and Peter Mitchell. 2017. *SDG TARGET 12.3 on Food Loss and Waste: 2017 Progress Report.* Washington, DC and Banbury: WRI/WRAP.

Luyckx, Karen. 2018. "Report: Expert Panel on the Risk Management of Using Treated surplus Food in Pig Feed." Expert Panel Report WP6 Task 6.3.3. REFRESH.

Mbow, Cheikh, Cynthia Rosenzweig, Luis G. Barioni, Tim G. Benton, Mario Herrero, Murukesan Krishnapillai, Emma Liwenga, et al. 2019. "Chapter 5: Food Security." In *Climate Change and Land: An IPCC Special Report on Climate Change, Desertification, Land Degradation, Sustainable Land Management, Food Security, and Greenhouse Gas Fluxes in Terrestrial Ecosystems*, 200. Switzerland: IPCC.

Messner, Rudolf, Hope Johnson, and Carol Richards. 2021. "From Surplus-to-Waste: A Study of Systemic Overproduction, Surplus and Food Waste in Horticultural Supply Chains." *Journal of Cleaner Production* 278 (January): 123952. doi:10.1016/j.jclepro.2020.123952.

Milford, Anna Birgitte, Arnstein Øvrum, and Hilde Helgesen. 2015. "Nudges to Increase Recycling and Reduce Waste." Discussion Paper, 1–27.

Møller, Hanne, Therese Hagtvedt, Nina Lødrup, Jens Kirk Andersen, Pernille Lundquist Madsen, Mads Werge, Ane Kirstine Aare, et al. 2016. *Food Waste and Date Labelling.* TemaNord. Nordic Council of Ministers. doi:10.6027/TN2016-523.

Mourad, Marie, and Steven Finn. 2019. "Opinion | France's Ban on Food Waste Three Years Later—Food Tank." *Food Tank*, June. https://foodtank.com/news/2019/06/opinion-frances-ban-on-food-waste-three-years-later/.

Newsome, Rosetta, Chris G. Balestrini, Mitzi D. Baum, Joseph Corby, William Fisher, Kaarin Goodburn, Theodore P. Labuza, Gale Prince, Hilary S. Thesmar, and Frank Yiannas. 2014. "Applications and Perceptions of Date Labeling of Food." *Comprehensive Reviews in Food Science and Food Safety* 13 (4): 745–69. doi:10.1111/1541-4337.12086.

Nordic Council of Ministers, Jarle Marthinsen, Peter Sundt, Ole Kaysen, and Kathrine Kirkevaag. 2012. *Prevention of Food Waste in Restaurants, Hotels, Canteens and Catering.* Nordic Council of Ministers. doi:10.6027/TN2012-537.

OECD. 2016. *Better Policies for Sustainable Development 2016: A New Framework for Policy Coherence.* OECD. doi:10.1787/9789264256996-en.

———. 2021. *Making Better Policies for Food Systems.* OECD. doi:10.1787/ddfba4de-en.

Papargyropoulou, Effie, Rodrigo Lozano, Julia K. Steinberger, Nigel Wright, and Zaini bin Ujang. 2014. "The Food Waste Hierarchy as a Framework for the Management of Food Surplus and Food Waste." *Journal of Cleaner Production* 76: 106–115. https://doi.org/10.1016/j.jclepro.2014.04.020.

Parker, Jeffrey R., Nita Umashankar, and Martin G. Schleicher. 2019. "How and Why the Collaborative Consumption of Food Leads to Overpurchasing, Overconsumption, and Waste." *Journal of Public Policy & Marketing* 38 (2): 154–71. doi:10.1177/0743915618823783.

Parry, Andrew, Stephen LeRoux, Tom Quested, and Julian Parfitt. 2014. *UK Food Waste—Historical Changes and How Amounts Might Be Influenced in the Future.* Banbury, UK: WRAP.

Parsons, Kelly, and Corinna Hawkes. 2019. *Brief 5: Policy Coherence in Food Systems.* Rethinking Food Policy: A Fresh Approach to Policy and Practice. London: Center for Food Policy, City, University of London.

Patinha Caldeira, C., V. De Laurentiis, and S. Sala. 2019. "Assessment of Food Waste Prevention Actions." Luxembourg: EUR 29901 EN, Publications Office of the European Union, ISBN 978-92-76-10190-1, doi:10.2760/101025, JRC118276.

Piras, Simone, Laura García Herrero, Stephanie Burgos, Flavien Colin, Manuela Gheoldus, Charles Ledoux, Julian Parfitt, Dominika Jaros, and Matteo Vittuari. 2018. "Unfair Trading Practice Regulation and Voluntary Agreements Targeting Food Waste." Deliverable D3.2. REFRESH.

Reeve, Belinda, Anne Marie Thow, Phil Baker, Jessica Hresc, and Serena May. 2020. "The Role of Australian Local Governments in Creating a Healthy Food Environment: An Analysis of Policy Documents from Six Sydney Local Governments." *Australian and New Zealand Journal of Public Health* 44 (2): 137–44. doi:10.1111/1753-6405.12968.

ReFED. 2016. *A Roadmap to Reduce U.S. Food Waste by 20 Percent—Technical Appendix.*

———. 2020. *Insights Engine Food Waste Monitor 2020 Methodology.* New York: ReFED.

ReFood. 2013. *Vision 2020: UK Roadmap to Zero Food Waste to Landfill.* London: Refood-SARIA Group.

REFRESH. 2018. "REFRESH Pilots First Surplus Food Shelf in the Netherlands | REFRESH." https://eu-refresh.org/refresh-pilots-first-surplus-food-shelf-netherlands.

———. 2019a. *Pigs Could Stop 14 Million Tonnes of Surplus Food From Being Wasted—Press Release.* The Netherlands: REFRESH.

———. 2019b. *Avoiding Food Waste Through Feeding Surplus Food to Omnivorous Non-Ruminant Livestock. Policy Brief.* The Netherlands: REFRESH.

———. 2019c. "Hungarian Pilot Project—Ugly but Tasty | REFRESH." https://eu-refresh.org/hungarian-pilot-project-ugly-tasty.

———. 2020. "Food Waste Reduction Training of PENNY Apprentices Successfully Completed | REFRESH." https://eu-refresh.org/food-waste-reduction-training-penny-apprentices-successfully-completed.

Reynolds, Christian, Andy Boulding, Henry Pollock, Nina Sweet, Jabier Ruiz, and Tanja Draeger de Teran. 2020. *Halving Food Loss and Waste in the Eu By 2030*. Berlin: WWF Deutschland, WRAP.

Reynolds, Christian, Liam Goucher, Tom Quested, Sarah Bromley, Sam Gillick, Victoria K. Wells, David Evans, et al. 2019. "Review: Consumption-Stage Food Waste Reduction Interventions—What Works and How to Design Better Interventions." *Food Policy* 83 (February): 7–27. doi:10.1016/j.foodpol.2019.01.009.

Samen Tegen Voedselverspilling. 2020. "Samen Tegen Voedselverspilling | Home." https://samentegenvoedselverspilling.nl/.

Schmidt, Karolin, and Ellen Matthies. 2018. "Where to Start Fighting the Food Waste Problem? Identifying Most Promising Entry Points for Intervention Programs to Reduce Household Food Waste and Overconsumption of Food." *Resources, Conservation and Recycling* 139 (December): 1–14. doi:10.1016/j.resconrec.2018.07.023.

Sheldon, Marissa. 2020. "South Korea Recycles Food Waste in Effort to Become Zero-Waste Society." March 18. www.nycfoodpolicy.org/food-policy-snapshot-south-korea-food-waste/.

Sinclair Taylor, Jessica, Julian Parfitt, and Dominika Jarosz. 2019. *Regulating the Role of Unfair Trading Practices in Food Waste Generation*. The Netherlands: REFRESH.

Smetana, Sergiy, Adriano Profeta, Anita Bhatia, and Volker Heinz. 2021. "Waste Food Not Eat: Food Waste Treatment or Obesity—Selection of Sustainable Strategies for Dealing With Food Waste and Obesity." *Research Square* (April). doi:10.21203/rs.3.rs-418092/v1.

Smith, Andrew F. 2020. "The Perfect Storm." In *Routledge Handbook of Food Waste*, edited by Christian Reynolds, Tammara Soma, Charlotte Spring, and Jordon Lazell, 37–54. Routledge. doi:10.4324/9780429462795-4.

Stöckli, Sabrina, Eva Niklaus, and Michael Dorn. 2018. "Call for Testing Interventions to Prevent Consumer Food Waste." *Resources, Conservation and Recycling* 136 (September): 445–62. doi:10.1016/j.resconrec.2018.03.029.

Stroecken, Rick. 2017. "Food Waste in the Fresh Produce Supply Chain." 950127812010. WAGENINGEN: MST-Group.

Sundin, Niina, Magdalena Rosell, Mattias Eriksson, Carl Jensen, and Marta Bianchi. 2021. "The Climate Impact of Excess Food Intake—An Avoidable Environmental Burden." *Resources, Conservation and Recycling* 174 (November): 105777. doi:10.1016/j.resconrec.2021.105777.

Sustainability Victoria. 2020. *The Path to Half: Solutions to Halve Victoria's Food Waste by 2030*. Victoria: Sustainability Victoria.

Thompson, Bethan, Luiza Toma, Andrew P. Barnes, and Cesar Revoredo-Giha. 2018. "The Effect of Date Labels on Willingness to Consume Dairy Products: Implications for Food Waste Reduction." *Waste Management* 78 (August): 124–34. doi:10.1016/j.wasman.2018.05.021.

Thow, Anne Marie, Stephen Greenberg, Mafaniso Hara, Sharon Friel, Andries du Toit, and David Sanders. 2018. "Improving Policy Coherence for Food Security and Nutrition in South Africa: A Qualitative Policy Analysis." *Food Security* 10 (4): 1105–30. doi:10.1007/s12571-018-0813-4.

Toti, Elisabetta, Carla Di Mattia, and Mauro Serafini. 2019. "Metabolic Food Waste and Ecological Impact of Obesity in FAO World's Region." *Frontiers in Nutrition* 6 (August): 126. doi:10.3389/fnut.2019.00126.

Turvey, Catherine, Meghan Moran, Jennifer Sacheck, Ashley Arashiro, Qiushi Huang, Katie Heley, Erica Johnston, and Roni Neff. 2021. "Impact of Messaging Strategy on Consumer Understanding of Food Date Labels." *Journal of Nutrition Education and Behavior* 53 (5): 389–400. doi:10.1016/j.jneb.2021.03.007.

UNEP DTU Partnership and United Nations Environment Programme. 2021. *Reducing Consumer Food Waste Using Green and Digital Technologies*. Copenhagen and Nairobi: UNEP DTU Partnership and United Nations Environment Programme.

University of Sydney. 2020. "Australian Local Food System Policy Database—Strengthening Food Systems Governance at the Local Level." https://law-food-systems.sydney.edu.au/policy-database/.

USDA. 2019. "USDA | OCE | U.S. Food Waste Challenge | Resources | Recovery/Donations." *U.S. Food Waste Challenge/Recovery/Donations*, March 3. https://web.archive.org/web/20190303095426/www.usda.gov/oce/foodwaste/resources/donations.htm.

USEPA. 2015. "The US Food Recovery Hierarchy." http://www2.epa.gov/sustainable-management-food/food-recovery-hierarchy.

Villarreal, B., D. Garcia, and I. Rosas. 2009. "Eliminating Transportation Waste in Food Distribution: A Case Study." *Transportation Journal* 48 (4): 72–7.

Wilson, Norbert L. W., Bradley J. Rickard, Rachel Saputo, and Shuay-Tsyr Ho. 2017. "Food Waste: The Role of Date Labels, Package Size, and Product Category." *Food Quality and Preference* 55 (January): 35–44. doi:10.1016/j.foodqual.2016.08.004.

World Bank. 2020. *Addressing Food Loss and Waste : A Global Problem With Local Solutions*. Washington, DC: World Bank.

World Resources Institute. 2016. *Food Loss and Waste Accounting and Reporting Standard*. Washington, DC: WRI.

WRAP. 2016. *Taking Action on Waste; Resources for Hospitality and Food Service Chefs and Support Staff*. Banbury: WRAP.

———. 2019a. *Healthy Sustainable Eating and Food Waste*. Edited by Prepared by GfK Social Research. Banbury, UK: WRAP.

———. 2019b. "The Courtauld Commitment 2025 | WRAP UK." www.wrap.org.uk/content/courtauld-commitment-2025.

———. 2020a. "Food Waste Reduction Roadmap | WRAP." https://wrap.org.uk/taking-action/food-drink/initiatives/food-waste-reduction-roadmap.

———. 2020b. *The Hospitality and Food Service Agreement Taking Action on Waste*. Banbury, UK: WRAP.

———. 2020c. *UK Progress Against Courtauld 2025 Targets and UN Sustainable Development Goal 12.3*. BCV011–005. Banbury: WRAP.

———. 2020d. *This Document Provides a Summary of the Methodology for the Household Simulation Model*. Banbury: WRAP.

———. 2020e. "Menu Planning for Preventing Food Waste | WRAP UK." www.wrap.org.uk/content/menu-planning-preventing-food-waste.

Part 2

International programmes

4 The contribution of social protection to reducing food loss and waste

Qiushi Yue, Daniella Salazar Herrera, and Omar Benammour[1]

Introduction

Our food systems[2] need urgent transformation to be inclusive, resilient, and sustainable. The number of people suffering from food insecurity and malnutrition continues to rise. In 2020, some 720 million to 811 million people were living in hunger globally, while nearly one in three people did not have access to adequate food (FAO et al. 2021, xii). Over 149 million children under five years old were stunted, 45 million wasted, and nearly 39 million overweight (ibid.). In sharp contrast to this are the high levels of food loss and waste (FLW). Approximately 14% of food is lost from production before reaching retail (FAO 2019, 22). At retail and consumption stages, around 17% of food is wasted (UNEP 2021, 20). COVID-19 confinement measures resulted in more FLW by disrupting food supply chains, limiting market access, and changing food-buying patterns (FAO 2020a, 1). The current levels of FLW represent a substantial economic cost for all the actors in the world's agri-food systems, contributing to the mismanagement of our natural resources and aggravating food insecurity and climate change.

Over the years, food systems have gone through tremendous changes. These changes involve food commodification, agricultural mechanisation, processing industrialisation, distribution reorganisation, and market globalisation (Caron et al. 2018, 4), often happening in the process of structural and agricultural transformation, urbanisation, and modernisation. The evolution has resulted in a significant rise in productivity and food quantity. At the same time, agriculture investments tend to prioritise staple crops and oilseeds, and maize, wheat, and rice represent over half of the global food supply from vegetal products (HLPE 2017, 25). As a result, non-perishable and energy-dense foods become more available, often at lower prices. The increase in productivity in food systems can spill over into the rural non-farm economy, potentially leading to more diversified and productive livelihoods in rural areas and improved access to services and infrastructure (UN DESA 2021, 52). The changes could translate into a decrease in poverty and food insecurity.

Despite increased productivity, food systems transformations in many countries have led to externalities such as increased malnutrition, environmental

DOI: 10.4324/9781003226932-7

degradation, and rural inequality (Benton and Bailey 2019, 1; FAO 2017b, xiv, 21; IFAD 2021, 15). Consolidated global and national value chains have given rise to stricter standards on food quality (FAO 2017b, 21, 38), which can be barriers for smallholders to access markets hence increased inequality. As cheap and energy-dense products become easily accessible, more people suffer from malnutrition, including obesity (Benton and Bailey 2019, 4). Cheaper food has also reduced the economic incentive to avoid FLW (ibid.). Cosmetic standards imposed by big retailers such as size, colour, and shape can also lead to safe and nutritious but 'ugly' food wasted, causing severe environmental impacts. To address these issues, we must put in place well-coordinated multisectoral policies and programmes to transition to sustainable and inclusive food systems.

This chapter examines the role of social protection in building inclusive and sustainable food systems, focusing specifically on its contribution to reducing FLW. It adopts a food system lens to understand social protection's role in shaping the complex range of activities and actors involved in food production, processing, distribution, consumption and disposal, and their social and environmental outcomes. It starts by analysing how social protection has the potential to enable inclusive and sustainable transformations, including its contributions to FLW reduction. Country case studies in Ireland, Costa Rica, the United States, and Brazil follow. The chapter concludes with concrete recommendations drawing on lessons from the cases while outlining directions for future research.

Social protection and FLW reduction

Social protection refers to 'a set of policies and programmes that addresses economic, environmental and social vulnerabilities to food insecurity and poverty by protecting and promoting livelihoods' (FAO 2017a, 6). Social protection is a fundamental human right. Nonetheless, only 46.9% of the world population enjoys at least one social protection benefit, and the remaining are not covered at all (ILO 2021, 19). In response to the COVID-19 crisis, governments planned or implemented nearly 4,000 social protection measures to protect lives and livelihoods (Gentilini et al. 2022, 5). However, many of these measures were one-off, phased out, and did not specifically target actors in the agri-food systems.

Social protection can support reducing poverty, which disproportionately affects rural households. It has a great potential for ensuring meaningful participation of poor and marginalised households in food systems' transformation processes. If coupled with nutrition messaging and education, social protection, such as cash transfers, can contribute to improved food security and access to healthy and diversified diets. Likewise, it can support livelihoods and adaptation to climate change through enabling investments in assets, technologies, and inputs. Social protection can also enhance the resilience of vulnerable households to shocks, reducing their reliance on negative coping mechanisms while improving sustainable natural resource management and agricultural practices.

Additionally, social protection can contribute to structural transformation by '. . . preparing households and individuals for livelihood changes by strengthening human capital accumulation and allowing investments in more risky but potentially more profitable activities' (FAO 2020b). The latter enables an inclusive structural transformation process that leaves no one behind.

Social protection can contribute to a more sustainable food system transformation by preventing and reducing FLW in different ways. Social protection programmes can facilitate fulfilling basic needs, enable productive investments, and help develop agri-food value chains of food otherwise lost or wasted. Social protection interventions can contribute to preventing food loss by improving small producers' access to food loss-reduction technologies and capacity building opportunities. Finally, in cases where FLW cannot be prevented, social protection can be a mechanism to enable surplus food redistribution. This chapter will focus mainly on the latter.

According to the 'Food-use-not-loss-or-waste' hierarchy, redistributing safe and nutritious food for human consumption is optimal when FLW cannot be avoided (FAO 2016, 5). The involvement of many actors in the food systems is essential for the success of food recovery and redistribution, including producers, food processors and manufacturers, retailers, food service sectors, charities, food banks, and social enterprises (European Commission 2017a, 8). Food banks are a key player in food redistribution. In 2020, food banks in 44 countries served 40 million people (Global FoodBanking Network 2021).

Globally, there has been growing recognition of food recovery and redistribution programmes. Guidelines and policies have been introduced to enable such processes. These include the European Union guidelines on food donation (European Commission 2017a) and a practical guide for food recovery and redistribution in Europe and Central Asia (FAO 2016). Some countries have integrated these initiatives into broader national social policies, including national social protection systems.

Despite these efforts, only a small proportion of surplus food is redistributed. Often this is due to legal, financial, and operational barriers, limited information available on the surplus food available, and a lack of matchmaking between surplus and those in need. Other constraints include a lack of organisation and an unstable supply of donated food and volunteers to carry out redistribution tasks. Similarly, there are shortages of cold chain and refrigeration equipment, essential for high-value perishable food items such as fish, fruits, and vegetables.

Food redistribution programmes, typically carried out by volunteers and NGOs, can become more effective and reach a more significant scale if they are linked with existing social protection systems and their delivery mechanisms and tools, such as registries or targeting methods. The use of social protection tools can improve the targeting of food redistribution programmes to the most food insecure by providing important socio–economic data, including through social registries. When food redistribution initiatives are embedded in government-led social protection systems, they can potentially tap into more resources, networks, and infrastructure, thus overcoming operational barriers.

Specifically, school feeding programmes can be a platform to redistribute food that complies with national safety standards but is considered 'ugly' for the market. When accompanied by education and behaviour change communication, such programmes can promote a gradual change in the culture of overemphasising cosmetic standards.[3] Embedding food redistribution initiatives within national social protection systems can also increase their sustainability, legitimacy, and prominence. Linking food redistribution with social protection delivery mechanisms helps identify and reach communities otherwise marginalised, enables food redistribution channels that support food loss reduction, encourages participation through food donation or sales, and increases the visibility of donations.

Some argue that linking food waste and redistribution with food insecurity may depoliticise hunger and hinder the fulfilment of the right to food by transferring the responsibility from the government to civil society. Some consider it 'regressive' that the voluntary sector performs the social protection duties of governments (Carher and Furey 2017, 18). Of particular concern is the normalisation of food aid as a response to food insecurity and poverty, particularly as the ability of the charity sector to meet people's needs is limited (Caraher and Davison 2019, 7). The United Nations Special Rapporteur Olivier de Schutter has rightly argued that food banks depend on donations and goodwill and should not substitute comprehensive national social protection programmes (Just Fair 2013, 7). Despite their limitations, local initiatives such as food banks have a great potential to address short-term hunger and reduce FLW. Their efforts represent social innovations that respond fast and offer concrete local solutions, and can be transformative if alliances and innovative partnerships are built with government-led social protection (Berti, Giordano, and Mininni 2021). In addition, they provide livelihood diversification opportunities and incentivise the local economy. Food redistribution initiatives can be leveraged and integrated into a broader national social policy framework to go beyond short-term impact by partnering with public institutions.

Overall, social protection and food redistribution programmes can have synergies at all stages of the food value chain. The following case studies have been selected for examination, including initiatives in Ireland, Costa Rica, the United States, and Brazil. The examples cover good practices in utilising surplus food from production to retailing.

FLW—country case studies

European Union effort to promote food recovery and redistribution

In the European Union (EU), around 88 million tonnes of food are wasted each year, accounting for 20% of the total food produced, costing an estimated €143 billion. In the meantime, 112 million citizens are at risk of poverty. Over 40 million cannot afford a quality meal with meat, fish or vegetarian equivalent every second day (European Commission 2020, 1).

The EU recognises food donations as a strategy to reduce food waste and promote a circular economy. Endorsed in 2017, the EU guidelines on food donation aim to support member states in adopting specific legislation to facilitate food donation in the Union. It contains examples of specific areas of legislation, focusing on food hygiene and other aspects, such as labelling and VAT. However, it is not clear if and how these redistribution programmes are associated with national social protection programmes.

The Fund for European Aid to the Most Deprived (FEAD) is one of the vehicles associated with these interventions. FEAD was established in 2014, with an allocation of €3.8 billion (€4.5 billion including national contributions) for 2014–2020. It is an EU programme aiming to reduce poverty in member states, including through providing food items to deprived persons. FEAD is considered a supranational instrument that provides social protection to vulnerable groups in the EU (Greiss et al. 2020, 622). In some countries, such as Ireland, FEAD was implemented in conjunction with food recovery and redistribution programmes led by civil society organisations, which has led to a more significant impact.

Combining food assistance and surplus food redistribution in Ireland

In Ireland, food poverty and food waste are two major social problems. It is estimated that Ireland wastes one million tonnes of food each year, with food waste in the commercial sector amounting to 303,000 tonnes per annum (Government of Ireland 2021, 1), while poverty has been rising, especially after the outbreak of the COVID-19 pandemic.

FEAD is managed by Ireland's Department of Employment Affairs and Social Protection (DEASP). Its objectives are to provide food assistance to the food insecure, such as homeless persons and children in low-income households while tackling food waste (European Commission 2017b, 32). To that end, DEASP has partnered with FoodCloud, a social enterprise that matches businesses with surplus food to local charities (Government of Ireland 2019, 3). This innovative partnership between a supranational food aid programme, FEAD, a national social protection ministry, DEASP, and food redistribution partners, including FoodCloud and local charities, has led to a greater impact.

Beneficiaries regularly receive nutrient-dense foods such as fish, meat, fruits, and vegetables from charities through FoodCloud's traditional redistribution programmes. At the same time, they also receive FEAD-funded non-perishable food products identified by DEASP, procured by FoodCloud and distributed through local charities. The food received allows the beneficiaries to allocate resources to meet other needs. Thanks to this arrangement, in 2019, over 195,000 people received 1,323 tonnes of EU-funded food through local charities (Government of Ireland 2019, 4). In the meantime, these charities collected over 482 tonnes of surplus food from FoodCloud, mainly perishable but high value and nutrient-dense food (ibid., 4).

In this process, greater impacts were created for all parties involved. Local charities improved the quality and quantity of food that they deliver to end recipients by accessing FEAD-funded food and redistributing surplus nutrient-dense food. The stable supply of food, in turn, helps charities build trust and long-term relationships with the end recipients. In addition, local charities were able to save resources and spend them on other services.

The interventions go beyond meeting the short-term needs of the vulnerable groups, as they are also provided with information on social services and directed to appropriate state agencies for support in such things as searching for employment. FEAD has been integrated into the National Action Plan for Social Inclusion of Ireland, focusing on enhancing charities' capacity to support the most vulnerable (European Commission 2018, 60). Despite this, an assessment of the initial operation of FEAD in Ireland concluded that the programme only reached a small number of recipients in some rural areas (European Commission 2018, 110).

The difficult scale-up of food redistribution in Costa Rica

Costa Rica is an upper-middle-income country with one of the lowest poverty rates in Latin America (World Bank 2020). However, food insecurity remains severe (25.5% before COVID-19), and malnutrition is a growing challenge, especially undernutrition and obesity of children (FAO 2020c).

The Ministry of Health developed a National Policy on Food and Nutrition Security 2011–2021 to expand different types of interventions, including the extension of social protection measures. The aim was to reduce poverty, food insecurity, and malnutrition. In parallel, interest in reducing FLW has grown for years. Around 40% of food is lost or wasted (El Mundo 2017). A National Policy on Sustainable Production and Consumption 2018–2030 was recently developed to manage food waste.

Given growing food waste, three different initiatives have been implemented to redistribute food surplus to poor households in the country, of which only one is government-led. This initiative is a direct redistribution scheme, without intermediaries, managed by the National Centre for Food Supply and Distribution (CENADA). CENADA is a governmental programme that runs a wholesale market to supply perishable products, such as vegetables and dairy products, to retail markets. The objectives of CENADA are to organise the market, reduce the organic waste within the markets, and improve food quality. Food redistribution is not mandatory and depends on the goodwill of each concessionary.

In this context, CENADA distributes only fruits and vegetables. It redistributed 234 tonnes between September 2020 and May 2021. CENADA faces multiple challenges such as the lack of an enabling legal framework, limited funds, and insufficient collaboration with civil society initiatives such as the Food Bank of Costa Rica (ABACOR) and the Alimentalistas. CENADA, and food redistribution in general, need to be strengthened to guarantee a more substantial impact. ABACOR, the other food redistribution initiative, which has played a crucial role in responding to the food crisis associated with COVID-19, has redistributed more than 259 tonnes of food surplus to 41,000 beneficiaries through community-based organisations.

The Costa Rican case remains a promising example in the region. It is based on solid alliances between food producers and distributors, volunteers, organisations, and beneficiaries. However, the insufficient legal framework for food donation limits its scale-up and institutionalisation within the national social protection system. There is no national food donation law or policy. This creates problems in setting up minimum requirements for food suppliers, a registration process and liability protection for food donations. It also represents a challenge for establishing clear food safety and quality regulations, including date labels, in case of donation, in coherence with the Codex Alimentarius and the General Health Law that regulates food quality and safety in the country. This lack of regulation is problematic as the food donators, considered 'food establishments' by law, do not have specific sanitary requirements in the General Health Law. This could become a risk for the consumers and a challenge for donors and food recovery organisations. The lack of liability protection for food donations is also a strong limitation to scaling up food surplus donations, despite an attempt to amend the General Health Law in 2016.

The COVID-19 pandemic did accelerate the creation of a specific regulation around food surplus donations, the COVID-19 Food Donation Guidelines. These guidelines helped clarify the donation procedure from wholesale, retail businesses, food banks, food distribution networks and social welfare organisations, and food quality and safety requirements, including date labels. However, it is not clear if the guidelines will remain relevant and in place in the future. Also, additional barriers to food surplus donation remain, such as the lack of incentives for surplus donations.

Finally, despite the recognition by the government and different stakeholders in Costa Rica that food surplus is an important social safety net for food insecure households, there are no clear linkages with the many national social protection schemes in place in the country.

Bycatch and by-products in fisheries—the role of social protection in reducing food loss in production and post-harvest stages

The fisheries sector is one of many contrasts and inequalities. While the industry is a crucial source of food, employment, and economic well-being for people, over 90% of those employed are in the small-scale fisheries sector, where poverty and food insecurity are prevalent (Béné, Macfadyen, and Allison 2007, 2).

All fisheries, particularly commercial ones, inevitably produce bycatch, part of which tends to be discarded. Although there is no internationally agreed definition, there is a consensus that bycatch is the 'catch that a fisher did not intend to catch but could not avoid, often did not want or chose not to use'

(FAO 2011). While bycatch is often inevitable, the amount caught and discarded, and thus wasted, can be reduced. Currently, despite representing about 2.5% of the food produced in weight globally, 30 to 35% of fisheries are wasted in most regions, usually through discards (Guillen et al. 2018, 6), thus generating food loss in a sector with high food insecurity.

Discards are defined as the percentage of the 'total catch that is thrown away or slipped' (FAO 2011). Often, this is due to a lack of commercial value, especially as discards would take up space in the cold chain on board that could be allocated to higher value target catches (Clucas 1997). Likewise, since regulations often prohibit bycatch from being retained, discarding becomes a mechanism to avoid violating these regulations. Quotas on landings also can incentivise discarding, as fishers forecast for higher value fish to be caught. Discarding also occurs because the gear affects the catch, but it does not reach the deck (Gillnett 2008, 45).

Discards represent a missed economic and food security potential, especially for small-scale fishing communities. Instead of being discarded, sustainable bycatch could be utilised and redistributed to improve the food security and nutrition of vulnerable and poor households. Social protection initiatives, particularly social assistance and public procurement processes, can facilitate this process, thus increasing the availability of food and enhancing small-scale producers' income.

Fish by-products refer to the 'secondary products that could be used for human consumption' (FAO 2013). For example, if the target product from a fish is the fillet, the rest, including the head, viscera, bones, skin and scales, could be considered by-products (Ahern et al. 2021, 11; FAO 2013). From the portion of fish that is utilised (and not discarded), almost half of it is a by-product. In most regions, the by-products tend to be wasted, representing a significant loss of micronutrients (Ahern et al. 2021, 11). Incorporating by-products in social protection initiatives can enhance nutrition in many communities. Social protection can also enable by-product processing by providing access to fish processing technologies and allowing investments in these productive endeavours.

Additionally, sustainable bycatch and by-products can also foster local economic development by transforming them for local consumption. They can be utilised and repurposed through commercialisation or donation, direct feed for aquaculture or livestock, used as fertiliser, transformed into fish meal or value-added products such as fortified fish sauce, and exported (Funge-Smith, Lindebo, and Staples 2005; Hutchinson et al. 2007). The repurposing of bycatch and by-products increases income and generates alternative livelihoods. For instance, women usually work in the post-harvest sector and are in charge of processing and transforming bycatch and by-products into artisanal processed fish products.[4] Linking bycatch and by-products that can be repurposed with communities in need can improve the food security and nutrition of those receiving and commercialising the products. The following case studies seek to show how social protection could provide an opportunity to recover and redistribute bycatch and by-products.

Alaska, United States

In Alaska, the government banned the discarding of major groundfish species and limited the catch percentage that is not used for human consumption (Clucas 1997).

In response to this ban, the National Oceanic and Atmospheric Administration's (NOAA) Fisheries and North Pacific Fishery Management Council established a Prohibited Species Donation Program in 1996, which covers halibut and salmon (Watson, Stram, and Harmon 2020, 2). It aims to donate the unavoidable bycatch of said species to maximise their value instead of discarding it. The donation programme is implemented by a non-profit organisation named SeaShare. It oversees the processing, transportation, certification, and distribution of food donations, relying heavily on voluntary partnerships and financial support from the seafood industry. SeaShare has delivered six million pounds of salmon and halibut bycatch through Feeding America, a hunger relief organisation. The latter is the United States' largest network of food banks, accounting for 23.5 million servings of seafood reaching food-insecure households over 27 years (NOAA 2020).

A survey conducted by Feeding America in 2014 found that around 14% of the population of Alaska and 20% of children are food insecure. This situation of vulnerability often results in the consumption of less expensive, less healthy, and less nutritious food. Therefore, this initiative fills the gap between the surplus of prohibited species bycatch and the need for nutritious food. Because it targets people who otherwise cannot acquire salmon or halibut given its high price, the programme does not create or entail competition with target salmon and halibut markets (NOAA 2020).

Overall, the programme provides food insecure people with access to quality, nutrient-dense food, which is limited in food banks. Without these donations, food banks would not be able to afford protein of this quality, which promotes good health by providing a complete protein high in Omega-3 while reducing future health risks (SeaShare undated).

Brazil

Brazil's shrimp fisheries are composed of several commercial target species. Due to net meshes' closure during trawling, low fishing gear selectivity, and lack of bycatch reduction devices, fishers catch a range of non-target species. Bycatch is diverse and includes fish, molluscs, and crustaceans, among other species that can have commercial value. In a study of the artisanal fisheries for seabob shrimp in the State of Santa Catarina, 216 species were identified as part of the bycatch. However, only that with a significant economic value and commercial size is landed, while the rest is discarded (Olinto Branco, Freitas Júnior, and Christoffersen 2015).

Processing the sustainably caught bycatch and by-products can generate additional revenues along the value chain and create an opportunity to use these products in public procurement programmes such as school meals.

The use of fisheries by-products has nutritional, economic, and environmental benefits when incorporated into school meals in the municipalities of Toledo and Marechal Candido Rondon in Paraná (Da Silva Leonel et al. 2019). A study conducted in these areas showed that incorporating fish by-products into school meals increased the nutritional value of meals and made diets more diverse. It also eliminated problems related to fish bones, especially with children. In fact, the low cost of fisheries by-products provided more meals at a lower cost and reached more children (Da Silva Leonel et al. 2019). Regular inclusion of fish by-products into school menus and meals guarantees an income for fisherfolk, which enables financial planning, including engagement with social security initiatives, among others. By sourcing fish by-products locally, the local economy is incentivised, increasing the incomes of fishery-dependent households (Da Silva Leonel et al. 2019).

Recommendations

The case studies have demonstrated that linking food recovery and redistribution with social protection can positively affect people's food security, nutrition, and income while reducing some of the environmental costs of FLW. The innovations and partnerships nurtured by existing food recovery and redistribution initiatives can help reduce poverty and food insecurity, empower small-scale producers, and reduce the environmental footprint of food production. There is a need for forging strong and innovative links between public institutions responsible for social protection, agriculture, nutrition and health, and actors in food recovery and redistribution, including food bank associations and networks, donors, redistributors, and beneficiaries.

There is also a need to learn from existing programmes and scale them up to better reach those in need. Institutional mechanisms should be put in place to create a pathway for food donations. As shown in Ireland, the collaboration between charities and social enterprise-led food redistribution and the EU food assistance programme has allowed for a stable supply of nutritious food to end recipients. In Alaska, a donation mechanism facilitates the consumption of fish potentially wasted by people who would usually not afford it and in a manner that did not affect the prices. In Costa Rica, food donation guidelines adopted during the COVID-19 pandemic sought to reduce hazards stemming from the quality of donated food in redistribution schemes. However, more permanent mechanisms and guidelines need to be adopted for the long-term sustainability of food redistribution.

Nutrition should be a key element when linking food redistribution and social protection. These initiatives must ensure the availability of nutrient-dense food. The goal is to address hunger, undernutrition, and emerging problems such as the growing prevalence of overweight and obesity resulting from the increased affordability of cheap calories. In the Irish case, the collaboration between FEAD and local NGOs has improved the nutritional value of the food packages, as most food distributed by FoodCloud is nutrient-dense perishable food. Similarly, in utilising fish by-products in school meals in Brazil, their nutritional value improved at a lower price. This made it possible to reach more children and generated additional income for fishery-dependent communities. In addition, nutrition education programmes are essential for consumers to access and choose healthy diets and for programme managers to provide healthy food.

While the examples presented here reveal a promising potential, social protection interventions should be complemented with programmes in other sectors to achieve impact at scale. A transition to more inclusive and sustainable food systems also needs a coherent set of complementary multisectoral policies, programmes and tools.

Similarly, fostering innovative public and private sector partnerships and alliances is critical to achieving transformative effects. In Ireland, the partnership between a government ministry DEASP, a social enterprise, local charities, and food enterprises has brought about positive changes in reducing hunger and FLW. In Alaska, the partnership between NOAA and the civil society organisations SeaShare and Feeding America enabled the redistribution of food that otherwise would have been lost and wasted. These bottom-up social innovations provide rapid solutions to local needs. They have a potentially transformative impact, by including promoting local solutions and empowering local organisations to participate in national policy processes.

Conclusions and discussion

Social protection can reduce poverty, improve food security and nutrition, and reduce FLW. Social protection can be an enabler for a sustainable and inclusive food systems transformation. The contribution of social protection has, however, remained under-tapped. This chapter has presented promising examples of how social protection can contribute to scaling up surplus food redistribution to reach needy people, positively impacting the environment, livelihoods, food security, and nutrition. In each case, innovative partnerships between the government, food enterprises, and communities were an enabling factor.

A long-term approach to reducing FLW through different measures remains essential. As mentioned earlier, food waste can be attributed to a system that externalises the real costs of food production (Haws, Reczek, and Sample 2017; Benton and Bailey 2019; Hendriks et al. 2021). To reduce the perverse consequences of our food systems, such as food waste, redefining the true value of food seems a promising initiative (United Nations Food System Summit 2021 Scientific Group 2021). Social protection can be instrumental in mitigating the potential negative social impacts of the transition. At this point, the potential role of social protection in promoting a true cost and price of food remains speculative. More research needs to be done to identify comprehensively social protection's role in sustainable food systems transformation.

Acknowledgements

This study was partially supported by the Social Protection Component of the Project 'Responsible use of fisheries and aquaculture resources for sustainable development' (GCP/GLO/352/NOR).

Notes

1 © Food and Agriculture Organization of the United Nations, 2022. 'The views expressed in this publication are those of the author(s) and do not necessarily reflect the views or policies of the Food and Agriculture Organization of the United Nations'.
2 Food systems is defined as

> [T]he entire range of actors and their interlinked value-adding activities involved in the production, aggregation, processing, distribution, consumption, and disposal of food products that originate from agriculture, forestry or fisheries, and parts of the broader economic, societal, and natural environments in which they are embedded.
>
> (FAO 2018, 1)

3 See Kenya's example of using ugly food which otherwise will be wasted to feed school children (Karimi 2017). www.wfp.org/stories/ugly-vegetables-destined-dump-are-now-helping-feed-thousands-schoolchildren-kenya
4 In the case of women in Colombia, they process and commercialise the bycatch from the shrimp fishery, making this, in most cases, their sole income (Garay et al. 2020; FAO & INVEMAR 2021).

References

Ahern, M. B., S. H. Thilsted, M. Kjellevold, R. Overå, J. Toppe, M. Doura, E. Kalaluka, B. Wismen, M. Vargas, and N. Franz. 2021. "Locally-Procured Fish Is Essential in School Feeding Programmes in Sub-Saharan Africa." *Foods* 10: 2080. https://doi.org/10.3390/foods10092080. www.mdpi.com/2304-8158/10/9/2080.
Béné, C., G. Macfadyen, and E. H. Allison. 2007. "Increasing the Contribution of Small-Scale Fisheries to Poverty Alleviation and Food Security." FAO Fisheries Technical Paper. No. 481. Rome, FAO. 125p.
Benton, T. G., and R. Bailey. 2019. "The Paradox of Productivity: Agricultural Productivity Promotes Food System Inefficiency." *Global Sustainability* 2: e6, 1–8. https://doi.org/10.1017/sus.2019.3.
Berti, G., C. Giordano, and M. Mininni. 2021. "Assessing the Transformative Potential of Food Banks: The Case Study of Magazzini Sociali (Italy)." *Agriculture* 11: 249. https://doi.org/10.3390/agriculture11030249.
Caraher, M., and R. Davison. 2019. "The Normalization of Food Aid: What Happened to Feeding People Well?" https://emeraldopenresearch.com/articles/1-3/v2.
Carher, M., and S. Furey. 2017. "Is It Appropriate to Use Surplus Food to Feed People in Hunger? Short-Term Band-Aid to More Deep-Rooted Problems of Poverty." Food Research Collaboration Briefing Paper. https://foodresearch.org.uk/wp-content/uploads/sites/8/2017/01/Final-Using-food-surplus-hunger-FRC-briefing-paper-24–01–17-.pdf.
Caron, P., et al. 2018. "Food Systems for Sustainable Development: Proposals for a Profound Four-Part Transformation." *Agronomy for Sustainable Development* 38: 41. https://doi.org/10.1007/s13593-018-0519-1.
Clucas, I. 1997. "A Study of the Options for Utilization of Bycatch and Discards from Marine Capture Fisheries." No. FIIU/C928. Rome, FAO.

Da Silva Leonel, A., M. Espagnoli GEraldo Martins, A. Feiden, A. de Grandi, A. da Silva, and E. Coutinho. 2019. "Uso de teconologias de processamento do pescado em cardápios escolares: viabilidade econômica." https://periodicos.sbu.unicamp.br/ojs/index.php/san/article/view/8653394/20777.

European Commission. 2017a. "Commission Notice of 16.10.2017. EU Guidelines on Food Donation." https://eur-lex.europa.eu/legal-content/EN/TXT/PDF/?uri=CELEX:52017XC1025(01)&from=EN.

———. 2017b. "Fund for European Aid to the Most Deprived." Diverse Approaches to Supporting Europe's Most Deprived. FEAD Case Studies 2017. www.priimk.lt/data/public/uploads/2018/02/2017-m.-gerosios-praktikos-katalogas.pdf.

———. 2018. "FEAD Mid-Term Evaluation." Final Report. VC/2016/0664.

———. 2020. "Food Donation in the EU." https://29september.eurofoodbank.org/wp-content/uploads/2020/09/Infographics_EN.pdf.

FAO. 2011. "International Guidelines on Bycatch Management and Reduction of Discards". p. 4. https://www.fao.org/3/ba0022t/ba0022t.pdf.

———. 2013. "Innovative Uses of Fisheries by-Products." 2. www.fao.org/3/bb213e/bb213e.pdf.

———. 2016. "Food Recovery and Redistribution." A Practical Guide for Favourable Policies and Legal Frameworks in Europe and Central Asia. Working paper. www.fao.org/uploads/media/Food_recovery_and_redistribution_guide.pdf.

———. 2017a. "FAO Social Protection Framework: Promoting Rural Development for All." www.fao.org/3/a-i7016e.pdf.

———. 2017b. "The State of Food and Agriculture: Leveraging Food Systems for Inclusive Rural Transformation." www.fao.org/3/I7658e/I7658e.pdf.

———. 2018. "Sustainable Food Systems: Concept and Framework." www.fao.org/3/ca2079en/CA2079EN.pdf.

———. 2019. *The State of Food and Agriculture 2019. Moving Forward on Food Loss and Waste Reduction.* Rome. www.fao.org/3/ca6030en/ca6030en.pdf.

———. 2020a. *Mitigating Risks to Food Systems During COVID-19: Reducing Food Loss and Waste.* Rome. www.fao.org/policy-support/tools-and-publications/resources-details/zh/c/1276396/.

———. 2020b. *The Role of Social Protection in Inclusive Structural Transformation.* Rome. www.fao.org/3/ca7333en/CA7333EN.pdf.

———. 2020c. *The State of Food Security and Nutrition in the World 2020: Transforming Food Systems for Affordable Healthy Diets.* Rome. www.fao.org/3/ca9692en/CA9692EN.pdf.

FAO, IFAD, UNICEF, WFP, and WHO. 2021. *The State of Food Security and Nutrition in the World 2021. Transforming Food Systems for Food Security, Improved Nutrition and Affordable Healthy Diets for All.* Rome: FAO. https://doi.org/10.4060/cb4474en.

FAO and INVEMAR. 2021. *La importancia de la labor femenina en la pesca y su acceso a servicios de protección social: El caso de las platoneras de Buenaventura.* Colombia. http://cinto.invemar.org.co/alfresco/d/d/workspace/SpacesStore/a34b81bf-a76b-46f8-9b58-a3f50d757420/LA%20IMPORTANCIA%20DE%20LA%20LABOR%20FEMENINA%20EN%20LA%20PESCA%20Y%20SU%20ACCESO%20A%20SERVICIOS%20DE%20PROTECCI%C3%93N%20SOCIAL:%20El%20caso%20de%20las%20platoneras%20de%20Buenaventura,%20Colombia?ticket=TICKET_25d00e62a24a66def500d41a1a266 5f68120b251.

Funge-Smith, S., E. Lindebo, and D. Staples. 2005. "Asian Fisheries Today: The Production and Use of Low Value/Trash Fish from Marine Fisheries in the Asia-Pacific Region." RAP PUBLICATION 2005/16.

Garay, A., F. Escobar, and M. Rueda, eds. 2020. *Estrategias para el Fortalecimiento de la Actividad de las Platoneras del Distrito de Buenaventura. Primer informa Técnico Final. FAO-INVEMAR.* Santa Marta: Instituto de Investigaciones Marinas y Costeras José Benito Vives de Andréis. 8p+anexos. http://cinto.invemar.org.co/alfresco/d/d/workspace/SpacesStore/864bc4ed-1cb9-4ee8-a48d-733bcafee975/PRY-VAR-017–019.pdf?ticket=TICKET_e4043bebc0afe565376a57da16799c93d04273ac.

Gentilini, U. et al. 2022. "Social Protection and Jobs Responses to COVID-19: A Real-Time Review of Country Measures." Living Paper Version 16. February 2, 2022. https://socialprotection.org/discover/publications/social-protection-and-jobs-responses-covid-19-real-time-review-country.

Gillett, R. 2008. "Global Study of Shrimp Fisheries." FAO Fisheries Technical Paper. No. 475. Rome, FAO. 2008.331p www.fao.org/3/i0300e/i0300e01a.pdf.

Global FoodBanking Network. 2021. "40 Million People Relied on GFN Food Banks for Meals Amid COVID-10 Crisis in 2020." www.foodbanking.org/40-million-people-relied-on-gfn-food-banks-for-meals-amid-covid-19-crisis-in-2020/.

Greiss, J., B. Cantillon, and T. Penne. 2020. "The Fund For European Aid to the Most Deprived: A Trojan horse dilemma?" *Social Policy and Administration* 55: 622–36. https://doi.org/10.1111/spol.12647.

Guillen, J., S. J. Holmes, N. Carvalho, J. Casey, D. Hendrik, M. Gibin, A. Mannini, P. Vasilakopoulos, and A. Zanzi. 2018. "A Review of the European Union Landing Obligation Focusing on Its IMplications for Fisheries and the Environment." *Sustainability* 10 (4). https://doi.org/10.3390/su10040900.

Government of Ireland. 2019. "FEAD Annual Implementation Report." www.gov.ie/pdf/?file=https://assets.gov.ie/99825/914b142e-0c18-40a9-9ef6-f754e595faf9.pdf#page=null.

———. 2021. "How Much Food Do We Waste in Ireland?" www.epa.ie/publications/circular-economy/resources/NWPP-Food-Waste-Report.pdf.

Haws, K. L., R. W. Reczek, and K. L. Sample. 2017. "Healthy Diets Make Empty Wallets: The Healthy Expesion Intuition." *Journal of Consumer Research* 43 (6): 992–1007. https://doi.org/10.1093/jcr/ucw078.

Hendriks, Sheryl, Mario Herrero, Adrian de Groot Ruiz, Hans Baumers, Pietro Galgani, Daniel Mason-D'Croz, Cecile Godde, et al. 2021. "The True Cost and True Price of Food. A Paper from the Scientific Group of the U.N. Food Systems Summit." United Nations Food Systems Summit 2021. www.researchgate.net/publication/355108393_The_true_cost_and_true_price_of_food_A_paper_from_the_scientific_group_of_the_UN_Food_Systems_Summit/link/615e901250be5507288c4009/download.

HLPE. 2017. "Nutrition and Food Systems." A Report by the High Level Panel of Experts on Food Security and Nutrition of the Committee on World Food Security. Rome. www.fao.org/3/i7846e/i7846e.pdf.

Hutchinson, S., G. Seepersad, R. Singh, and L. Rankine. 2007. *Study on the Socio-Economic Importance of By-Catch in the Demersal Trawl Fishery for Shrimp in Trinidad and Tobago.* Department of Agricultural Economics and Extension Faculty of Science and Agriculture. St. Augustine, Trinidad: The University of the West Indies. www.fao.org/fishery/docs/DOCUMENT/rebyc/trinidadtobago/UWI_MALMR_ByCatch_Report_Final_ver3.pdf.

IFAD. 2021. "Rural Development Report." Transforming Food Systems for Rural Prosperity. www.ifad.org/documents/38714170/43704363/rdr2021.pdf/d3c85b6a-229a-c6f1-75e2-a67bb8b505b2?t=1631621454882.

ILO. 2021. *World Social Protection Report 2020–22: Social Protection at the Crossroads-in Pursuit of a Better Future.* Geneva: ILO. www.ilo.org/wcmsp5/groups/public/@dgreports/@dcomm/@publ/documents/publication/wcms_817572.pdf.

Just Fair. 2013. "Freedom from Hunger: Realizing the Right to Food in the UK." www.equallyours.org.uk/wp-content/uploads/2013/03/Freedom-from-Hunger.Just-Fair-Report.FINAL_..pdf.

Karimi, Martin. 2017. "Ugly Vegetables Destined for the Dump Are Now Helping to Feed Thousands of Schoolchildren in Kenya." *World Food Programme*, 2017. www.wfp.org/stories/ugly-vegetables-destined-dump-are-now-helping-feed-thousands-schoolchildren-kenya.

NOAA. 2020. "Seafood Bycatch Donation Relieves Hunger and Reduces Waste." *NOAA*, October 2020. www.fisheries.noaa.gov/feature-story/seafood-bycatch-donation-relieves-hunger-and-reduces-waste.

Olinto Branco, Freitas Júnior, and Lindsey Christoffersen. 2015. "Bycatch Fauna of Seabob Shrimp Trawl Fisheries From Santa Catarina State, Southern Brazil." doi:10.1590/1676-06032015014314.

Pérez González, Karla. 2017. "En Costa Rica 40% de Alimentos Se Desperdicia o Desecha Antes de Ser Consumido." *El Mundo.* www.elmundo.cr/costa-rica/costa-rica-40-alimentos-se-desperdicia-desecha-consumido/.

SeaShare. undated. *Share the Sea.* SeaShare. www.seashare.org/.

UN DESA. 2021. *World Social Report 2021: Reconsidering Rural Development.* New York: United Nations Department of Economic and Social Affairs.

UNEP. 2021. *Food Waste Index Report 2021.* Nairobi. www.unep.org/resources/report/unep-food-waste-index-report-2021.

United Nations Food Systems Summit 2021 Scientific Group. 2021. "The True Cost and True Price of Food." United Nations Food Systems Summit 2021.

Watson, J., D. Stram, and J. Harmon. 2020. "Mitigating Seafood Waste Through a Bycatch Donation Program." www.frontiersin.org/articles/10.3389/fmars.2020.576431/full.

World Bank. 2020. "Latin America and the Caribbean." https://databank.worldbank.org/data/download/poverty/33EF03BB-9722-4AE2-ABC7-AA2972D68AFE/Global_POVEQ_LAC.pdf.

5 Reducing food loss in rural development projects. Examples from IFAD's investments

Romina Cavatassi, Robert Delve, and Giuseppe Maggio

Introduction

Elaborating a policy pathway to eradicate food insecurity remains a top priority for the agenda of developing and advanced economies around the globe. There is widespread agreement among policymakers, practitioners, and scholars on the need of a holistic approach aimed at radically transforming the current food system to tackle the complex set of interconnected challenges it reflects (IFAD 2021).

The COVID-19 pandemic has negatively impacted our food system. Pandemics create both demand and supply shocks in all economic sectors, to varying degrees and at different rates (Bloom, de Wit, and Carangal-San Jose 2005). From a food supply perspective, the COVID-19 pandemic has caused unprecedented disruptions to local, national, and global food supply chains through lockdowns and transport restrictions, causing economic losses, increasing the risk of social unrest, and reducing household food security (Laborde et al. 2020). Production is further compromised by the changes in climate, especially by the increased frequency of weather shocks reducing agricultural yields, encouraging weed and pest proliferation, and increasing the volatility in food prices (Nelson et al. 2009). From a food demand perspective, recent projections suggest that from the current 7.8 billion people, the global population may be reaching 8.5 billion in 2030 and 9.7 billion in 2050 (UN DESA 2019). Yet, despite improvements in global food security and poverty reduction, COVID-19 has reversed some of these gains, with the most recent State of Food Insecurity, indicating up to 800 million people do not have enough food to eat (FAO 2021).

In this context, it is important to note the contribution of food loss to food security and nutrition. According to FAO (2019), every year about 14% of food is lost before reaching the market. All agricultural commodities are affected by food loss, including vegetable, fruits, cereals, legumes, meat, dairy, and fish. The magnitude of the losses depends on several factors, including the geographical region and the type of value chain. For example, in Sub-Saharan Africa, about 13.5% of the grain production is lost along the value chain, while the percentage increases up to 50% for fruit and vegetables (FAO 2011).

DOI: 10.4324/9781003226932-8

IFAD, in collaboration with FAO and WFP, supports the use of the Food Loss Analysis methodology, a tool that identifies the points along the value chain where food loss is occurring so that corrective actions can be taken. In parallel to the causes of food losses being different for every crop and in every country, so are the solutions (e.g. chilling, cold storage, use of hermetic storage bags). The current COVID-19 pandemic has decreased the efficiency of the food supply chains and therefore increased global food loss, as the frequent lockdowns and slowdown in transportation have increased the loss of perishable agricultural, meat, and fisheries products.

It is also very important to note that food losses affect the livelihoods of people well beyond its direct effect on increasing household food insecurity: FAO estimates that about 8% of global annual emissions, or 1.5 Gigatonnes of CO_2 per year, are generated producing food that never reaches the consumers' table (FAO 2011). Reducing food losses[1] therefore is a critical step in transforming our food system and improving food security without putting additional pressure on the natural resource base and on the environment.

IFAD's mandate is focused on supporting rural development and ensuring an equitable, inclusive, and sustainable transformation of rural livelihoods. Through its Strategic Framework (2016–2025), IFAD has recognised these challenges and has outlined the principles of engagement, overarching goals and strategic objectives that guide its operations. IFAD implements its strategy through three mutually reinforcing strategic objectives (SOs): (a) increase poor rural people's productive capacities (SO1); (b) increase poor rural people's benefits from market participation (SO2); (b) and strengthen the environmental sustainability and climate resilience of poor rural people's economic activities (SO3) (IFAD 2016). The focus of IFAD operations remains rural transformation for smallholder producers: farmers, pastoralists, small fishers, and food processors. In particular, IFADs actions are aimed at improving the conditions of vulnerable and marginalised groups, such as women, indigenous people, and youth.

Most small-scale producers and rural entrepreneurs can't afford to invest in food loss reduction interventions like improved post-harvest storage technologies or infrastructure and need access to affordable financial instruments to support these investments. For example, an IFAD-supported study conducted in four African countries found that although many suitable loan products were available, in practice they were inaccessible to most smallholder farmers. There were various reasons for this: many financial institutions did not have branches in rural areas; interest rates were too high; and the risk of borrowing without price and insurance guarantees was too great for smallholder farmers (IFAD 2019). IFAD is encouraging private sector investments in food loss reduction efforts at both local and national levels through its various rural finance interventions. This includes their Private Sector Engagement Strategy and collaboration with private banks, microfinance institutions, and the public sector to develop appropriate financial instruments for smallholder farmers and SMEs (Delve 2021).

Many IFAD programmes have implemented activities aimed at reducing food losses in developing countries. These investments include the construction of on-farm and off-farm post-harvest infrastructure, provision of drying, storage, and processing equipment and delivery of capacity building trainings to actors along the food value chains. Other interventions have aimed at improving market access and access to rural finance (IFAD 2019; Delve 2021).

This chapter presents a set of examples of IFAD's investment in food loss reduction implemented in several regions and across different value chains. We draw from more recently designed and ongoing projects as well as from projects that have completed and whose impacts have been measured through Impact Assessment approaches. Key insights and policy messages conclude the chapter.

IFAD action to reduce food loss

Reducing food losses to achieve sustainable food systems is among the key actions in the 2030 Sustainable Development Goal (SDG) Agenda. SDG target 12.3 is 'to reduce food losses along production and supply chains, including post-harvest losses' by 2030. IFAD has fully committed itself to Target 12.3 through its participation of the IFAD President as one of the 12.3 Champions coalition. Since 2011, IFAD has taken concrete actions, together with other multilateral organisations and foundations, to specifically accelerate food loss reduction in developing countries.

Around 12% of the annual IFAD disbursement on loans and grants (approximately US$100 million per year) targets actions aimed at reducing food losses (IFAD 2019). The majority of these funds have been targeted at upgrading post-harvesting infrastructures, such as post-harvest equipment, collection centres and storage warehouses, to improve the road network systems and build packaging facilities, allowing food value chain actors to minimise the different stages food losses along their food supply chains. In addition, IFAD funds have targeted post-harvest equipment, supported the purchase of improved post-harvest drying and cooling machines, storage, processing, and transport equipment, and delivered capacity buildings to enable producers and processors to adopt improved food loss reduction technologies.

The following projects supported by IFAD in collaboration or partnership with other donors and organisations document progress at reducing food losses. Examples were selected from projects supporting crop, fish, and livestock production where impact assessments have been conducted or from projects that have been ongoing for many years and for which evidence is available.

IFAD operations in the fishery sector

The fish value chain is one of the value chains with the highest food losses because of the high degree of perishability of its products. Some examples of IFAD investments to reduce losses in this value chain are described below.

The Coastal Community Development Project (CCDP)—Indonesia

The CCDP has targeted the fish market and the livelihood of thousands of people in Indonesia. The country has the third largest fishing sector in the world, with an estimated fish production of about six million tonnes per year. Despite its volume, the Indonesian fishing sector still struggles to grow at its potential and small-sale fishers achieve a limited income. This is due to the poor level of infrastructure and high inefficiencies across the value chain, resulting in their catches being poorly preserved and reaching the market in poor condition. According to official statistics, about 35% of the Indonesian seafood get loss or wasted before reaching the final consumer (FAO 2020).

The CCDP project has been implemented between 2013 and 2017, across 12 coastal districts, with the objective of increasing capabilities in marine and coastal resources management of fishers and other actors in the fisheries value chain. To achieve this objective, the programme supported investment in new equipment, such as motorised boats, to increase their area of operation, and implemented trainings on processing practices and on packaging. Processing and packaging brings a dual benefit for fishers, increasing the time of storage and realising a higher market price, as processed fish is sold at a higher price and has a wider market demand. Support was also given to the development of a network of small enterprises, to be led by women and to employ mostly women, producing, among others, traditional smoked and sun-dried offerings, fish paste, and fish-flavoured snacks such as crackers and shredded fish. Besides these interventions, other activities have included an increase in the conservation of coastlines through favouring the mangrove plantation and rotational rules for fishing points, as well as the support to aquaculture and ecotourism activities, which have provided an increased contribution in terms of enhancement of the sustainability of the value chain.

Cavatassi, Mabiso, and Brueckmann (2019) conducted an extensive evaluation analysis of the CCDP project and assessed the impact of project participation on several dimensions of the IFAD Strategic Objectives (SOs) and to food loss reduction. Their analysis found that fishing productivity of participants increased by 79% compared to a control group. The project participants also have observed an improvement of market access by 28% and a reduction in PHLs by 5%. Also, CCDP was effective in strengthening coastal resource governance and government policies and procedures towards increased responsibilities and management of the sector. Overall, CCDP achieved its economic objectives of increasing the efficiency and sustainability of the whole value chain, for example by providing refrigeration technology that reduced overfishing by farmers, who normally adopted an over-fishing policy to cover their expected losses before they could market their catches (Cavatassi, Mabiso, and Brueckmann 2019; Mabiso 2019).

PROPESCA—Mozambique

IFAD has committed to also reduce FLW from fish in Sub-Saharan Africa, as for example with the project PROPESCA in Mozambique. The project's goal is to improve the livelihood and income of people in the fishery sector of Mozambique. The project has focused on the artisanal fisheries, with the development objective of allowing artisanal fishers and other operators in the value chain to generate more returns in terms of sales in a sustainable way.

Mozambiquans consume fish in three different forms other than fresh—salted, dried, or smoked. However, because of the high investment costs, some of these preservations are implemented only by large-scale actors, while the small-scale fishers and intermediaries are exposed to potential losses at all the stages of the value chain. Poor infrastructural conditions and lack of adequate equipment (e.g. ice makers, fridges, and refrigerated trucks) are among the major causes of food losses that fisheries experience. Similarly, inappropriate storage practices and low volumes of storage equipment cause large losses for dried and salted fish.

Given that losses may occur at each stage of the value chain, PROPESCA targeted a wide range of value chain actors, from fishers and processors, to transport operations and marketers. PROPESCA implemented trainings, demonstrations, and long-term technical assistance to increase the skill levels of participants. A large part of the investment targeted the improvement of storage and trading facilities, including the provision of fridges and refrigerated trucks to increase the refrigerating capacity. PROPESCA invested in reducing the more indirect causes of food losses, for example management and maintenance of 525 km of rural roads, expansion of rural electrification through establishment of 127 km of electric lines linking markets, suppliers, and the national grids. These infrastructural works have been complemented with the installation of alternative power supply structures, including solar panels to guarantee a continuous power supply for cold storage and ice making equipment. Also, alternative power systems have been installed on the different islands where the project has also established new fish markets. Provision of electric power resulted in an increase in the supply of fresh and frozen fish market, which was sold at a higher price compared to dry fish.

PROPESCA constructed 15 market structures and restored 16 market facilities, which now have access to water, electric power, and sanitation, and provided support to the creation of more than 2,700 credit groups, to allow fishermen to access to a sustainable network of financial services. In terms of impact, beneficiaries of PROPESCA have observed a reduction in production losses across all parts of the value chain. PROPESCA contributed significantly to improving the efficiency of the targeted fish value chains. Project beneficiaries reported a drop in post-production losses as a result of the introduction of improved fish handling, preservation, and processing facilities and techniques. The increase in ice production capacity and the improvement of rural roads will also contribute to reduce losses, particularly for higher value fish. The reduction of post-production losses coupled with the productivity increases generated by the project is expected to lead to a substantial increase in the volume and value of the fish marketed by beneficiaries. As of 2018, the yearly value of higher value fish marketed by fishers in the project area increased from US$55 million to US$204 million, while for dried fish and fresh fish the value of yearly sales are expected to increase by project completion from US$31.5 million to US$42 million and from US$14 million to US$31.5 million, respectively.

The implementation of the project has been associated with a 10% increase of the total fishery revenues in the provinces where the project was implemented (IFAD 2020). At beneficiary level, it was observed a shift of ownership from perishable and low cost means of transport and work, such as bicycles and rowing boats, to more modern and efficient assets, such as motorbike, cars, and motorised boats. A similar trend has emerged for household appliance and access to services. For example, the beneficiaries using oil lamp for lightening decreased from 49% to 16%, while the share of households using electricity increased from 29% to 46%.

According to the project completion report, PROPESCA has increased food accessibility and lowered the level of food insecurity in the areas of intervention. In particular, the percentage of households able to purchase food increased by 25% to 33.6%, accompanied by a reduction of those that found it sometimes difficult to access food, from 52.2% to 43.7%. This results from the increased in revenues for beneficiaries, through the improved market accessibility and storage, and by the higher physical supply of fish in the market. Finally, the benefits of the project appeared to spill over beyond the direct beneficiaries themselves, as the infrastructural expansion has generated a large group of indirect beneficiaries, who could access to renovated and improved infrastructures, electricity, and new lines of credit through the financing institutions.

IFAD operations in the crop sector

A key element to reduce food loss in crop systems is the promotion of on- and off-farm post-harvesting technologies also in the agricultural sector.

Climate-Resilient Post-Harvest and Agribusiness Support Project (PASP)—Rwanda

The PASP development objective was to increase smallholder incomes through facilitation of improved market linkages that promoted increased agricultural production from crops and dairy and reduction in losses in a changing climate. PASP's primary target group was rural smallholder farmers engaged in production and primary processing in maize, beans, cassava, Irish potatoes (IPs), horticulture, and dairy value chains.

Before PASP, PHLs were one of the greatest sources of inefficiency in agricultural production with losses estimated at about 30% of harvested products across all value chains. These losses were further compounded by the heavy reliance on rainfed agriculture and vulnerability to climate change. PASP interventions on climate smart post-harvest infrastructure and investments were considered an opportunity for improving crop productivity and resilience in more uncertain climatic and economic conditions.

PASP significantly contributed to reducing poverty levels through reduction of PHLs and improved market linkages. This was achieved by construction of post-harvest infrastructure and facilities, training farmers in climate smart good agriculture practice (GAP) particularly in post-harvesting handling and selling stages, empowerment of cooperatives, improving market linkages, and promotion of sustainable climate resilient technologies. The final project impact survey (IFAD 2020b) found that PHLs had reduced significantly for the targeted crop and dairy value chains. For example, quantitative losses in the IP value chain reduced from 37% to 10% and qualitative losses from 30% to 10%; in cassava, losses reduced from 35% to 13%; and dairy value chain PHLs were reduced from 18% to 4%. For beans, qualitative losses reduced from 23% at baseline to 9% at end line. In addition, PASP achieved a 26% increase in net income for project beneficiaries.

The final impact survey established an improvement in household food security, and this was assessed through changes in eating habits of beneficiary households. It was found that 75.6% of beneficiary households reported an improvement in food availability and eating habits. For example, there was a reduction in the number of households that had only one meal a day from 37% at baseline to 21%. Further, the percentage of beneficiary households that had at least two meals and three meals a day increased by 12% and 3%, respectively.

Timor-Leste Maize Storage Programme

Promoting the reduction of food losses during the post-harvesting period can provide a substantial contribution towards food security. Between 2011 and 2015, IFAD implemented the Timor-Leste Maize Storage Programme (TLMSP) targeting maize farmers in the upland territories. Timor-Leste is one of the poorest countries in the world; about 70% of Timor-Leste's population relies on agriculture to obtain their livelihood, and about 95% of this experienced at least one hungry season without staple foods IFAD (2010). Malnutrition and preventable diseases are common among children and youths, who also represent the majority of the population in the rural areas (54%).

Maize and root crops are the main sources of food for the rural population. In particular, maize accounts for 36% of the total crop production and to a similar percentage to household's consumption. Maize also has high storage losses associated with the traditional storage methods used by households. Before the project implementation, it was estimated that rodents and weevils accounted for up to 15% loss of stored maize during the post-harvesting period. This loss is equivalent to a cost of about $17.5 million, or about 31,000 metric tonnes of maize at the national scale.

The objective of TLMSP was to stabilise food availability among maize growers in rural areas, reduce food losses, and increase their level of food security. To achieve these three objectives, the beneficiary farmers of TLMSP could purchase grain storage drums at a subsidised cost and receive capacity building trainings on their use and maintenance. Being made of hard plastic and being air-tight, the drums were ideal for preventing food losses from rodents and weevils. The drums have a lifespan of 25 years and do not require any additional treatment or maintenance. The subsidised cost was designed to incentivise the beneficiaries and involved a US$10 contribution and a project contribution of US$40. This has increased the responsibility of participants in the care and maintenance of the drums and led to a high rate of adoption rate.

Overall, 23,000 farmers purchased more than 41,300 steel drums (IFAD 2016). The analysis of the project impact found that, thanks to the technology delivered to the farmers, post-harvest maize losses have decreased from 15% to about 1% of the total maize harvested. This result has translated to an increase availability of 80 kg of maize per family, corresponding to a total of 1,079 metric tonnes available for the 23,000 beneficiaries every year. According to the impact assessment of the project, the level of food insecurity of participants has also decreased steadily, with the likelihood of beneficiary households experiencing a first hungry season reducing from 95% to 33%, and the likelihood of a second hungry season passing from 31% to 6% (IFAD 2016). Other results have suggested that both chronic malnutrition (−3.3%) and underweight (−14.1%) were sensibly lower among children under five years belonging to beneficiary household.

PNAAFA—Lower Guinea and Faranah

The Rural Development: National Programme to Support Agricultural Value Chain Actors—Lower Guinea and Faranah Expansion (PNAAFA-LGF) is an expansion of a national programme aiming at improving farmers' productivity and food security through the support and capacity building of farmer organisations working in vegetable and rice value chains. The PNAAFA-LGF focused on increasing the post-harvest activities by sensitising farmer federations and farmer cooperatives to submit proposals for value chain development activities in Lower Guinea that involved public and private sector actors. In total, the PNAAFA-LGF targeted 53,303 households (117,918) producers along the value chains, with 56% of beneficiaries being women, and 37% youth.

The PNAAFA-LGF targeted reducing food loss through training sessions (86% women) on processing and transformation of more than 25 vegetables. This increased the lifespan of these vegetable from a few weeks to in some cases, more than six months. A key nutritional result was that this increased diet diversity and smoothed consumption of vegetables throughout the year. This transformation increased revenues for beneficiaries, for example many were able to receive a price three times higher for a kilogram of processed product, compared to selling the raw product. The programme has also contributed to improve the quality of infrastructures to allow them to access the market. For example, the project has built rural infrastructure (e.g. 70 storage warehouses, sorting sheds, and river crossings and rural roads).

Reducing food losses and fostering food transformation contributed to a substantial increase of beneficiaries' income. According to the completion impact assessment, 82% of beneficiary households declared that their income doubled as a consequence of the project, while for 11.5% income tripled (IFAD 2013). According to 31% of households, this was possible due to the improved production allowing more marketable product. Overall reducing food loss through the promotion of food transformation has also had an indirect effect on food security, which improved in terms of both quantity and quality of food consumed by the beneficiaries, the number of meals per day increased by 97%, while about 19% of households declared to have improved the quality of their meals. This has also contributed to a reduction in the share of children under five suffering from malnutrition, from 35% to 29%.

IFAD's operations in livestock

Livestock systems represent another key sector where food loses can be greatly reduced both along the value chain, through better post-harvest and handling facilities and technologies, and through cooling facilities. In addition, livestock systems are also at the centre of attention due to their contribution to GHG emissions (estimated at about 14.5% of all anthropogenic GHG emissions, IPCC, 2021). This is expected to further increase due to increasing global demand for meat and livestock products. The effort is thus to invest in livestock systems that are instrumental in the transition towards circular agricultural systems where food losses are dramatically reduced, increasing the productivity per unit of livestock through better feed, veterinary services, and pasture management, and through careful and attentive restoration of pasture and degraded land.

Smallholder Dairy Commercialization Programme—Kenya

The Smallholder Dairy Commercialization Programme (SDCP) was designed to address constraints in the smallholders' milk sector in Kenya by increasing smallholders' production, productivity, and participation in milk markets and reducing food losses along the milk and dairy value chain. It did this through training dairy groups, offering technical support for household dairy production and developing milk-marketing value chains. The first phase of the SDCP (July 2006 to March 2013) was implemented in 27 divisions in nine counties across central and central-western Kenya. The second phase ran from December 2015 to March 2020.

The SDCP trained beneficiary dairy groups on organisational and enterprise skills and helped them establish and maintain links with extension systems, input providers, and output purchasers. In addition, the project improved dairy groups access to financial services by promoting competitive investment grants designed to improve dairy business activities and techniques. Through these activities, the SDCP established sustainable dairy enterprises, enabled group members to obtain financial services, reduced transaction and input costs, raised output prices, and increased beneficiaries' production and market knowledge. To achieve higher production and productivity, SDCP increased the number of more productive livestock, and improved their health by providing technical support on artificial insemination, animal disease prevention and disease management, fodder production, feeding practices, and dairy enterprise management practices. Furthermore, the programme increased dairy producers' access to the processing sector and improved the linkages of small-scale milk producers, traders, and processors with local milk markets. To this end, the project invested in improving market infrastructure, such as milk-cooling facilities and improved road infrastructure, and in developing marketing skills by training milk-marketing groups and beneficiaries and setting up low-cost market information systems. The project supported 13,132 dairy groups, created eight milk-cooling and processing facilities, and established 6,123 fodder-bulking sites.

By improving access to appropriate post-production facilities and markets, SDCP has reduced milk losses by 26% in the project area. On the basis of current milk prices, the value of the amount of milk saved is KES 24.5 million (US$240,000) per year. Combined with the increases in milk yields generated by the adoption of production technologies, this result has led to a significant improvement in the marketing of milk. Downstream, the expected results include a 50% increase in the quantity of milk delivered to the processing industry and a 20% increase in the amount of value-added milk marketed. The improvement of milk marketing resulted in a positive increase in the incomes, livelihoods, and nutrition of 63,000 households. As of March 2019, the average income increased from KES 130/day (2009 baseline) to KES 720/day for 80% of smallholder dairy farmers and 50% of small traders targeted by the project.

Both the qualitative and quantitative analyses conducted reported a significant reduction of milk losses thanks to better grazing and managing techniques coupled with cooling and processing facilities and better access to the market (Cavatassi and Brueckman 2019). It is important to note that the private sector has been instrumental in implementing the programme, especially in providing market linkages for the dairy groups: two of the largest dairy-processing firms have offered support to some of the dairy groups in terms of marketing and technical support for high-quality milk handling and the operation of milk-bulking facilities. This finding suggests that partnership and involvement with the private sector could create good synergies that would increase the project's impacts and lead to a significant reduction in food loss.

The Rwanda Dairy Development Project

The Rwanda Dairy Development Project (RDDP) was designed to increase the nutritional status and incomes of poor households relying on dairy subsector as a pathway out of poverty. The project started in 2016 in 12 districts and ended in 2022 and had a total budget of US$65.1 million. RDDP's aim was to raise rural smallholder incomes through more productive and profitable dairy production obtained via sustainable intensification, better infrastructure, and improved market access.

In particular, the project's theory of change was based on the importance of changing to a 'climate-smart dairy production' approach, where dairy farmers learnt practices and production methodologies to sustainably produce higher quantities of good quality milk, whilst adapting to climate change. Climate-smart dairy farming was pursued through the adoption of more sustainable practices and technologies; this involved (i) installation of roof top tanks for rain water collection (to increase water availability and reduce time spent collecting water); (ii) improved access to high-quality dairy inputs, such as forage and other feeds, access to veterinary services, AI, and breeding techniques; (iii) adoption of green technologies, such as solar and biogas for energy generation; and (iv) support to milk collection and marketing, coordinating services for input supply, increasing and strengthening infrastructure needed for processing milk and dairy products.

Assessment of the project has found the importance of green and sustainable technologies to reduce food losses. For example, the solar energy installation at milk collection centres and milk processing units has provided a cheap source of energy for chilling milk, as well as for cooling milk products.

The final evaluation of the impact of RDDP on reduction of food losses is not yet available. However, there are several studies that report on this project and the sustainability of the dairy sector in Rwanda (see Taiwo, Olaniyan, and Ndagijimana 2019; Habiyaremye et al. 2021).[2] These analyses have shown that RDDP is successfully raising beneficiaries' income; it has also enhanced beneficiaries' access to credit and extension services. The role of more efficient and empowered farmers' organisation is showing to be fundamental in enhancing access to input and veterinary services.

Lessons and recommendations

The projects illustrated earlier provide a set of examples for stakeholders, policymakers, and practitioners in project design and implementation on how best to reduce food loses and contribute to the Agenda 2030 and the SDGs. Reducing food loss should be a key priority in developing countries as a pathway to reduce hunger, to increase incomes, and to reduce emissions while increasing access and affordability of food.

Lesson 1: Governments should put in place mechanisms, policies, and financing to facilitate collaboration and coordination amongst a wide range of stakeholders and partners (e.g. private sector, rural finance providers, NGOs, and farmers' organisations) to achieve improved livelihoods and food security through the reduction of food losses. Coordination should include not only farmers/fishers/breeders, processors, traders, retailers, but also members of the trade cooperatives and professional associations. Improving the coordination among these actors helps to identify the major sources of food losses along the value chain and on which intervention points' policy should be developed. A better connection with the value chain actors will also allow to understand whether the promoted technologies or practices will be adaptable to the local context and reduce handling, transportation, and transaction costs, thereby increasing gross margins. Improved dialogue between value chains actors and policymakers helps the design of appropriate capacity building training and technical assistance to ensure a medium- and long-term uptake of the promoted technologies.

Lesson 2: Capacity building in the promotion of good practices in food storage and management, safe food handling, on-farm storage and optimising consumption, and processing are all key to reducing food losses.

Lesson 3: Access to finance remains a crucial requirement to allow smallholders and fishers to invest in technology and equipment, which can reduce their post-harvest and food losses. An alternative solution that may be considered is the introduction of shared credit liability along the value chain. Financial and credit companies should better understand and price their products based available collaterals of the smallholder producers, especially in developing countries, where the available asset guarantees are minimal.

Lesson 4: Training farmers and enhancing their skills should remain a priority of any intervention on reducing food loss. A lack of awareness and capacity is a main cause of food losses in developing and developed countries. Since each stage of the food value chain may become a source of food loss, trainings should be designed to target all the possible operations in the value chain, from harvesting to processing and marketing. Government and policymakers should not underestimate the role that data may have for identifying where food loses occur within the food value chain. As FAO (2019) suggests, lack of accurate data is among the causes of mis-targeting of policies, and of the slowness of the interventions in the policy arena. With this, it is also necessary to promote well-established and new methodologies to estimate food losses within a value chain, such as the FAO food loss assessment methodology, which has been developed to increase the accuracy of policy intervention.

Lesson 5: Investments in infrastructure including storage, cooling facility, transport, and handling equipment to ensure longer shelf life are crucial to effectively reduce food loses. This is particularly relevant for highly perishable food such as vegetables, fish, and dairy products. In rural development interventions, it is essential to invest and put in place actions to promote improved equipment and on-farm storage structures. Some of these, such as hermetic bags and metallic/plastic drums, are easily accessible by farmers. Others may be needed at community level, for example building of collective storage facilities, which can help in reducing food losses among farmers who are unable to access their own on-farm storage facilities. Given that the vast majority of losses in grain production occur during the storage, increased availability of these technologies into the market at a subsidised price may contribute to a reduction in food losses. Besides the reduction in food losses, improving the storage of grain and dried products can help with intra-seasonal volatility in price. Many farmers, for example, prefer to avoid the risk of losing their produce and thus sell it as soon as they harvest it. With an improvement in the storage system, producers could store their product while waiting for price to increase. Others, however, may require larger investments that may also be difficultly covered, such as refrigeration structures as in CCDP. For this reason, some initial investment is needed and can be covered through private-public partnership, especially for agricultural sub-sectors specialised in the production of highly perishable and fresh commodities, such as fishery and vegetables.

Supporting investments in food processing are crucial in triggering transformative processes in the value chain. Processing stretches the lifespan of the produce, allowing the same product to sell at higher prices, as shown in the agricultural products in the PNAAFA-LGF programme. However, for specific value chains, improvements in storage and processing may occur only through an improvement in rural infrastructure, like storage facilities or feeder roads. As shown by PROPESCA, investment in the improvement and maintenance of a road network remains essential to connect producers to the market, reduce food waste, and increase the efficiency in food distribution across the food value chain. Given that the majority of the producers operate in rural areas with inadequate access to electricity, the objective of reducing food losses through increased processing and storage facilities will only occur through large structural investments in power supply.

Notes

1 Food waste is a topic very much connected to reducing food losses. Given IFAD's mandate and beneficiaries, that is to improve rural peoples' livelihood and promote rural development, the most relevant and impactful area of intervention is related to food losses rather than waste and it is the focus of the present chapter.
2 A potential limitation of these studies relies on the fact that these focus on the contribution effect rather than on the attribution effect, that is, they analyse the income pathways of beneficiary households without comparing them to a control group.

References

Bloom, E., V. de Wit, and M. J. Carangal-San Jose. 2005. *Potential Economic Impact of an Avian Flu Pandemic on Asia.* Asian Development Bank. http://hdl.handle.net/11540/2165.

Cavatassi, R., and P. Brueckman. 2019. *Smallholder Dairy Commercialization Project, Policy Brief.* Rome, Italy: IFAD.

Cavatassi, R., A. Mabiso, and P. Brueckmann. 2019. *Impact Assessment Report: For the Coastal Community Development Project, Republic of Indonesia.* Rome, Italy: IFAD.

Delve, R. 2021. "Tackling Food Loss for Sustainable Food Systems." www.ifad.org/en/web/latest/-/intl-day-food-loss-2021.

FAO. 2011. *Global Food Losses and Food Waste—Extent.* Rome, Italy: Causes and Prevention.

———. 2019. *The State of Food and Agriculture 2019. Moving Forward on Food Loss and Waste Reduction.* Rome. www.fao.org/state-of-food-agriculture/en.

———. 2020. *The State of World Fisheries and Aquaculture 2020.* Rome. www.fao.org/publications/sofia/en/.

———. 2021. *The State of Food Security and Nutrition in the World 2021.* Rome. https://www.fao.org/documents/card/en/c/cb4474en.

Habiyaremye, N., E. A. Ouma, N. Mtimet, and G. A. Obare. 2021. "A Review of the Evolution of Dairy Policies and Regulations in Rwanda and Its Implications on Inputs and Services Delivery." *Frontiers in Veterinary Science* 8.

IFAD. 2010. *Timor-Leste Maize Storage Programme Project Design Report.* Rome, Italy: IFAD.

————. 2011. *Artisanal Fisheries Promotion Project (PROPESCA). Project Design Report.* Rome, Italy: IFAD.

————. 2013. *Programme National d'Appui aux Acteurs des Filières Agricoles—extension Basse-Guinée et Faranah (PNAAFA-extension BGF).* Rome, Italy: IFAD.

————. 2016. *Timor-Leste Maize Storage Programme Project Completion Report.* Rome, Italy: IFAD.

————. 2019. *The Food Loss Reduction Advantage: Building Sustainable Food Systems.* Rome, Italy: IFAD.

————. 2020. *Artisanal Fishery Promotion Project (PROPESCA) Completion Report.* Rome, Italy: IFAD.

————. 2020b. *Climate-Resilient Post-Harvest and Agribusiness Support Project (PASP) Project Completion Report.* Rome, Italy: IFAD.

————. 2021. *Transforming Food Systems for Rural Prosperity. IFAD Rural Development Report.* Rome, Italy: IFAD.

Laborde, D., W. Martin, J. Swinnen, and R. Vos. 2020. "COVID-19 Risks to Global Food Security." *Science* 369 (6503): 500–2.

Mabiso, A. 2019. *Coastal Community Development Project Policy Brief, Republic of Indonesia.* Rome, Italy: IFAD.

Nelson, G. C., M. W. Rosegrant, J. Koo, R. Robertson, T. Sulser, T. Zhu, and D. Lee. 2009. "Climate Change: Impact on Agriculture and Costs of Adaptation (Vol. 21)." International Food Policy Research Institute. United Nations Department of Economic and Social Affairs. 2019 Revision of World Population Prospects.

Taiwo, O., O. Olaniyan, and A. Ndagijimana. 2019. "Effects of Rwanda Dairy Development Project on the Livelihood of Dairy Farmers in the Western Province of Rwanda." *African Journal of Sustainable Development* 9: 85–111.

UN DESA. 2019. *United Nations, Department of Economic and Social Affairs, Population Division.* World Population Prospects 2019.

6 The European Union and the fight against food waste and losses

From policy to practice

Fabrizio D'Angelo

Introduction

The European Union (EU) is one of the bigger legislative actors in the world. With more than 400 legislative acts only in 2019, the EU influences directly its member states and indirectly the entire world.

Food waste has not always been at the centre of the EU legislative works. With the adoption of the SDGs in 2015, the legislative and policy activism related to food waste and losses became greater and greater. The EU became one of the leading actors in implementing the *2030 Agenda for Sustainable Development* (United Nations 2015), starting with important policy proposals such as the *EU Circular Economy package* (European Commision 2015) and later the *EU Green deal* (European Commission 2019c). Food waste and losses became a clear target to fight, and new policy instruments were needed to undertake this mission. One of the main initiatives coming from this policy input is the *EU Food Waste and Losses Stakeholders' platform*, an extraordinary forum put in place to create common standards, procedures, and proposals to tackle this big problem in a common and shared way. Thanks to these proposals, the EU has now a more comprehensive and developed framework to fight food waste and losses. However, further binding initiatives, with fixed and mandatory targets, will come in the next years.

The first part of this chapter is composed of six sections, and it will focus on the main policies and practical outputs coming from the EU legislative and policy activity.

If, from a policy point of view, a lot of work has been done in the last years, what the EU Institutions are concretely doing to fight against food waste and losses? What did they put in place to reduce food waste and comply with their political recommendations? The second part of this chapter is composed of two sections, and it will focus on some projects and initiatives carried out by the EU institutions in their daily food and catering operations. This is an occasion to highlight how the EU administration is caring about this problem and how it is trying to solve it.

DOI: 10.4324/9781003226932-9

The Fusions study about food waste in Europe: Brussels, we have a problem!

FUSIONS (Food Use for Social Innovation by Optimising Waste Prevention Strategies) is a project about working towards a more resource-efficient Europe by significantly reducing food waste. The project ran for four years, from August 2012 to July 2016. It was funded by the European Commission Framework Programme 7 (www.eu-fusions.org/).

Among the deliverables of this project, the 'Estimates of European food waste levels' has been the first step towards a common and comprehensive European policy on food waste and losses. The project delivered the first EU common definition of food waste: Fractions of '*food and inedible parts of food removed from the food supply chain to be recovered or disposed of (including— composted, crops ploughed in/not harvested, anaerobic digestion, bioenergy production, co-generation, incineration, disposal to sewer, landfill or discarded to sea)*' (FUSIONS 2016, 2).

The study 'Estimates of European food waste levels', published in March 2016, presents estimates for food waste arising in the EU-28. Estimates of food waste were sought for 2012. This was the first exercise trying to have an EU-28 estimation of food waste along with a common European methodology. The estimates have been obtained using a combination of national waste statistics and findings from selected research studies.

It was clear that the data presented in this study had a relatively high uncertainty due to the limited number of underlying studies of sufficient quality available. It is important to underline that it was the first attempt to build a study on existing data, adjusting that to a common definition and then finding valid ways of upscaling and producing an EU-28 data set for food waste (FUSIONS 2016, 3).

The collection and analysis of data from across Europe for this study generated an estimate of food waste in the EU-28 of 88 million tonnes. The sectors contributing the most to food waste are households (47 million tonnes ± 4 million tonnes) and processing (17 million tonnes ± 13 million tonnes). These two sectors account for 72% of EU food waste.

Despite the uncertainty and the difficulties related to the collection and liability of the data collected during this study, the EU institutions and member states were finally aware of the huge amount of food wasted in Europe. This study opened the eyes of European legislators about a hidden major problem: why are we wasting all this food in Europe? What are the costs related to food wastage? What can be improved? What do we need to monitor to reduce food waste?

The need to understand more about this issue started increasing. The lack of common analytical tools and methodologies became evident. This study had the merit to be the evidence-based lever for the launch of the common EU policy against food waste and losses.

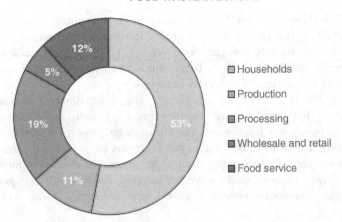

Figure 6.1 Split of EU-28 food waste in 2012 by sector; includes food and inedible parts associated with food.

Source: adapted from FUSIONS (2016)

The Circular Economy package: where the EU fight against food waste begins

The EU communication 'Closing the loop—An EU action plan for the Circular Economy' has been published in December 2015 (European Commission 2015). This communication set up an action plan with the aim to accelerate the transition to a more circular economy and minimise the generation of waste as an essential contribution to the EU's efforts to develop a sustainable, low-carbon, resource-efficient, and competitive economy.

The EU Circular Economy action plan is an instrument implementing the SDGs by 2030, in particular Goal 12 (with the target of halving per capita food waste at the retail and consumer level), and reducing food losses along production and supply chains, regarding sustainable consumption and production (European Commission 2015, 2–3).

In the circular economy communication, for the first time at EU level, food waste was defined as 'an increasing concern in Europe'. The production, distribution, and storage of food were identified as sectors using natural resources and generating environmental impacts. Some aspects such as the financial losses and the social impacts have also been raised as major problems related to food waste.

The food waste measuring methodologies were one of the most important issues identified by the action plan. The FUSIONS project showed that food waste takes place all along the value chain: during production and distribution, in shops, restaurants, catering facilities, and at home. During the data collection made by FUSIONS, there was no harmonised, reliable method to measure food waste in the EU. This made it particularly hard to quantify and to have a clear picture of the problem. Addressing the measurement issue was an important step towards a better understanding of the problem, a coherent monitoring and reporting as well as effective exchange of good practices across the EU. This is the reason why the Commission decided, for the first time, to elaborate a common EU methodology to measure food waste in close cooperation with member states and other stakeholders (European Commission 2015, 14–15).

The communication defined the main priorities linked to the achievement of the SDG target on food waste:

• develop a common EU methodology to measure food waste and define relevant indicators. It will create a platform involving member states and stakeholders in order to support the achievement of the SDG targets on food waste, through the sharing of best practice and the evaluation of progress made over time.
• take measures to clarify EU legislation relating to waste, food, and feed and facilitate food donation and the use of former foodstuff and by-products from the food chain in feed production without compromising food and feed safety; and
• examine ways to improve the use of date marking by actors in the food chain and its understanding by consumers, in particular the 'best before' label (European Commission 2015, 15).

EU Platform on food losses and waste: towards a common European approach on food waste and losses

The Communication on Circular Economy (European Commission 2015) called on the Commission to establish a Platform dedicated to food waste prevention. Thus, the EU Platform on Food Losses and Food Waste (FLW) was established in 2016, bringing together EU institutions, experts from the EU countries and relevant stakeholders selected through an open call for applications.

The mandate of the Platform, initially foreseen to end on 31 October 2019, has been extended until the end of 2021 in order to allow this expert group to pursue its work and ongoing projects over a 5-year period.

The Platform supports the Commission, member states, and all actors in the food value chain, including consumer and other non-governmental organisations, in taking action to prevent food losses and food waste without compromising food safety, feed safety, and/or animal health.

The Platform's work covers areas such as definitions and measurement framework for food waste; monitoring of food waste levels and progress made by all actors towards the achievement of SDG 12.3; implementation and application of EU legislation related to waste, food, and feed to ensure the highest value use of food resources (in line with a 'food use hierarchy').

In addition to plenary meetings, the Platform also operates in sub-groups to examine specific aspects and/or questions related to food waste prevention. As provided for in the Terms of Reference of the Platform, the Chair of the Platform may set up sub-groups for examining specific questions. At the inaugural meeting of the Platform, it was agreed that four sub-groups would be established in order to support the Commission's work in relation to food donation, food waste measurement, action and implementation, date marking, and food waste prevention (European Commission 2019b, 4). The food donation and food waste measurement sub-groups are further analysed here below.

The food donation sub-group

The sub-group has two main tasks: the preparation of EU food donation guidelines for donors and receivers of food surplus, and the identification of practices, guidelines, and rules existing in member states in relation to food donation for sharing with Platform members.

Following consultation with the food donation sub-group, the Commission has adopted EU food donation guidelines in order to facilitate the recovery and redistribution of safe, edible food to those in need. The guidelines seek to facilitate compliance of providers and recipients of surplus food with relevant requirements laid down in the EU regulatory framework (e.g. food safety, food hygiene, traceability, liability, VAT), and promote common interpretation by regulatory authorities in the EU member states of EU rules applying to the redistribution of surplus food (European Commission 2017).

The food waste measurement sub-group

The Commission has been delegated to establish a common methodology to measure food waste levels in the EU, as well as a reporting format for the EU countries to inform on progress made over time. The Delegated Decision establishing a common EU methodology to measure food waste entered into force on 17 October 2019 and was drafted in consultation with the food waste measurement subgroup. The first data collection on food waste was undertaken by member states in 2020, in view of reporting on national food waste levels by mid-2022. The EU reporting framework will help standardise reporting of food waste levels by business and contribute to global monitoring of the Sustainable Development Goal Target (12.3).[1]

Article 1 of the delegated act foresees that the amounts of food waste shall be measured separately for the following stages of the food supply chain: (a) primary production; (b) processing and manufacturing; (c) retail and other distribution of food; (d) restaurants and food services; (e) households (European Commission 2019a). The identification of common measurement stages has been set as main priority in order to improve the quality of EU data on food waste.

Article 2 of the delegated act sets the common methodology to be applied for the food waste measurement. According to the EU Methodology, member states shall: measure each year the amount of food waste generated in a full

Table 6.1 Methodology for in-depth measurement of food waste.

Stage of food supply chain	Methods of measurement				
Primary production	–Direct measurement	–Mass balance			– Questionnaires and interviews – Coefficients and production statistics – Waste composition analysis
Processing and manufacturing					
Retail and other distribution of food			–Waste composition analysis	Counting/ scanning	
Restaurants and food services					Diaries
Households					

Source: Adapted from European Commission 2019.

calendar year; measure the amount of food waste for a given stage of the food supply chain using the methodology set out at least once every four years; for the first reporting period, member states shall measure the amount of food waste for all stages of the food supply chain using the methodology. The amounts of food waste shall be measured in metric tonnes of fresh mass (European Commission 2019a).

Annex III of the Delegated decision established specific methods of measurement according to the different stages of the food supply chain (European Commission 2019a; see also Chapter 1). The different methods can only be applied to the stages as shown in Table 6.1.

The different methods set by the Platform are:

- Direct measurement (weighing or volumetric assessment): Use of a measuring device to determine the mass of samples of food waste or fractions of total waste, directly or determined on the basis of volume. It includes measurement of separately collected food waste.
- Scanning/Counting: Assessment of the number of items that make up food waste, and use of the result to determine the mass.
- Waste composition analysis: Physical separation of food waste from other fractions in order to determine the mass of the fractions sorted out.
- Diaries: An individual or group of individuals keeps a record or log of food waste information on a regular basis.

The Platform provided also other methods when there is no direct (physical) access to food waste or when direct measurement is not feasible:

- Mass balance: Calculation of the amount of food waste on the basis of the mass of inputs and outputs of food into and out of the measured system, and processing and consumption of food within the system.

- Coefficients: Use of previously established food waste coefficients or percentages representative for a food industry sub-sector or for an individual business operator. Such coefficients or percentages shall be established through sampling, data provided by food business operators or by other methods

Moreover, member states data, collected according to the common EU food waste measurement methodology, will be reported to the EU by using a specific reporting format. All the collected data will be accompanied by a quality check report, in order to help verify the quality of the data and improve data collection in the future.

The EU Platform on Food Losses and Food Waste will continue to play a key role in mobilising action to reduce FLW across the EU as part of the Farm to Fork Strategy. In order to re-establish the Platform and ensure continuity of work as of 2022, the Commission launched a new public call for applications for private sector organisations and invited public entities to join its work for another 5-year term (2022–2026). Interested organisations were invited to apply until 23 July 2021.

EU waste framework directive

The Waste Framework Directive entered into force in 2008 and was then revised in 2018. The revised version sets the basic concepts and definitions related to waste management, including definitions of waste, recycling, and recovery.

This Directive also sets some binding targets for the EU. By 2020, the preparing for re-use and the recycling of waste materials (such as paper, metal, plastic, and glass) from households shall be increased to a minimum of overall 50% by weight. By 2020, the preparing for re-use, recycling, and other material recovery, including backfilling operations using waste to substitute other materials, of non-hazardous construction and demolition waste shall be increased to a minimum of 70% by weight. Finally, by 2025, the preparing for re-use and the recycling of municipal waste shall be increased to a minimum of 55%, 60%, and 65% by weight by 2025, 2030, and 2035, respectively.[2]

The waste framework directive, for the first time in an EU legislative document, gives clarification on the definition of food waste. The Directive takes as reference Article 2 of Regulation (EC) No. 178/2002 (the European Food Law): 'food' (or 'foodstuff') means any substance or product, whether processed, partially processed or unprocessed, intended to be, or reasonably expected to be ingested by humans. 'Food' includes drink, chewing gum, and any substance, including water, intentionally incorporated into the food during its manufacture, preparation, or treatment.[3] Therefore, food waste is all the 'food' that has become waste (art. 3, 4a).[4]

An important recommendation made by the Directive is that member states should take measures to promote prevention and reduction of food waste in line with the 2030 Agenda for Sustainable Development, adopted by the United Nations (UN) General Assembly on 25 September 2015, and in particular its target of halving per capita global food waste at the retail and consumer levels and reduce food losses by 2030.

The Directive also makes it mandatory to set an EU common reduction target of 30% by 2025 and 50% by 2030 of the global per capita generation of food waste. This target has not been approved yet by the member states and it will be defined and approved after the first results of the EU food waste data to be released in 2023.

A crucial aspect of this directive is the obligation for member states to measure progress made in the reduction of food waste on the basis of the data collected through the implementation of the EU common methodology elaborated by the EU Platform on Food losses and Food waste.

By 31 December 2023, the Commission shall examine the data on food waste provided by member states with a view to considering the feasibility of establishing a Union-wide food waste reduction target to be met by 2030 on the basis of the data reported by member states in accordance with the common methodology.

Eventually, Article 29(2a) of the Directive asks the member states to adopt specific food waste prevention programmes within their waste prevention programmes.[5]

The Green deal and the Farm to Fork Strategy: it is time for a green revolution in the EU

In December 2019, the European Commission published the Communication entitled the *European Green Deal*, confirming the EU leadership in the fight against climate change. This Communication resets the Commission's commitment to tackling climate and environmental-related challenges and defines several fields of immediate action in order to achieve the EU common objective to be climate neutral by 2050.

Among the key policies presented in the Communication, a specific strategy for sustainable food systems has been proposed: *The Farm to Fork Strategy* (European Commission 2020). The Farm to Fork Strategy is at the heart of the Green Deal. It addresses in a comprehensive way the challenges of sustainable food systems and recognises the links between healthy people, healthy societies, and a healthy planet. The strategy is also central to the Commission's agenda to achieve the United Nations' SDGs.

Building the food chain that works for consumers, producers, climate, and the environment is one of the main priorities of the Farm to Fork Strategy. The strategy sets a number of actions needed to achieve its objectives in this field. One of the main actions is reducing FLW all along the food chain.

The strategy underlines the fact that tackling FLW is key to achieving sustainability. The strategy's action plan foresees two main actions to tackle food waste at EU level:

- Proposal for binding EU-level targets for food waste reduction, expected by 2023
- Proposal for a revision of EU rules on date marking ('use by' and 'best before' dates), expected by the end of 2022

The Commission confirms in its strategy the commitment to halving per capita food waste at retail and consumer levels by 2030 (SDG Target 12.3). Using the new methodology for measuring food waste and the data expected from Member States in 2023, it will set a baseline and propose legally binding targets to reduce food waste across the EU (European Commission 2020).

From 'opinions' to practice: The European Economic and Social Committee (EESC) and the European Committee of the Regions (CoR) at the forefront of the fight against food waste

In the early 2015, EESC and CoR became the first EU bodies implementing an internal policy and procedures in order to tackle food waste within their catering operations.

EESC and CoR are two consultative bodies of the European Union. EESC represents the European civil society (entrepreneurs, trade unions, NGOs, etc.) and the CoR represents the European local and regional authorities. Both Committees are in charge of adopting political and technical opinions related to legislative proposals made by the European Commission and other European institutions. Both Committees occupy the same premises and they have some joint services in order to improve their synergy and the budgetary efficiency.

In 2014, the Eco-management and Audit Scheme service (EMAS) and the Catering service, part of the joint services of both Committees, decided to participate into a project promoted by the Brussels-Capital region 'Cantines durables', called later '*Good Food Strategy*' (Brussels Environment 2015). This project aimed at improving the sustainability of the catering sites, promoting healthier diets, introducing organic and vegetarian food and new ways of managing food stocks. This was the beginning of a project, which allowed the two bodies to become a leading example of sustainable good practices and a pioneer among the other EU institutions in the field of food sustainability and food waste reduction.

Food waste prevention measures: monitoring and evaluation within the Committees' premises

The Committees have several catering sites: three cafeterias, one 'à la carte restaurant', several VIP rooms, several spaces for cocktails and buffets, and one canteen serving on average 500 meals per day.

At the beginning of the project, it was very difficult to understand the nature of the food waste generated and its main causes. The complex nature of different types of activities along with the few available infrastructures for the catering services did not allow having a standardised monitoring approach to all the catering operations.

The food waste reporting was set up in 2014 using a tool—the 'waste calculator'—created in collaboration with an external consultant. This is a monthly table showing, day by day, the amount of portions left over for each type of dish served in the canteen. The Committees applied the scanning technique, which has been chosen as one of the common EU methodologies for the food waste measurement (European Commission 2019a).

In order to better explaining the methodology applied by the Committees, here is a practical example. For the dish of the day, known as the 'Daily', the Committees receive the number of leftover portions of proteins, vegetables, and starches. One portion means one individual ration. Leftovers are therefore not weighed, but scanned (the number of leftover portions are identified) and counted up at the end of service by a member of the kitchen staff. The Committees decided to apply this methodology because of the lack of infrastructure, space, and time, allowing the kitchen staff to provide this service along with their other routine tasks. The number of meals wasted is estimated by aggregating the remaining portions together to 'reconstruct' a dish from the protein/starch/vegetable leftovers. The data related to the number of meals sold are provided by the catering contractor. The contractor sends to the catering team the number of meals sold each month, which allows them to fine-tune the figures. These data (once gathered and processed) allow the catering team to estimate waste.

During the monitoring and measurement phase, some inconsistencies have been seen, reported, and rectified, but data and the main trends are generally reliable. The main difficulty in measuring waste accurately was that the catering team did not have precise information on the total quantities produced. They receive monthly statements of leftover portions, but they cannot link them directly to the number of dishes produced. The catering team therefore had to find a way of estimating the total quantity produced. This estimate was made by adding together the number of meals sold and the number of meals wasted.

In order to fight food waste, the Committees also put in place other tools than the monitoring system:

- **Prediction monitoring system**: adapting production on the base of the consumption of previous years. This system bases its prediction on data collected in the previous years and gives an estimate of potential clients attending the canteen. Therefore, if there is a correspondence between a specific day of the week and a specific meeting where in the past there was a high level of attendance, there is a high probability of having more clients at the canteen. It allows adapting the use of raw products during the production phase and avoiding food scarcity and food waste at the same time.
- **Weather monitoring system**: adaption production on the base of weather conditions: there is a strict relation between nice weather and clients' volume in the canteen. In sunny days, the canteen attendance is lower than during rainy days.
- **Warming up and cooling down techniques**: keeping food cold or warm and preparing it for consumption only when needed. These techniques are used to make sure that the unconsumed products can be reused safely for other preparations. Warming ovens and rapid coolers are needed in order to put in place food safety technics without any danger.

According to the 2018 and 2019 figures, food waste at the canteen of the Committees (in the production and consumption phase) does not exceed 5%. In the previous years, it was possible to see a clear evolution from around 20% to less than 5% of food waste in the Committees' canteen. Even if the results only cover the production and consumption phase at the site level, there is a clear evidence of the evolution and the functioning of good practices and monitoring tools.

Food donation procedure

In 2015, the Committees were the first EU bodies to organise and put in place a food donation procedure with the aim of reducing food surplus waste while helping people in need. The Committees, the catering contractor, and a Brussels social restaurant signed an agreement in order to deliver food surplus coming from the Committees' buffets to people in need.

For practical reasons, in the first phase of the project, only sandwiches were donated. The catering team encountered some consistent difficulties: respecting the food safety measures imposed by AFSCA (the Belgian food safety agency) and logistical problems such as access to the Committees' premises and security, and the delivery of food to the charities.

The key aspect for the success of the food donation project was the implementation of good practices in order to control the cold chain and ensure that the food was delivered in perfect and safe conditions. Small infrastructure investments were needed to comply with the regulations in the field. Surplus sandwiches are stored in the fridge, waiting to be donated. Between 2015 and 2018 more than 12 000 sandwiches have been donated to charities (EESC and COR 2021).

In 2017, phase 2 of the project has been launched: the food donation was extended to all other buffets and not only sandwiches. Moreover, in order to overcome problems related to the delivery, as the charities were not always able to collect the surplus food, the Committees organised a bike delivery, allowing to donate the surplus food in a flexible way without transportation constraints and producing zero CO_2 emissions. Between 2017 and 2018, more than 800 kg of other types of food than sandwiches have been donated to charities and disadvantaged people (EESC and COR 2021).

Continuous improvement of waste reporting remains an objective, with the focus on holding regular discussions with the contractor. The Committees explored new possible measurement methodologies and new tools available now in the market with the hope of implementing them in the near future. Quality monitoring will be continued, as it provides many lessons and, just on its own, enables action to be taken on the causes of waste. Eventually, in parallel with the fine tuning of the measurement tools, the food donation project which started with the donation to a Brussels social restaurants of sandwiches and hot meals that have not been sold during buffets (and which have remained in the fridge), will be enlarged to the few unused food generated by the production in the canteen. The monitoring of food waste has made it possible to highlight the minimum amount of leftovers possible. The Committees want these leftovers to be managed more responsibly.

The Council of the European Union: how a big institution deals with food waste within its premises

The Council of the European Union is one of the biggest actors in the EU legislative process. It is responsible of the European Parliament and the European Commission of the EU policymaking and it takes a major role in representing the member states governments at EU level. The Council hosts around 1,500 staff members.

With regard to its catering infrastructures, the Council has three cafeterias and three canteens. More the size of the institution is big and more is difficult to change routine mechanisms without a strong political will. In this context, the Council had to wait a strong political push before starting good practices within its premises.

In 2016, the Council made a political commitment to a series of initiatives such as improving monitoring of food waste, raising awareness among population, improving the understanding and use of date marking (also among consumers), and facilitating the donation of unsold food products to charities (Council of the European Union 2016).

Following its political commitments, the Council catering team started to collaborate with the catering contractor in order to put in place a monitoring and measurement system within its catering operations.

The Council put in place an annual food waste measurement system, based on the production of dishes, sales, recovery (food left in the cold room), and losses (food displayed to customers in hot pots, salad bar and refrigerated display case). The system allows the chef to know the losses or the excessively high recovery and thus adapt his orders and production.

The goal is to bring the production as close as possible to the sale and avoid losses. To do this, the chef bases himself on customer habits, an estimate of the number of meeting rooms occupied and his knowledge of the dishes that always appeal. During the service, he follows with all the cooks the quantities of the different dishes cooked and decreases them when the end of service approaches or the number of customers is lower than expected (for instance, at the end of the service, cooking per minute on the grill). The kitchen team is asked to check the main waste remaining on the plates. This makes it possible to control the unsuitable quantity and/or the random cooking of the food placed on the plates. The action plan is implemented daily, first checking the estimate of the quantities for the day and then recovering meat, fish, and vegetables that have remained at temperature in the cold room. Some products can be reused for other preparation.[6]

According to 2019 figures, the waste produced in the Council's canteen in the production phase was between 5% and 10% on average on the overall food production. This low percentage is given thanks to the recuperation techniques put in place by the kitchen staff (European Council, Catering memo, internal working document).

Conclusions

The EU policy on food losses and waste greatly evolved over the last ten years, passing from a hidden problem, with zero policy measures in place, to a major issue to consider in order to reach sustainability and reduce carbon emissions in Europe. The main problem of the EU policy remains the consistency of the EU-wide comprehensive data on FLW and the level of implementation of the EU recommendations in the different member states.

Even if tools have just been created, it is not clear yet whether the data collected by the different member states will allow to clearly understand the overall food waste generation in Europe. This means that a lot of work needs still to be done in order to proper implement the policy tools and the FLW methodology. Moreover, even if there is a binding recommendation to estimate and report on food waste in the EU, the difference in the degree of accuracy and quality in the data reporting can be important from country to country.

However, the fact of having a specific set of policy tools, binding targets, and a proper system of monitoring and measuring food and losses puts the European Union at the front row of the fight against FLW at international level.

Finally, regarding the degree of the policy implementation for the reduction of food waste in the EU institutions premises, a lot of work has to be done. Only few EU institutions have a clear policy against food waste and constantly monitor food waste in their daily catering operations. A stronger collaboration between catering services and sustainability services within the EU institutions will be extremely beneficial to put the fight against food waste among the top priority of the EU administration.

Notes

1 The EU website on food waste measurement is available at https://ec.europa.eu/food/safety/food-waste/eu-actions-against-food-waste/food-waste-measurement_en.
2 https://ec.europa.eu/food/safety/food-waste/eu-actions-against-food-waste/food-waste-measurement_en, European Commission website.
3 Art. 2, REGULATION (EC) No 178/2002, European Union, 2002.
4 Art. 3, 4a), DIRECTIVE (EU) 2018/851, European Union, 2018.
5 Art. 29, par. 2°, DIRECTIVE (EU) 2018/851, European Union, 2018.
6 Some examples of products that can be reused: the salad bar and the protein part, soups, hot vegetables; the peels of certain organic vegetables are dried in the oven after washing as a garnish for dishes, parsnips, sweet potatoes, carrots; the bread is made into croutons as a soup garnish. The food surplus of the kitchen staff's meal, on Fridays, at the end of the day, is given as a donation to the Red Cross. The products that cannot be reused in the kitchen go into anaerobic digestion.

References

Brussels Environment. 2015. "Good Food Strategy. Towards a Sustainable Food System in the Brussels-Capital Region." https://document.environnement.brussels/opac_css/elecfile/BRO_GoodFood_Strategy_ENGL.pdf.

Council of the European Union. 2016. "Food Losses and Food Waste—Council Conclusions." https://data.consilium.europa.eu/doc/document/ST-10730-2016-INIT/en/pdf.

EESC and COR. 2021. "Environmental Results 2020 Data." www.eesc.europa.eu/sites/default/files/files/qe-af-21-001-en-n_0.pdf.

European Commission. 2015. *Closing the Loop—An EU Plan for the Circular Economy*. Brussels: European Commission. https://eur-lex.europa.eu/resource.html?uri=cellar:8a8ef5e8-99a0-11e5-b3b7-01aa75ed71a1.0012.02/DOC_1&format=PDF.

———. 2017. "Mandate of Sub-Group Established Under the EU Platform on Food Losses and Food Waste to Support EU Activities to Facilitate Food Donation." https://ec.europa.eu/food/system/files/2018-12/fw_eu-actions_subgroup-mandate_food-donation.pdf.

———. 2019a. "Commission Delegated Decision (EU) 2019/1597 of 3 May 2019 Supplementing Directive 2008/98/EC of the European Parliament and of the Council as Regards a Common Methodology and Minimum Quality Requirements for the Uniform Measurement of Levels of Food Waste (Text with EEA Relevance.)." https://op.europa.eu/it/publication-detail/-/publication/241cf6a4-e103-11e9-9c4e-01aa75ed71a1/language-en.

———. 2019b. "EU Platform on Food Losses and Food Waste—Terms of Reference." https://ec.europa.eu/food/system/files/2019-11/fw_eu-actions_flw-platform_tor.pdf.

———. 2019c. "The European Green Deal." https://eur-lex.europa.eu/legal-content/EN/TXT/?qid=1576150542719&uri=COM%3A2019%3A640%3AFIN.

———. 2020. "Farm to Fork Strategy. For a Fair, Healthy and Environmentally-Friendly Food System." https://ec.europa.eu/food/system/files/2020-05/f2f_action-plan_2020_strategy-info_en.pdf.

FUSIONS. 2016. *Estimates of European Food Waste Levels*. Stockholm. www.eu-fusions.org/phocadownload/Publications/Estimates of European food waste levels.pdf.

United Nations. 2015. "2030 Agenda for Sustainable Development." https://www.un.org/sustainabledevelopment/development-agenda/.

Part 3

National policies

7 Did France really ban food waste? Lessons from a pioneering national regulation

Marie Mourad

Introduction

While French people are often portrayed as fine gourmets that enjoy their dishes to the last bite, they are no exception when it comes to discarding large quantities of food. Like in other industrialised countries, the production and distribution of large volumes of food, transported over long distances through various intermediaries, inevitably generates large volumes of waste. Establishing a definition and accurate numbers on food waste is complex (Chaboud and Daviron 2017), but the French Agency for the Ecological Transition (ADEME) estimated in 2016 that the French food system generated ten million tonnes of FLW, the equivalent of 150 kilos per person and per year. This would represent 15.3 million tonnes of CO_2 and 16 billion euros. From farm to fork, the sectors of food production, processing, distribution, and consumption may represent 32%, 21%, 14%, and 33%, respectively, of this waste (ADEME 2016).

In this context, French policymakers have engaged in a 'fight' against food waste since 2013. The country made a commitment to halve food waste by 2025, in line with European directives. France's goal precedes the UN SDGs' target of halving food waste by 2030. Rallying social, economic, and environmental concerns, the French government took the opportunity to be exemplary on this issue. In 2016, France became the first country to pass a national law specifically against food waste, referred to as 'Loi Garot' after the National Assembly member who submitted the law proposal. This policy was also the first to adopt a formally strong and binding language, obligating supermarkets to set up partnerships for food donation and prohibiting the voluntary destruction of edible food. As it earned significant international attention and even ranked France the number one country in terms of food sustainability (BCFN 2017), the media often portrayed it as a complete 'ban' on food waste (Chrisafis 2016). But did France really ban food waste? And what can policymakers from other countries learn from the French experience?

This chapter reviews the negotiation, creation, and implementation of this French regulation over the past ten years, along with its most recent evolutions and impacts. The analysis is based on the author's Ph.D. research (Mourad

DOI: 10.4324/9781003226932-11

2018), which includes more than 130 interviews with French and European experts and stakeholders and the observation of roundtables and meetings related to the food waste policy-making process between 2013 and 2021. In addition, the chapter draws on a case study of a Californian food redistribution regulation that was inspired by the French one and adopted in 2020. In California, the author carried out interviews with policymakers, participated in the law-making process and drafting of guidance documents, and, as an independent consultant, supported local governments in the implementation of the law.

Through the analysis of the elaboration and implementation of French food waste policies, this chapter questions the relative efficacy of different types of policy instruments. In the case of food waste, policy approaches have been classified as either regulatory or 'suasive', including communication, education, and voluntary agreements. These two approaches can be combined with both market-based measures, that is taxes and subsidies, and public services, that is public infrastructures, databases, and common spaces (Giordano, Falasconi, and Pancino 2020). While the French 2016 law had a formally strong regulatory component, the analysis shows that it was largely suasive and relied on symbolic messaging and voluntary engagement, in addition to financial incentives. Yet, it has had significant impacts and served as a model internationally, as shown by the California regulation. Beyond regulations themselves, public policies have unequally prioritised different steps in a hierarchy of competing solutions, namely prevention of waste at the source, redistribution of food to people, and recycling (Mourad 2016; Papargyropoulou et al. 2014). This chapter challenges policymakers' focus on food donation and redistribution, at the expense of prevention measures and structural changes that would address overproduction, access to quality food, and more generally the way we value our food and the resources to produce, distribute, and prepare it.

First, the analysis will review the creation and expansion of French food waste policies, notably through a national multi-stakeholder collaboration, the 2016 law itself, subsequent policies, and finally the California law it helped inspire. It will then address the impacts of these policies on food redistribution networks and the quality of donated goods, on the sales of soon-to-be-expired discounted products, and on prevention strategies. The conclusion draws lessons from the French case to design and implement impactful food waste policies in other countries.

Beyond the ban: the creation and expansion of French food waste policies

The 'Loi Garot', unanimously voted by the Parliament in February, 2016, made France the first country to have a national regulation specifically labelled as 'fighting food waste'. Even if it was portrayed by many as a sudden and drastic 'ban', it was the result of a long and collaborative process that produced many policy measures against food waste.

Prior policies and the 'National Pact' against food waste

France did not wait until 2016 to have policies aimed at redistributing surplus food, even if they were not tied to 'waste'. Since the 1980s, the country has had significant fiscal incentives that encourage businesses to donate food to charity organisations. The tax reduction amounts to 60% of the inventory value of donated goods (up to 0.05% of a company revenue), which was the highest in the European Union in 2014 (European Economic and Social Committee 2014). For example, Spain had a similar incentive but only for 35% of the value of donations. These incentives have been reinforced since 2013 to apply to farmers, food processors, and logistics operators. The latter can now benefit from tax reductions when they provide free transportation services to deliver donations, for example.

If food redistribution policies were backed by strong financial instruments, the ones on waste prevention mostly relied on awareness campaigns. The French Environmental Agency started its 'Let's reduce our waste' campaign in 2009, which included messages around food waste. It led to another campaign 'We've had enough waste' in 2016, which targeted food waste among professionals as well as consumers. The Ministry for Agriculture and Food has also developed anti-food waste campaigns over the last few years, which provide citizens with tips to plan meals, shop, cook, eat their leftovers, or even use traditionally uneaten parts of produce like carrot tops. By mostly focusing on individual practices, these campaigns tend to place the responsibility on consumer behaviours rather than structures that lead them to waste. This policy approach aims at transforming consumer demand to indirectly change business practices (Dubuisson-Quellier 2016).

If the 2016 Loi Garot seemed like a coercive turn, it actually evolved from several years of workshops as part of the National Pact against Food Waste, started in 2012 by Garot, then minister of Agrifood Systems. This multistakeholder process ensured the participation of various actors, including environmental non-profits, consumer organisations, food assistance organisations, and representatives of the agrifood, retail, and food service sectors. The goal was to reach a consensus on solutions to food waste, explicitly without 'stigmatising' one actor or the other.

Yet participants, ranging from volunteers in a food charity to public relation professionals representing a network of 40,000 food companies, did not have the same influence in the discussions. The imbalance of power between organisations with often divergent interests allowed dominant actors, such as the ones that controlled large portions of the food system, to shape the 'apparent consensus' in a way that favoured their own interests, as more marginal participants did not overtly disagree (Cloteau and Mourad 2016; Urfalino 2007). Large food companies maintained the idea that consumers were responsible for the largest share of food waste and should be the target of communication campaigns. At the same time, they rejected proposals to change promotional offers or packaging formats that may lead their clients to overbuy and waste.

Since representatives of the retail sector largely dominated the discussion, it is all the more surprising that the law would establish a strong ban on super-market waste.

Not a real ban? The symbolic power of the Loi Garot

The law gained attention for its obligation for supermarket donations, but this was only one provision among others.

The regulation notably established that all large food businesses—and not only supermarkets—had to follow the hierarchy of preferred solutions to food wastage: first, preventing food surplus, then, redistributing edible food to feed humans, after, feeding animals, and otherwise composting or using inedible food for anaerobic digestion to generate energy. Incinerating or sending food to landfill should be the last resort. Technically, this measure remained suasive in the sense that public services in charge of insuring such prioritisation had no capacity to actually monitor compliance: 'We cannot have an officer hidden behind each supermarket's garbage!', said one representative of the French Ministry of Agriculture and Food in 2015.

What was actually 'banned', at least formally, was for supermarkets above 400 square metres (a reasonably small threshold covering the vast majority of French supermarkets) to 'voluntarily destroy edible food', for example by pouring bleach or other chemical products on the food in the garbage. Breaking this rule may lead to fines of up to €3,750. However, without any surveillance of supermarkets' garbage cans, the regulation remained 'only coercive in its wording', as the National Coordinator of Food Waste Policies put it in 2018. No financial sanctions have been levied as of today, and even if they were, their amount is negligible for most supermarkets as a proportion of their annual sales. This ban on destroying food was therefore mostly symbolic.

The idea that the law made donations 'mandatory', the provision which gained the most attention is only partly true. The regulation mandates that supermarkets above 400 square metres sign an agreement with food assistance organisations to donate their excess edible, unsold products. Yet, the obligation to sign a contract obligates neither that supermarkets donate a minimum quantity of their unsold products nor give at regular intervals. As such, a supermarket could theoretically comply by donating one box of chocolates per year.

This limitation partly echoed the request of Food Bank representatives, who actually did not request mandatory donations and claimed in 2014 they did 'not want to become the garbage bin of the supermarkets by collecting low-quality products'. The founder of an organisation aimed at improving food access criticised a 'race to save kilos of food' and the measurement in numbers of meals or 'kilos per poor', with no indication of quality. Indeed, food assistance organisations often receive donations that are blemished, damaged, near or past their expiration date, or just nutritionally inappropriate. As a result, they incur additional costs to cull and dispose of some of the donated food.

The law does not establish mandatory inspections of supermarkets to prevent this type of 'donation dumping'. Moreover, food redistribution organisations have received limited financial and logistical support to expand their capacity, such as staff, storage, and/or refrigeration space, for additional donations.

In the end, the regulatory language of the 2016 law may be formally strong and binding, but its successful implementation mostly relied on voluntary engagement from private actors—supported by strong pre-existing tax incentives. The co-founder of a Paris-based food redistribution organisation suggested in 2018 that the law had not changed anything apart from the intensity of media coverage. Still, food waste reduction efforts are becoming the norm without the need for heavy-handed regulation, as businesses feel threatened by 'this mediatic buzz we all dread', as one supermarket Public Relation manager explained in 2017. Besides, the law required food waste prevention curriculum in classrooms and in professional training programmes. Such provisions gained less attention than the supposed 'supermarket food waste ban', but they have the potential to prevent, and not only redistribute, food waste.

Food waste policies after 2016

French food waste policies did not end with the 2016 regulation. In 2018, as part of a law on sustainable food, the obligation to set up partnerships with food redistribution organisations and the prohibition on voluntarily destroying edible food were extended to large food service operations (cafeterias serving more than 3,000 meals) and food manufacturers (with annual revenues exceeding 50 million euros). In 2020, the same requirements were extended to the wholesale sector as part of a law on the 'circular economy'.

In an effort to improve the quality of donations, an additional ordinance (*décret*) required supermarkets and other donors to sort products beforehand to avoid transferring this work to food assistance organisations, and to only donate products up to 48 hours before their expiration date. Companies have to implement training for their staff, track the quality of donated goods, and take notes of defects that recipients mention.

In addition, the 2018 and 2020 laws required the food service and industry sectors, respectively, to measure and analyse the amount of food they waste. These mandatory 'diagnostics' aim at preventing the production of excess food rather than donating it. Commercial restaurants must offer containers or 'doggy bags' for their clients to bring leftovers home. The 2020 law finally established a 'label' to reward businesses taking action against food waste, starting with supermarkets and food service establishments that were also mandated to halve food waste by 2025, while other sectors have until 2030 to meet this goal.

An international offshoot: the California case

As the supposed 'French ban on of food waste' gained attention from the media and food waste activists, policymakers abroad took it as an inspiration.

In the United States, California was the first state to pass regulations against edible food waste in 2016, as part of a climate law called Senate Bill 1383 (SB1383). Local policymakers took France as a case study throughout the rule-making process in the following years, which established the state-wide goal of redistributing 20% of edible food currently going to landfill by 2025. Starting in 2022, the largest 'commercial edible food generators' (supermarkets exceeding 930 square metres or two million dollars in sales, food service providers, wholesalers, and distributors) will have to sign formal partnerships with food redistribution organisations. In 2024, the same requirements will apply to restaurants (with more than 250 seats or larger than 460 square metres), hotels, large venues, and events (stadiums, concert halls, etc.), and public cafeterias in the governmental, health, or school sectors.

As opposed to the French law, which does not have any quantitative requirement, the Californian law requires businesses to donate the 'maximum amount' of their surplus edible food that would otherwise be thrown away. It also has a much larger scope by including smaller restaurants and hotels, even though it does not include food manufacturing businesses. The implementation process differs from the centralised French approach, as it places the burden on cities and local counties to ensure that businesses in their jurisdiction comply with these requirements. Local jurisdictions are also required to provide financial and logistical resources to increase food redistribution capacity, for example by increasing storage space or refrigerated transportation. These additional requirements suggest that California policymakers tried to avoid some short-falls of French policies, which did not directly guarantee that food recipient organisations would have sufficient capacity to redistribute donations.

Policy impacts: a focus on redistribution at the expense of prevention?

After almost five years of implementation, it is possible to draw lessons from French policies. The French National Assembly and Ministry of Agriculture have carried out evaluations of the law's impact (Melchior and Garot 2019; Ministère de l'Agriculture et de l'Alimentation 2019), while food redistribution companies in search of business opportunities have also tried to assess how public policies changed the new 'market' for food redistribution and food waste prevention.

The development of food donations and redistribution networks

Despite limited financial and logistical support, representatives of both food assistance organisations and food businesses observed that donation quantities increased by up to 30% in 2017. A study led by a food redistribution start-up showed that the percentage of supermarkets donating unsold products rose from 66% prior to 2016 to 94% in 2018 and 96% in 2019. More than half of them donated every day, thus reducing both supermarkets' and food banks' need to discard highly perishable products (Comerso 2018, 2019). The national food bank network reports that with 2,700 supermarkets distributing more than 46,000 tonnes per year, donations have become a larger share of their food supply. Even if public authorities have not yet monitored what businesses donate versus throw away, these results confirm that donations have significantly increased in the wake of the law.

The law—and increased awareness on food waste—has also spawned additional partnerships between local businesses and food assistance organisations. New food redistribution start-ups like Comerso and Phenix charge food companies a fee to find donation recipients, while optimising logistical resources to collect and redistribute even small quantities of fresh and prepared food. These food waste reduction companies generally offer 'all in one' services, including staff training, operational strategies to minimise losses, logistical and fiscal assistance with donations, or organic waste recycling. The sustainability manager of a large supermarket chain indicated in 2018 that these solutions had been particularly helpful for stores in rural areas that were unable to reach local charities.

Still, more than 90% of food businesses do not pay for this type of redistribution services and rely on the main food bank network, local food assistance organisations, or recently created food redistribution non-profits that also play an intermediate role between donors and recipients. For example, the Chainon Manquant ('Missing Link') redistributes food from supermarkets, caterers, and large events (sports, concerts, etc.) in the Paris area through a network of volunteers and its fleet of refrigerated trucks. Even actors who traditionally did not donate their surplus food, such as caterers who feared food safety issues or in some cases did not want to have their brand names associated with food assistance (as one Parisian high-ended caterer explained in 2016), have started donating food in the last few years.

In the meantime, more and more organisations have created innovative ways to rescue products such as blemished fruits and vegetables, stale bread, or even by-products that were not considered edible. For example, since 2016, 'Rebelle' jams—a play on words on rebel and re-belle, meaning beautiful again—transform unsold, overripe, or blemished fruit from supermarkets into handmade jams. The company established partnerships to close the loop by selling the jam in the very supermarkets that donate their fruit. Its production kitchen in an underprivileged suburb of Paris employs workers who were long-term unemployed. Other social enterprises have developed similar initiatives, some of which 'upcycle' by-products like stale bread that can become beer or—the other way around—barley 'spent grains' from the brewing process that can be transformed into flour and baked goods.

These evolutions are part of a global mobilisation against food waste and a renewed interest in food redistribution, pushed by activists, entrepreneurs, and policymakers across the world. In California, where recent food redistribution regulations are yet to be implemented, many start-ups and non-profits have also emerged to collect, transform, or redistribute food in innovative ways.

For example, Replate charges businesses to redistribute their food by hiring drivers that were already on the road, like the ones working for Uber or food delivery companies. In California, Renewal Mills 'upcycles' okara (soy grain protein et fibre leftover from the tofu-making industry) into flour, brownies, and cookies. Nonetheless, the strong commitment of French businesses and in particular supermarkets, which were the first targets, demonstrates the impacts of the Loi Garot. It is significant that up to 10% supermarkets were paying for a food redistribution service in 2019, while these services like Replate are still marginal in California.

Quantity, not quality?

Unsurprisingly, managing large quantities of food remained a 'daily challenge' for food assistance organisations, which received only limited and sporadic financial support to manage the additional food donated in response to the law. Food banks and pantries in the United States and other countries are similarly challenged. When they have to discard uneaten, donated food (and bear the disposal costs), even more resources are wasted to move food that should never have been produced.

According to the French Coordinator of Food Waste policies in 2018, the ordinance requiring supermarkets to cull products and donate packaged items 48 hours before their expiration dates had helped improve the quality of donated food. However, a representative of a French food bank explained that they still had to throw away approximately 20% of the total food they received. At the national level, Food Banks reported in 2018 that they threw away 11% of their food, as opposed to 8% in 2016, which suggests a decrease in the quality of donations (Melchior and Garot 2019). They also indicated that most products were donated less than 48 hours before their expiration date, in contradiction with regulatory requirements.

The director of the non-profit that criticised food donation measurement in 'kilos per poor' insisted that policies pushed towards donating higher volumes and weight, without considering the material and nutritional quality of the food. Many representatives of food assistance organisations, both in France and in the United States, regularly complain about receiving products that are 'second-class', 'junk food', or just 'weird', such as new flavours of yogurt, chips, or soda that failed their entry on the market. More than 80% of newly introduced products fail (Nielsen 2015), and large quantities of them end up on the food banks' shelves. Nutritionally, even if donations of fruits and vegetables were on the rise in 2019, food banks did not receive enough produce or protein to offer a diet that matches national nutritional recommendations. Fourteen percent of the products they distribute have added fat, salt, and sugar, while it is recommended to consume less than 2.5% (Ministère de l'Agriculture et de l'Alimentation 2019). Bread and pastries are among the products that food assistance organisations receive in too large quantities relative to their clients' need, and often have to throw away themselves.

As relatively high tax incentives play an important role in encouraging donations, French representative Garot advocated for additional regulations that would tie such incentives to the quality of the food so that it is not blemished or expired, for lack of consideration of its nutritional quality. One of his proposed provisions was to reduce fiscal incentives for products donated closer to their expiration dates. But this regulation was rejected and tax incentives are still based on quantity rather than quality. Both in France and in the United States, donors and food assistance organisations estimate the financial value of their donations, for tax purposes, based on a formula applied to the weight of the food and not its cost. Food bank representatives in the two countries pointed to donations of soda as an example of a 'heavy food' that generated high incentives for donors regardless on its impact on the populations receiving the 'food'.

Many food justice advocates have criticised these policies as linking food waste reduction efforts to food assistance. This 'philantrocapitalist' approach promotes the charitable efforts of donors and maintains overproduction, without challenging power imbalances and unequal distribution of resources (Riches 2018; Bishop and Green 2008). In the United States, the ties between the main food bank networks and large food corporations, which donate their food but also fund most of their operations, are even described as a 'hunger industrial complex' that perpetuates not only overproduction and waste but also 'hunger', malnutrition, and obesity (Fisher 2017). In France too, food waste policies have prompted discussions about the appropriateness of charitable donations, supported by generous tax reductions, that do not guarantee the food security or dignity of recipients. In particular, the push to generalise and formalise food redistribution through formal agreements tends to exclude small-scale organisations or grassroots groups, which have been particularly important in fighting for food justice and supporting their local communities.

An unexpected outcome: selling at all cost before donating

Even if French policies largely focused on donations, many businesses, unexpectedly, have actually begun selling more of their soon-to-be-wasted products at a discounted price before donating them.

In 2014, many supermarkets did not want to discount their products because having a 'low cost' image would negatively impact their business. The head of Corporate Sustainability at an urban supermarket chain indicated in 2014: 'It wouldn't work for us because we are a premium supermarket, it's not our approach'. Other supermarkets did not want to group discounted items in one place to avoid attracting clients that would only buy these products. Some store leaders mentioned the risk that employees would voluntarily let food items reach their expiration date in order to discount them and have their family and friends (or themselves) buy them.

But as food waste prevention gained more attention, discounting products became a more attractive strategy for supermarkets. The founder of Zero Gâchis

(Zero Waste), a French start-up helping supermarkets with their discount sales through a dedicated mobile app, explained in 2014: 'We changed the way it was presented. Before, it was the corner of the poor, with big yellow tags and red prices. Now, it's not for someone who struggles to make end meets, but for people who consume sustainably'. Taking advantage of growing consumer awareness around food waste, discount sales have become a new 'sustainable consumption' market niche, allowing supermarkets to optimise their sales of an overabundance of items while highlighting their environmental and social commitments.

In 2019, more than 90% of supermarkets reported discounting soon-to-expire products (Comerso 2019). Discounts were particularly effective for highly perishable, high-value foods, such as fish, meat, and dairy (Comerso 2019; Phénix 2021). These sales tend to generate comparable revenues to the donation tax credit while making food more affordable for clients.

Beyond supermarkets, many businesses such as bakeries, restaurants, and hotels have turned to start-ups like Too Good to Go, which allows them to post on a mobile app the products they have available at a discount at the end of the day. The free app allows individuals to see, for example that their neighbourhood bakery is offering ten leftover pastries for a few euros and commit to pick them up. Founded in 2013, Too Good to Go has had a tremendous success and claimed to have 42 million users in 15 countries in 2021. In France, the company partners with 20,000 businesses and has nine million registered users. With its slogan 'save food, save the planet', the social enterprise targets environmentally conscious consumers along with more opportunistic ones looking for a good bargain. It provides tools to educate consumers and has mobilised a network of French cities to advocate for food waste reduction policies, including changes in the expiration date system. In 2021, the app spread to New York and San Francisco.

The success of these new discounted food markets may increase access to more affordable food, but it also has contributed to the recent decline in the overall quality of food donations, which had initially improved in the first year of implementation of France's food redistribution law. Businesses try to sell their commodities to the last minute, especially fresh products like fruits, vegetables, dairy, meat, and fish. If these are generally expensive, they would also be of great nutritional value for food assistance organisations. Meanwhile, the unsold products they donate are 'on their last leg', as a food bank representative put it in 2021. Thus, the quality of donations may have increased right after the 2016 law, benefiting from higher awareness around food waste, but it has decreased in the following years.

A difficult shift towards prevention

While fire sales and efficient redistribution operations are appealing, they fail to prevent unnecessary production in the first place. They even perpetuate a norm of abundance, in which supermarket shelves are always full and food is conveniently accessible at all times, in countries where production levels almost double what would be nutritionally appropriate. In both France and the United States, available food exceeds 3,500 calories per person daily, while recommended consumption is on average 2,000 calories per day. Optimising current processes and redistributing existing surplus are not enough. In order to conserve resource inputs and minimise environmental and social negative externalities along the food supply chain, reducing excessive production is necessary.

To promote prevention among food system actors as well as consumers, the French 2016 law required professional training programs and schools to provide curricula addressing food waste and promoting the value of food in the French gastronomic tradition. Most prevention measures relied on voluntary engagement and did not compel businesses to change their practices. But these measures, along with consumer awareness campaigns, remain a 'weak' form of prevention compared to structural changes that would target the generation of surplus at the root (Mourad 2016).

As early as 2015, a regulation required large companies to include actions to fight food waste as part of their CSR public reports, but there was no obligation of quantified results—especially because data on food waste still remain highly confidential. Given that more than 60% of supermarket directors indicated that they were not familiar with the concept of Corporate Social Responsibility in 2019 (Comerso 2019), relying on voluntary business commitments may not be sufficient. During the National Pact against food waste, activists and citizen groups advocated for concrete requirements on food businesses, such as clarifying their expiration date system, reducing portion sizes at restaurant and cafeterias, and stopping 'buy one get one free'-like promotions that push consumers to buy more than they need. However, most of these proposals were rejected and not included in later regulations.

Nonetheless, the most recent French regulations in 2018 and 2020 suggest a potential shift towards prevention measures, with an anti-food waste label highlighting businesses with the best practices, and mandatory 'diagnostics' and measurement of food waste in the food service and food processing sectors. 'What gets measured, gets managed' has been a slogan of food waste reduction for many years. The UN Sustainable Development Target 12.3, dedicated to halve food waste, encourages business to take a 'Target-Measure-Act' approach to food waste, based on measurement and voluntary commitments. US-based company Leanpath, founded in 2004, offers solutions to the food service sector to weigh and analyse all the leftovers, in order to improve purchases and meal preparation. The company has proven very successful in decreasing levels of overproduction and waste. In France, thousands of restaurants and food service operations have already committed to measure their waste and take action through a partnership with ADEME.

The French food service sector exemplifies the possibility of improving food quality while reducing waste. Many cafeterias have already committed to improving the taste and nutritional content of their meals, which contributes to reducing waste as clients are more likely to finish their plates, and businesses can in turn reinvest savings from food waste reduction in higher quality products. The 2018 food sustainability regulation also requires large food service operations to source a minimum proportion of organic and local products and to offer more vegetarian alternatives. While shorter supply chains may reduce the amount of waste generated by successive intermediaries and additional transportation, going away from animal products is an indirect form of food waste reduction as fewer resources are needed to produce the same amount of calories. These pioneering efforts, still out of the policy agenda across the Atlantic, not only reduce waste but also progressively re-value food.

Conclusions and discussion

The examination of the multi-stakeholder process that led to drafting the French regulation reveals how dominant actors in the food systems were able to influence the 'seemingly consensual' decisions (Urfalino 2007; Cloteau and Mourad 2016). This result confirms what has been observed in international roundtables on other topics such as sustainable soy or palm oil, where large firms imposed their views on farmers and non-profit environmental organisations despite the proposed inclusiveness of the process (Fouilleux 2013). As a result, some topics remained excluded from the conversation over the years. For example, the definition of food waste did not consider the variable use of resources to produce food, such as animal products that 'convert' 1,700 calories into 500 calories, which environmental scientists have characterised as a form of waste (Smil 2004). While food availability largely exceeds nutritional needs in most industrialised countries, the consumption of additional or 'unnecessary' calories is not accounted for as waste (Blair and Sobal 2006). Finally, even if significant quantities of products have to be discarded to guarantee a certain level of food safety, the priority of food safety was never questioned—and is even less so now in the wake of a global pandemic.

Overall, the French food waste policy strongly emphasised food donation and led to an increase in food redistribution. Yet, critiques have shown that the latter may solve neither food waste nor food insecurity (Fisher 2017; Riches 2018). In terms of prevention, French policies encouraged marginal optimisations of business processes, while sidelining structural changes in the food system that would reduce waste at the source. Similarly to what happened with climate change or obesity (Comby 2015; Bergeron, Castel, and Nouguez 2014), communication campaigns have placed the responsibility on consumer behaviours rather than changing the structures that lead them to pollute, gain weight, or in our case, to waste food.

Despite its limitations, the French policy can serve as a model for other countries, as it was for California. 'Banning' the destruction of edible food—still not food waste as a whole—was its most symbolic feature, and it played a key role in raising awareness on the issue. Its most coercive provision, at least formally, was mandating partnerships for food redistribution between businesses and food redistribution organisations. California drew on this approach and added the requirement to distribute a 'maximum amount' of food, with the binding state-wide goal of redistributing 20% of food previously sent to landfill, and a plan to improve the capacity of food recipient organisations. One challenge that many countries will face in their food waste reduction policies is to provide sufficient resources to actually support the implementation of these redistribution systems. One solution could be to significantly increase taxes on food going to waste, in order to generate funding potentially mobilisable for food waste redistribution as well as prevention and recycling.

In addition, future food waste policies in France, California, and other countries will need to strengthen their focus on prevention. Measuring waste is a first step, and recent French regulations have started implementing this. As a second step, food companies may need to make data more transparent, as a way to break the stigma on waste and to share best practices. While the UN SDGs have engaged in this process, no country has yet required businesses to publish data on food waste. Finally, public policies will need to further regulate company practices. Most business models still rely on producing and wasting large volumes of cheap food, pushed onto the consumer through advertising, packaging, large portions, and promotional offers. Unequal power relationships between retailers and suppliers also lead farmers to overproduce in order to meet strict requirements of their buyers, including aesthetic criteria for fruit and vegetables. Despite recent regulation such as the EU Directive on Unfair Trading Practices, these power imbalances still result in high levels of food waste at both the production and consumption levels.

Finally, a true prevention of food waste will require a profound transformation of our food systems. Many solutions exist, such as sustainable and regenerative agriculture, or alternative systems of distribution at a smaller scale with fewer intermediaries, which may generate less waste and help revalue our food and those who produce it. French policies have started supporting these alternatives, even if they remain marginal. But such changes need to happen at the European and global levels, as food companies are in competition with one another. Thinking of innovative alternatives has also become crucial in a fast-changing sector where consumers are further and further disconnected from producers. For example, online purchases and food delivery keep increasing, even more so due to the recent pandemic, which may or may not lead to more 'impulse buying' and waste.

Future evolutions are unknown, but preventing food waste may require changing social norms towards less food consumption (including of animal products) and abundance. We may need to revisit the over-convenience that leads to waste, to the benefit of food quality and authenticity. The French experience thus encourages policymakers globally to re-value, rather than just redistribute or re-sell, food.

References

ADEME. 2016. *Pertes et gaspillage alimentaires : l'état des lieux et leur gestion par étapes de la chaîne alimentaire.* Angers, France: ADEME. https://librairie.ademe.fr/dechets-economie-circulaire/2435-etat-des-lieux-des-masses-de-gaspillages-alimentaires-et-de-sa-gestion-aux-differentes-etapes-de-la-chaine-alimentaire.html.

BCFN. 2017. "2017 Food Sustainability Index." Barilla Center for Food and Nutrition. www.barillacfn.com/m/pdf/FoodSustainabilityIndex2017GlobalExecutiveSummary.pdf.

Bergeron, Henri, Patrick Castel, and Etienne Nouguez. 2014. "Lutter Contre l'obésité En Gouvernant Les Conduites Des Consommateurs." *Questions de Santé Publique* (25) (juin): 1–4.

Bishop, Matthew, and Michael Green. 2008. *Philanthrocapitalism: How the Rich Can Save the World.* 1st ed. New York: Bloomsbury Press.

Blair, Dorothy, and Jeffery Sobal. 2006. "Luxus Consumption: Wasting Food Resources Through Overeating." *Agriculture and Human Values* 23 (1): 63–74.

Chaboud, Géraldine, and Benoit Daviron. 2017. "Food Losses and Waste: Navigating the Inconsistencies." *Global Food Security* 12 (March): 1–7. https://doi.org/10.1016/j.gfs.2016.11.004.

Chrisafis, Angelique. 2016. "French Law Forbids Food Waste by Supermarkets." *The Guardian,* February 2016. www.theguardian.com/world/2016/feb/04/french-law-forbids-food-waste-by-supermarkets.

Cloteau, Armèle, and Marie Mourad. 2016. "Action publique et fabrique du consensus ; la 'lutte contre le gaspillage alimentaire' en France et aux Etats-Unis." *Gouvernement et action publique* (1) (March): 63–90. https://doi.org/10.3917/gap.161.0063.

Comby, Jean-Baptiste. 2015. *La question climatique : Genèse et dépolitisation d'un problème public.* Paris: Liber.

Comerso. 2018. *Baromètre 2018 de La Valorisation Des Invendus En Grande Distribution.* Paris, France: Comerso/Ipsos.

———. 2019. *Distribution/Retail: Objectif Zéro-Déchet.* Paris, France: Comerso/Ipsos.

Dubuisson-Quellier, Sophie, ed. 2016. *Gouverner les conduites.* Paris: Presses de Sciences Po.

European Economic and Social Committee. 2014. "Comparative Study on EU Member States' Legislation and Practices on Food Donation." www.eesc.europa.eu/en/our-work/publications-other-work/publications/comparative-study-eu-member-states-legislation-and-practices-food-donation.

Fisher, Andy. 2017. *Big Hunger: The Unholy Alliance Between Corporate America and Anti-Hunger Groups.* Cambridge, MA: The MIT Press.

Fouilleux, Ève. 2013. "Normes transnationales de développement durable." *Gouvernement et action publique* 1 (1): 93–118.

Giordano, Claudia, Luca Falasconi, and Barbara Pancino. 2020. "The Role of Food Waste Hierarchy in Addressing Policy and Research: A Comparative Analysis." *Journal of Cleaner Production* 252: 119617. https://doi.org/10.1016/j.jclepro.2019.119617.

Melchior, Graziella, and Guillaume Garot. 2019. "Rapport d'information sur la mise en application de la loi n° 2016–138 du 11 février 2016 relative à la lutte contre le gaspillage alimentaire (Mme Graziella Melchior et M. Guillaume Garot)." In *Commission des affaires économiques.* Paris: Assemblée Nationale. www.assemblee-nationale.fr/dyn/15/rapports/cion-eco/l15b2025_rapport-information.

Ministère de l'Agriculture et de l'Alimentation. 2019. "Évaluation de l'application des dispositions de la loi du 11 février 2016 relative à la lutte contre le gaspillage alimentaire, et du décret d'application du 28 décembre 2016." Synthèse. Paris, France. https://

agriculture.gouv.fr/gaspillage-alimentaire-evaluation-de-lapplication-des-dispositions-prevues-par-la-loi-garot.

Mourad, Marie. 2016. "Recycling, Recovering and Preventing 'Food Waste': Competing Solutions for Food Systems Sustainability in the United States and France." *Journal of Cleaner Production* 126 (July): 461–77. https://doi.org/10.1016/j.jclepro.2016.03.084.

———. 2018. "La lutte contre le gaspillage alimentaire en France et aux Etats-Unis : mise en cause, mise en politique et mise en marché des excédents alimentaires." In *These de doctorat de sociologie*. Paris: Institut d'études politiques. www.theses.fr/2018IEPP0014.

Nielsen. 2015. *The Nielsen Breakthrough Innovation Report*. USA: The Nielsen Company. https://www.nielsen.com/wp-content/uploads/sites/3/2019/04/nielsen-us-breakthrough-innovation-report-2015.pdf.

Papargyropoulou, Effie, Rodrigo Lozano, Julia K. Steinberger, Nigel Wright, and Zaini bin Ujang. 2014. "The Food Waste Hierarchy as a Framework for the Management of Food Surplus and Food Waste." *Journal of Cleaner Production* 76: 106–15. https://doi.org/10.1016/j.jclepro.2014.04.020.

Phénix. 2021. *Le Baromètre de l'anti-Gaspi: Les Invendus et Leur Valorisation En Supermarché et Hypermarché*. Paris, France: Phénix.

Riches, Graham. 2018. *Food Bank Nations: Poverty, Corporate Charity and the Right to Food*. Oxford, UK: Routledge. www.routledge.com/Food-Bank-Nations-Poverty-Corporate-Charity-and-the-Right-to-Food/Riches/p/book/9781138739758.

Smil, Vaclav. 2004. "Improving Efficiency and Reducing Waste in Our Food System." *Environmental Sciences* 1 (1): 17–26. https://doi.org/10.1076/evms.1.1.17.23766.

Urfalino, Philippe. 2007. "La Décision Par Consensus Apparent: Nature et Propriétés." *Revue Européenne Des Sciences Sociales* 45 (136): 47–70.

8 Food waste policy in Italy

From decision to implementation

Simone Busetti

Introduction

Italy has a long and pioneering history of fighting food waste. The first regulations on food donations date back to the 1990s, and the policy has constantly evolved since with its latest reform in 2016. As a result, Italy now offers a wide range of policy tools against food waste: regulations, economic incentives, institutions, information, and education programmes. This chapter traces the evolution of the policy and provides an in-depth analysis of selected tools to determine what works, what does not work, and which improvements are possible.

Food waste in Italy is at the crossroads of different policy sectors. It involves administrations from the local to the national levels and brings together different policy sectors. Over the years, social assistance—the use of surplus food to help people in need—has undoubtedly been a major goal for Italian policymakers. However, sustainability issues are progressively becoming more important, especially since the launch of the National Plan for Food Waste Prevention in 2014. The chapter represents such varied perspectives by analysing interventions implemented at different territorial scales (local, regional, national) and spanning social, environmental, and agricultural policy.

The chapter is organised as follows: The next section briefly reviews research on food waste quantification in Italy. Then a descriptive section presents the evolution of policy with a specific focus on the 2003 Good Samaritan Law (law 155) and the 2016 Food Waste Law (law 166). Six sections follow with an in-depth analysis of selected tools: fiscal and bureaucratic incentives, discounts on waste taxes, new regulations on food after the best-before date, institutions, production of data and software solutions to improve logistics.

The chapter draws on information from a desk analysis of secondary sources and 12 semi-structured interviews with key stakeholders. The reviewed documents include academic journals, research reports, government briefs, and administrative documents. Six interviews were conducted in-person for previous research (Busetti 2019) and six were explicitly conducted for this chapter using video conferencing.[1]

DOI: 10.4324/9781003226932-12

The policy problem: quantifying Italian food waste

Compared with other European countries, the best estimates rank Italy third worse in terms of total food waste (10.5 kilotonnes) and 11th for the per capita amount, with 179 kg of waste per capita each year, equal to the EU27 average (data estimated for 2006, see European Parliament 2013; European Commission 2010). According to the same data, food wastage in Italy is estimated to occur disproportionately along the food chain: production/manufacturing (54%), household (26%), food service and catering (15%), and retail (5%) (European Parliament 2013). Using FAOSTAT data from 2011, Priefer, Jörissen, and Bräutigam (2016) provided slightly different estimates for the origins of Italian food waste: 38% from agricultural production, 8% from postharvest handling and storage, 10% from processing and packaging, 6% from distribution, and 38% from consumption. Yet, in both cases, most food waste is produced in production and consumption.

Although there are no official statistics at the national level, several studies are available that shed light on different features of Italian food waste. In terms of the total waste, the ISPRA research centre recently provided an innovative estimate of *systemic waste*, measured in calories (ISPRA 2018). Systemic waste is the part of production that exceeds the dietary requirements and ecological capacity. This includes unconventional food waste sources such as overeating, edible food used for animal feed, or non-yields. Between 2007 and 2015, the average systemic food waste in Italy was estimated at 4,160 kcal wasted per person per day. If one considers an average nutritional requirement of 2,480 kcal per person, the total calories produced would be 6,640, of which 62.7% are wasted along the food chain (ISPRA 2018).

Other studies provide estimates for single stages of the food chain. Concerning agriculture, statistics by the National Institute of Statistics (ISTAT) reveal that in 2020, about 1.3 million tonnes of products were unharvested, accounting for approximately 2.4% of total agricultural production (CREA 2021). Concerning retail, research by a national supermarket company calculated that unsold products in 2016 represented 1.4% of the total food retailed (Coop 2016). The research also offered a measure of the impact of food donations on the avoidance of food waste. Once unsold products recovered by charities were considered, the unsold products to be disposed of decreased from 1.4% to 1.11%, equivalent to €107.3 million (Coop 2016).

Finally, several methods have been used to measure the food waste produced by Italian households. For instance, Tua, Grosso, and Nessi (2017) carried out a compositional analysis of waste samples at treatment plants to analyse urban waste. On average, food waste represented 15% of total waste, by weight, of which 28% was considered avoidable. Since 2013, the Waste Watcher Observatory has performed a yearly survey of perceived household food waste; this was estimated to be 595.3 grams per week in 2022, up compared with results from the previous year (Waste Watcher 2022). Finally, the National Observatory for Food Surplus, Recovery and Waste recently performed its first systematic

Table 8.1 Chronology of the Italian food waste policy.

Year	Main policy and institutional changes
1972	All donations become VAT-exempted
1997	Food donations are not part of company profits
1999	Donated food is considered destroyed and eligible for VAT deductions
2003	Good Samaritan Law is approved by Parliament (law 155/2003)
2012	National fund for needy people and Permanent Coordination Table
2014	National Plan for Food Waste Prevention (PINPAS)
2015	Guidelines for charities concerning recovered food
2016	Food Waste Law (law 166/2016)
2016	National Table for Fighting Food Waste
2017	National Observatory on Food Surplus, Recovery and Waste
2018	Guidelines for food waste prevention in canteens

Source: Created by author.

survey using a methodology developed by van Herpen et al. (2019), leading to their estimate of 370 grams per week as the average Italian household food waste (Scalvedi and Rossi 2021).

A brief history of the Italian policy

In tracing the evolution of the food waste policy in Italy, we may identify two pivotal moments: the approval of the Good Samaritan law in 2003 and the adoption of the Food Waste Law in 2016. Table 8.1 provides a chronology of the main policy changes, most of which are analysed in depth in the following sections.

After progressive tax relief was brought in during the 1990s, a major reform of food recovery came with the adoption of law 155 in 2003, also known as the Good Samaritan Law. Modelled on the 1996 law in the United States (see Chapter 12), law 155 was a true revolution for the recovery and distribution of food—the first of such laws to be approved in Europe.

The law has only one article stating that non-profit organisations that recover food to distribute to people in need are considered equal to final consumers. This simple provision has enormous consequences. First, it means that donors are free from all liability after donation to food rescue organisations. They remain responsible for the production and manufacturing phases and must donate safe products but they are legally protected from harmful consequences of donated food, which instead fall under the responsibility of food rescue organisations. The second major consequence of the law is that recovery organisations (now considered equal to final consumers) must comply with procedures that are much simplified compared to the previous law.[2]

The Good Samaritan Law reassured donors that donating was not risky and smoothed out the donation process and bureaucracy. The law was particularly effective for recovering fresh and perishable food such as cooked meals produced by retailers, catering services, and canteens (schools, hospitals, firms).

This food has high value as it typically contains more resources than raw food and can be immediately used to feed people. However, it also needs to be recovered and redistributed quickly, making safety and liability issues major concerns that the law contributed to settling. Coop—one of the biggest food retailers in Italy—started its corporate food recovery programme straightaway in 2003, in consequence of the law (Coop 2016). That same year, Banco Alimentare, the leading Italian food rescue organisation, founded a new programme called Siticibo to exploit the new opportunities offered by the law. Only considering food recovered from canteens and restaurant services, Siticibo redistributed 2.6 million meals, 800 tonnes of bread, and 900 tonnes of fruit in the first ten years—all food that would have been disposed of without the law (Banco Alimentare 2013).

The second radical change in Italian food waste policy came in 2016 when the Italian Parliament passed law 166/2016 about 'food donation and redistribution for social solidarity and reduction of food waste' (Food Waste Law). The bill was proposed in April 2015 and—after plenary and committee meetings in both chambers—unanimously approved in August 2016.

The law is the product of an extraordinary political moment for food issues in Italy. In 2015, the city of Milan hosted the Universal Expo 'Feed the Planet, Energy for Life', which highlighted the unparalleled window of opportunity for policy change, especially regarding food and nutrition issues. To mention only the major reforms of 2016, in addition to the food waste law, Italy passed a law on social agriculture, one on biodiversity and a National Plan for organic food (Busetti and Dente 2018).

Yet, the 2016 Food Waste Law did not come out of a temporary fashion for food but was the product of long-term preparation that dated back some years. In 2014, the Ministry of the Environment approved the National Plan for Food Waste Prevention (PINPAS). The plan contained ten priority actions to reduce surplus food (Ministry of the Environment 2014) and started a broad consultation with food actors about the adequacy of the existing regulations and the prospect of introducing standard systems of measuring food waste. A position paper resulting from the consultation discussed several proposals for improving the food waste policy (PINPAS 2015), most of which were to be the backbone of the 2016 law: the explicit possibility to donate food after the best-before date, the streamlining of the donation bureaucracy, and the possibility to provide discounts on local waste taxes proportional to food donations.[3]

The new law systematised existing regulations into a coherent bill and expanded the fight against food waste with new tools. Table 8.2 presents a summary of the provisions introduced in 2016.

Reducing the costs of donations: fiscal and bureaucratic incentives

In 1972, decree 633 included donations among VAT exempt transactions, which benefitted food banks and recovery organisations, which did not have

Table 8.2 The 2016 Food Waste Law.

Main innovations of the 2016 Law Against Food Waste	
Definitions	- The law distinguishes between food surplus (unsold products due to lack of demand) and food waste (non-commercialised products) and establishes the priority of their use for human consumption. - The law clarifies the difference between the date of minimum durability and the use by date, specifying that food after the best-before date is eligible for donation.
New organisations can recover and redistribute food	- Before the law, only a specific kind of not-for-profit organisation (so-called ONLUS) benefitted from the existing normative and fiscal framework for donations. The law now includes all public and private organisations established to pursue unified goals, not for profit.
New goods become eligible for food donations	- Mislabelled food - Food after the best-before date - Bread and bakery products that were baked more than 24 hours ago - Surplus directly collected on farms - Confiscated goods
New institutions	- The law establishes the National Table for Combating Food Waste (see below). This is a coordinating panel tasked with putting forward policy proposals, supervising monitoring and evaluation activities and promoting good practices. The Table is a relabelling of the existing Permanent Coordination Table established in 2012.
Communication and research	- Awareness and communication campaigns and dedicated programmes on public TV, radio, and multimedia services - Three-year public fund to finance research and innovation to reduce food waste
Streamlined bureaucracy of donations	- Donations can be reported to fiscal authorities through online channels. - Only one monthly communication is needed for all donations in the past month. - Communication is unnecessary for individual donations in a month amounting to less than €15,000.
Discounts on waste taxes	- Municipalities can establish voluntary waste fee discounts for donors.

Source: Created by author.

to pay VAT on received goods. In 1999, law 133 introduced VAT deductions: fiscally, donated food was considered equal to destroyed goods, and donors could enjoy a return on the VAT already paid on that food. This favourable fiscal regime included food not on sale or not marketable because of packaging or labelling issues, a reduced shelf life, or other commercial reasons. Finally, in 1997, decree 460 established that food donations were no longer to be considered part of company profits. Overall, these provisions did not provide a special incentive to donate but granted donated goods the same fiscal treatment as destroyed goods, thus eliminating the awkward situation where destroying food was more convenient than donating or recovering it.

Law 166/2016 further facilitated recovery by streamlining the bureaucracy involved in donating food. Before 2016, food donors had to provide detailed information about donations to the fiscal authority five days in advance. Though preliminary communications were not needed for donations below about €5,000 or perishable food of modest value, the donation bureaucracy was burdensome: all deliveries were to be planned and communicated in advance and sent with detailed transportation documents describing all the goods donated. The 2016 law simplified procedural burdens significantly. It eliminated all preliminary communications and required only one cumulative communication per month relating to all the donations made in the last 30 days. Furthermore, it expanded the communication-free remit from €5,000 to €15,000 and simplified the transportation documents (e.g. requiring only the total weight of donations to be specified).

These simplifications were significant for small shops with diverse surplus and little management capacity (Busetti 2019). In commenting on the reform, the social policy manager at Coop supermarkets highlighted how small retail outlets had struggled with the former bureaucratic requirements and could finally implement the corporate donation programmes that Coop had started in 2003 (Bruzzone 2018).

Overall, the combined effect of fiscal and bureaucratic provisions favours donations over destruction. However, other alternatives—such as disposal and recycling—still appeal in terms of costs. Donations entail a heavy start–up cost: a company needs to allocate employees to select and store products, provide space to store donations, and organise pickups and deliveries (Busetti 2019). While disposal costs are already factored in companies' expenses (Alexander and Smaje 2008), the Italian fiscal benefits do not make donations particularly convenient versus disposal (Baglioni, De Pieri, and Tallarico 2016; PINPAS 2015). A different argument applies to recycling, which is certainly more consolidated within companies' routines, but may entail sorting activities equal to those required by donations. On the positive side, however, we should not forget that donations certainly have the advantage of enhancing a company's image of corporate social responsibility—an immaterial gain that can be of great benefit to companies.

To conclude on the Italian incentive system, two notes of caution are worth mentioning. First, in the case of large-scale franchise companies, local shops under the franchise have no autonomy to manage their incoming and outgoing food and cannot decide to start a donation process in the absence of a central company programme or explicit permission from the central management. Considering these cases, when policymakers design an incentive system, they should pay attention to the possible mismatch between the producers of waste (the individual shops) and the decision-makers able to agree to start donations (the company management). Bureaucratic simplifications, for instance, may help individual shops and favour the correct implementation of donation processes on the ground but provide no direct incentive to the company management to decide to start donations. More generally, actively promoting company-level agreements may be essential for future food waste reduction. As an example, in Italy, the increased salience of food waste after the 2015 Expo pushed several companies to launch donation programmes and sign national agreements with food recovery organisations, which automatically committed several shops at once and thus had a considerable effect.

A final point concerns a possible blind spot in the current system of incentives. Food recovery organisations and food banks are key implementers of the policy but have financial, logistical, technological, and personnel constraints (Kantor et al. 1997; De Boeck et al. 2017). They not only have to collect and deliver food but also need to ensure necessary safety measures are upheld in both its storage and transportation. Increasing amounts of food donations will necessarily increase their costs, even more so for perishable fresh food that must be redistributed quickly or food in need of special management, such as that in an unbroken cold chain. Some kind of support for food recovery organisations—for instance, a tax cut related to their technological or facility updates or logistics solutions such as the one described in Chapter 14—may thus be essential to increase the quantity and quality of food they recover.

Rewarding donors? Municipal discounts on the waste collection tax

Law 166/2016 established that municipalities could voluntarily grant food donors a reduction of the local waste tax. The logic of the reduction appeared obvious: following the 'pay-as-you-throw' principle, donors waste less and should pay less. Also, new donors may be encouraged to start donating to enjoy the tax reduction. Though there are no evaluations available, interviews reveal that its design and implementation are problematic and the likely impact negligible.[4]

By law, the waste tax in Italy should cover the city's waste disposal service cost in full. The tariff includes two parts: one is fixed and covers investments and fixed costs while the other is variable and covers the service cost. A discount of waste taxes based on food donations affects the variable part of the tax in proportion to the expected savings on the management costs of the service.

Existing tax reductions—such as those for paper—follow this logic. The company asking for a reduction does not use the municipal service but has their waste managed by a private operator. This typically happens with waste categories produced in significant volumes, that are easily recyclable and which can be profitably managed by private companies. In these cases, the municipality saves part of the service cost (there is no need to collect a certain proportion of waste) and can grant a corresponding discount on the variable part of the tax. Does this logic apply to donated food? Unfortunately, no.

The problem with food donations is that they only represent a fraction of the total organic waste produced by urban food operators (for instance, in the

2016 data from Coop reported earlier, donations accounted for 20% of the total surplus). The municipality will still need to collect the remaining organic waste from donors without a significant change in the frequency of the waste disposal service. The very nature of food waste and food donations thus poses a substantial limit on the tax reduction that municipalities can offer. In addition, the discount cannot be given as a lump sum but should be proportional to the amount of food donated. This requires donors to certify their food donations with the municipality, with a noticeable increase in the administrative burden.

Interviews with municipal managers confirm that the incentive is negligible; it cannot promote a change in the behaviour of potential donors or in any significant way compensate for the costs of donating. If such reductions are to really convince new donors, municipalities should increase the tax cuts significantly. However, this increase would not be proportional to their cost savings for the service, thus creating the need to establish a subsidy for donations that risks financing wasters instead of incentivising waste prevention.

Institutionalisation: the National Table for Fighting Food Waste

In 2012, following the global financial crisis, the government established a national fund for needy people. The fund entails the direct purchase of food, covers part of the cost of food distribution, and also includes food donations. Together with the fund, the Ministry of Agriculture set up a Permanent Coordination Table with advisory functions for the management of the national fund, which is also in charge of making policy proposals regarding food donation and recovery, promoting innovation and monitoring surplus food and waste. In 2016, law 166 transformed the Table into the National Table for Fighting Food Waste.

The Table brings together five ministries (agriculture, environment, employment, economy, health) and representatives of the main actors involved in the prevention, production, and redistribution of food waste and loss: producers, distributors, retailers, food banks, and charities.

Thanks to its broad membership, the Table allows complete oversight of food losses and waste, which affords it excellent potential to promote innovations and fine-tune legislative changes. New proposals can be discussed in advance with all the interested actors, which gives the Table the scope to integrate different perspectives (environmental, fiscal, health, and social) and anticipate implementation problems. The Table may also help with technical adjustments, such as harmonising regulations and procedures across different ministerial administrations (for instance, fiscal and environmental ones).

Yet, though it is a permanent institution established by law, the Table meets only occasionally; it is convened politically to consult on specific issues (e.g. recently, the social emergency due to COVID-19). This norm of occasional engagement limits the potential advantages of having such an institution and makes it beholden to the sensitivity of the political leadership, who may choose when and if to convene it. In addition, all parties maintain their institutional interests without the Table having its own institutional identity; it can serve policymakers to hear different perspectives, but is prone to be dominated by conflicting pressures.

Data production and information: the Observatory on Food Surplus, Recovery and Waste

In 2017, the Ministry of Agriculture established the National Observatory on Food Surplus, Recovery and Waste as part of the Research Council for Agricultural Research and Economics (CREA). The Observatory is tasked with collecting and disseminating best practices and producing data on food surplus and waste. Both activities aim to provide decision-makers with solid knowledge and contribute to designing more effective interventions, including those directly promoted by the Observatory: awareness campaigns, information leaflets, dietary guidelines, and education initiatives.

In 2018, the first report of the Observatory (OERSA 2019) surveyed good practices implemented across the food chain, reported barriers highlighted by stakeholders, and suggested possible innovations and improvements to the current policy. The report also reviewed databases and measurements produced by companies, associations, and academics. The Observatory is now working to coordinate the existing databases on food losses and waste and make some of them accessible on its website.

One of the main activities of the Observatory is administering the survey of household food waste on a representative sample of Italian families (Scalvedi and Rossi 2021). The survey was first administered in 2019 and will be repeated periodically every two years (data for 2021 are yet to be released). The focus on consumers is considered essential for informing preventive measures since consumers' behaviour may influence the entire supply chain. Therefore, the survey not only inquires about households' quantities of waste but also collects policy-relevant information on cognitive and behavioural factors underlying food waste. A couple of examples may highlight the importance of building such an evidence base.

Compared to other EU countries, Italians dispose of comparatively smaller quantities of partly used food because they typically store and eat leftovers. Instead, the largest proportion of consumers' food waste (43.2%) is that which is not used at all, such as unopened packages and perishable products (fruit, yoghurt, eggs, and potatoes). This suggests that education campaigns should focus on overbuying, to promote more careful planning of grocery shopping and—in light of the high prevalence of fresh products—provide information on how to store food properly and understand when a product is still edible.

Another interesting finding is the low importance of environmental concerns related to food waste. For Italian consumers, wasting food is a negative emotional experience unrelated to sustainability issues but instead to ethical considerations and traditional values (especially for older generations).

This finding suggests that effective preventive strategies should stress the ethical aspects of wasting food rather than its ecological consequences.

Finally, these data may also enhance the government's ability to reach the right targets of awareness and education campaigns. For example, the 2019 survey revealed that families who waste more also have worse nutritional habits. These data suggest that nutritional advice and food waste messages should be coupled. This strategy not only improves efficiency (with the delivery of multiple messages to a coherent target) but also allows food waste communication to become part of a consolidated and long-standing network of initiatives (alongside those related to nutrition), hence widening their target. Accordingly, the Government Guidelines for a Healthy Diet now include a chapter on sustainable diets with suggestions for reducing food waste (CREA 2018). Similarly, food waste is now part of all training initiatives on nutrition held by CREA with medical doctors and local health authorities.

Enlarging the scope of donations: the best-before date

The 2016 law introduced the possibility to donate new kinds of food, such as mislabelled, confiscated food or bread after 24 hours from its baking. In some cases, such as bread, new streams of donations could finally start and entire categories of products are now recovered instead of being disposed of. Among these provisions, the law clearly distinguishes between the date of minimum durability (best-before date) and the use-by date, clarifying that food after the best-before date can be safely donated for human consumption.

The lack of safety concern associated with passing the best-before date was established before the law came into effect, but there was a long-standing ambiguity about the status of such food, especially whether or not it could be donated. Without an explicit legal provision, this uncertainty led to resistance from donors, food banks, and even health authorities, which hampered food recovery (PINPAS 2015). The law is undoubtedly the first step towards introducing a new perception of best-before dates, but its impact should be put into perspective, especially in the short term.

The relevance of this new regulation depends on the amount of food past the best-before date that is primed to be disposed of but could be donated: the greater this quantity, the bigger the impact of the reform. A review of the waste produced at different stages in the food chain may provide a rough estimate of this quantity. As we know from the above section on quantification, according to different estimates, consumers and producers account for about 80% of total food waste. Consumers are not targeted by the policy, while in the case of producers, passing the best-before date is certainly not a reason for wasting food (especially if one considers agriculture).

Garrone, Melacini, and Perego (2014) report the reasons for the production of surplus food by Italian manufacturers and distributors. In both cases, passing the best-before date is not a major cause of surplus. For instance, manufacturing companies generate 66.9% of their surplus because the food reaches the internal sell-by date, a percentage that amounts to 48.7% in the case of distributors (Garrone, Melacini, and Perego 2014). This date is usually set at a proportion of the shelf life, giving retailers enough time to sell their products and consumers enough time to consume them. The other reasons for surplus generation, such as aesthetic criteria or non-compliance with packaging or other commercial standards, apply to food products equally well within the best-before date.

In conclusion, the legal provision for donating food after the best-before date will mainly target retailers. Although we do not have data for Italy, Leb-ersorger and Schneider (2014) performed a sorting analysis of discarded food in Austrian retail outlets and reported that products that went unsold due to passing the best-before date or use-by date amounted to approximately 28% of the food discarded.

Another point worth mentioning about food past the best-before date con-cerns possible resistance from donors, food banks, and even people in need. This resistance was widely reported in our interviews and occurs for different reasons. First, manufacturers are sensitive to the reputational consequences of donations (Baglioni, De Pieri, and Tallarico 2016). They fear that donating food after the best-before date may backfire and hurt, rather than enhance, their reputation. Indeed, news that the company is providing disadvantaged people 'second-class' food that is no longer marketable may not benefit them in terms of social responsibility. Second, in the case of food banks and food recov-ery organisations, resistance is both a matter of organisation, for the difficulty of managing this food, and social, to provide fragile people with high-quality food with a long shelf life. Alexander and Smaje (2008) described a similar situation in the case of FareShare franchises, which treat use-by and best-before dates as virtually equal when screening donations. Finally, interviews with food banks report that beneficiaries are said to be resistant both because they do not trust the safety of food past the best-before date and because they feel mis-treated with lower quality food that other people would not buy or eat.

Notwithstanding their differences, a common reason regards a persistent and generalised stigma about food past the best-before date, be it because of misplaced fears and doubts regarding safety or just for prejudice about taste and social perception. This means that the legal backing offered by the law will likely not change things in the short term, though it could nonetheless represent the first step towards a new culture and understanding of the best-before date.

This cultural leap certainly cannot rely only on new regulations. It has become all the more common in recent years to find corners in supermarkets where food close to the best-before date is sold at a discounted price. Some of the major supermarket chains in Italy are also promoting this food through smartphone apps (Maconi 2020). On the one hand, these commercial prac-tices might negatively impact the quality of donations; the food is sold until the very last day of market utility and then donated legally under the law (see also the discussion in Chapter 7). On the other hand, however, these practices may have the positive effect of increasing the attention consumers pay to food waste and contributing to familiarising people with the perception that the best-before date is flexible, illustrating that most food at this point is safe and perfectly edible. Finally, they can also answer a social purpose, allowing some fragile people to buy discounted food in a supermarket instead of receiving aid in a soup kitchen or food bank.

Optimising logistics: the information system for withdrawals in the Emilia Romagna region

Overproduction is a common risk in agriculture. It happens because of exceptional situations like the Russian embargo in 2014 and also due to more ordinary events like simple weather fluctuations. The EU Common Agricultural Policy (CAP) protects farmers from these risks by compensating them for products' withdrawal in the case of overproductions that would create market imbalances. The CAP also provides an incentive for food recovery; if products are distributed to charities for free, producers receive greater compensation than in the case of withdrawals ending in product transformation or destruction.

An evaluation of this system is beyond the scope of this chapter, but several concerns have been raised about whether the EU incentives are contrary to food waste prevention (European Court of Auditors 2019). Nonetheless, at present, large quantities of food are withdrawn from the market and can be either delivered to charities or diverted to options ranked lower in the food waste hierarchy. The EU compensations aim at ensuring food recovery, but are they all that is needed?

Withdrawals regard fresh food, which is highly perishable and suddenly becomes available in significant quantities. Producers' associations must contact charities and organise the delivery while charities must receive and manage single deliveries of several tonnes of food. The process requires more than an economic incentive; it requires planning, logistics, and professional management.

In 2012, the Emilia Romagna region developed a software solution to facilitate matching the demand with the supply of food withdrawn from the market.[5] Figure 8.1 shows the market withdrawals paid for by Agrea, the regional agency that manages the software. Histograms show the tonnes of food divided by destination, and the dotted line represents the percentage recovered, expressed as the value of the food in euros. Even without considering the years 2014–2017, which were most affected by the Russian embargo, huge quantities of food can be seen to have been withdrawn from the market.[6] Fortunately, most of it was successfully recovered.

With the new information system, producers' associations register their data at the start of the year and publish weekly quantities of food available complete with all logistical information. Charities also access the software and view data about overproductions and deliveries. All operations are instantly tracked, and the region can easily control withdrawals and distribute payments. The software provides information about which products are available, where and when

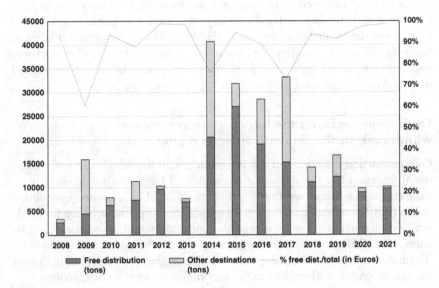

Figure 8.1 Market withdrawals and food recovery.
Source: Agrea 2022.

they can be delivered, and who can potentially receive them. Data for past years also inform charities about potential overproductions coming soon.

Although the portion of food recovered has increased with the implementation of the software, it is difficult to prove its impact. Interviewees testified to its general optimisation in the management of overproductions. Certainly, the software is a significant upgrade compared to when producers' associations called charities without notice, hunting for one that could receive 30 tonnes of tangerines within a couple of days. As a further clue of its effectiveness, other regions in Italy have started to use the software, and it also received funding through the Horizon 2020 project 'Low in Food' as a good practice to be disseminated in other European countries (https://lowinfood.eu/).

As mentioned, the software does not address food waste prevention but targets its recovery. Having said that, the region now has ten years of micro-level data that may allow for 'predicting the unexpected', that is at which point in the year overproduction of a specific product is more likely to happen. These data may also help distinguish exceptional overproductions from recurrent ones that might be addressed using different tools (such as incentives to switch part of the production to other products). Of course, a reformulation of market withdrawals would be a task for decision-makers at the EU level, not for the regional bodies. However, it is worth noting how careful monitoring and optimisation of food recovery may help us design better preventive strategies if these data are used to support policy formulation.

Conclusion and policy implications

Over the past couple of decades, Italy has incrementally built what now appears to be a broad and coherent set of solutions for fighting food waste: incentives, regulations, information tools, and new institutions. This section summarises the key messages of the chapter that may be useful for designing and implementing similar tools in other contexts.

Regarding the design of incentives for donations, policymakers should work on limiting both financial and administrative burdens and consider the relative costs of more consolidated options such as disposal or recycling. These incentives should be precisely targeted, considering both producers of waste (retailers) and the company management deciding whether to launch a donation programme. Interestingly, discounts on local waste taxes do not appear to be particularly effective. Yet, the possibility of providing incentives to charities, such as tax cuts for technological updates, is worth considering. Food banks are critical implementers of food donation programmes, and such incentives, as well as other forms of support, would increase their capacity without funding food wasters.

Moreover, creating new institutions explicitly dedicated to food waste can increase the knowledge available about the design and implementation of related policy, improve the drafting of new legislation, and increase the advocacy and attention afforded to the food waste problem itself. The Italian institutions mentioned in this chapter are new to the scene and not particularly strongly developed. However, they have potential for opening up a forum to discuss legislation (the Table) and creating an agent to integrate food waste into the broader issue of healthy and sustainable nutrition (the Observatory).

Ensuring a proper evidence base is a staple of policy design. Most existing research investigates the magnitude of the food waste problem. These efforts need to be complemented by a more solid evidence base of policy-relevant information about the causes and mechanisms of food waste at different stages of the supply chain. More precise data will inform tailored and effective policies. The analysis of consumers led by the Observatory and that suggested for withdrawals in the Emilia Romagna Region provide two examples of how new data may improve policy.

Beyond this, the design of dedicated public programmes is another resource that administrations can deploy to fight food waste. The software technology for improving logistics in the Emilia Romagna region provides a good example of how regulation and incentives can be complemented by supporting the management capacity of producers and charities. However, there is certainly great scope to further expand technology use, tailor policy, and increase resource efficiency.

A final note concerns reputation and stigma about the best-before date. This analysis showed that the amount of related food waste is limited and occurs mainly at the retail stage. The new legal provision helps avoid the legal uncertainty that previously impeded donations but cannot necessarily over-come the reputational and organisational barriers in the short term. Looking to the future, education and awareness programmes, along with greater familiar-ity with this food in supermarkets, may complement existing regulations and promote further acceptance.

Notes

1 All interviews lasted approximately one hour and discussed design and implementation issues concerning the current policy. List of interviews: Interview 1: Municipal manager; Interview 2: Food recovery organisation; Interview 3: Food bank; Interview 4: Super-market manager; Interview 5: Food franchise manager; Interview 6: Food waste expert; Interview 7: National Observatory on Food Surplus, Recovery and Waste; Interview 8: Municipal manager; Interview 9: Food recovery organisation; Interview 10: Regional manager; Interview 11: Regional Food Recovery Organisation; Interview 12: Food donor, national supermarket company.
2 Yet, this does not mean that hygiene norms are bypassed. In fact, in 2015, the Ministry of Health also validated operational guidelines for charities prepared by Caritas Italiana and Banco Alimentare dealing with hygiene and safety issues concerning recovered and redistributed food (Ministry of Health 2015).
3 Other proposals were to be applied by other means, such as the elaboration of guidelines for food waste prevention in canteens (Ministry of Health 2018).
4 The very approval of the tax reduction was problematic. The government provided no technical direction on how municipalities could design the discount in compliance with the existing waste regulations. In addition, the discount had no financial support. Both issues created a range of doubts and uncertainties that discouraged many municipalities from passing the reduction.
5 See https://agricoltura.regione.emilia-romagna.it/servizi-online/come-fare-per/gestione-crisi-e-ritiri-dal-mercato.
6 To put these numbers into perspective, in 2020, Banco Alimentare, the leading national food bank, distributed about 100 tonnes of food across the whole country (www.bancoalimentare.it).

References

Alexander, Catherine, and Chris Smaje. 2008. "Surplus Retail Food Redistribution: An Analysis of a Third Sector Model." *Resources, Conservation and Recycling* 52 (11): 1290–98. https://doi.org/10.1016/J.RESCONREC.2008.07.009.

Baglioni, Simone, Benedetta De Pieri, and Tatiana Tallarico. 2016. "Surplus Food Recovery and Food Aid: The Pivotal Role of Non-Profit Organisations. Insights From Italy and Germany." *VOLUNTAS: International Journal of Voluntary and Nonprofit Organizations* 28 (5): 2032–52. https://doi.org/10.1007/S11266-016-9746-8.

Banco Alimentare. 2013. "La Legge 155/2003, Una Legge Italiana All'avanguardia Al Fine Di Incoraggiare Le Donazioni Di Cibo Cotto e Fresco Ai Più Poveri [Law 155/2003, an Italian Law to Enhance Donations of Fresh and Cooked Food for the Poor]." www.bancoalimentare.it/sites/bancoalimentare.it/old-files/Legge_155_20032(2).pdf.

Boeck, E. De, L. Jacxsens, H. Goubert, and M. Uyttendaele. 2017. "Ensuring Food Safety in Food Donations: Case Study of the Belgian Donation/Acceptation Chain." *Food Research International* 100 (October): 137–49. https://doi.org/10.1016/J.FOODRES.2017.08.046.

Bruzzone, Mauro. 2018. "Coop. Un Volano per Far Crescere Le Donazioni [Coop. A Fly-Wheel to Make Donations Increase]." In *Dallo Spreco Al Dono [From Waste to Gift]*, edited by Patrizia Toia. www.patriziatoia.info/images/ebooks/dallo_spreco_al_dono.pdf.

Busetti, Simone. 2019. "A Theory-Based Evaluation of Food Waste Policy: Evidence From Italy." *Food Policy* 88. https://doi.org/10.1016/j.foodpol.2019.101749.

Busetti, Simone, and Bruno Dente. 2018. *EXPOst. Le Consequenze Di Un Grande Evento [EXPOst. The Consequences of a Big Event]]*. Bologna: Il Mulino. https://doi.org/10.4/JQUERY-UI.MIN.JS.

COOP. 2016. "Libro Bianco COOP Sullo Spreco Alimentare. [White Paper COOP on Food Waste]." www.coopnospreco.it/wp-content/uploads/2019/03/libro_bianco_ancc_coop.pdf.

CREA. 2018. "Linee Guida per Una Sana Alimentazione [Guidelines for a Healthy Nutrition]." www.salute.gov.it/imgs/C_17_pubblicazioni_2915_allegato.pdf.

———. 2021. "L'agricoltura Italiana Conta 2021." https://cnbbsv.palazzochigi.it/media/2429/itaconta-2021_ita_web.pdf.

European Commission. 2010. "Preparatory Study on Food Waste Across EU27." https://doi.org/10.2779/85947.

European Court of Auditors. 2019. "Farmers' Income Stabilisation: Comprehensive Set of Tools, but Low Uptake of Instruments and Overcompensation Need to Be Tackled." www.eca.europa.eu/Lists/ECADocuments/SR19_23/SR_CAP_Income_stabilisation_EN.pdf.

European Parliament. 2013. "Technology Options for Feeding 10 Billion People Recycling Agricultural, Forestry & Food Wastes and Residues for Sustainable Bioenergy and Biomaterials." www.europarl.europa.eu/RegData/etudes/etudes/join/2013/513513/IPOL-JOIN_ET(2013)513513_EN.pdf.

Garrone, Paola, Marco Melacini, and Alessandro Perego. 2014. "Surplus Food Recovery and Donation in Italy: The Upstream Process." *British Food Journal* 116 (9): 1460–77. https://doi.org/10.1108/BFJ-02-2014-0076.

Herpen, Erica van, Lisanne van Geffen, Mariska Nijenhuis-de Vries, Nancy Holthuysen, Ivo van der Lans, and Tom Quested. 2019. "A Validated Survey to Measure Household Food Waste." *MethodsX* 6 (January): 2767–75. https://doi.org/10.1016/J.MEX.2019.10.029.

ISPRA. 2018. "Spreco Alimentare: Un Approccio Sistemico per La Prevenzione e La Riduzione Strutturali [Food Waste: A Systemic Approach for Structural Prevention and Reduction]." www.isprambiente.gov.it/files2019/pubblicazioni/rapporti/RAPPORTO-SPRECOALIMENTARE_279_2018.pdf.

Kantor, L. S., K. Lipton, A. Manchester, and V. Oliveira. 1997. "Estimating and Addressing America's Food Losses." *Food Review* 20 (1): 2–12.

Lebersorger, S., and F. Schneider. 2014. "Food Loss Rates at the Food Retail, Influencing Factors and Reasons as a Basis for Waste Prevention Measures." *Waste Management* 34 (11): 1911–19. https://doi.org/10.1016/J.WASMAN.2014.06.013.

Maconi, Caterina. 2020. "La Lotta Allo Spreco Alimentare Passa Da Un'app [Fighting Food Waste with a Smartphone App]." *La Repubblica*, February 4, 2020. www.repubblica.it/economia/rapporti/osserva-italia/le-storie/2020/02/04/news/la_lotta_allo_spreco_alimentare_passa_da_un_app-247594305/.

Ministry of Health. 2015. "Manuale per Corrette Prassi Operative per Le Organizzazioni Caritative [Handbook of Correct Practice for Charities in Recovery, Collection and Distribution of Food]]." www.salute.gov.it/imgs/C_17_pagineAree_1187_listaFile_item-Name_1_file.pdf.

———. 2018. "Linee Di Indirizzo Rivolte Agli Enti Gestori Di Mense Scolastiche, Aziendali, Ospedaliere, Sociali e Di Comunità, Al Fine Di Prevenire e Ridurre Lo Spreco

Connesso Alla Somministrazione Degli Alimenti [Guidelines for Preventing Food Waste in Canteens in Schools, Companies, Hospitals and Social Institutes]." www.salute.gov.it/imgs/C_17_pubblicazioni_2748_allegato.pdf.

Ministry of the Environment. 2014. "PINPAS. Piano Nazionale Di Prevenzione Degli Sprechi Alimentari [PINPAS. National Plan for Food Waste Prevention]." www.mite.gov.it/sites/default/files/archivio_immagini/Galletti/Comunicati/PINPAS 10 MISURE PRIORITARIE 5 GIUGNO 2014.pdf.

OERSA, Observatory on Food Surplus Recovery and Waste. 2019. "Ricognizione Delle Misure in Italia e Proposte Di Sviluppo [Survey of Policy Options and Proposals of Development]]." www.crea.gov.it/documents/59764/0/Osservatorio+CREA+O-ERSA+WEB.pdf/c93f0266-e5f7-e2f3-e581-32797328bb3b?t=1559138880594.

PINPAS. 2015. "*La Donazione Degli Alimenti Invenduti: Verso La Semplificazione Normativa [The donation of unsold food products. Towards simplifying the regulation]*." https://www.mite.gov.it/sites/default/files/archivio_immagini/Galletti/Comunicati/alma_mater_bologna/Position%20paper%20sulla%20donazione%20degli%20alimenti%20invenduti.pdf.

Priefer, Carmen, Juliane Jörissen, and Klaus Rainer Bräutigam. 2016. "Food Waste Prevention in Europe—A Cause-Driven Approach to Identify the Most Relevant Leverage Points for Action." *Resources, Conservation and Recycling* 109 (May): 155–65. https://doi.org/10.1016/J.RESCONREC.2016.03.004.

Scalvedi, Maria Luisa, and Laura Rossi. 2021. "Comprehensive Measurement of Italian Domestic Food Waste in a European Framework." *Sustainability* 13 (3): 1492. https://doi.org/10.3390/SU13031492.

Tua, Camilla, Mario Grosso, and Simone Nessi. 2017. "The 'REDUCE' Project: Definition of a Methodology for Quantifying Food Waste by Means of Targeted Waste Composition Analysis. " *Rivista Di Economia Agraria* LXX2 (3): 289–301. https://oajournals.fupress.net/index.php/rea/article/view/9928/9925.

Waste Watcher. 2022. "ITALIA." www.sprecozero.it/wp-content/uploads/2022/02/Il-caso-Italia-2022-4-febbraio-2022.pdf.

9 Food waste policy in Romania

A case study

Cristina Vasilescu

Introduction

Fighting food waste has become a pressing issue on the public agenda at both EU and global levels due to its environmental, social, and economic impacts. Romania is no exception to this.

With 6,000 tonnes of food wasted per day and over two million tonnes over a year, Romania occupies ninth place in the EU for food wasted after countries with a higher population and income level (European Parliament 2016). Despite the fact that around half of Romanians spend on average 40% of their income on food (EPC Consultanță de Mediu 2016) and that 23.4% live in poverty (National Institute of Statistics 2020) having limited access to food, Romania wastes on average 130 kg of food per inhabitant (Ecopolis 2019). While food waste increased by 36.5% between 2010 and 2016 (Antoneac et al. 2019), the general opinion is that food waste has decreased or maintained at the same level (Dumitru et al. 2021).

In a 2019 study, CNEPSS shows that food waste occurs especially in households: 49% of the total waste compared to 37% in the food industry, 5% in public food, and 2% in the agricultural sector. Another study (Dumitru et al. 2021) underlines those consumers produce 41% of food wasted in Romania. The different figures on the distribution of food waste along the food chain point out the low reliability of data on food waste, as also confirmed by other studies (Ecopolis 2019; UN 2021). While representatives of the food industry underline that consumers are responsible for most of the food wasted in Romania, interviewed civil society organisations (NGOs) pinpoint that consumers seem to be the major responsible for food waste, also due to a high level of underreporting of food waste in the food production and process chain.

Several studies have tried to portray food wasters in Romania. The typical food waster in Romania is male, under 35 years old, with a high level of education and income (Iorga et al. 2017) and resident in urban areas (CNEPSS et al. 2019). Cantaragiu (2019) points out that women are more prone to save food due to guilty feelings related to social inequalities (i.e. young women) and financial responsibility (i.e. adult and older women). Other studies (Pocol et al. 2020) sustain that the feeling of guilt does not act as an incentive to saving

DOI: 10.4324/9781003226932-13

food, as food wasters do not recognise themselves as responsible for food waste but, on the contrary, tend to blame others for it. Pocol et al. (2020) point out that information on food (e.g. conservation, understanding of labels) and habits are more significant in predicting the food waste level than socio-demographic variables. Furthermore, the study also reveals that people who have experienced life in the countryside have been involved in food buying and cooking, and in eating food leftovers in their childhood, tend to pay more attention to saving food than those who did not have such experiences.

As shown in Table 9.1, when it comes to the causes of food waste in Romania, they are of various types: behavioural, legal/policy, and logistic/administrative.

Table 9.1 Food waste causes

Type	Food waste cause
Behavioural	Lack of information on food waste prevention: • 60% of the consumers have no information on food waste and do not understand labels (Caprita 2016); • 69% of the surveyed food production, process, and distribution actors do not have specific knowledge on food waste prevention and reduction (Dumitru et al. 2021); • This information gap is due to the absence of the food waste topic from formal and informal education (chapter interviews). Moral attitude towards food after the Communist regime: • The passage of the Romanian society from restricted access to food during the communist regime to a high availability of food after it fell has pushed consumers to buy large quantities of food even when not needed, without paying attention to its quality, seasonality or provenance. According to interviewees, the large quantity and cheapness of food are the only things that count for many Romanians. 'Aggressive' commercial campaigns of food retailers: • In a context where people focus on food quantity and reduced prices, the aggressive commercial campaigns of food retailers induce consumers to buy food they do not need, which often ends up as waste (chapter interviews). Indeed, in 14% of cases analysed by CNEPSS et al. (2019), food waste is due to buying food in excess. Limited interest of food chain actors in the prevention and reduction of food waste, even though not all interviewees agree on it (see the paragraph Food waste causes).
Legal/policy	Uncertainty of the legal framework on food waste (further details in the paragraph Food waste causes) Administrative burden on food chain actors (see the paragraph Food waste causes) Strict regulations on consumption of food labelled 'best before' after expiry: • The 2005 Governmental Decision 984/2005 on food safety uses the general term 'validity term expired', forbidding food donation/commercialisation after this term, while the 2018 consumers' protection law specifies that food can be commercialised only within the 'use by'/'best before' dates.

Type	Food waste cause
Logistical/ administrative	Underdevelopment of the network of food organisations managing food waste (see the paragraph Food waste causes) Limited facilities for collecting, managing, and reusing organic waste, which makes it difficult to recycle and reuse organic waste (interviews; EC 2019)

Source: interviews and literature

To fight food waste, the Romanian authorities have adopted four measures: the 2014 National Plan for Fighting Food Waste (Ministerului Agriculturii şi Dezvoltării Rurale—MADR- 2014); the 2030 Sustainable Development Strategy (Romanian Government 2018), including food waste among its objectives; the adoption of the 2016 law on food waste (Parlamentul României 2016a); and the 2021 Emergency Ordinance 92 on waste management (Guvernul României 2021). However, despite the declared objective of reducing and preventing food waste, the concrete measures adopted by Romanian authorities in this direction remain quite limited. The Romanian Plan for fighting food waste has not been updated since 2014, while the Romanian Sustainable Development Strategy does not foresee any specific measures to achieve the food reduction and prevention target. The most important measure relates to the 2016 law on food waste. The adoption of the 2021 emergency ordinance on waste management further strengthens some of the provisions of the law on food waste (e.g. food donation) and introduces the 'polluter pays' principle and the use of the hierarchy of waste management. As this latter regulation has been adopted only recently, this chapter will focus on the analysis of the 2016 law on food waste. The chapter will explore its effectiveness in dealing with the food waste problem, with the aim to provide indications for future policy actions. Furthermore, the chapter will also include a set of successful practices to prevent or reduce food waste delivered by NGOs.

The chapter draws on a desk analysis of literature on food waste in Romania, and five online interviews with representatives of NGOs in the food sector and the food industry. Despite attempts to connect with Romanian authorities in charge of fighting food waste, it has not been possible to obtain their point of view.

Food waste policy approach in Romania: the Romanian food waste law

As mentioned previously, the 2016 food waste law remains the main measure undertaken by the Romanian authorities to reduce and prevent food waste.

This chapter focuses on the analysis of its effectiveness in preventing and reducing food waste, pointing out its main strengths and weaknesses.

Background of the law design and implementation

Until the drafting of the 2016 law on food waste, Romanian authorities paid at best limited attention to food waste prevention and management, as wasted food was not considered as manageable rubbish. While Romanian authorities almost ignored the topic, several Romanian NGOs had started to push forward food waste prevention and reduction through information, education, and non-perishable food collection through donations made under the sponsorship law, allowing for sponsorship through goods.

In 2014, in the context of the European Year against Food Waste and EU commitments to prevent and reduce food, the Ministry of Environment announced the need to adopt a specific strategy in this area. The same year, the design of the strategy was transferred from the Ministry of Environment to the Ministry of Agriculture and Rural Development, which announced the adoption of a National Plan for Fighting Food Waste (MADR 2014).

Seizing this window of opportunity, several NGOs initiated a dialogue with the Ministry of Agriculture to enhance policy development in this area. While the plan was adopted in 2014, interviewees revealed that the intentions of the Ministry to undertake the concrete actions foreseen by the plan were more declarative than real. To push the process forward, NGOs looked for political support, which was obtained from a member of parliament who coordinated the initiation of a law proposal against food waste sustained by 52 parliamentarians (Parlamentul României 2016b). The new law, drafted with the strong support of NGOs (Ecopolis 2019 and interviews), was adopted in 2016. It foresaw the obligation for all actors along the food chain to take measures for preventing and reducing food waste, including through food donation to specifically registered operators. The mandatory nature of the law created discontent among food industry actors. Food industry actors were also concerned by the lack of clarity of food receivers' responsibilities and the risk of developing parallel circuits of food commercialisation due to the possibility offered to food receivers to sell their products (interviews). Civil society interviewees suggested that food industry actors used these arguments instrumentally to block a law they considered inconvenient.

The law entered into force in May 2017, but it could not be applied due to the absence of the methodological norms. Finally, it was suspended in June 2017. However, a proposal for changing the law was initiated in September 2017 (Parlamentul României 2017) and ended in 2018 with the adoption of a new law (Parlamentul României 2018). The new law eliminated the compulsory nature of food waste prevention and reduction measures, which were now only recommended. The sole obligation of food actors consisted of drafting and reporting on a yearly plan to prevent and reduce food waste, submitted to MADR. However, the law foresaw no control and transparency mechanisms for the drafting and reporting of these plans. The law also forbade the selling of food close to the expiry date, which caused heated debates between the food industry and social enterprise actors. A mediation was found with the introduction of an exception from this provision for NGOs and social enterprises.

Even though the law was adopted in 2018, the methodological norms for its concrete application were approved only in February 2019 (Parlamentul României 2019). According to interviewees, food industry actors were happy with the new law, while civil society representatives were profoundly disappointed by it. The new law presented several shortages that made its application difficult: the omission of food banks from food donation beneficiaries; the requirement for a registered contract for the transfer of food; payment of VAT for food transferred, but not for food destroyed; exclusion of the 'polluter pays' principle. A new correction of the law was needed to eliminate these shortages. In July 2020, law 131 was adopted (Parlamentul României 2020). It recognises food banks among beneficiaries of food donations, foresees a less complex contract model, introduces fiscal advantages for food businesses that transfer food, including through donations, and specifies food receivers' responsibility for ensuring the respect of the food hygiene and safety norms after the receipt of the food.

Objectives and measures

As adopted in 2016 and later modified, the food waste law aims to contribute to the EU objective of reducing food waste by 50% until 2030, by introducing specific measures for the prevention and reduction of food waste along the entire food chain.

The law is expected to also produce a reduction in costs related to the ecological footprint of small and medium enterprises (SMEs), food for socially assisted people, and the management of organic waste. For achieving these outcomes, the 2019 Methodological Norm foresees two main categories of measures: a set of general measures targeted to all actors in the food chain, and a set of specific measures targeted to the food production, process, distribution, commercialisation, and hotel/restaurant/café (HORECA) sectors.

Both general and specific measures include the efficient use of resources and adaptation to climate change, education, and information to consumers on food waste prevention and reduction, research, development, and innovation of products and processes, traceability of food and adaptation to the market conditions. In addition, specific measures also foresee the creation of a FIFO system ('first in, first out') for product stocks and the valorisation and elimination of food waste according to the waste management hierarchy (in the HORECA sector). General measures pay specific attention to the quantification of food waste, the planning and reporting on food waste prevention, and reduction through yearly plans, and donation of food fit for human consumption to operators managing food excess at least ten days before the expiry date. Food unfit for human consumption can be donated after a risk assessment has been undertaken by the food donor, while perishable food can be donated only to social canteens. NGOs and social enterprises that receive food can commercialise it to the final consumer at a reduced price to cover the staff and operation costs; they have to present a yearly activity report on the food donations received.

The law intends that businesses along the food chain should try to undertake at least two of these measures before destroying the wasted food.

Main results, and success and failure factors of the law on food waste

According to the interviews held, the law has produced limited results so far, in particular due to its recent (since 2019) and limited application on the ground. Several reasons explain its limited implementation.

Interviewees consider that the voluntary nature of the law hinders the development of the food waste prevention and reduction system. However, it is not clear whether a mandatory law could reverse the situation, at least in the short term, considering the food receivers' still limited capacity of managing excess food. While the law on food waste recommends food donations, it does not cover any kind of measure to develop food receiver networks. Currently, there are only five food banks in Romania that cover big and medium-size cities. They are self-funded through schemes such as donations and projects, which often limits their access to significant and continuous resources for development. Other food receivers are local NGOs, public administrations, the local networks of churches, or the Somaro social stores. However, often these organisations do not have the capacity to redistribute large quantities of food. Furthermore, while there is a high concentration of NGOs in large cities that can redistribute food, in small towns their presence is less intense, hindering food donations.

The still limited interest in food waste prevention and reduction by many businesses along the food chain is another explanation for the limited implementation of the law. From some interviewees' point of view, this is due to three main reasons: businesses' lack of knowledge on the societal effects of food waste and its prevention and reduction; their limited sense of belonging to the community; and their fear of incurring fines in case of food donations, fuelled by the high level of corruption in the Romanian public administration and the 'paper-based' mentality of public staff. In particular, this latter aspect triggers a zero-risk bias (i.e. a preference for absolute certainty), which makes them consider destruction the preferred option for managing wasted food.

However, the opinions of the interviewees on businesses' limited interest in saving food are divergent. Interviewed representatives of the food industry claim that businesses are extremely interested in preventing and reducing food waste. On the contrary, interviewed NGOs consider that only a limited number of companies are interested in taking measures to prevent and reduce food waste. This latter point of view seems to be confirmed by the findings of studies on this topic (Dumitru and Burghiu 2019). To what extent businesses along the food chain are interested in preventing and reducing food waste remains an open issue for debate, against the lack of national data on it. The mandatory reporting on plans to prevent and reduce food waste, brought in by the law on food waste, could represent a relevant source of information. However, currently (December 2021), these plans are not available on the MADR website (MADR 2014). Interviewees reveal that, despite several requests to civil organisations to publish these plans, this has not yet happened. The recent emergency ordinance on waste management that also sets mandatory obligations for reporting on waste management in the food sector might fill in this information gap.

The limited financial incentives to save food indicated by the law is another reason why its implementation is slow. The last changes to the law overcame the payment of the VAT issue and introduced fiscal advantages for food donors. However, according to interviewees, these are not sufficient to incentivise businesses to adopt measures to prevent and reduce food waste. Furthermore, interviews with civil society organisations reveal that donors find it more convenient to donate food through the general law on sponsorships than through the law on food waste, as fiscal advantages seem to be higher and the administrative burden lower.

Interviews with food receivers revealed that the high administrative burden triggered by the law also hinders its implementation. The law requires that food receivers have to report on each quantity of food received. As many food receivers are small NGOs with limited permanent staff and rely on volunteers, a high level of reporting is considered excessive even though its relevance is recognised. In this context, some food receivers prefer to use the sponsorship law for food donations, as it does not include complex reporting. While the use of the food sponsorship law allows food to be saved, it does not favour data collection on the prevention and reduction of food waste.

The uncertainty of the legal framework is another explanation for the limited implementation of the law. Food industry actors raised questions regarding the lack of clarity of the law about food donors' responsibilities on food safety after its donation. Even though the last version of the law tries to solve this issue by specifying that food receivers are '(. . .) in charge of the respect of the hygiene of the food receipt after the donation' (law 131/2020), it does not explicitly exclude food donors' responsibility in this area. This represents a barrier to food donation for businesses, in particular due to their fear of incurring into fines. In addition, food safety authorities from the various counties interpret the law differently, for example according to interviewees, in some cases food safety authorities accept that food is transferred for animal consumption, while in others they do not. Another issue that seems to create confusion among food donors and receivers regards the last day possible for receiving and commercialising or donating food received. Interviewees point out that while the food waste law allows food donation at any time in the previous ten days before the minimal validity date, regulations adopted by the food safety authority seem to forbid the transfer of food close to expiry in the last five days of the minimum validity term.

Despite the food waste law allowing NGOs to act as food receivers, they face difficulties in obtaining all the authorisations needed, as many of the rules in the food sector refer to businesses and not to NGOs. Often, public staff in charge of releasing these authorisations do not know exactly how to manage this issue, which causes different interpretations of the same rules across territories.

Uncertainty of the legal framework triggers an aversion to ambiguity for both food donors and receivers, which hinders the application of the law on food waste.

Another reason explaining the limited implementation of the law regards the reduced direct contacts between food receivers and businesses in the food sector. Even though the law provides for a register of food receivers available on the MADR website, according to interviewees, it is largely unknown among businesses in the food industry. Interviewees reveal that contacts with food donors occur mostly through personal contacts and through the food banks, which activate trust mechanisms favouring collaboration. However, according to interviewees, the capacity of food banks to act as intermediaries between food donors and receivers is still limited. Furthermore, the lack of opportunities for repeated interaction between food donors and receivers, which could activate trust mechanisms even in the absence of previous personal contacts, does not allow for building new trusted collaborations.

Limited waste management infrastructure at local level (Comisia Europeană 2019), which prevents the composting or transformation into biogas of food wasted, adds to the previous barriers to the implementation of the law.

It is also worth noting that most public debates related to the law on food waste focused more on food transfer than on other measures indicated by the law. These include awareness-raising and education targeted to businesses and consumers, which are equally important for saving food. While NGOs have always tackled this issue, public actions in this area are still limited. This may be due, on the one hand, to an issue of capacity (economic, knowledge, etc.) and on the other hand to the intensity of public institutions' interest in this topic. As pointed out by one of the interviewees, while the law put food waste prevention and reduction on the agenda of public institutions, much has yet to be done to get public officials really committed to the objectives of the law.

While some of the interviewees consider that the law on food waste 'represents only a point ticked off on the list of Romanian commitments deriving from EU policies' (interviewees), others acknowledge that, despite its limits, the law also presents some achievements. The main achievement is having put the topic of food waste prevention and reduction on the agenda of both public institutions and businesses in the food sector. At the beginning of the drafting process of the law, food saving was a topic for civil society organisations and partially for multinational companies as a consequence of their original group policy on food waste in Europe. Nowadays the topic is more diffused along the food chain businesses, even though it still has not managed to contaminate the entire sector. For instance, two of the interviewees point out that, in the last few years, they have also started to receive food from small neighbourhood shops or small producers, which were absent from this process previously. This increased interest (even though limited to some businesses) in food waste prevention and reduction has been triggered in particular by the higher prominence of the topic. This has been favoured by strong debates on the food law in the media, and by civil society organisations' strong lobby for the adoption of the law on food waste.

Another achievement of the law regards the design of a legal framework for food waste prevention and reduction. Even though the law is far from being perfect, it represents a starting point for a further development of the topic in particular in the context of the 2021 National Recovery and Resilience Plan.

The existence of a register that can put food donors and receivers in contact is another achievement of the law. If properly communicated, the register can be a useful tool for triggering trust mechanisms between food donors and receivers, as being registered and acknowledged by the Ministry certifies the reputation of food receivers.

Mandatory plans on measures proposed and taken for preventing and reducing food waste are also considered particularly relevant for saving food, on the condition that they are publicly available. Indeed, the adoption of plans on a complex topic such as food waste allows people to design concrete and specific actions towards a goal, harnessing their resources for accomplishing that plan. In addition, reporting on achieved results allows businesses to note how they can reach the complex objective of gradually preventing and reducing waste. Furthermore, their transparency could activate a pre-commitment mechanism, as once committed publicly towards the achievement of a specific goal, it would be much more difficult to give it up especially in a context where companies rely extensively on social rewards.

Exemplary practices in food waste prevention and reduction in Romania: the role of the Romanian civil society

The fact that the law on food waste has not yet fully achieved its objectives does not mean that food waste prevention and reduction has remained idle in Romania. For instance, food banks in Romania have redistributed over 5,076 tonnes of food for an overall amount of 2,758,294,168 RON and fed 135,000 people (Banca pentru Alimente website 2021).

As detailed previously, the Romanian civil society had a relevant role not only in making the topic of food waste salient for the Romanian context, but also in pushing it forward concretely through specific projects and interventions.

The fiches below present two examples of practices successful in preventing food waste, selected based on the interviews recorded and the literature review.

Table **9.2** Examples of practices successful in preventing food waste

Title	*CLUJ FOOD BANK*
Duration	*Since 2018*
Leader	*'Banca pentru Alimente Cluj'*

Territory	Cluj County and nearby counties (Sibiu, Alba Iulia, Bistriţa)
Objectives and rationality	Gather food in excess from businesses along the food chain to redistribute them to people in need.
	The Food Bank was developed originally as an action of the Food Waste Combat Project, developed by JCI Active Citizens Cluj, with the aim to contribute to preventing and reducing food waste in Romania. While initially the project focused on raising awareness on food waste and on educating people on how to prevent and reduce it, in 2017 the decision to create a food bank was taken in the context of the new law on food waste. The project was promoted by a series of people already involved in social and environmental projects in Cluj County. The creation of the Food Bank was carried out with the support of Lidl and the European Federation of Food Banks.
Target groups	Public and private social organisations targeted to people in need
Governance	While initially part of the Food Waste Combat project by JCI, the Food Bank became a completely autonomous organisation in 2019.
	The Bank acts in partnership with: Lidl; the European Federation of Food Banks; the Romanian Association of Food Banks of which is part; the Municipality of Cluj-Napoca; the Institute for Circular Economy and Environment (IRCEM); citizens. While Lidl and citizens mobilise financial resources to support the Bank, the other partners offer knowledge and legal resources.
	Until 2021, the Bank had established a partnership with 20 food producers, distributors and retailers, most of which are multinational companies or large Romanian companies. However, in the last few years the Bank has also partnered with small food businesses.
Actions/ measures/ activities	Collection of excess food and its redistribution to social organisations targeting people in need. The Food Bank also organises food donation campaigns—in particular, jointly with supermarket chains.
Main outcomes	• Around 120 organisations benefited from the food collected by the Bank in 2021. • The food saved from waste increased from 8.4 tonnes in 2018 to over 370 tonnes in 2021. • Voluntary work amounted to 1,000 hours in the first eight months of 2021. • Each one1 RON invested by the Bank corresponded to seven RON of social impact.
Main success factors	• Self-effectiveness of the team leading the project; the team developed confidence in its capacity to influence the fight against food waste in Cluj. • Strong support from the local community; the support was favoured by a good reputation of both the organisation promoting the project and the team leading it. It was also encouraged by the increase in the relevance of the food waste prevention and reduction topic in the city, as well as in the creation of a sense of community responsibility on this topic. This was achieved through awareness raising, and information and education activities put in place by the food waste combat project.

Title	CLUJ FOOD BANK
Duration	*Since 2018*
Leader	*'Banca pentru Alimente Cluj'*

Main success factors	• Active participation of relevant food donors in the Cluj area; this was favoured in particular by a number of issues. These include the gain in social image of companies, respect of international pre-commitments of the group (in particular for multinational companies), financial gains resulting from saving money for the neutralisation of food, and fiscal advantages offered by the law.
Links	https://foodwastecombat.com/ https://bancadealimentecluj.ro/

Title	SOMARO ASSOCIATION—SOCIAL STORE
Duration	*Since 2010*
Leader	*Somaro Association*

Territory	National
Objectives and rationality	Objectives: • Support people at risk of poverty to have access to primary goods (e.g. food, clothes) and to increase their self-effectiveness and dignity; • Enhance circular economy. The Romanian social stores draw on the experience of the Soma social stores in Austria. The concept behind it is based on vulnerable people increasing their self-effectiveness capacity if social organisations work with them, and not for them. For Somaro, this means offering people in need the opportunity to buy food, clothes and other items as any other person would. In addition, in a context of increasing consumerism, many products that could be reused but risk being thrown out due to faults in packaging, bad appearance, storing limits, expiry date, etc. Somaro collects these goods sells them at a nominal price to people in need. To prevent the reselling of products bought by clients, clients can buy products a maximum of three times a week and the value of their purchases cannot exceed a certain limit.
Target groups	People at risk of poverty selected with the support of public authorities.
Governance	Katharina Turnauer Privatstiftung, ERSTE Foundation, ISOVOLTA AG, and SoMA Austria have created the association, which is now an independent leader of the social stores. The Austrian Embassy in Romania, local municipalities and Social Care and Child Protection offices support Somaro. Somaro works in partnership with numerous food donors, most of which are multinational food companies.
Actions/ measures/ activities	• Collection, storage and commercialisation of excess food or food close to expiry to people in need at low prices; • Collection, storing and commercialisation of other products.
Main outcomes	• Three social stores opened in Romania. • Around 5,000 beneficiaries benefit from the Somaro social stores. • Over 1,000 families buy food daily from the social stores. • Collection and redistribution amounts to around 300–400 tonnes of food yearly.

(Continued)

Table **9.2** (Continued)

Title	*SOMARO ASSOCIATION—SOCIAL STORE*
Duration	*Since 2010*
Leader	*Somaro Association*
Main factors favouring effectiveness	• Financial incentives offered by the law, in particular the sponsorship law; • Social rewards for companies engaged in food donation; • Pre-commitments on food waste prevention and reduction (usually multinational companies, undertaken mainly at international level).
Links	http://somaro.org/

Conclusions and policy implications

With the strong push and support of the Romanian civil society, Romanian authorities faced food waste prevention and reduction, in particular through the adoption of a specific law on food waste. The law had a tortuous process being approved for the first time in 2016—but blocked until 2018 following pressure from food industry actors—and changed twice (in 2018 and 2020). The law became operational in 2019 with the adoption of the methodological norms.

The effectiveness of the law presents light and shadows. The law has contributed to providing a legal framework for food saving, to increase the salience of food waste prevention and reduction, and to creating tools for putting food receivers in contact with potential donors. However, its full effectiveness in preventing and reducing food waste has been hindered primarily by its delayed and limited application on the ground.

The limited implementation of the law is explained by various factors: uncertainty of the legal framework; limited financial advantages compared to other laws (e.g. sponsorship law); limited organic waste reuse infrastructure; limited businesses' interest in the food waste topic, despite some progress in the last years; and voluntary implementation of the law. However, not all interviewed actors acknowledge these latter two aspects as barriers to the implementation of the law. Furthermore, the higher focus on food transfer than on raising awareness on and educating businesses and consumers to save food also hinders the effectiveness of the law. The under-communication of the food register introduced by the law combined with the lack of dialogue opportunities between food receivers and potential food donors also hinders food saving, as it results in limited food donors' knowledge of, and trust in, food receivers. The lack of public measures supporting the development of food receiver networks and capacities also limits food saving in Romania, as food banks face difficulties in developing their capacity of managing large quantities of food donated and their geographical coverage. Finally, the lack of engagement of local actors (such as municipalities) in the design of the law has resulted in a lack or—at best limited—commitment towards supporting food waste prevention and reduction.

Nevertheless, several companies—particularly multinationals—have undertaken specific measures to fight food waste by selling food close to the expiry date at reduced prices or donating it to food receivers. Food donation has been favoured in particular by pre-commitments of businesses in fighting food waste. In particular, at the international level for multinational groups, this has involved fiscal advantages—especially in the context of the sponsorship law— and the good reputation of food receivers. When working with small businesses (e.g. neighbourhood shops, local farmers), the interest in community well-being triggered by the sense of belonging to the respective community represents a relevant driver for food donation.

The Romanian case provides us with several lessons to be considered for future policy actions. Food waste prevention and reduction necessitates a stable and clear legal and regulatory framework that leaves no room for different interpretations across public administrations involved in this area. In the presence of a high capacity to manage food in excess at the same level across the country, the legal provisions on saving food should be mandatory. In line with the EU recommendations to pay attention to the shelf life of products, the legal framework should clarify the use of 'best before' and 'use by' labels and encourage food transfer of food labelled 'best before' even after the expiry of its validity term. Furthermore, the legal framework should also introduce the 'polluter pays principle' to discourage food waste along the entire chain (i.e. from businesses in the food sector to consumers).

The Romanian case shows that the adoption of a legal framework is not sufficient for ensuring food waste prevention and reduction. The legal framework should be accompanied by integrated policy measures in various fields (e.g. education, waste management, economics, ICT). Raising awareness and knowledge on, and educating about, food waste prevention and reduction among businesses, public staff, and consumers is paramount for increasing food saving. This aim can be achieved through formal education, such as the introduction of the food waste prevention and reduction in the school curricula from kindergarten. It can also be achieved through informal education such as involvement of both children and adults in food production, messages on food waste prevention displayed in restaurants, and information campaigns within companies. In addition, guidelines on how to save food for consumers and businesses, exchanges of good practices between actors in the food sector, and online platforms on food waste prevention or reduction can be used.

Furthermore, the introduction of a monitoring system—also through specific apps—that can provide reliable data on food waste along the entire food chain (from businesses to consumers) is also particularly useful for increasing people's awareness of the food wasted or saved. The provision of financial incentives also sustains the uptake of food waste prevention and reduction measures. However, such incentives should be significant to trigger actors' interest in saving food. In addition, measures targeting the extension, development, and increase in the capacity of food receivers to manage food should also be adopted to incentivise food donations. Moreover, the improvement in sustainable waste management at the local level (e.g. through biogas or composting infrastructure) can also contribute to food waste reduction.

The adoption of an integrated policy approach requires a multilevel governance framework. Thus, wide partnerships should be created, including

Table 9.3 Social mechanisms for triggering food waste prevention and reduction in the Romanian context

Level of deployment	Mechanism	Brief definition	Example in the Romanian case
Fully deployed mechanisms	Focusing events	Events that catalyse attention on a specific policy issue	The 2014 European Year against Food Waste: an opportunity to put the food waste topic on the public agenda
	Salience	A feature of some things to make them stand out and attract people's attention	Increased attention to the food waste topic following its strong presence in the media
	Sense of belonging	Need to get attention to and from others; feel part of a specific group	Small producers/retailers engaged in food donations following their sense of belonging to the community
	Reputation	People's higher adhesion to a certain initiative in the presence of a reputable source	Good reputation of the promoters of the Cluj Food Bank enhanced food donations and people's participation in the initiative
	Pre-commitment	Method of self-control used to reduce preferred choices at a later stage	Food donations of multinationals in Romania adapted to respect commitments set by their international groups
	Stick and carrots	Provision of incentives and sanctions to determine changes in behaviours	Financial incentives (in particular, the sponsorship law) enhanced food donations
	Zero-risk bias	Preference for certainty	Fear of food businesses of incurring fines in the case of food donations due to uncertain provisions of the law on food waste combined with the 'paper-based' mentality of public staff favoured food neutralisation
	Trust	Reliance on the actions of another party	The lack of trust of food donors in receivers regarding food conditions after donations combined with zero-risk bias increased preference for food neutralisation
Potential mechanisms	Emotions	Intense feeling towards an issue/object producing behavioural changes	Triggering childhood memories and emotions related to experience in the countryside can induce good food habits
	Naming and shaming	Public disclosure of a failing/deviant party followed by a public sanction, such as shaming	The publication of plans for food waste prevention and reduction, and their results, may encourage businesses to reach their targets to avoid naming and shaming
	Feedback	Information on results	Reporting on plans for food waste prevention and reduction can enhance encourage commitment of food actors over a long period of time

Source: Author's elaboration based on interviews and literature

local public bodies and citizens. Partnerships should be based on transparency, accountability, and equal participation of all actors. Furthermore, to foster trust and coordination between the various actors along the food chain, intersectoral and multilevel steering groups should be established.

Finally, the Romanian case also provides indications on social mechanisms that trigger virtuous behaviours in food waste prevention and reduction, to be considered in designing policies in this area.

References

Literature

Antoneac, Andreea, Ionut L. Petre, Maria Nica, and Adrian S. Iana. 2019. "Food Waste Analysis in Romania in Comparison to the European Union." *Annals of Faculty of Economics* 1 (1): 227–39.

Banca Pentru Alimente. 2021. https://bancapentrualimente.ro/.

Cantaragiu, Ramona. 2019. "The Impact of Gender on Food Waste at the Consumer Level." *Studia Universitatis 'Vasile Goldis' Arad. Economics Series* 29 (4): 41–57. www.sciendo.com/article/10.2478/sues-2019-0017.

Caprita, Diana. 2016. "Reducing Food Waste in Order to Become the Zero Hunger Generation." *International Conference on Competitiveness of Agro-food and Environmental Economy Proceedings, The Bucharest University of Economic Studies* 5: 187–201. https://ideas.repec.org/a/aes/icafee/v5y2016p187-201.html.

Centrul Naţional de Evaluare şi Promovare a Stării de Sănătate, Institutul Naţional de Sănătate Publică, Centrul Regional de Sanatate Publica Targu Mures, Direcţia de Sănătate Publică Judeţeană Suceava. 2019. "Analiză de Situaţie." www.dspsv.ro/uploads/PromovareaSanatatii/Alimentatie%202019/Analiza%20de%20situatie%202019%20-%20Ziua%20Nationala%20a%20Alimentatiei%20si%20a%20Combaterii%20Risipei%20Alimentare.pdf.

Comisia Europeană. 2019. "Evaluarea punerii în aplicare a politicilor de mediu." Raport de ţară. https://ec.europa.eu/environment/eir/pdf/report_ro_ro.pdf.

Dumitru, Ionel, and Alexandru-Gabriel Burghiu. 2019. "Romanian Food Waste Analysis." *New Trends in Sustainable Business and Consumption Basiq International Conference Proceedings*, 441–48. https://basiq.ro/wp-content/uploads/2019/06/BASIQ-2019-Conference-proceedings.pdf.

Dumitru, Oana M., Corneliu S. Iorga, and Gabriel Mustatea. 2021. "Food Waste Along the Food Chain in Romania: An Impact Analysis." *Foods* (10): 1–11. https://doi.org/10.3390/foods10102280.

Ecopolis. 2019. "Studiu de fundamentare a politicilor publice privind risipa alimentară." Unpublished Report.

EPC Consultanţă de Mediu. 2016. "Studiul privind risipa de hrană în România, pe lanţul de distribuţie, de la producători şi importatori la consumatorii din mediul urban." http://foodwaste.ro/wp-content/uploads/2016/11/Studiu-privind-risipa-de-hran%C4%83-%C3%AEn-Rom%C3%A2nia-_MMV_sinteza.docx.

European Parliament. 2016. "Tackling Food Waste. The EU's Contribution to a Global Issue." www.europarl.europa.eu/RegData/etudes/BRIE/2016/593563/EPRS_BRI(2016)593563_EN.pdf.

Guvernul României. 2021. "Ordonanţă de urgenţă nr. 92 din 19 august 2021 privind regimul deşeurilor." https://legislatie.just.ro/Public/DetaliiDocumentAfis/245846.

Iorga, Corneliu S., Laura Apostol, Nastasia Belc, Caludia E. Mosoiu, Lavinia M. Berca, Oana M. Niculae, and Mona E. Popa. 2017. "Profile of High Risk Wasting Food Consumer in Romania." *Scientific Bulletin. Series F. Biotechnologies*, no. XXI: 301–7. https:// bioresurse.ro/blogs/rezultate/profile-of-high-risk-wasting-food-consumer-in-romania.

Ministerului Agriculturii și Dezvoltării Rurale. 2014. "Planul Național de Acțiune pentru combaterea." *Risipei Alimentare*. www.madr.ro/docs/ind-alimentara/risipa_alimentara/ planul-national-de-actiune-pt-combaterea-risipei-alimentare-in-ro.pdf.

National Institute of Statistics. 2020. "Relative at-risk-of-poverty rate by gender." http:// statistici.insse.ro:8077/tempo-online/#/pages/tables/insse-table.

Parlamentul României. 2016a. "Legea nr. 217 din 17 noiembrie 2016 (*republicată*) privind diminuarea risipei alimentare." https://legislatie.just.ro/Public/DetaliiDocument/183792.

———. 2016b. "Raport asupra propunerii legislative privind diminuarea risipei alimentare." www.cdep.ro/pls/proiecte/upl_pck2015.proiect?idp=16473.

———. 2017. "Ordonanță de urgență nr. 45 din 30 iunie 2017 pentru suspendarea Legii nr. 217/2016 privind diminuarea risipei alimentare." https://legislatie.just.ro/Public/ DetaliiDocumentAfis/190679.

———. 2018. "Lege nr. 200 din 20 iulie 2018 pentru modificarea și completarea Legii nr. 217/2016 privind diminuarea risipei alimentare." https://legislatie.just.ro/Public/ DetaliiDocumentAfis/203111.

———. 2019. "Normele metodologice de aplicare a Legii nr. 217/2016 privind diminuarea risipei alimentare." https://legislatie.just.ro/Public/DetaliiDocument/232442.

———. 2020. "Lege nr. 131 din 15 iulie 2020 pentru completarea alin. (8) al art. 270 din Legea nr. 227/2015 privind Codul fiscal și pentru modificarea Legii nr. 217/2016 privind diminuarea risipei alimentare." https://legislatie.just.ro/Public/DetaliiDocumentAfis/227838.

Pocol, Cristina B., Margaux Pinoteau, Antonio Amuza, Adriana Burlea-Schiopoiu, and Alexandra-Ioana Glogovet. 2020. "Food Waste Behavior Among Romanian Consumers: A Cluster Analysis." *Sustainability* (12): 1–17. www.mdpi.com/2071-1050/12/22/9708.

Romanian Government. 2018. "Romania's Sustainable Development Strategy 2030." http:// dezvoltaredurabila.gov.ro/web/wp-content/uploads/2019/03/Romanias-Sustainable-Development-Strategy-2030.pdf.

UN. 2021. "Food Waste Index." Report 2021. www.unep.org/resources/report/unep-food-waste-index-report-2021.

Interviews

- Representative of Mai Mult Verde Association, October 2021
- Representative of Mai Bine Association, October 2021
- Representative of Somaro Association, October 2021
- Representative of the Cluj Food Bank, October 2021
- Representative of Romalimenta, October 2021

10 Japan's practices on food waste reduction

Chen Liu

Introduction

Reducing food loss and waste (FLW) has become a global issue. Japan was one of the first countries to address FLW issues by launching a policy initiative focused on FLW management in 2000. Following the introduction of this initiative, the amount of FLW initially decreased, but this has levelled off in recent years (Liu et al. 2016). FLW remains a critical issue, owing to the country's low food self-sufficiency rate and shortage of available landfill sites for waste disposal. It is estimated that the annual amount of FLW generation in Japan is 25.31 million tonnes, of which the amount of *food loss*, which is food that can be eaten but is thrown away, was 6.00 million tonnes in fiscal year 2018 (Ministry of the Environment 2021). Out of these 6.00 million tonnes, 3.24 million tonnes came from the business sector, mainly from substandard products, returned goods, unsold goods and leftovers, and 2.76 million tonnes came from the household sector, mainly from leftovers, untouched food (direct disposal), and over-peeling (excessive removal). To achieve the Sustainable Development Goal (SDG) 12.3, Japan has set a national target of halving *food loss* from the total in 2000 by the year 2030. This chapter will introduce an overview of policies related to FLW (Food Waste Recycling Act in 2000 and Act on Promotion Food Loss and Waste Reduction in 2019), trends on FLW generation, and good practices being undertaken to reduce FLW in Japan by governments at both the national and local levels as well as by the private sector.

Definition of the 'Food Loss' and 'Food Waste' in Japan

According to the SOFA (The State of Food and Agriculture 2019) published by the Food and Agriculture Organization of the United Nations (FAO 2019),

(1) Food Loss is the reduction in the quantity or quality of food caused by the decisions or actions of food suppliers in a chain excluding retailers, food service operators, and consumers; and
(2) Food Waste refers to the reduction in quantity and quality of food caused by the decisions and actions of retailers, foodservice operators, and consumers.

DOI: 10.4324/9781003226932-14

However, in Japan, the term '*food loss*' (食品ロス) is used to refer to 'food that is still edible but is discarded for some reason', regardless of the source. It consists of three categories: 'direct disposal' (untouched food), 'leftover food' and 'excess removal' (e.g. peeling vegetables too thickly). It was divided into two main categories, business and household, thereby combining the FAO definitions of 'Food Loss' and 'Food Waste', but edible and possibly avoidable. To avoid misunderstanding, it will be henceforth referred to as *food loss*.

Another technical term often used in Japan is '*food waste*' (食品廃棄物). The Food Recycling Law, which is explained below, defines '*food waste*' as 'food that is disposed of after it has been used for food or without being used for food' and 'food that is obtained as a secondary product in the process of manufacturing, processing or cooking food and that cannot be used for food'. This includes animal and vegetable residues from food manufacturing and processing, expired food that is left unsold and discarded at the distribution stage, cooking scraps, and leftovers from the food service industry and households. This is the sum of the FAO definitions of 'Food Loss' and 'Food Waste', but not including on-farm and post-harvest 'Food Loss'.

Historical evolution of government policies/actions related to FLW

There are two laws directly related to FLW: the Law for Promotion of Recycling and Utilization of Recycled Food Resources (Food Recycling Law) enacted in 2000 (MAFF 2013), and the Act on Promotion Food Loss and Waste Reduction (Food Loss Reduction Promotion Law) enacted in 2019 (e-GOV 2019). The Food Recycling Law was enacted with the aim of reducing and recycling '*food waste*' generated by food-related businesses (manufacturers, wholesalers, retailers, restaurants, etc.). In the event that a business's efforts are significantly inadequate, recommendations, public announcements, and orders are issued, and penalties are also stipulated. On the other hand, the Food Loss Reduction Promotion Law stipulates the roles of the national government, local governments, businesses, and consumers in promoting the reduction of *food loss*. While the Food Recycling Law is a law for businesses, the Food Loss Reduction Promotion Law is a law aiming at 'a national movement in which various entities cooperate'. The law is based on the idea of a 'national movement of various actors', which includes national and local government support for consumer and business education, knowledge dissemination and awareness-raising, support for initiatives, and support for food bank activities. Both laws are soft laws that aim to promote voluntary initiatives rather than regulatory approaches.

Food Recycling Law

Japan has developed a Fundamental Plan for Establishing a Sound Material-Cycle Society (2003, revised in 2008, 2013 and 2018) based on the Basic Act for Establishing a Sound Material-Cycle Society (Law number 110 of the year

2000, hereinafter referred to as the 'Basic Act') and has implemented related measures in a comprehensive and structured manner, in order to develop a 'sound material-cycle society' where the consumption of natural resources is reduced and the environmental load is minimised to the extent possible. Under this umbrella act, several specific recycling laws have been developed, including containers and packaging, home appliances, food waste, construction waste, end-of-life vehicles, and small home appliances.

As one of the specific recycling laws, the Food Recycling Law was enacted in 2001, and revised in 2007 and 2015. The Food Recycling Law sets out rules for the reduction of food waste, which includes both edible and inedible waste, and the recycling of food waste, so that waste can be used as animal feed and fertiliser, or to generate energy. The usages are prioritised in the order of animal feed, fertilisers, oil and fat products, and finally, 'heat recovery' through methanation, if all other treatments are difficult. A target for efforts on implementation of the food waste recycling rate by food related businesses was set in 2000. In addition, the law requires companies with large volumes of food waste generation (more than one million tonnes per year) to conduct mandatory regular reporting on food waste-related data (food waste generation, sales, recycle amount, recycling rates) to the Ministry of the Environment (MOE) every year since 2007. Moreover, the law sets 'reference generation units' (from April 2014 to March 2019) in order to further reduce the generation of food waste for 31 specific business type (meat product manufacturers, noodle manufacturers, prepared food manufacturers, food/drink wholesalers, various food retailers, convenience stores, dining/restaurants, bars, cafes, fast food stores, hotels, school lunch and hospital food groups, etc.)

In addition, to promote recycling of food waste into feed and fertiliser, the Japanese government has introduced a certification and registration system for businesses that produce feed and fertiliser from food waste including the 'Eco-feed' registration system and the 'Food Recycle Mark' certification system. As of March 2018, 28 companies had been certified for 49 products under the 'Eco-feed' label, and 13 fertiliser production companies had been licensed under the 'Food Recycle Mark'. Furthermore, based on the revised Food Recycling Law in 2007, a 'Recycling Loop' has been promoted, and this requires food-related business to purchase farm products grown using food waste-derived compost/animal feed. The 'Recycling Loop' is a kind of a certification system to create a business plan for a waste exchange network on food recycling. Having been certified as part of the Recycling Loop, companies in the loop are exempt from requiring authorised permission as waste transporters under the Public Cleansing and Waste Management Law, resulting in 50 companies coming under exemption (as of the end of April 2019).

Food Loss *Reduction Promotion Law*

While the Food Recycling Law has not been very effective in either addressing the downstream of the food supply chain, or involving consumers and households, the purpose of the Food Loss Reduction Promotion Law aims to comprehensively promote the reduction of *food loss* by establishing basic policies as 'social efforts to prevent food that can still be eaten from being wasted' in cooperation with a wide range of stakeholders. The role of the government is to comprehensively promote the reduction of *food loss* by establishing a basic policy, and then local governments must endeavour to establish a *food loss* reduction promotion plan based on the law. As for some basic measures, the national government and local public entities are charged with carrying out dissemination and awareness-raising, providing support for the efforts of food-related businesses, etc., carrying out surveys and other research, and supporting food bank activities.

Food Loss *Reduction Target*

In the Fourth Basic Plan for Establishing a Sound Material-Cycle Society (decided by the Cabinet in June 2018), the reduction target for household *food loss* (to halve the 2000 level by 2030) is set, while the same reduction target for business *food loss* across the different stages of the supply chain is set in the Food Recycling Law (announced in July 2019), including reducing *food waste* associated with recycling by 95% for food manufacturers, 75% for wholesalers, 60% for retailers, and 50% for restaurants by March 2025.

National Movement for the Reduction of Food Loss *(No-Foodloss Project)*

On October 2013, the Ministry of Agriculture, Forestry and Fisheries launched the No-*Foodloss* Project as a cooperative initiative between six Ministries in Japan: Consumer Affairs Agency, Government of Japan (CAA), Cabinet Office, Ministry of Education, Culture, Sports, Science and Technology: Japan (MEXT), Ministry of Agriculture, Forestry and Fisheries (MAFF), Ministry of Economy, Trade and Industry (METI) and Ministry of the Environment (MOE). The No-*Foodloss* Project aims at reforming the behaviour and raising the consciousness of all food stakeholders, by supporting the adoption of loss reduction models in every step of the food supply chain where loss is generated. The actions taken include providing support to initiatives by local governments and to food banks, promoting the use of doggy bags, and launching a series of pilot projects. These include trial attempts to loosen deliver-by dates, to extend use-by dates and to develop strategic communication among retailers, mass media, and SNS services to develop new consumer awareness strategies.

The No-*Foodloss* Project makes use of a campaign character called 'Rosu-non' (Loss-non) in some cafeterias, restaurants, convenience stores, and super-markets in order to appeal to the wider public, advocate for change in habits, and provide support to national initiatives. In addition, October has been designated as '*Food Loss* Reduction Month' and 30 October as '*Food Loss* Reduction Day' to promote and raise awareness of efforts to reduce *food loss* in an intensive and regular manner.

Current status of FLW in Japan

In Japan, the related statistical data on food consumption and food waste generation can be downloaded from the Portal Site for Official Statistics of Japan (e-Stat 2021). For example, the data on food demand are based on the food balance sheet compiled by MAFF. The data on food waste generated by the manufacturing, wholesaling, retail, restaurant/catering industries, and by households are a result of the mandatory reporting requirement put into effect following the revision of Japan's Food Recycling Law in 2007. This was based on survey data and reports found in the Statistical Survey on Food Waste, produced by the Statistics Department of MAFF and MOE. The data on end-of-life management of food waste are based on the statistical data on waste management produced by the Statistics Department of MOE. It is worth noting that the annual data are based on Japan's fiscal year (FY), which starts in April and ends in March of the following year.

On the basis of the above officially published data, the current status of food waste in Japan in 2018 is summarised in Figure 10.1, and the trend of recycling rate in food industry (food manufacture, food wholesaler, food retailer, and restaurant) between 2008 and 2019 is shown in Figure 10.2. Highlights are as follows:

1)   It is estimated that Japan discarded approximately 25.31 million tonnes of food annually (including 8.30 million tonnes of by-products such as soybean meal and bran which have been sold commercially as animal feed or fertiliser). Out of these, 17.65 million tonnes are from the food industry (7.69 million tonnes are collected as general waste from business activities), while 7.66 tonnes are from households.

2)   Although the generation of FLW by the food industry is a major contribution to the total FLW, the reducing and recycling rate is higher than 80%. Out of those 17.65 million tonnes of FLW generated by the food industry, 9% is reduced through dehydration treatment, 51% is recycled as feed, 12% is recycled as fertiliser, 8% is recycled as energy (waste-to-energy, etc.), and only 19% is treated by incineration or landfill as waste.

3)   Out of those 17.65 million tonnes of FLW generated by the food industry, the food manufacturing industry accounted for the largest share at 14.00 million tonnes (79%), followed by the food service industry at 2.15 million tonnes (12%), food retailing at 1.22 million tonnes (7%), and food wholesaling at 0.28 million tonnes (2%), with recycling rates of 95%, 31%, 51%, and 62%, respectively, in 2018. Although the contribution of food manufacturing is substantial, the recycling rate is also high. On the other hand, the disposal rate remains quite high in the catering activities and retail, despite the recycling rate improving since 2010.

4)   The amount of food waste generated by households is estimated at 7.66 million tonnes, out of which 93% is treated by incineration or landfill as waste while only 7% is recycled.

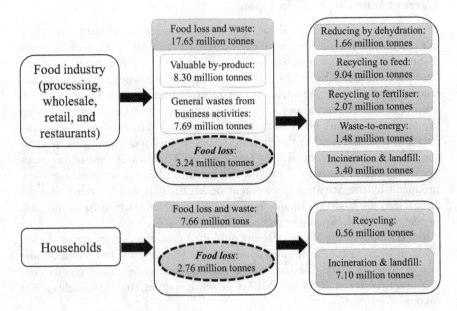

Figure 10.1 Generation and treatment status of food loss and waste in Japan in 2018.
(Data source: MOE (2021))

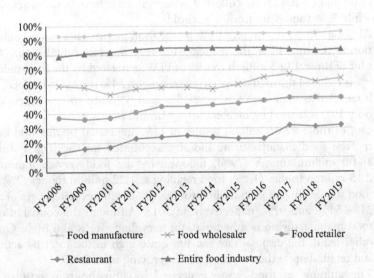

Figure 10.2 Trend of recycling rate in food industry between 2008 and 2019.
(Data source: MOE (2021))

5) Of the total 6.00 million tonnes related to *food loss*, 3.24 million tonnes came from the food industry and another 2.76 million tonnes from individual households; as an average of 47 kg per person per year, 130 g per person per day, roughly equivalent to a daily bowl of rice.

Good practices by local government, business, and civil society

The following practices have mainly been compiled on the basis of examples presented on MAFF official websites (MAFF 2021) and the Consumer Affairs Agency (MAFF 2021).

Practices by local government

Local governments are implementing various initiatives to reduce *food loss*. For example,

(1) Oki Town, located in southern Fukuoka Prefecture in the Kyushu region of Japan, introduced a scheme to recycle kitchen waste as local resource and turn it into liquid fertiliser for farming. The Oki Recycling Center, 'Kururun', a biogas plant equipped with a methane fermentation system, started to operate in the town in October, 2006. All of the organic waste generated in the town (both by households and businesses), as well as human waste (including septic tank sludge) is separated and collected. Methane fermentation is carried out at Kururun, where the electricity produced by methane gas covers 70% of the electricity demand for the facility. Nicknamed Kuruppi, digestive liquid is used as fertiliser by farmers and in private gardens in the town. Rice (Kan-no-megumi, Circle of Blessings), oil (Kan-no-kaori, Circle of Flavor), and vegetables grown using Kuruppi are used for school lunches or preferentially sold to town residents at reasonable prices. What town residents eat turns into human waste and septic tank sludge, and returns again to Kururun (Liu, Onogawa, and Premakumara 2018).

(2) Fukui Prefecture was the first prefecture in Japan to launch the 'Oishii Fukui Tabekiri Undo (Eat All You Can)' movement, a campaign to encourage people to prepare and eat up dishes using delicious local ingredients. It includes (1) cooking delicious food at home, in hotels, restaurants, etc., using Fukui's ingredients; (2) eating up the cooked dishes; and (3) if there are any leftovers, they can be used at home as new ingredients in new dishes, or taken home to eat at home after eating out. The local government has been working together with the Fukui Prefectural Federation of Women's Associations, the largest consumer organisation in the prefecture to raise awareness among citizens. Specific calls to citizens include the following at home to (1) check the fridge before you go out shopping; (2) buy only what you need, in bulk or by weight; (3) once a week set aside a

'fridge clear out day' (a day to use up food that is nearing its expiry date); (4) find out how much you can eat (the right amount); (5) know your family's schedule and cook only what you need; (6) use up food by making use of parts of it that have always been thrown away; and (7) store the food in a way that allows you to eat it all. When eating out, (1) if you feel you cannot eat a full portion, ask 'Can I have a small portion'? Additionally, if there is an ingredient you are unable eat, ask the waiter, 'Can you leave out the "-"'? (2) If you can't finish all the food you ordered, ask the waiter if you can take it home. During a banquet, (1) inform the restaurant of the gender and age of the people present, and order the right amount of food; (2) allow time to eat without leaving your seat, for example 30 minutes at the beginning and ten minutes at the end of the banquet; (3) divide the food from the table with the most food left over to the table with the least food; (4) the organiser or host should ask the guests to 'leave no food uneaten' during the banquet; (5) make sure that no food is left over, for example by ordering food that is not at risk of food poisoning to be packed to go. The campaign has been running since 2006, and since its implementation, the percentage of *food loss* in combustible waste has decreased from 11.6% in 2009 to 9.4% in 2014. In 2016, Fukui Prefecture called on all local governments in Japan to join the network, and the National Delicious Food Campaign Network Council was established. The main pillars of the network's activities are information-sharing and dissemination and national joint campaigns, and as of 15 June 2020, 422 local governments have joined the network.

(3) According to a citizen's questionnaire survey conducted in 2014, responses to the question 'Why do we have untouched food'? included 'I bought too much food and could not use it all' and 'I forgot to keep it in the refrigerator'. In order to reduce the amount of 'untouched food', especially to prevent people from forgetting to use food, which is close to its best-before dates, or which is easily damaged such as meat and vegetables, Yokohama City in Kanagawa Prefecture designated the 10th and 30th of every month as days to check the contents of the refrigerator, thus implementing the 'Refrigerator 10/30 Movement'. This campaign includes (1) the distribution of publicity leaflets and magnets; (2) the distribution of magnet sheets to attach to refrigerators and a monitoring survey; and (3) a call on Twitter for people to check their fridges on the 10th and 30th of each month. According to the results of the monitoring survey, it was found that about three-quarters of respondents checked their refrigerators on the 10th or 30th of each month, as they were reminded by the magnets stuck on their fridges, and that about 68% of the respondents used the food they found when it was near the expiration date or when it was damaged. It shows that the 'Refrigerator 10/30' campaign has a positive effect on reducing *food loss* in households. In addition, on the 10th and 30th of each month, the City of Yokohama tweets to its 4,000 followers on the Yokohama Environment Twitter feed to remind them to check their refrigerators and to introduce 'Recipes for using up seasonal vegetables'.

(4) Matsumoto City in Nagano Prefecture has been promoting the 'Let's Eat Up Everything! 30/10 Campaign', which is intended to reduce leftovers by encouraging people to remain seated at banquet events and enjoy eating for at least 30 minutes after the toast and ten minutes before the banquet ends. The city distributes logoed stickers and coasters to restaurants and halls to raise awareness, and also recognises restaurants and companies that encourage *food loss* reduction as official members of the campaign. In addition, the city recently started a new initiative calling on restaurants to offer smaller portions of the dishes on their menu for the elderly and those who cannot eat much. These are known as 'platinum menus' and are posted on the city's website. These campaigns serve as opportunities for citizens to revisit their everyday practices (banquets in this case) to see where and why losses are generated. Similar movements to the 30/10 Campaign are spreading nationwide.

Practices by business

(1) Efforts of the food industry to review the 'one-third rule'

The 'one-third rule' is a widespread commercial practice in the food distribution sector in Japan, and has been identified as one of the main reasons for FLW generation. This rule stipulates that the period from the date of manufacture to the best-before date is divided equally into thirds between the food manufacturer, retailer and consumer in the food distribution process, with the first third being the delivery deadline and the second third being the sales deadline (Figure 10.3 (a)). Incidentally, in Japan, whether a 'best-before' date or a 'use-by' date should be indicated on processed foods is determined by the 'ease of deterioration' of the food, according to the 'Guidelines for the indication of food expiration dates' established by the Ministry of Health, Labour and Welfare (MHLW) and the Ministry of Agriculture, Forestry and Fisheries (MAFF) in 2005. The 'best-before' date is set for foods whose quality is considered to be less susceptible to deterioration, while the 'use-by' date is set for foods whose quality is considered to be more susceptible to deterioration. If the wholesaler fails to deliver the goods to the retailer within the first third delivery deadline, or the retailer fails to sell the goods within the second third sales deadline, the goods are returned, removed or disposed of, even though there is still plenty of time left for them to be used. The one-third rule has been implemented as a commercial practice due to the fact that Japanese consumers are overly conscious of best-before dates, and manufacturers are trying to reduce the risk. In response to this problem, in 2012, the Working Team for the Commercial Practices Examination for the Reduction of Food Loss and Waste (hereafter Working Team) was established to review the business practice of the 'one-third rule' and create a policy-based solution for a delivery deadline among food manufacturers/wholesalers/retailers, in collaboration with the national government (Cabinet Office, Consumer Affairs Agency (CAA), MAFF, Ministry of the Environment (MOE), Ministry of Economy, Trade and Industry (METI) and private enterprises. The Working Team recommends easing the allowable delivery period to half (Figure 10.3 (b)), and urges companies to take action. For the manufacturer, this has the advantage of avoiding wasteful production and also reducing inventories. On the other hand, extending the delivery deadline is a major concern for retailers, as it also means shortening the sales deadline.

MAFF has presented the results of a demonstration in which the delivery deadline was reduced from one-third to one-half. The results showed that food manufacturers were able to reduce the production of perishable products and the disposal of unshipped products, while distribution centres were able to reduce the number of expired products and the number of returned products. At retail outlets, where there was concern about shortened best-before dates, there was no increase in the disposal of beverages and confectionery with a shelf life of 180 days or more. In addition, according to a survey conducted by the Institute of Distribution Economics in 2016, when 17 food retailers who relaxed the delivery deadlines for processed food products were surveyed, 0% of the respondents reported that the 'discount loss rate' and 'waste loss rate' had worsened. The empirical results show that this is an effective means of reducing waste.

According to a survey by the Working Team, 186 retailers have relaxed their delivery deadlines in 2021. In addition to the growing trend in food

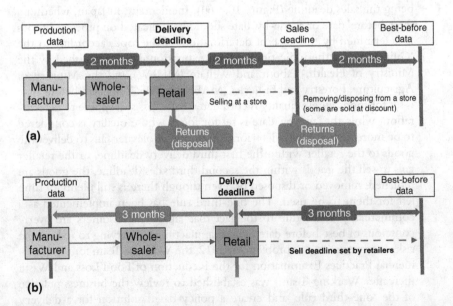

Figure 10.3 Review of 'one-third rule' (in the case that the best-before period is six months).
(a) Current (b) Revised

supermarkets, the relaxation is also beginning to spread to drugstores and pharmacies. In addition, the number of retailers who have eased delivery deadlines for a wide range of processed food items (retailers who have eased delivery deadlines for soft drinks, confectionery with a best-before date of 180 days or more, cup noodles, bagged noodles, retort pouches, and all other processed food items) came to 83, or 44.6% of the total. Consumer cooperatives and convenience stores accounted for more than 60% of the total, indicating that ambitious efforts are being made.

However, there is a variation in the adoption status by regional and product characteristics, and the burden on wholesalers and manufacturers at the source of shipments is also an issue. Given this situation, it is important to take a cross-institution, holistic approach to reduce food waste throughout the supply chain and to gain consumer understanding.

(2) Efforts of the food industry to review best-before dates

Efforts to review best-before dates by not only extending the best-before date (163 items in 2015) but also changing the display from best-before date to best-before month (115 items in 2015) has been implemented by the food industry.

In Japan, best-before dates are set by multiplying the actual number of days a product lasts by a 'safety factor', which is often 0.8. In other words, the best-before date is 20% less than the period of time in which the product is normally good to eat. One of the main reasons for the short shelf life is the aim of the manufacturer to reduce the risk, as can be seen from the name 'safety factor'. Once a product has left the hands of the manufacturer, it is difficult to trace how it is stored at each stage of distribution, sale, and consumer. This means that the food is not always stored in the most appropriate way as envisaged at the time of production. Therefore, as a safety measure, manufacturers set an excessively short shelf life.

The best-before date labels on many products are shown in years, months, and days. On the other hand, retailers may not be able to deliver products because they have an earlier best-before date than the products in their stock (another commercial practice existing in Japan that not to deliver products with a best-before date older than that of products already delivered), which increases the likelihood that the products that cannot be delivered will be disposed of. Therefore, it is expected that the best-before date will be indicated in a generalised manner, such as in years and month or daily (keeping the yearly, monthly, and daily indications, but unifying the indication of the day, e.g. in units of ten days) so that the best-before dates of the products in stock and the products to be delivered will be the same, which will lead to a reduction of *food losses*.

As of 2021, the number of companies that have introduced the 'best-before month' is 233, with efforts spreading among manufacturers of canned and bottled foods, retort pouches, soft drinks, confectionery, and seasonings.

In addition, MAFF has also designated 30 October as the 'National Day for Reviewing Business Practices' and announced the companies that are working on easing delivery deadlines and generalising the labelling of best-before dates. There is a growing momentum in the public and private sectors to review business practices. At the same time, the Consumer Affairs Agency has announced that it will launch a campaign from 1 February 2021 to raise awareness of the fact that 'best-before' dates are 'best-before' dates for tasty food.

(3)   Product Demand Forecasting Business (Japan Weather Association 2021)

From ice cream and soft drinks to 'oden' hotpot and steamed buns, there are many products for which demand is greatly influenced by weather and temperature. Not only do retailers have to predict sales and decide how much to order in advance, but wholesalers also have to predict how much retailers will order. The Japan Weather Association uses weather data to provide highly accurate forecast information on demand, and promotes the sharing of information between manufacturers, wholesalers, and retailers, using social networking services such as Twitter to incorporate consumers' experiences of the day, such as whether they are feeling 'hot' or 'cold', in its analysis to improve the accuracy of demand forecasts. Tofu, for example, takes two days from the time the soybeans are soaked in water to the time the product is ready. Because of its short shelf life, supermarkets place orders of tofu the day before they are due to stock up, but manufacturers have to anticipate orders from retailers before they can start production. The tendency of each company to overestimate the amount of orders and production due to the fear of running out of stock also increases the amount of waste. Disparate demand forecasting in the manufacturing, wholesale, and retail sectors contributes to *food losses*. In response to these problems, the provision of highly accurate demand forecast information using weather data and the sharing of information between manufacturers, wholesalers, and retailers is being promoted.

By using not only weather forecast data but also big data such as sales data and analysing it with the latest technology such as AI, it is possible to predict the quantity of goods needed in the future. Shops also manage their sales accordingly, but it is inevitable that unpredictable factors such as the weather will result in surpluses. However, manufacturers, wholesalers, and retailers can cooperate with each other to prevent shortages and reduce stock levels by working together on everything from product planning and sales planning to demand forecasting and stock replenishment. It has been reported that food waste from Yose-Tofu has been reduced by 30% per year through the use of the Japan Weather Association's service.

Practices by civil society

(1)   Food banks

Food bank organisations collect uneaten food from food producers, wholesalers, and shops, and distribute it to social-welfare organisations, such as orphanages and self-support facilities for the homeless and disabled. They collect and distribute uneaten food, including food that cannot be sold due to mislabelling, broken packaging, dead stock of limited-time sales, and surplus stock. Food bank organisations in Japan have a relatively short history. The first food bank started its activities around the year 2000 (Second Harvest Japan 2012), and the number of food banks increased rapidly in the second half of the 2010s, and now there are more than 110 food banks operating in Japan. They deal with 7,398 tonnes of food a year, which is a small portion of the total amount of food wasted. The reasons for this are considered to be: (1) lack of infrastructure (offices, warehouses, delivery vehicles, etc.); (2) lack of manpower; (3) lack of operating costs; (4) lack of know-how; (5) lack of recognition; (6) legal risks associated with food donation; and (7) lack of cooperation with the government (CAA 2019).

However, recently, especially since the outbreak of COVID-19, the importance of food banks has increased. This is due to the fact that emerging problems of people in need of social support, such as the homeless, underage orphans, and single-parent families. The government made a guideline about how to handle food donated to food banks, in order to ensure food quality and traceability, so that food banks get high reliability from food-related businesses and can handle more food.

(2) Food drive

A 'food drive' is an initiative to collect untouched food from households and donate it to those in need. The main differences between a food drive and a food bank are: (1) the food drive is for items that are not used at home, which are not necessarily 'left over'; (2) prepared foods from supermarkets and convenience stores are not eligible. Donations to food banks and food drives are not yet common in Japan, but in recent years many local authorities have organised food drives and some have set up permanent food drive boxes. Food drives are also held at businesses, supermarkets, temples, and shrines. This is a growing activity in which individuals can also participate, which could work as a medium to connect people with the less visible problems that affect the most vulnerable people in the local community. Some examples of specific initiatives include

- Consumer Co-operative Pal System

  Every week, the cooperative delivers individual food items to its members by car and at the same time collects surplus food from households. The collected food is given to the food bank in the prefecture.

- Large supermarkets such as Muji

  A box is placed at the entrance to the supermarket where shoppers can drop off surplus food from their homes. The food bank then takes the surplus food and donates it to those in need.

- Otera Oats Club

  The support group gathers information on the number of children in single parent households, gives their addresses to Otera Oyatsukurabu, and shares information on provision of the nearest support with the temple. With this information, temples receive offerings of food from households before it goes bad, and cooperate with support groups for single-parent households across the country to provide 'Osusowake' or food distribution. It is said that 447 temples cooperate with this scheme, and their stance is to take a step back and support the groups from behind.

(3) Salvage parties

Events called salvage parties have been organised in Tokyo and several other places since 2013 and have attracted considerable attention. The participants bring foodstuffs and ready cooked foods that would otherwise not have been used, and prepare food together with the other participants. Some of this food is unwanted seasonal gifts received from friends or relatives but which is not to the taste of the recipient, or something that the recipient does not know how to use. These salvage parties bring together the uneaten food and foodstuffs with the knowledge and skills of the participants. In this way, the uneaten food items are turned into delicious and enjoyable meals, and this provides opportunities for communication among the participants. Salvage parties can be held for the following occasions such as an event to think about FLW, community gatherings, for company social events and team building, and at school classes or cultural festivals.

Conclusions and discussion

Japan's Food Waste Recycling Law and related initiatives have made progress in encouraging recycling and waste minimisation among food industries since 2001. In particular, the total amount of FLW and the total amount of waste incinerated or disposed of in landfill have gradually decreased (Liu et al. 2016). In terms of reducing *food loss*, about 90% of businesses have achieved the reference generation units set by MOE and MAFF in 2014 (MAFF 2021). However, since the target value was set at a relatively low level that most businesses could easily achieve, the reduction in the amount of *food loss* generated is limited.

When looking at the recycling rate in 2019 against the five-year target set for the period 2014–2019 by industry, the food manufacturing industry reached its target of 95%. The food wholesaling industry achieved 64% against a target of 70%. Food retailing improved slightly, at 49% against a target of 51%. The food service industry stood at 32% against a target of 50% (MOE 2021).

With the exception of food manufacturers, the recycling rate for food industries has not met their recycling targets: this is especially the case for restaurants. The food service industry generates small amounts but a variety of food waste. This waste contains a lot of salt and oil, and is prone to contamination by foreign objects such as chopsticks and toothpicks, making food waste recycling more difficult.

On the other hand, there are two main impediments to the food recycling industry: one is the economic rationality of the collection fees charged by food waste recycling businesses, which are higher than the collection fees charged by municipalities for general commercial waste, causing food-related businesses to choose to dispose of their food waste in general waste, thus preventing them from collecting the food waste necessary for food recycling businesses; another is that in some cases, it is difficult to secure land for food recycling businesses due to lack of local understanding.

In recent years, the amount of *food loss* generated by both food industries and households has remained stable at around three million tonnes each year since the 2010s (see Figure 10.4). In 2019, a target was set to halve the amount of *food loss* along the whole supply chain by 2030 compared to 2000. With a further reduction of around 15–20% over the next 10 years or so, Japan could achieve the target (see Figure 10.4). However, FLW remains a critical issue, especially in light of the country's low rate of food self-sufficiency, the shortage of available landfill sites for waste disposal, and the national directives for establishing a sound material-cycle society. Further efforts to systematically reduce food loss and waste are urgently needed across all stages of the food supply chain, both in the upstream section of food supply (i.e. on-farm and post-harvest) and the downstream section of food supply (restaurants) and at the consumer level. A number of unaddressed issues and challenges remain:

(1) Existing laws/measures do not address FLW that is generated at the farm level, although this aspect of FLW is more easily recycled as animal feed and fertiliser.

(2) Although almost half of *food loss* is generated by households and treated using incineration/landfill, there is not much room left for further recycling, meaning that it is very difficult to prevent and reduce FLW through behaviour change. This is due to several factors. First, waste disposal is carried out at the municipal level, and incineration is the main treatment method for municipal solid waste including household waste in Japan (Approx. 80%). Although waste separation practices are well established in Japan, few local governments currently collect household food waste separately from other waste, Secondly, the scale of the crop/animal farming system in Japan is declining and the market for feed/fertiliser recycled by FLW is considered to be limited, if no actions to resuscitate the agricultural sector are taken. How to further prevent and reduce FLW to achieve the 2030 target is still a major challenge.

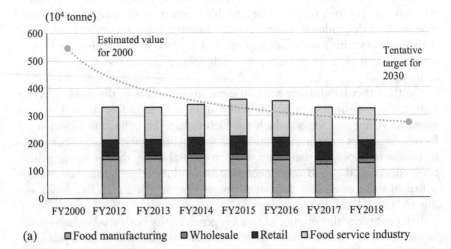

(a)   ▫ Food manufacturing   ▫ Wholesale   ■ Retail   ▫ Food service industry

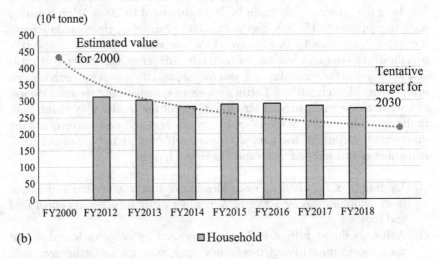

(b)   ▫ Household

Figure 10.4 Trend of *food loss* generation and reduction target for 2030.

(Data source: MAFF (2019))

(3) Significant quantities of FLW are generated by supply chains originating outside of Japan, and, in the light of Japan's continued and increasing reliance on food imports, these chains require further study.

References

CAA. 2019. "Current Status and Issues of Food Bank Activities." chrome-extension://
dnkjinhmoohpidjdgehjbglmgbngnknl/pdf.js/web/viewer.html?file=https%

3A%2F%2Fwww.caa.go.jp%2Fpolicies%2Fpolicy%2Fconsumer_education%2Fmeeting_materials%2Fassets%2Freview_meeting_002_191126_0014.pdf (in Japanese).

———. 2021. "Knowing and Learning About *Food Loss*." chrome-extension://dnkjinhmoohpidjdgehjbglmgbngnknl/pdf.js/web/viewer.html?file=https%3A%2F%2Fwww.caa.go.jp%2Fpolicies%2Fpolicy%2Fconsumer_policy%2Finformation%2Ffood_loss%2Fefforts%2Fassets%2Fefforts_220614_0001.pdf/ (in Japanese).

e-GOV. 2019. "Act on the Promotion of Reduction of Food Loss (Act No. 19 of 2019)." https://elaws.e-gov.go.jp/document?lawid=501AC1000000019.

e-Stat. 2021. "Portal Site of Official Statistics of Japan." www.e-stat.go.jp/en.

FAO. 2019. *The State of Food and Agriculture 2019. Moving Forward on Food Loss and Waste Reduction*. Rome. Licence: CC BY-NC-SA 3.0 IGO.

Japan Weather Association. 2021. "The Eco+Logi Project." https://ecologi-jwa.jp/en/concept/.

Liu, C., Y. Hotta, A. Santo, M. Hengesbaugh, A. Watabe, Y. Totoki, D. Allen, and M. Bengtsson. 2016. "Food Waste in Japan: Trends, Current Practices and Key Challenges." *Journal of Cleaner Production* 133. https://doi.org/10.1016/j.jclepro.2016.06.026.

Liu, C., K. Onogawa, and D. G. J. Premakumara. 2018. "Paradigm Shift From Incineration to Resource Management, and Town Development." September. www.ccet.jp/sites/default/files/2018-10/THE CASE OF OKI TOWN_web.pdf.

MAFF. 2013. "MAFF Website on Food Recycling Law." www.maff.go.jp/j/shokusan/recycle/syokuhin/index.html (in Japanese).

———. 2019. "Release of the Amount of *Food Loss* 2012–2019." chrome-extension://dnkjinhmoohpidjdgehjbglmgbngnknl/pdf.js/web/viewer.html?file=https%3A%2F%2Fwww.maff.go.jp%2Fj%2Fpress%2Fshokusan%2Fkankyoi%2Fattach%2Fpdf%2F210427-4.pdf (in Japanese).

———. 2021. "What Is the *Food Loss*." www.maff.go.jp/j/shokusan/recycle/syoku_loss/161227_4.html (in Japanese).

MoE. 2021. "Announcement of Estimated Amount of Food Waste and Food Loss in Japan (FY 2018)." www.env.go.jp/press/109519-print.html (in Japanese).

Second Harvest Japan. 2012. *Report of the Commissioned Work to Promote Food Bank Activities*. Tokyo: Second Harvest Japan (in Japanese).

11 The political economy of anti-food-waste in China

From anti-corruption to enhancing food security

Xiaohua Yu

Introduction

The literature has intensively shed light on food waste in China (e.g. Li et al. 2022; Lu et al. 2022; Min, Wang, and Yu 2021). However, it mainly measures the loss and waste (Li et al. 2022), or studies the determinants (Min, Wang, and Yu 2021; Li et al. 2021; Ding et al. 2022) or the implications for environmental resources or economic policies (Song et al. 2015; Yu and Abler 2014, 2016). China recently has been taking a massive campaign against food waste, and the institutional background and political motivations have not been well elaborated.

Unlike other countries where the main purpose of food waste reduction is located on food security and ecological concerns, China started from food waste reduction as a pillar of anti-corruption campaign in 2012. Food waste was regarded as corruptive behaviour for governmental officials. Traditionally, frugality shall be a merit of governmental officials when China was not a rich country. The reduction of food waste and loss was only limited in the scope of government-related restaurants or expenditures at first.

After the US-China economic conflict in 2018, China realised that its food security heavily depends on the international market, particularly the US market. In order to reduce strategic dependence on international food market, China started to take strict policies to reduce food waste as a tool for enhancing food security. Anti-food-waste switched its strategic focus from the governmental system to the general public. In August 2020, President Xi Jinping gave a specific instruction to prohibit food waste. The People's Congress then swiftly passed the 'Anti-Food-Waste Law of the People's Republic of China' on April 29, 2021, just six months after the instruction. The law came into force immediately after the pass. It evidences that the Chinese government is now taking a serious step to tackle the issue of food waste, which is regarded as an important policy to support food security.

Food security is a top policy priority for the Chinese government. As the largest population in the world, the Chinese government believes that food supply in China cannot solely rely on international markets. President Xi Jinping emphasised many times that 'Chinese should hold their own rice bowl, which should be filled with cereals produced by Chinese'.[1]

DOI: 10.4324/9781003226932-15

After the economic reform in 1978, in company with rapid economic growth, consumers climb in the food ladder, switching from a diet dominated by starch food to a diet with more animal products. Due to limited endowment of natural resources, such as land and water, we can observe an increasing trend of food imports in the past decades. Particularly after China's access to WTO in 2001, the imports of food increased drastically. In 2020, China imported more than 140 million tonnes of food. Such an increasing trend of food import makes Chinese government nervous. Chinese leaders worried that if one day the international market could not supply such a huge amount of food to China, Chinese people could suffer from starvation, it would cause social unrests immediately and could undermine the governance of the Communist Party of China.

Recent researches find that food waste and loss is very substantial in China. Chinese grains suffer from 8% to 10% food waste and loss in the post-harvest process stage (Lu et al., 2022; Li et al., 2022). According to the China Health and Nutrition Survey (CHNS), Chinese Consumers per capita wasted 16 kg of 415 kg of total consumed food products. Vegetable products contributed 31% and 54% of total consumption and total waste respectively, followed by rice at 22% and 13%, respectively (Song et al. 2015). In other words, Chinese consumers wasted 8.7% vegetables and 2.3% rice. In total, more than 10% of the food is wasted or lost in the whole food supply chain. An effective reduction of food waste and food loss implies that China could reduce its strategic dependence on international market and ensure better food security.

In addition, frugality has always been regarded as a traditional good virtue. Chinese government hence promotes food waste reduction as a promoting of the traditional frugal virtue in addition to anti-corruption and enhancing food security (Fig. 1).

Different from other countries, the massive anti-food-waste campaign in China is a top-down movement driven by a few factors, such as ensuring food security, promoting traditional frugal virtue, and carrying out anti-corruption.

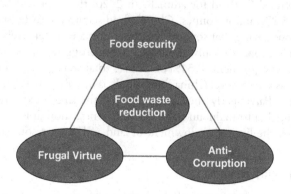

Figure 11.1 Institutional Framework of Anti-Food Waste in China.

In the past years, China has built up a comprehensive institutional system to tackle food waste. Some policies worked very well, while some not. This paper will introduce the policy background and progress, discuss some practical difficulties and offer some lessons and experiences for the future policy and other countries as well.

Food security: a foundation of national security

Status quo of food security

Food is the life of the people. Chinese government regards food security as a foundation of national security. The long history in China has offered the governments a lesson: if the food supply was insufficient, it would cause social unrests, undermining the legitimacy of the government. Historically, many dynasties were overthrown by uprises of their people due to famines. It was estimated that the big famine in the period from 1959 to 1961 killed more than 30 million people, mainly due to inappropriate policies (Kung and Lin 2003). This has been a historical stain for the Communist Party of China.

After the economic reform in 1978 introduced market economy and open-up policy, Chinese consumers became wealthier and demanded more and better food (Yu and Abler 2009, 2014, 2016). China is seeing a nutrition transition, and the traditional starch-dominated diet is gradually replaced by the western-style animal-products-dominated diet (Tian and Yu 2015; Yu and Abler 2016). It is projected that food demand in China could reach the peak in 2030, and the total demand for grains could be more than 850 million tonnes (Zhou et al. 2020).

We can observe a gradually increasing trend of food import in China in recent years in company with increasing domestic production. According to the database of China's custom, in 2020, the total imports of various types of grains reached 142.62 million tonnes, accounting for 21.3% of total domestic production. The main product of the imported grain is soybeans, which is made for soymeal for feed for animals. In 2020, the imported soybeans hit a record of 103.27 million tonnes. China's food security actually shows as 'feed security'. Considering that soybean yield per unit area is relatively lower compared to staple food, it is only about 1/3. Converting the imported food into arable land, it is equivalent to 51% of China's total arable land. The food security situation is very severe. China food supply is heavily dependent on international markets. Particularly, the United States is the largest exporter to China.

China struggled to maintain food self-sufficiency, though it is an impossible mission, given the limited endowment of land and water resources.

Food security policy in China

Food security has always been the foundation of national security. Resolving the problem of food is always the top priority of governing the country. Since

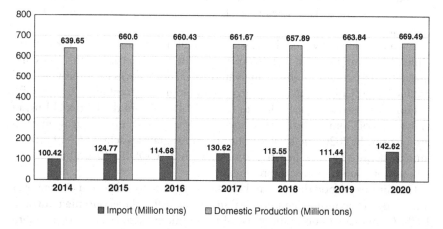

Figure 11.2 Grain production and import in China (2014-2020).
Source: National Bureau of Statistics of China

the 18th National Congress of the Communist Party of China, in which President Xi Jinping was elected as the new leader of China, food security is further emphasised and regarded as a foundation of national security. The 2013 Central Rural Work Conference of the Communist party clearly put forward the new food security concept: 'ensure basic self-sufficiency in grains and absolute security of cereals'.

China has the largest population of 1.4 billion in the world. The government thought that only by basing itself on food self-sufficiency can it ensure food security and then manage the overall situation of economic and social development. If there is a major food shortage in China, it will be difficult for the world to increase production capacity in a short time to meet the needs, and 'the good situation of social and economic development may be interrupted'. In other words, if there was no food security, the rapid economic development in China would be undermined.

China attaches great importance to food security and has successively introduced various policies, continuously increasing investment in land quality improvement, agricultural infrastructure, agricultural technologies, and offering huge subsidies to farmers and local governments to produce food (Yu and Zhao 2009).

First, China set up the strictest arable land protection institutions by setting up a red line of '1.8 billion mu of permanent arable land' (120 million hectares of land). Converting the arable land to construction land should be compensated by the same size of arable land converted from other construction land or deserted land. China invested heavily to increase land quality, such as levelling the land or providing irrigation systems. From 2016 to 2020, the central government arranged approximately 120.5 billion yuan in subsidies for protection of arable land fertility each year. This is so called 'Land for food (cang liang yu di)'.

Second, China invested heavily in agricultural technologies. Particularly, China is focusing on the technologies of seeds and mechanisation. Seeds and agricultural machines are still main technological bottlenecks for improving food production in China. This is so called 'Technologies for food (cang liang yu ji)'.

From 2004 to 2020, according to the official data from the National Bureau of Statistics of China, China has achieved a 17-year consecutive increase in grain production. In 2020, the total output of various grains reached 669.49 million tonnes, despite various negative shocks, such as COVID-19 outbreaks, and catastrophic floods in Henan province.

Conditions of food demand and food security are not static and change over time with the economic and political situations. After the economic reform in 1978, China saw a continuously rapid economic growth over 40 years. With the consumers' income continuing to increase, food consumption structure is transformed and upgraded. Consumers demand more animal-based food products such as eggs, milk, and meat. In turn, it requires more grains to be used as feed products. Due to the limited resource endowment of land and water resources, food supply and demand are in a tight balance, and food imports have been steadily increasing in the past decades (Figure 11.3).

In 2020, China's total imports of various types of grains reached 142.62 million metric tonnes, accounting for 21.3% of total domestic grain output. The United States is the largest food exporting country to China. The main imported food is soybeans. As aforementioned, if the imported food is converted to land resource, it is about half of Chinese arable land. Food self-sufficiency is already an impossible mission.

Increasing food import, on the one hand, helps China to save domestic resources and break the resource constraints to develop economy. On the other hand, in the background of a series of China-US economic conflicts after 2018, China is worried that the United States could weaponise food export and put China's national security and economic development at risk.

In addition to 'land for food' and 'technologies for food' policies, how to further dig food supply potential in China? Chinese government realised that food waste is still a big problem in China. Reduced food waste implies that it could increase effective supply in China.

Food waste in China: a threat or a solution to food security

Shift of food waste focus in China

As Chinese consumers get wealthier, food waste is increasing. Food waste reduction is critical to combat hunger and ensure food security, and reduce water, energy, and other resources' inputs.

FLW could happen in each stage of the whole food supply chain from the initial production, through harvest, transport, process, and retail, down to the final restaurant, and household consumption (FAO 2011; Li et al. 2022). FLW is a global phenomenon, but differs in characteristics in development stages and cultural backgrounds. The low-income and under-developed countries often have more loss in the harvest and storage stage due to premature harvest in order to tackle food insufficiency between seasons, and low harvest technologies and improper storage facilities. However, the high-income and developed countries are prone to have more food waste at the process and consumption stage, as the consumers tend to throw away more part of the food which is still eatable, and purchase more food than they could eat up (FAO 2011).

China is an emerging country, transferring from a low-income to a high-income country. In 2020, per capita GDP in China had reached 72,447 yuan, or about 10,500 USD, close to the threshold of $12,696 for the high-income countries defined by the World Bank.[2] At the end of 2020, China also announced that absolute poverty had been eliminated. Hunger is no longer an issue for Chinese people. In such a background, food waste emerges as an issue as more food waste is observed in a relative affluent society. Both food loss at the production stage and food waste at consumption stage are severely increasing.

Measurements of food waste in China

Estimated by the FAO (2011), annually about one-third of the global food supply, mainly in developed countries, has been lost and wasted. It is a great threat to global food security. China, as an emerging country, also sees an increasing food waste, though less than the global average FLW. There has been a large body of literature measuring food waste and loss in China at different stages, and their policy impacts (Yu and Abler 2014, 2016). Food waste studies require detailed survey data, and there has been a large body of related literature.

Food waste at postharvest stage

First, Li et al. (2022) conducted a meta-analysis of 57 researches to synthetically study food waste in each stage of postharvest from harvest, transportation, drying, storage, processing, and distribution in China.

Li et al. find that (1) 2.7–3.9% loss for rice, 2.3–4.7% loss for wheat, 2.3–2.7% for corn at the harvest stage; (2) 0.9% loss for rice, wheat and corn at the transportation stage; (3) 1.4–1.85% loss for rice, 1.4% loss for wheat and corn at the drying stage; (4) 1.2–2.0% loss for rice, 1.75–3.2% loss for wheat, 1.87–4.5% for corn at the storage stage; (5)1.73% for rice, and 2.2–3.3% for general grains at the processing stage, (6) 0.79% for rice, and 1.0–1.5% for general grains at the processing stage. In sum, the total loss for the post-harvest stage is 6.9–8.4% for rice, 7.8% for wheat, 9.0% for corn, and 7.9% for general grains. In a word, we can see the total food loss rate for grains ranges from 6.9% to 9.0%, and the medium value is 8%.

Lu et al. (2022) conducted a survey of 3,000 households from 2015 to 2019 in 25 provinces and found that the food loss rates are different for grains, vegetables, and fruits, and specifically 7.9% food loss for grains, which is consistent with Li et al. (2022). However, the loss rates for vegetables and fruits are relatively higher, 27.7% and 13.2%, respectively. They find that the FLW could be reduced by 40–60% if appropriate policies are taken.

Food waste in consumption

Income is a major determinant or food waste. As income grows, food waste for consumers increases.

The China Health and Nutrition Survey (CHNS) is a major source for studying food waste in the literature. Song et al. (2015) finds that per capita average food consumption (waste) is 415 kg (16 kg), and the vegetables, rice, wheat, and the rest (pork, legumes, and fruits) represent 128.65 kg (8.64kg), 91.3 kg (2.08 kg), 58.1 kg (2.24 kg), and 62.25 kg (2.08 kg), respectively. If we calculate the waste rate, the waste rate is 3.86% for all products; and 6.72%, 2.28%, 3.86%, and 3.34% for vegetables, rice, wheat, and the rest (pork, legumes, and fruits).

Min, Wang, and Yu (2021) calculated the food waste and their calories equivalent for the years 2004, 2006, and 2009. They find that per capita food waste is 127.67 grams per three days, or 15.5 kg per year. It is consistent with Song et al. (2015). They also find that per capita food waste annually in 2004, 2006, and 2009 is 18.56 kg, 14.21 kg, and 14.03 kg, respectively. If the waste can be converted to calories per day, and they equivalently are 52.31 kcal, 35.27 kcal and 38.89 kcal.

Li et al. (2021) had a survey of 207 rural households in 21 villages, and they find that rural households have significantly lower food waste. Per capita food waste is only 8.7 grams per meal, or 26.1 grams per day for three meals, or 9.5 kg per year. It is significantly lower than the CHNS survey.

Wang et al. (2017) use a direct weighing method and a survey of 3,557 tables in 195 restaurants in four case cities of China in 2015, and find that food waste per capita per meal in the four cities was 93 g, consisting mainly of vegetables (29%), rice (14%), aquatic products (11%), wheat (10%), and pork (8%). This equals approximately 11 kg/cap/year and is not far from that of Western countries, although per capita GDP of China is still much lower. Though restaurant consumption is not a daily activity for Chinese consumers, their occasional consumption still has a substantial waste, in comparison to 16 kg waste per year at home consumption.

If we combine the waste in the postharvest stage and consumption stage, we can conclude that China had at least 11% loss for cereals and 35% loss for vegetables. There are sizable spaces for food waste reduction.

Determinants of food waste in China

Food waste could happen at all stages of the whole supply chain. At the production stage, farm size is still relatively small, and a large harvest combines with less waste cannot be applied. Farmers are just released from hunger and poverty so that premature harvest also happens for those relatively poor farmers. Particularly, more than 300 million farmers are conducting off-farm employment, and off-farm income is a dominating income source, so that they may not be timely available for harvest. Early or late harvest also causes more FLW.

As Chinese rural and urban consumers have different consumption structure, rural consumers clearly have lower food waste. There are a few reasons. First, rural consumers have lower income; second, rural consumers are close to agriculture, and have the tradition of food saving virtue; third, rural food waste could be used as feed for domestic animals, such as pigs, chickens, and pets (Qi, Lai, and Roe 2021). Hence, rural households always have an efficient way to consume food.

Income does not necessarily increase food waste. Common wisdom says that rich consumers may tend to waste more food, as food's marginal costs are lower for them. However, Li et al. (2021) find that lower income households in rural China, on the contrary, have a higher waste rate than the higher income group. It is possible that (1) poor households may purchase lower quality, unprocessed and more perishable food, which lead to higher loss or waste, and (2) lower income household may not have refrigerators to store food and hence have higher food waste.

Li et al. (2021) and Jiang et al. (2018) additionally find that family size, age structure, health status, and whether having pets or not are significant determinants for food waste of households in rural China.

Min, Wang, and Yu (2021) suggest that dietary knowledge and education play significant roles in food waste in addition to rural-urban differences. Zhao and Yu (2020) use a randomised trial to find that parent nutrition knowledge is important for family health and nutrition status.

These studies provided important information for policy-making to effectively reduce food waste.

Food waste reduction policies in China: a top-down political campaign

China started the political campaign against food waste at the end of 2012 when President Xi Jinping was elected as the General Secretary of the Communist Party. The campaign moves forward from a pure anti-corruption campaign to a food security enhancing policy. In this section, we will analyse the policy evolution. Table 11.1 shows the major policies in China related to food waste reduction.

Anti-corruption and anti-food-waste

After President Xi took the power, in order to stabilise his position, purge his political opponents, and change the behaviours of corruptive officials, he started a massive political campaign against corruption.

In December 2012, the Communist Party of China issued two regulatory documents: The Eight Regulations of the 18th CPC Political Bureau

Table 11.1 Regulations on Food Waste Reduction in China after 2012

Time	Government bodies and regulations	Contents related to food waste reduction
Dec. 4, 2012	The Eight Regulations of the 18th CPC Political Bureau on Improving Work Style and Keeping Close Contact with the People, ('Eight Regulations of the Central Committee'),	Article 8: Strictly practice frugality, and incorruptive political activities; strictly implement the regulations on housing and vehicle equipment related to work and living conditions.
Dec. 26, 2012	According to the eight regulations, officials from Zhejiang Province created another 'six prohibitions', which were later adopted by the Communist Party of China. ('six prohibitions').	Article 4: Strictly forbidden to offer money or goods to officials; and strictly prohibit extravagance, lavishness, waste in practice.
Nov.25, 2013	The State Council: 'Regulations on the Party and Government Organization to Strictly Save and Oppose Waste'	Article 65 stipulates to completely prohibit the governments from extravagance and waste
Mar. 18, 2014	The General Office of the Central Committee of the Communist Party of China and the General Office of the State Council issued the 'Opinions on Strict Saving and Opposing Food Waste'	Eight articles in detailed regulations on saving and opposing food waste'. Specifically, (1). To eliminate waste of meals during public-related activities; (2). To promote frugal meals in the canteen of the public-related institutions; (3). To implement a scientific and civilised food consumption model; (4). To reduce food loss and waste in all links of the food supply chain; (5). To promote recycling and re-utilization of food waste; (6). To improve publicity and education for food waste reduction; (7). To improve food-waste-reduction related laws and regulations; (8). To strengthen supervision and inspection for food waste reduction.
Aug. 11, 2020	'Prohibit Food Waste" instruction by President Xi Jinping,	Xi Jinping requires that food waste should be resolutely prohibited, and an atmosphere of 'waste is shameful and saving is proud' should be created in the whole society.
Apr. 29, 2021	On 29 April 2021, the 24th meeting of the Standing Committee of the 13th National People's Congress voted to pass the 'Law of the People's Republic of China on Anti-Food Waste', which came into force on the date of promulgation.	32 articles of the law lay out the general legal framework to regulate food waste in China, mainly aiming at food waste and loss reduction at consumption and sales links, and at the same time properly handling the relationship with relevant laws such as the Food Security Law that is being drafted for food waste and loss reduction in production, processing, storage and transportation, etc.

Time	Government bodies and regulations	Contents related to food waste reduction
Jul. 29, 2021	Notice of the Office of the State Council on the Implementation of the 'Law of the People's Republic of China on Anti-Food Waste'	Government offices at different levels should (1) Actively carry out publicity and training;(2) Improve relevant laws, regulations and standards; (3) Improve the supervision and inspection work mechanism to reduce food waste.
Oct. 29, 2021	The public report of The Fifth Plenary Session of the Nineteenth Central Committee of the Communist Party of China.	Explicitly mentioned 'Carrying out food saving actions'.
Oct. 31, 2021	The General Office of the Central Committee of the Communist Party of China and the General Office of the State Council issued the 'Food Saving Action Plan'	28 articles. In order to implement the requirements of the Fifth Plenary Session of the 19th Central Committee of the Communist Party of China on "carrying out food saving actions" and promote the implementation of the "Law of the People's Republic of China on Anti-Food Waste",
26. Nov. 2021	The General Office of the State Council Issued '14th Five-Year' Plan on Cold Chain Logistics Development.	The Plan specifically states that China will build a " 'Four Horizontal and Four Vertical' National Cold Chain Logistics Backbone Channel Network". The Plan also points out that 'Promoting the high-quality cold chain logistics is an important mean to reduce post-production losses of agricultural products and waste in food circulation, expand high-quality market supply, and better meet the people's growing needs for a better life'.

Source: Collected by the author.

on Improving Work Style and Keeping Close Contact with the People, (briefly 'Eight Regulations of the Central Committee'), and 'six prohibitions'. The two documents clearly stated that 'practice frugality, and incorruptive political activities', and 'Strictly prohibit extravagance, lavishness, waste in practice'. 'Waste' (including food waste) behaviours of officials are regarded as a corruptive behaviour, and were punished by the party and government.

One year later, the State Council issued 'the Regulations on the Party and Government Organization to Strictly Save and Oppose Waste' in November 2013. It further regulated the governments to reduce waste and save resources.

In the massive anti-corruption movement, thousands of different levels of officials have been purged and arrested.[3]

After two years of the anti-corruption campaign, the General Office of the Central Committee of the Communist Party of China and the General Office of the State Council issued the 'Opinions on Strict Saving and Opposing Food Waste'. It is the first time to specifically look at food waste issues in government agents or public-related organisations. The opinions said:

> A large population and relatively insufficient land resources are the basic national conditions in China, and food supply and demand have been in a tight balance for a long time. However, under the influence of unhealthy trends such as ostentation, lavishness, and face-saving, coupled with the imperfect supervision system, the phenomenon of food waste is widespread, and the people strongly oppose this. Strict frugality and combating food waste are not only urgent needs to ensure national food security, but also important measures to promote the traditional virtues of diligence and frugality of the Chinese nation and accelerate the construction of a resource-saving and environment-friendly society. In order to implement the "Regulations of Party and Government Organs on Strictly Saving and Opposing Waste", we will further promote the work of combating food waste.

After this campaign, all government-related expenditure on food and lodging has been strictly checked by the Discipline Inspection Departments of the Communist Party of China, and the Auditory Departments of the government. For instance, the governments implemented very detailed food expenditure regulations, though slightly various in different regions, generally including: (1) Luxury liquors and wines were forbidden to serve in public-related dinners; (2) Per person expenditure on food and the number of dishes ordered were limited under a certain amount; (3), Any reimbursements of unnecessary food expenditure were prohibited. Any violations of these regulations will be punished as corruption, and the related officials could suffer different punishments, varying from promotion freezing to dismissal. Such a campaign substantially reduced food waste and loss in public-related food expenditures. Before, over-order as a Chinese tradition of hospitality was prevailing due to a soft budget, and caused plenty of food waste and loss in public-related restaurants.

This document lays out the policy targets of the anti-food-waste campaign: to ensure food security, to promote traditional virtues of diligence and frugality, to combat corruptions, and to construct a resource-saving and environment-friendly society.

Food security enhancement

After President Xi Jinping entered into his second term in 2017, his position was stabilised, while Donald Trump became the US president in 2016, and China and the United States started the economic conflicts in 2018.

President Xi realised the importance of food security in China. As China has been increasingly importing food, food supply in China is strategically dependent on imports from international markets, particularly from the United States, which is the largest agricultural exporter to China. As political tension between China and US increases, China is worried about a possible weaponisation of food exports by the United States, though the probability is very low.

President Xi raised the policy of food security to a very high level, as a foundation of national security. Chinese government endeavours to increase domestic food supply by different measures. Now, reduction of food waste is again raised by President Xi in August 2020. Reducing food waste and loss could marginally increase food supply for the people. In an instruction, Xi Jinping required that food waste should be resolutely prohibited, and an atmosphere of 'waste is shameful and saving is proud' should be created in the whole society.

After this instruction, different government bodies again started to move swiftly.

On 29 April 2021, the 28th meeting of the Standing Committee of the 13th National People's Congress voted to pass the 'Law of the People's Republic of China on Anti-Food Waste', which came into force on the date of promulgation. After the instruction of President Xi in August 2020, a national law already passed all legislation procedures and came into force within six months. It shows both the efficiency of Chinese government and the importance of food waste reduction in China.

On 29 July 2021, the Office of the State Council issued a notice on the Implementation of the 'Law of the People's Republic of China on Anti-Food Waste'. It required each level of government body to act swiftly to execute the law. Governments and public-related agents should be a model for food waste reduction.

On 29 October 2021, the public report of The Fifth Plenary Session of the Nineteenth Central Committee of the Communist Party of China once again reiterated 'Carrying out food saving actions' from the party's perspective.

On 31 October 2021, The General Office of the Central Committee of the Communist Party of China and the General Office of the State Council issued the 'Food Saving Action Plan', which gave the detailed instructions for carrying out 'Law of the People's Republic of China on Anti-Food Waste' for each level of government bodies.

This action plan has 28 articles, which specifically include the measures in all dimensions for food waste reduction: (1) To strengthen the loss reduction in agricultural production link; (2) To strengthen the reduction of grain storage link; (3) To strengthen the loss reduction in the grain transportation link; (4) To accelerate the advancement of food processing links to save food and reduce losses; (5) Resolutely curb waste in catering consumption; (6) Vigorously promote technological innovation in food saving and loss reduction; (7) To strengthen the publicity, education, and guidance of food saving and loss reduction.

After issuing the 'Food Saving Action Plan', it is expected that governmental bodies at different levels will follow this plan, and allocate budget and manpower to carry out these actions in the coming years. For instance, investment in food waste reduction techniques, such as more efficient harvest combines will be subsidised; food storage facilities will be upgraded; and food waste in restaurants will be inspected. Particularly, the cold-chain logistics will be a major instrument for post-harvest food waste reduction.

Shortly after issuing the Food Waste Reduction Action Plan, the General Office of The State Council announced 'The'14th Five-Year' Plan on Cold Chain Logistics Development' as an important support. In this plan, China will ambitiously invest in building a ' "Four Horizontal and Four Vertical" National Cold Chain Logistics Backbone Channel Network' to connect all domestic cold-chain logistics hubs with international ones.

Since 2012, the Chinese government under the leadership of President Xi has established a comprehensive legal and regulatory system on food waste reduction. According to 'the Food Saving Action Plan', by 2025, the measures on food waste and loss reduction in all links of the food chain should be refined and reformed, and the promotion of food waste and loss reductions should achieve more obvious and concrete results.

Barriers to food waste reduction: macro policy and micro costs

China has made comprehensive policies to reduce food waste as food waste reduction has been regarded as an important tool to enhance food security and promote the good virtues of diligence and frugality. China wishes to reduce strategic dependence on international food markets. The campaign on food waste reduction is a typical top-down policy.

The section "Measurements of food waste in China" already showed that restaurant consumption had a high rate of food waste. The government regulates that consumers in restaurants should eat up all ordered food, which is called 'Empty Plate Movement'. Governments can punish consumers and restaurants if there are leftovers.

Many local governments have created different guidelines for 'The Empty Plate Movement', and most of them are non-compulsory. For instance, Beijing City implemented guidelines separately for nine different sub-scenarios with different characteristics[4]: social catering stores, government canteens, primary and secondary school canteens, college canteens, hospital canteens, star-rated hotels, country homestays, collective dining and delivery companies, and local government representative offices in Beijing. The guidelines instruct food facilities through precise use of ingredients, change of business models, better publicity and customer guidance, and long-term supervision and implementation, to change the food environment, and to encourage consumers and food facilities to reduce food waste together. While a few local governments made compulsory policies to offer price discounts for consumers' behaviour of 'Empty Plate', and fine food providers who encourage consumers to over-order food.[5]

Particularly, canteens in government facilities or in public-related organisations, such as schools and hospitals, should strictly follow the regulation to reduce food waste. It still can be counted as an anti-corruption action.

However, how to reduce food waste in the post-harvest supply chain and private home consumption still faces a few hurdles.

Top-down policy and grassroots participation

Clearly, the top-down food waste reduction campaign is firstly driven by anti-corruption campaign and then food security.

In China, most ordinary consumers are not involved in the policy making process, and have nothing to do with anti-corruption campaign, as citizens are not allowed to freely participate in political issues. Therefore, the early stage of food waste reduction as an anti-corruption campaign only occurred at the government organisation, and did not actively motivate the participation of the grassroots.

Even though now food waste reduction campaign is driven by the political motive of enhancing food security, consumers' behaviour cannot be self-motived. Food security is a public good, and consumers cannot feel the importance under the situation of sufficient food supply. The generations born after the Great Famine between 1959 and 1961 do not have the hunger memory, and they do not understand the meaning of food security in person.

The chinese government also tries to promote food waste reduction as a traditional virtue of diligence and frugality. It is true that in the traditional agricultural society of China, food supply was not sufficient, and diligence and frugality were good virtues. However, after more than 40 years of rapid economic growth, Chinese consumers were released from hunger, and enjoyed a good life in a relatively affluent society. The behaviour of frugality is not regarded as a good virtue, rather as a symbol of poverty.

In addition, China now suffers from high economic inequality with a Gini coefficient of 0.465.[6] The polarised society also poses difficulty to reduce food waste: the rich do not want to reduce it, and the poor do not have room to reduce.

How to motivate the grassroots to actively participate in food waste reduction is a challenging policy issue in the future.

Macro policy and micro costs

The aforementioned section "Measurements of food waste in China" already showed that food waste in China is relatively low in comparison to other developed countries. The postharvest loss for grain accounted for 8%, and the home consumption accounted for 3%. Recovering these loss and waste could be very costly (Wang et al., 2015). Assume the utility function of food waste is

$$U = B\,(w,\,p,\,z) - C(w,\,z) \tag{1}$$

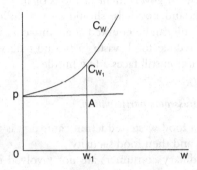

Figure 11.3 Food Waste Reduction and its costs.

where B is the benefit function of food waste reduction w, price p, and other variables z, C is the cost function for food waste reduction.

The optimal waste is given by the first-order-condition, $B_w(w, p, z) = C_w(w, z)$. Under the market equilibrium, $B_w(w, p, z) = C_w(w, z) = p$.

We can depict the marginal cost of food waste reduction in Fig. 3. Given the price p, we assume the baseline of food waste TW. If the government wants to reduce food waste by W_1, the marginal cost of the food should rise to Cw_1. There are two possibilities to reach the equilibrium: The first policy choice is to raise the food price to Cw_1, and the second policy choice could be that the government subsidises the cost of food waste reduction, which is the area $PACw_1$. This shows that food waste reduction is costly. A key to policy success is who bears the cost of food waste reduction.

According to the theoretical framework, governments could take a few measures. It is important to create a new food environment to reduce food waste with economic incentives.

In the postharvest stage, the government could invest or subsidise to develop new technologies, such as the cold-chain logistics system to reduce the marginal cost of food waste reduction. In private household consumption, government could promote food waste reduction by increasing the psychological price of foods (Bao, Dai, and Yu 2018; Ding et al. 2022), for instance, by showing the hunger memories of the generations who suffered from the Great Famine, and reminding the consumers of hunger in low-income countries, such as in African countries.

Conclusion

A large body of literature has shed light on food waste in China, with the main focus on the measurements and the determinants. China started a massive top-down policy campaign against food waste in 2012, after President Xi Jinping took power. However, the institutional change behind food waste reduction has not been well studied.

The massive campaign against food waste was at first initiated politically by anti-corruption movement, as wastes, especially food waste with public expenses, were regarded as a corruption of the officials. Later, as President Xi stabilised his position in his second term after 2017, China started to conflict with the United States.

After the economic reform in 1978, with rapid economic growth, China saw an increasing trend of food import. In 2020, China imported more than 140 million tonnes of food, of which more than 100 million tonnes are soybeans, and the United States is the largest exporting country to China. If converting all the food into land, it is about 50% of the total arable land in China. China is worried about possible weaponisation of the food trade by the United States due to the heavy strategic dependence on the United States.

China is regarding food security as a foundation of national security. Against such a background, China turns the campaign of food waste reduction into a tool to enhance food security from 2020. So far, China has set up a comprehensive institutional system for reducing food waste. Particularly, a key event is that the standing Committee of the People's Congress of China passed the Law on Anti-Food Waste in April 2021.

Under the strong leadership of the Communist Party of China, China put strong regulations on food waste reduction in restaurants and government-related canteens. Food waste in restaurants can be punished with fines, and food waste in government-related canteens is regarded as a corruption.

However, the success of food waste reduction still faces a couple of hurdles. First, the campaign has not motivated the active participation of the grassroots as China is not a democratic society and the severe income inequality hinders the effectiveness of the policy. Second, food waste reduction incurs high costs. Food waste rate is not so high: about 8% for the post-harvest supply chain, and 3% for household consumption. How to economically compensate the costs for the players in the postharvest stages and the private consumers is still a question for the future policy effectiveness.

Notes

1 Source: Xinhua News Agent: www.xinhuanet.com/politics/2015-08/25/c_128164006.htm.
2 Source: World Bank. https://data.worldbank.org/.
3 Source: BBC. www.bbc.com/zhongwen/simp/chinese-news-41719314.
4 Source: Beijing Municipal Commerce Bureau. http://sw.beijing.gov.cn/tpxw/202009/t20200922_2075671.html.
5 Source: National People's Congress of the People's Republic of China. www.npc.gov.cn/npc/c30834/202202/b7d15f9375d447f884729b99c2a4ae47.shtml.
6 Source: 'China Household Survey Yearbook' (2020 edition. Page 22) published by China Statistical Press.

References

Bao, T., Y. Dai, and X. Yu. 2018. "Memory and Discounting: Theory and Evidence." *Journal of Economic Dynamics and Control* 88 (March 2018): 21–30.

Ding, Y., S. Min, X. Wang, and X. Yu. 2022. "Memory of Famine: The Persistent Impact of Famine Experience on Food Waste Behavior." *China Economic Review* 73 (June 2022): 101795. https://doi.org/10.1016/j.chieco.2022.101795.

FAO. 2011. *Global Food Loss and Food Waste-Extend, Cause and Prevention.* Food and Agriculture Organization of the United Nations (FAO), Room. www.fao.org/3/i2697e/i2697e.pdf.

Jiang, J.-Q., T. Yu, Z.-H. Wang, D.-M. Qi, and W.-Z. Huang. 2018. "Analyzing the Size and Affecting Factors of Household Food Waste in China." 2018 Conference, July 28–August 2, Vancouver, British Columbia 277551, International Association of Agricultural Economists.

Kung, J., and J. F. Lin. 2003. "The Causes of China's Great Leap Famine, 1959–1961." *Economic Development and Cultural Change* 52 (1): 51–73.

Li, C., et al. 2022. "A Systematic Review of Food Loss and Waste in China: Quantity, Impacts and Mediators." *Journal of Environmental Management* 303 (1): 114092.

Li, Y., L. Wang, G. Liu, and S. Cheng. 2021. "Rural Household Food Waste Characteristics and Driving Factors in China." *Resources, Conservation and Recycling* 164 (3): 105209.

Lu, S., G. Cheng, T. Li, L. Xue, X. Liu, J. Huang, and G. Liu. 2022. "Quantifying Supply Chain Food Loss in China With Primary Data: A Large-Scale, Field-Survey Based Analysis for Staple Food, Vegetables, and Fruits." *Resources, Conservation and Recycling* 177 (7): 106006.

Min, S., X. Wang, and X. Yu. 2021. "Does Dietary Knowledge Affect Household Food Waste in the Developing Economy of China?" *Food Policy* 98: 101896.

Qi, D., W. Lai, and B. Roe. 2021. "Food Waste Declined More in Rural Chinese Households with Livestock." *Food Policy* (98): 101893.

Song, G., M. Li, H. M. Semakula, and S. Zhang. 2015. "Food Consumption and Waste and the Embedded Carbon, Water and Ecological Footprints of Households in China." *Science of the Total Environment* 529: 191–97.

Tian, X.*, and X. Yu. 2015. "Using Semiparametric Models to Study Nutrition Improvement and Dietary Change With Different Indices: The Case of China." *Food Policy* 53: 67–81.

Wang, L., et al. 2015. "Study on Theories and Methods of Chinese Food Waste (Zhong guo shi wu lang fei yan jiu de li lun yu fang fa tan xi) (in Chinese)." *Journal of Natural Resources* 30 (5): 715–24.

———. 2017. *The Weight of Unfinished Plate: A Survey Based Characterization of Restaurant Food Waste in Chinese Cities." Waste Management* 66: 3–12.

Yu, X., and D. Abler. 2009. "The Demand for Food Quality in Rural China." *American Journal of Agricultural Economics* 91 (1): 57–69.

———. 2014. "Where Have All the Pigs Gone? Inconsistencies in Pork Statistics in China." *China Economic Review* 30: 469–84.

———. 2016. "Matching Food with Mouths: A Statistical Explanation to the Abnormal Decline of Per Capita Food Consumption in Rural China." *Food Policy* 63: 36–43.

Yu, X., and G. Zhao. 2009. "Chinese Agricultural Development in 30 Years: A Literature Review." *Frontiers of Economics in China* 4 (4): 633–48.

Zhao, Q., and X. Yu. 2020. "Nutrition Knowledge, Iron Deficiency and Children Anemia in Rural China." *Journal of Development Studies* 56 (3): 578–95.

Zhou, D., X. Yu, D. Chen, and D. Abler. 2020. "Projecting Meat and Cereals Demand for China Based on a Meta-Analysis of Income Elasticities." *China Economic Review* 59: 101135.

12 History and legacy of the U.S. Good Samaritan Food Donation Law

Emily M. Broad Leib and Ariel Ardura

I. Introduction

Food loss and waste (FLW) is one of the greatest challenges facing our food system and the environment, with one-third of food lost or wasted along the supply chain each year (UN Food & Agriculture Organization 2011, 4), much of which remains safe and edible. The Food Recovery Hierarchy developed by the U.S. Environmental Protection Agency, which highlights the priorities for reducing FLW, suggests that feeding surplus food to people is the second most prioritised route for such food, behind preventing food waste at the source (U.S. Environmental Protection Agency 2021a). Supporting food donation is a popular and logical solution to redirect safe, surplus food into the hands of those who need it most.

However, a significant barrier to the donation of safe surplus food is the fear among donors that they will be found liable if someone becomes sick after consuming donated food. In 1996, in order to address such fears, the United States passed the Bill Emerson Good Samaritan Food Donation Act ('Emerson Act'), the first global law providing immunity from liability for food donors and intermediary organisations that distribute donated food. Providing food donors and food rescue organisations with liability protection is a powerful tool to encourage food donation. Such protection limits the likelihood that these actors will be held legally or financially responsible for any harm caused by donated food, provided they act in accordance with relevant laws.

When introduced, the Emerson Act was a global innovation that increased the profile of donating safe surplus food; over time, the Emerson Act and successive legislation supporting food donations, such as tax incentives, have made the United States a leader in food donation. As evidence, Feeding America, the national network of food banks in the United States, has around 200 food banks in all 50 states and distributes four billion meals per year (Feeding America 2021).

The Emerson Act is a global model, with many countries in recent years proposing or enacting similar laws to protect food donors. Nevertheless, the Emerson Act suffers from some challenges, including a lack of awareness about the Act and a lack of clarity regarding some of its provisions. Twenty-five years

DOI: 10.4324/9781003226932-16

after its passage, there are still many businesses in the United States who do not donate due to confusion regarding, or lack of knowledge about, the Act. With rising global awareness about food waste and increasing food insecurity spurred by disruptions to the food system due to the SARS-CoV-2 pandemic, exploring the future of the Emerson Act is more relevant than ever. As more countries consider enacting a similar law, there are some ongoing challenges and questions pertaining to the Emerson Act that they should keep in mind, as well as opportunities for the United States to amend the Act to continue to see the benefits Congress hoped for at the time of its passage.

This chapter will begin with background as to FLW in the United States, as well as the history and overview of the Emerson Act. It proceeds to lay out some of the benefits of the Act and its innovations, before analysing the challenges that still plague the Act. The chapter then explores some of the other laws and policies in the United States that build upon the Act to support increased food donation. The chapter closes with an analysis of the Act's legacy, describing several other countries that have passed similar laws in recent years.

State of US FLW

Each year, the United States produces a huge amount of food that goes uneaten or unsold—over 80 million tonnes (ReFED 2021a). Of that, 54 million tonnes of food end up in landfills or otherwise go to waste (ReFED 2021a). The cost to grow, process, transport, and dispose of this wasted food totals $285 billion each year (ReFED 2021a). Food is wasted at each stage of production: some food never leaves the farm (or another source), while other foods spoil or are otherwise wasted by producers, wholesalers, and retailers (Cantor 1997). The largest single source of food waste in the United States takes place at the household level (ReFED 2021b), similar to findings globally (UN Environment Programme 2021).

The United States simultaneously experiences high rates of food insecurity. Approximately 13.8 million households in the United States—comprising about 10.5% of the U.S. population—experienced food insecurity in 2020, meaning that they lacked access to a sufficient amount of food to lead an active, healthy lifestyle (U.S. Department of Agriculture Economic Research Service 2021).

In addition to negative impacts on food security, FLW generates environmental costs. The land allocated to grow food, the use of scarce resources like water, the fossil fuels used to ship it, and the space used to store it are all wasted when food ends up in a landfill. To illustrate, food waste consumes 14% of all fresh water and 18% of cropland in the United States (ReFED 2020). As it decomposes, this food emits methane, a GHG 25 times more potent than carbon dioxide over a ten-year period (U.S. Environmental Protection Agency 2021b). In 2015, the U.S. Department of Agriculture (USDA) and the U.S. Environmental Protection Agency (EPA) jointly announced a national food waste reduction goal, aiming to cut U.S. food waste by 50% by the year 2030 (U.S. Environmental Protection Agency 2015). In April 2019, the USDA, the EPA, and the Food and Drug Administration (FDA) launched the Federal Interagency Food Loss and Waste Collaboration (formerly entitled the 'Winning on Reducing Food Waste Interagency Strategy') (U.S. Environmental Protection Agency 2019). The United States has also attempted to address food waste through laws, regulations, and guidance, with some of the strongest policies worldwide in several areas (Harvard Law School Food Law and Policy Clinic n.d.). These efforts evince a growing interest to reduce food waste by the U.S. government.

The United States has been a global innovator and leader in offering protection from liability due to potential harm from food donations. In 1996, the U.S. Congress was the first national government to create such protection when it enacted the Bill Emerson Good Samaritan Food Donation Act ('Emerson Act'). A significant barrier to food donation is the fear among donors that they will be found liable if someone becomes sick after consuming donated food. By enacting the Emerson Act, the U.S. government took a very public and substantial step to ensure that no surprise liability will arise if, despite good faith efforts on the part of donors and intermediaries in the food donation chain, a food recipient falls ill.

The Emerson Act provides comprehensive civil and criminal liability protection for food donors and nonprofit organisations that distribute food donations to those in need, as long as they act without gross negligence or intentional misconduct (42 U.S. Code § 1791). As described in more detail below, the Act also specifies that in order to be eligible for liability protection, donations must be intended for ultimate distribution to needy individuals, who must not pay anything of monetary value for the donated food (42 U.S. Code § 1791).

In addition to the Emerson Act's liability protection, all 50 states in the United States offer liability protection for food donation. Indeed, the U.S. government based the Emerson Act on earlier innovations that percolated up from the state level. While the Emerson Act's protection is strong and comprehensive, several U.S. states offer additional protections not offered under the Emerson Act. It is important to note, however, that the federal protection in the Emerson Act offers a floor of federal protection; this means that states cannot offer any less protection than that offered under the Emerson Act; they can only offer additional protection (U.S. Department of Agriculture 1997, 1).

Background on Emerson Act

Genesis of the Emerson Act

The Emerson Act was the first national law of its kind when it was enacted in 1996. The United States legal system is divided between the federal government and the 50 states and the District of Columbia. The federal government is a government of limited powers, and only has authority in areas laid out in the U.S. Constitution. States have authority over any areas not granted to the U.S. government, or in areas where the national government has not acted.

In general, federal authority to regulate food stems from the 'Commerce Clause', which provides Constitutional power for the federal government to regulate any goods and products—such as food—that move in interstate commerce (U.S. Const. art. I, § 8, cl. 3). Food donors or nonprofit intermediaries technically could face civil or criminal consequences if someone were to fall ill from donated food. Liability from these food-related injuries would most likely arise under civil tort law claims in which an end recipient who was harmed by the food sued a food donor or nonprofit organisation. Tort law covers claims brought by a party harmed due to the action or inaction of another party. In the United States, state law generally addresses questions of tort liability (Lewis 2019); however, legal scholars generally agree that the Commerce Clause allows the federal government to enact national reforms to tort law that affect intrastate commerce, because tort suits generally affect interstate commerce (Every CRS Report 2010).

However, because tort law is typically considered a state matter and governed under state statutes and state court decisions, liability concerns regarding harms due to donated food also bubbled up from the state level. This is in part because the United States is a fairly litigious country, meaning that companies have reason to fear litigation from consumers who are harmed by their products. In addition, this fear may be even greater for food products, because of how courts in the United States determine liability for those products. Whether a food manufacturer or retailer was negligent is generally a fact-based question that looks at whether that business utilised reasonable care. However, for food products, state courts across the United States generally apply a 'strict liability' standard, with a strong presumption that the company should be held liable and forced to pay for any harm, as long as the plaintiff proves that they consumed the product and they suffered an illness or injury (Fortin 2009). Indeed the U.S. House of Representatives report that accompanied the passage of the Emerson Act found that '[a]ll fifty states generally hold one who distributes food or any other defective product, the defective aspect of which causes injury, to be strictly liable, which means liable even in the absence of negligence' (U.S. Congress. House. 1996).

The Emerson Act was based on a groundbreaking state law enacted in the state of California in 1977 that did two things: it offered immunity from liability for food donors (but not nonprofit intermediaries), as long as they did not act with gross negligence, and it offered food donors a tax deduction for food that was donated (Morenoff 2002, 109–10).

Within a decade of California's law, every other state in the country had also enacted some liability protection for food donations (Morenoff 2002, 108). However, this led to another problem: discrepancies between state laws led to confusion and an inability for national or regional food businesses to develop common protocols (Morenoff 2002, 116–17).

In 1990, the U.S. Congress took action to attempt to address the wide variation among state laws by enacting a federal Model Good Samaritan Food Donation Act (U.S. Department of Agriculture 1999). The Model Act was nonbinding, but presented template language that states could adopt, in an effort to drive more uniformity amongst state laws. Unfortunately, the Model Act was adopted by only one state (University of Arkansas 2013), and businesses continued to complain about the variations among state laws (Haley 2013).

In 1995, Representative Danner of Missouri introduced legislation to turn the Model Good Samaritan Act into binding national law (Morenoff 2002, 125). Danner sought co-sponsorship from Representative Bill Emerson to show bipartisan support (Haley 2013). Emerson later became ill and passed away before the bill became law, leading Congress to name the legislation in his honour (Haley 2013). The legislation passed Congress and was signed into law in October 1996 (Morenoff 2002, 125).

How the Act works

The Emerson Act provides a baseline of federal protection from civil and criminal liability to both food donors and the nonprofit organisations involved in distributing food donations (42 U.S.C. § 1791 1996). The Act explicitly protects individuals, businesses, nonprofit food recovery organisations, the officers of businesses and nonprofit organisations, and gleaners (individuals who harvest donated agricultural crops for a nonprofit organisation that distributes the food to the needy) (42 U.S.C. § 1791 1996). The Act protects donations to any nonprofit organisations, whether formally incorporated (as a 501(c)3 or other nonprofit structure) or not (42 U.S.C. § 1791 1996, (b)(9)). With respect to gleaners, the Act not only protects against liability arising from the consumption of donated food, but also protects the property owner from liability related to injuries the gleaner might sustain while on the property (42 U.S.C. § 1791 1996, (c)-(d)). A separate federal law also explicitly grants liability protection to schools and local educational agencies that donate excess food to a 501(c)3 nonprofit organisation (42 U.S.C. § 1758).

The Emerson Act protections apply to donors and nonprofit intermediaries as long as several criteria are met.

First, the donation must be made in good faith (42 U.S.C. § 1791 1996, (c)(1)), meaning that the food donor and nonprofit organisation intended to donate and distribute safe food products.

Second, the donor must donate to a nonprofit organisation that distributes the food to needy populations. Direct donations from the donor to needy individuals are not protected by the Act (42 U.S.C. § 1791 1996, (c)(1)).

The donor also must donate either 'apparently fit' grocery products or 'apparently wholesome food', meaning products or foods that meet 'all quality and labeling standards imposed by Federal, State, and local laws and regulations', even if they are not 'readily marketable due to appearance, age, freshness, grade, size, surplus, or other conditions' (42 U.S.C. § 1791 1996, (b)(1–2)). If a food does not meet all federal, state, and local standards, the donor can still be protected by the Emerson Act as long as they follow the reconditioning procedures set out in the Act. Under those procedures, the donor must inform the non-profit of the nonconforming nature of the product (42 U.S.C. § 1791 1996, (e) (1)); the nonprofit must agree to recondition the item so that it is compliant (42 U.S.C. § 1791 1996, (e)(2)); and the nonprofit must be knowledgeable of the standards for reconditioning the item (42 U.S.C. § 1791 1996, (e)(3)).

Finally, the ultimate recipients cannot pay anything of monetary value for the donated food. However, if one nonprofit provides donated food to another nonprofit for distribution, the Act allows the first nonprofit to charge the distributing nonprofit a nominal fee to cover handling and processing costs (42 U.S.C. § 1791 1996, (e)(3)).

In addition to meeting the above requirements, in order to receive liability protection, donors or nonprofit organisations may not act with gross negligence or intentional misconduct (42 U.S.C. § 1791 1996, (e)(3)). Gross negligence involves 'voluntary and conscious conduct (including a failure to act)' by a person or organisation that knew when the donation was made that the donated food was likely to have harmful health impacts (42 U.S.C. § 1791 1996, (b)(7)). Intentional misconduct means donating 'with knowledge . . . that the conduct is harmful to the health or well-being of another person' (42 U.S.C. § 1791 1996, (b)(8)). The Act gives little guidance on what activities qualify as gross negligence or intentional misconduct; however, it is clear that to receive protection the food donor or food recovery organisation should not donate or facilitate the distribution of donated food that it knows is likely to be harmful or dangerous.

The Emerson Act offers a generous grant of protection. As noted above, for food products, courts generally apply a 'strict liability' standard. This means that there is a presumption that the company was liable, as long as the plaintiff proves that they consumed the product and suffered an illness or injury. The Emerson Act changes the liability standard with respect to donations of food or grocery products from strict liability (for food) or ordinary negligence (for grocery products) to the more egregious gross negligence or intentional misconduct standards.

A donation beyond that which is protected by the Emerson Act is not necessarily prohibited by law, as long as the food meets all food safety laws. For example, while the Emerson Act only protects donations made by a donor to a nonprofit organisation that then distributes the food to those in need, a food donor can legally donate wholesome food directly to a needy individual. However, such a donor will not receive the Emerson Act's liability protection, though they may be protected under state law (42 U.S.C. § 1791 1996, (c)(1)).

The impacts of the Act

The Emerson Act has enjoyed political popularity, ensured a general positive sentiment towards food donation by potential donors, supported the growth of food banks, and has not fostered any negative outcomes. However, the Act faces several challenges and there are ample opportunities to improve upon the Act both within the United States or as more countries consider similar legislation.

Positive contributions of the Emerson Act

As noted above, the Act and its predecessors demonstrate innovation and responsive policymaking in the face of an acknowledged challenge to food donation. Legislators were able to listen to constituents, develop thoughtful legislation, and come together across party lines to enact it.

In addition, the Emerson Act is one of the most cost-effective policies when it comes to food donation and recovery (Harvard Law School Food Law and Policy Clinic n.d.), because it costs very little to implement. Unlike a tax credit or tax incentive (which reduce government revenue), a grant or subsidy to develop food donation infrastructure (which require governmental funds to resource), or a penalty on food waste (which costs money to enforce), the Emerson Act merely changes the structure of private rights, making it more difficult for a harmed party to bring a legal claim.

The Emerson Act also serves an 'important symbolic purpose' (Morenoff 2002, 132)—it helps to show parties that food donation is legal and socially beneficial. This can be important where, as in the United States, food safety laws do not specifically mention food donation as an allowed practice. Offering protection for those businesses and intermediaries who follow all relevant food safety laws can ensure parties that donation is a priority for the relevant government actors.

The Emerson Act has also impacted willingness to donate on the part of companies. According to one account, the Act enabled 7–11 to increase its food donations 'by as much as 150% over two years' (Morenoff 2002, 131). The effectiveness of the Emerson Act is also evidenced by the fact that companies frequently ask for information about the Act's protections and how they apply to their donation models. Around the country, stakeholders in various states regularly hold presentations and information sessions on the Emerson Act in order to spread awareness about its protections and ease donor and donee concerns about their liability. It is further demonstrated by the prevalence of food banks across the country—as previously noted, Feeding America's network includes 200 or so food banks across the country (Feeding America 2021).

Lastly, the Emerson Act is a success because it has not increased harm to beneficiaries of donated food. In California, other states, and the Congressional debate over the Emerson Act, a major point of contention was the concern that offering liability protection would make businesses feel they could pass along unsafe food. Yet, in the more than 40 years since enactment of the California law and the 25 years since passage of the Emerson Act, no major foodborne illness outbreaks have been attributed to donated food. The Emerson Act and similar state laws also have not been tested in court because there have been no claims filed due to donated food (Morenoff 2002, 132).

Challenges with the Emerson Act

Despite its overall success, the Emerson Act suffers from several weaknesses. One weakness is that many businesses fail to donate food because they do not know about the liability protections available to food donors under the Emerson Act. As noted previously, a 2016 survey conducted by the Food Waste Reduction Alliance (FWRA) found that 50% of food manufacturers, 25% of retailers and wholesalers, and 39% of restaurants cite liability as a barrier to food donation (Food Waste Reduction Alliance 2016, 17, 24). This is true for two primary reasons: lack of awareness and lack of clarity. As a result, donors still fear the possibility of being sued over their donated food.

Another challenge facing the Emerson Act is its outdated view of food donation, which can hamper innovation in food recovery and donation. On top of the protection provided by the Emerson Act, states also provide their own liability protection for food donors and food recovery organisations (Harvard Law School Food Law and Policy Clinic 2016, 6). All 50 states had enacted state liability protection acts prior to the Emerson Act, and many states offer protections that broaden than those afforded by the Emerson Act. These state laws can be instructive to show some of the issues with the Emerson Act, particularly as many of these state laws have been updated in recent years.[1]

Lack of awareness

The Emerson Act additionally falls short due to its longevity; passed over 25 years ago, many of today's business leaders are not aware that the Act even exists. Further, Congress never delegated authority over the Emerson Act to any agency, so there was no governmental office or actor working to raise and maintain awareness about the Act. To remedy this lack of awareness about the Emerson Act, in 2018, Congress mandated the creation of a Food Loss and Waste Liaison within USDA to 'raise awareness of the liability protections afforded under the Emerson Act' (U.S. Department of Agriculture 2021) (Agriculture Improvement Act, H.R. 2, 115th Cong. § 12504 2018, (e)(1)). The Food Loss and Waste Liaison publishes information about the protections offered in the Emerson Act (U.S. Department of Agriculture 2021). While this is a positive development, the lack of awareness about the Emerson Act continues to pose a challenge.

Lack of clarity

Despite the intention for brevity and clarity, many provisions and terms in the Emerson Act are ambiguous or open to interpretation. No food donor or intermediary has been sued for damages caused by donated food, which means donors do not know how a court would apply the Act because there are no judicial opinions interpreting the Act (Harvard Law School Food Law and Policy Clinic 2013). The fact that the U.S. Congress did not delegate authority over the Emerson Act to any agency also means there have never been any implementing regulations or guidance interpreting the language of the Act. However, as noted earlier, in 2018, the U.S. Congress called on the newly formed Food Loss and Waste Liaison in USDA to answer questions about the Act. As a result of this mandate, USDA released responses to basic frequently asked questions on the Emerson Act, but the FAQs simply reiterate what is already in the legislation and do not address many of the deeper interpretive questions that have been raised about the Act (U.S. Department of Agriculture n.d.).

The lack of guidance from a court or a federal agency leads to confusion among potential food donors, who want to be sure they will receive liability protection before they make donations. For example, donors often have questions about whether specific unmarketable food qualifies as 'apparently wholesome food' for purposes of protection. This is the case, for example, with food past its 'best before' or 'sell by' date.

Another frequent question is how 'needy individuals' are defined. As the Emerson Act does not provide a definition, donors and nonprofits often worry that they may not meet this provision of the Act. Some argue that the criteria for determining who is a 'needy individual' or other similar terminology should be up to the discretion of the non-profit organisation or food recovery program serving those individuals. Most individuals and families accept food donations as a last resort, and if they self-identify as needy or meet the criteria of the distributing non-profit organisation, the donation should be protected.

Another point of confusion revolves around the 'quality and labeling' standards that must be met by donated foods in order for the donor or intermediary to receive protection. The language in the Emerson Act requires that all such standards be met, but neglects to define or clarify those standards in any way. As such, donors, nonprofits, and local health departments are often confused as to what standards to apply (Munger 2018). It might make more sense for the Emerson Act to instead require that foods meet all 'safety and labeling standards'. Interpreting the term 'quality' as referring only to food safety is consistent with typical food donation liability protection goals of encouraging food donors to donate foods that are safe for consumption and preventing the waste of such food; it ensures harmony between the liability protection and other national food safety laws.

As noted above, many potential donors report that the biggest barrier to their donation is fear of liability, evidencing a lack of knowledge about the Emerson Act protections or a lack of clarity on their provisions (Food Waste Reduction Alliance 2016). The absence of clear instructions to food donors leads to missed opportunities for food donations and, consequently, more senseless food waste.

Outdated protection can reduce innovation

The Emerson Act specifies several types of donations that will not be protected. For example, the Act does not protect direct donation made by a food donor to a person in need. It also does not protect donations if the end recipient is required to pay or give anything of value. These provisions, while reflective of the food donation practices in place at the time the Act was passed, today can hamper beneficial opportunities to reduce food waste.

The Emerson Act only protects food donors if they give food to a nonprofit organisation, which then distributes the food to needy individuals (42 U.S.C. § 1791 1996, (c)(2)). Under the Act, donors cannot receive protection if they donate directly to those in need. This restriction was likely added to ensure the safety of donated food by ensuring that food passes through a nonprofit organisation that is adept at handling and safely distributing foods; however, in reality it likely has little effect on ensuring food safety and instead serves to hinder food donation. First, most food donations come from food establishments that have undergone food safety training and licensure and know how to safely handle food donations. Further, perishable food is often difficult to route through an intermediary because if it does not get into the hands of a recipient quickly it will spoil. While the Emerson Act does not protect direct donations, roughly ten states in the United States provide liability protection for donations made directly to individuals in need, and the experiences from those states show that the protection has not resulted in food safety concerns.[2]

Further, Emerson Act protection is only available when food is given to the end recipients for free or 'without requiring anything of monetary value from the recipient' (42 U.S.C. § 1791 1996, (b)(3)). This restriction inhibits the operation of nonprofit food rescue models that aim to sell food at a low price, such as social supermarkets. However, the facilities and resources needed to successfully recover and process surplus food make donation costly for both donors and food recovery organisations. Organisations that sell foods at a low price can provide an alternative for low-income customers who cannot use food pantries or are looking for ways to supplement their pantry use. Donations to these organisations are not protected under the Emerson Act, which serves as a disincentive for food donors to give to those organisations as opposed to organisations that distribute food for free. While the Emerson Act does not protect this, over 15 U.S. states[3] provide liability protection to food rescue organisations that sell donated food to the end consumers at a level sufficient to 'cover the cost of handling such food', thereby enabling them to support many models of food donation (Mass. Gen. Laws ch. 94, § 328 2017).

Emerson Act's liability protection builds a supportive foundation for food donation, but alone cannot incentivise increased donation

The Emerson Act provides a floor to show that food donation is allowed, desirable, and will not subject donors to unexpected liability. In its day, it was an innovative solution to a challenge inhibiting safe food donation and, as described, was the first such national law enacted around the globe. However, liability protection for food donation provides only a starting place as it does not actually incentivise or require donation. More can be done to economically incentivise donation and overcome other barriers, such as cost and concern over protecting the brand. The United States has shown leadership in two other areas that move beyond liability protection and into promoting food donation—tax incentives for food donation, which exist federally and under several state laws, and penalties for food waste, which exist in a growing number of the U.S. states.

The United States—and various other nations—encourage food donation through tax incentives. The costs associated with food donation often serve as a barrier to food being donated, as food donors must allocate time and money to train staff as well as harvest, package, store, and transport surplus food that otherwise would be discarded. As a result, it is sometimes less expensive, and easier, for farmers, businesses, and private individuals to throw away food rather than donate food. Tax incentives can provide significant support for food donation efforts and for the reduction of FLW. U.S. taxpayers who donate food are eligible for an enhanced tax deduction (I.R.C. § 170, (e)(3)(C)).[4] For other in-kind products, a U.S. taxpayer may claim a tax deduction in the amount of the property's basis (I.R.C. § 170, (e)(1)) (26 C.F.R. § 1.170A—4 2018, (a)(1)) (I.R.S., Department of the Treasury 2018), which is usually the cost to the business to acquire the product. The enhanced tax deduction for food donation provides an extra incentive for donation of food products by allowing the donating business to deduct the lesser of (a) twice the basis value of the donated food or (b) the basis value of the donated food plus one-half of the food's expected profit margin (if the food were to be sold at fair market value) (I.R.C. § 170, (e)(3) (B)) (26 C.F.R. § 1.170A—4 2018, (b)(4)). This deduction can amount to as much as twice the general deduction. Further, under the enhanced deduction, all businesses may claim a deduction of up to 15% of their taxable income for food donations (I.R.C. § 170, (e)(3)(C)(ii)). In addition, a growing number of states are realising they can spur increased food donation by providing state-level tax incentives that are tailored to farms and businesses within their states (Harvard Law School Food Law and Policy Clinic 2016).

Another way to increase donation is to make it too costly waste; for example, by implementing penalties on food going to waste or requiring that food is diverted to other beneficial uses either via food donation or recovery. While there is no national law penalising food waste or requiring its diversion in the United States, a growing number of U.S. states and localities are taking action to reduce food waste and increase food donation.[5] Several states and localities have enacted organic waste bans or waste diversion requirements, which impose penalties for excess food sent to landfills. By placing restrictions on food waste disposal, organic waste bans can drive food waste generators to increase donation and explore other sustainable practices, such as food waste prevention, donation, and recycling food waste through composting and anaerobic digestion. For example, the state of Massachusetts saw a 22% increase in food donation in the first three years after its organic waste ban went into effect (Pink 2018), and in Vermont, food donation nearly tripled in the first three years of its waste ban (Vermont Agency of Natural Resources & Vermont Department of Environmental Conservation 2019).

While liability protection can serve as an initial step to encourage food donation and assure food donors they will not be subject to costly liability, it may not be enough to really spur donation without being paired with other policies that create a financial incentive or motivation to donate safe, surplus food.

The legacy of the Emerson Act

Since the passage of the Emerson Act in the United States, a number of other countries have enacted their own Good Samaritan laws for food donation, particularly in recent years. Several countries' laws emulate the U.S. law by providing comprehensive protection to both food donors and food recovery organisations. For example, in Argentina, a 2018 amendment to the Food Donation Law (Food Donation Law (Law No. 25989), Art. 9) established comprehensive liability protection for food donors and food recovery organisations, as long as those actors are not negligent (Harvard Law School Food Law and Policy Clinic 2020). Israel's 2018 Food Donation Encouragement Law (5778–2018, § 2) provides food donors and intermediary organisations with criminal and civil liability protection, provided they comply with applicable laws and are not negligent (Leket Israel 2018). Several other countries, such as Italy (Legge 25 giugno 2003, n. 155) and Peru (Ley No. 30498, 2016), offer liability protection only to food donors, but not to food recovery organisations or other intermediaries.

On the basis of the growing global interest in food waste and food recovery, it seems likely that governmental protection from liability for food donations will only increase in popularity. Countries interested in enacting or enhancing their own liability protection laws for food donation can build on the strengths of the Emerson Act and also improve on it. Enacting national liability protection laws will likely provide a boost to food donation, as was seen immediately after the enactment of the Emerson Act. However, to truly encourage food donation, countries should develop methods to ensure public awareness of the protections. Further, to guarantee clarity, countries should appoint a governmental agency to be in charge of the law's implementation and provide clear guidance on the law's provisions. Countries can also take a more forward-looking approach in terms of the types of innovative food donation and recovery methods they protect, or can take steps to ensure an implementing agency updates the protections periodically to best meet contemporaneous needs and best practices.

Conclusion

The Emerson Act is a pioneering model law that has made an important contribution to the field of food donation and recovery, both in the United States and globally. In the United States, It has played a vital symbolic role in assuring companies that food donation has strong government support and protection, and is a strikingly cost-effective policy for increasing food donation. It has a net positive impact as it has increased food donation but has not caused harm to beneficiaries. Yet, the Act has not been able to reach its full potential for several reasons: most notably, the lack of awareness of the Act, the lack of clarity about several of its provisions, and the absence of government department equipped to respond to questions about its coverage. Currently, new models of food donation and recovery are not well-protected under the Act, so it may stifle innovation. Finally, liability protection for food donations may be necessary, but insufficient on its own, to provide the financial incentives needed to make food donation a standard practice at scale. Time will tell how the United States and other countries iterate on the Emerson Act and strengthen its protections as they work to achieve national and global FLW reduction goals.

Notes

1 See, e.g., Haw. Rev. Stat. § 145D-2; 21 R.I. Gen. Laws Ann. § 21–34.1–2; Tenn. Code Ann. § 53–13–101.
2 Ariz. Rev. Stat. Ann. § 36–916 (Arizona); Cal. Civ. Code § 1714.25 (California); D.C. Code § 48–301 (D.C.); Minn. Stat. Ann. § 604A.10 (Minnesota); Nev. Rev. Stat. § 41.491 (Nevada); N.H. Rev. Stat. § 508:15 (New Hampshire); N.M. Stat. Ann. § 41–10–1–3 (New Mexico); Tenn. Code Ann. §§ 53–13–102 (Tennessee); Vt. Stat. Ann. tit. 12, § 5761–5762 (Vermont).
3 Alaska Stat. § 17.20.346 (Alaska); Ariz. Rev. Stat. Ann. § 36–916 (Arizona); Ark. Code Ann. § 20–57–103 (Arkansas); Conn. Gen. Stat. Ann. § 52–557L (Connecticut); D.C. Code § 48–301 (D.C.); Ga. Code Ann. § 51–1–31 (Georgia); Iowa Code Ann. § 672.1 (Iowa); M.G.L.A. 94 § 328; 105 Mass. Code Regs. 520.119 (Massachusetts); Mich. Comp. Laws Ann. § 691.1572 (Michigan); Mont. Code Ann. § 27–1–716 (Montana); Neb. Rev. Stat. § 25–21,189 (Nebraska); N.H. Rev. Stat. § 508:15 (New Hampshire); N N.J. Stat. Ann. § 24:4A-1—A5 (New Jersey); N.C. Gen. Stat. Ann. § 99B-10 (North Carolina); Okla. Stat. Ann. tit. 76, § 5.6 (Oklahoma); Or. Rev. Stat. § 30.890 (Oregon); R.I. Gen. Laws Ann. § 21–34–1–2 (Rhode Island); Tex. Civ. Prac. & Rem. Code Ann. § 76.001–004 (Texas).
4 In order to qualify for the enhanced tax deduction, several criteria must be met: the donation must go to a domestic 501(c)3 charitable organisation that uses the food solely for the care of the ill, needy, or infants;[4] the recipient organisation must use the donated food in a manner consistent with the organisation's 501(c)(3) exempt status;[4] the food must be given to the end recipient for free;[4] the donor must receive from the recipient organisation a written statement attesting to the value of the donated food;[4] and the food must met all federal food safety requirements. I.R.C. Section 170(e)(3)(C).
5 See, for example Cal. Pub. Res. Code § 42649.81, 2018; Conn. Gen. Stat. § 22a-226e (2016); 310 Mass. Code Regs. 19.017(3) (2016).

References

Cantor, Linda S., et al. 1997. "Estimating and Addressing America's Food Losses." *Food Revolution* 20. http://gleaningusa.com/PDFs/USDA-Jan97a.pdf.
Every CRS Report. 2010. "Federal Tort Reform Legislation: Constitutionality and Summaries of Selected Statutes." January 28. www.everycrsreport.com/reports/95-797.html.
Feeding America. 2021. "Our Work." www.feedingamerica.org/our-work.
Food Waste Reduction Alliance. 2016. "Analysis of U.S. Food Waste Among Food Manufacturers, Retailers, and Restaurants." www.foodwastealliance.org/wp-content/uploads/2013/05/FWRA-Food-Waste-Survey-2016-Report_Final.pdf.

Fortin, Neal D. 2009. *Food Regulation: Law, Science, Policy, and Practice*, 606–7. NJ: Wiley.

Haley, James. 2013. "The Legal Guide to the Bill Emerson Good Samaritan Food Donation Act." Ark. L. Notes 1448, August 8. http://media.law.uark.edu/arklawnotes/2013/08/08/the-legal-guide-to-the-bill-emerson-good-samaritan-food-donation-act/.

Harvard Law School Food Law and Policy Clinic. 2013. "Legal Fact Sheet: The Bill Emerson Good Samaritan Food Donation Act." www.chlpi.org/wp-content/uploads/2013/12/Emerson-Act-Legal-Fact-Sheet.pdf.

———. 2016. *Keeping Food Out of the Landfill*. https://chlpi.org/wp-content/uploads/2013/12/Food-Waste-Toolkit_Oct-2016_smaller.pdf.

———. 2020. *Argentina Legal Guide: Food Donation Law and Policy*. June. https://www.foodbanking.org/wp-content/uploads/2020/06/Argentina-Legal-Guide.pdf.

———. n.d. "The Global Food Donation Policy Atlas." https://atlas.foodbanking.org/atlas.html.

I.R.S., Department of the Treasury. 2018. "Charitable Contributions: For Use in Preparing 2017 Tax Returns." January 24. www.irs.gov/pub/irs-pdf/p526.pdf.

Leket Israel. 2018. "Law Passed to Promote Food Donations in Israel." *Leket Israel*, October 23. www.leket.org/en/law-passed-to-promote-food-donations-in-israel/.

Lewis, Kevin M. 2019. *Introduction to Tort Law*. Washington, DC: CRS in Focus.

Morenoff, David L. 2002. "Lost Food and Liability: The Good Samaritan Food Donation Law Story." *Food & Drug Law Journal* 57.

Munger, Sarah. 2018. "Bill Emerson's Makeover: Reforming the Bill Emerson Good Samaritan Food Donation Act." *Vermont Journal of Environmental Law* 64: 75–76.

Pink, Kevin. 2018. "Food Rescue and Donation Continue to Increase Across Massachusetts." *Recycling Works Massachusetts*, June 20. httwww.recyclingworksma.com/food-rescue-and-donation-continue-to-increase-across-massachusetts/.

ReFED. 2020. "27 Solutions to Food Waste." https://perma.cc/W55W-R67S.

———. 2021a. "Roadmap to 2030: Reducing U.S. Food Waste by 50% and the ReFED Insights Engine." 3. https://d1qmdf3vop2l07.cloudfront.net/brawny-garden.cloudvent.net/hash-store/a013dff6534d1409dcf3fe652a4691fc.pdf.

———. 2021b. "The Challenge: Explore Food Waste." https://refed.org/food-waste/the-challenge/#where_does_food_waste_occur.

UN Environment Programme. 2021. "Food Waste Index Report 2021." 8. www.unep.org/resources/report/unep-food-waste-index-report-2021.

UN Food & Agriculture Organization. 2011. "Global Food Losses and Food Waste—Extent, Causes, and Prevention." 4. www.fao.org/3/ai2697e.pdf.

University of Arkansas. 2013. "Legal Guide to Food Recovery." https://law.uark.edu/documents/2013/06/Legal-Guide-To-Food-Recovery.pdf.

U.S. Congress. House. 1996. "Bill Emerson Good Samaritan Food Donation Act. Economic and Educational Opportunities Committee." 104th Cong. www.congress.gov/congressional-report/104th-congress/house-report/661/1.

U.S. Department of Agriculture. 1997. "Memorandum from the Office of Legal Counsel, U.S. Department of Justice, to James S. Gilliland, General Counsel." March 10. www.justice.gov/file/19846/download.

———. 1999. A Citizen's Guide to Food Recovery. www.google.com/books/edition/_/nwhTcWv27PsC?hl=en&gbpv=1&pg=PR1.

———. 2021. "Good Samaritan Act Provide Liability Protection for Food Donations." March 9. www.usda.gov/media/blog/2020/08/13/good-samaritan-act-provides-liability-protection-food-donations.

———. n.d. "Frequently Asked Questions About the Bill Emerson Good Samaritan Food Donation Act." www.usda.gov/sites/default/files/documents/usda-good-samaritan-faqs.pdf.

U.S. Department of Agriculture Economic Research Service. 2021. "Household Food Insecurity in the United States in 2020." www.ers.usda.gov/webdocs/publications/102076/err-298.pdf?v=1265.8/.

U.S. Environmental Protection Agency. 2015. "EPA and USDA Join Private Sector, Charitable Organizations to Set Nation's First Food Waste Reduction Goals." www.usda.gov/wps/portal/usda/usdamediafb?contentid=2015/09/0257xml&printable=true.

———. 2019. "Winning on Reducing Food Waste Federal Interagency Strategy." www.epa.gov/sustainable-management-food/winning-reducing-food-waste-federal-interagency-strategy.

———. 2021a. "Food Recovery Hierarchy." www.epa.gov/sustainable-management-food/food-recovery-hierarchy.

———. 2021b. "Understanding Global Warming Potentials." www.epa.gov/ghgemissions/understanding-global-warming-potentials.

Vermont Agency of Natural Resources & Vermont Department of Environmental Conservation. 2019. "Biennial Report on Solid Waste." January 15. https://dec.vermont.gov/sites/dec/files/wmp/SolidWaste/Documents/Universal-Recycling/2019-DEC.Biennial.Report.on_.Solid_.Waste_.pdf.

Part 4

Local initiatives

13 Social innovation for food waste reduction

Surplus food redistribution

Anna R. Davies and Alwynne McGeever

Introduction

In certain countries, such as France and Italy, new regulations are encouraging retailers to reduce their food waste, particularly through the redistribution of edible surplus food they generate (Vaqué 2017). Social innovation around utilising, and not wasting, surplus food is a vibrant arena of action, with grassroots initiatives in this area both well established and emerging, particularly in urban areas (Edwards 2020; Davies 2019; Davies and Evans 2019). Collecting and repurposing surplus food can happen throughout the supply chain from gleaning before the farm gate, to receiving donations of surplus from food businesses and rescuing wasted food from bins (Edwards and Mercer 2007, 2012). Weymes and Davies (2018) identified over 400 surplus food redistribution activities in 100 cities around the world. They analysed what kinds of surplus food was being redistributed, and found that fresh fruit and vegetables, tinned, packaged, and prepared food products and meals were roughly evenly shared across initiatives, with meat and fish making up the smallest proportion of redistributive activities due to food safety concerns. Two-thirds of initiatives intercept surplus food at the retail stage, followed by produce at the upstream production and supplier stages (22%) and the downstream food service sector (20%) (Weymes and Davies 2018). Surplus food redistribution (SFR) initiatives are diverse; they can be informal in structure, or operate as charities, social enterprises, associations, and clubs as well as for-profit companies. Despite this diversity, all operate within a dynamic and not always supportive policy environment (Davies, Cretella, and Franck 2019) and have to manage collaborations with public and private sectors (Davies et al. 2016).

Strategies within Europe are beginning to address the issue of food waste and edible surplus, with the issue flagged in diverse documents from the Farm to Fork Strategy (European Commission 2020a) and the EU Circular Economy Action Plan (European Commission 2020b), which includes EU food donation guidelines (European Commission 2017). Meanwhile, the EU Platform on Food Losses and Food Waste, established in 2016, seeks to support all actors in defining measures needed to prevent food waste; sharing best practice; and evaluating progress made over time. Policies to enable food redistribution are

DOI: 10.4324/9781003226932-18

multi-scalar in nature with drivers emerging at supranational (e.g. European), national, and sub-national levels and cut across a wide range of government departments (from waste to community development). Key policy implementation tools include voluntary public-private agreements; fiscal incentives such as tax reductions on donated food; fines for wasting edible food; Good Samaritan laws that protect food donors from liability; food safety guidelines for donors and charities using food donations; traceability laws for the donated food; grants for redistribution solutions; and government led awareness campaigns about food waste and redistribution (see Deloitte et al. 2020).

In this chapter, we focus on SFR initiatives working to connect donors and recipients of food surplus that utilise digital technologies to mediate and up-scale their activities (Davies 2019). While food waste reduction is a major driver of these activities, motivations for SFR activities frequently go far beyond this to include environmental, social, economic, and political motivations for action (Weymes and Davies 2019). Interrogating illustrative cases from Dublin, London, and Barcelona in terms of their form, function, governance, and impacts, this chapter discusses key challenges and opportunities facing these initiatives. This research demonstrates a need for enhanced sustainability impact assessment (SIA) reporting amongst SFR initiatives in order to identify the contributions such activities make to food waste reduction and beyond.

Case studies

Dublin, Ireland

National policy context

As of 2018, 8% of the Irish population are considered at risk of food poverty (CSO SILC survey 2018). Ireland does not have a national food waste strategy, but has committed to developing a national food waste prevention programme within six months of passing the Circular Economy Bill 2021 (Department of the Environment, Climate and Communication [DCCE], 2021a). Until this food waste focused policy is delivered (in 2022), policy treatment of SFR is referenced across different policy documents relating to climate change, waste management, and food safety, all implemented by separate departments and government agencies.

Ireland's five-year roadmap for managing waste, 'A Waste Action Plan for a Circular Economy: Ireland's National Waste Policy 2020–2025' (DECC 2020) includes a dedicated section on food waste, with specific attention to SFR. The plan explicitly commits action according to the food waste hierarchy (Papargyropoulou et al. 2014), prioritising prevention and human consumption of surplus food over alternative waste valorisation options like animal feed, anaerobic digestion (AD), and compost. The plan relies on voluntary commitments from private food businesses to use the 'Environmental Protection Agency (EPA)

Food Waste Charter' (EPA 2017) in order to donate their surplus edible food. Signatories of the Charter make a pledge to measure, reduce, and report on their food waste. As part of their commitments, each participating food retailer has engaged with SFR programmes (EPA 2017). However, commitments to action are limited to investigating opportunities to simplify, regulate, and enable surplus food donation (DECC 2020, 25). No explicit actions to create new legislation, incentives, levies, or targets are developed or committed to.

Additionally, while Ireland's Climate Action Plan 2019 commits to halving food waste by 2030, it does not give details on what actions will achieve this, beyond committing to developing a strategy in the future with the food sector and FoodCloud (a surplus food redistributor operating across Ireland). In 2021, an update on interim actions indicated that there would be two policy documents forthcoming which would include reference to support for SFR: a 'National Agri-Food Strategy' and a 'Food waste prevention roadmap', but with little detail forthcoming on their content. While extensive levies are considered for single-use plastics in the Climate Action Plan, there are no levies considered for disposal of edible food.

Elsewhere, the Food Safety Authority of Ireland (FSAI), the government authority responsible for coordinating and enforcing food safety legislation in Ireland, has produced specific guidelines for food businesses donating foods, charities receiving food donations, food banks, and for the safe assembly of food parcels. Currently, policy tools for SFR in Ireland are scattered across different government departments and national state agencies. The siloed treatment of different aspects of the supply chain and waste streams of the food system challenges coordination to maximise all of the SFR opportunities from farm to fork. Policy ambition is also lacking in relation to enforcing levies or funding supports to prevent waste of edible food. Specific commitments are limited to voluntary agreements from the private sector and preliminary investigations into future policy supports.

In the absence of strong leadership on reducing food waste from governing authorities at all scales, new innovative actors are emerging and creating novel ways to use edible surplus, from enterprises such as Cream of the Crop—a commercial enterprise which uses surplus food to make ice cream in Dublin— to FoodCloud a food surplus redistribution hub and logistics social enterprise that has, in less than ten years, gone from supporting connections between one retailer and one community group to supporting SFR between hundreds of food retailers and community groups across Ireland and the United Kingdom.

Case study: FoodCloud

FoodCloud is Ireland's largest redistribution social enterprise, collaborating with food producers, manufacturers, and retailers to re-distribute surplus food to over 800 community and charity partners. FoodCloud's vision is a world where no food goes to waste. Their mission is to 'transform surplus food into opportunity to make the world a kinder place' (FoodCloud 2021).

SCALE AND IMPACT

Founded in 2013, FoodCloud has redistributed the equivalent of 4.4 million meals, reaching 180,000 individuals (FoodCloud 2020). FoodCloud's private partners include five of the largest supermarket chains in Ireland. FoodCloud is particularly innovative in its use of technology to smooth the logistics that can complicate food redistribution. Its 'Foodiverse' platform connects available surplus food with community and charity partners in Ireland, and the technology has been rolled out to support FareShare in the United Kingdom, OzHarvest in Australia, Banki Zywnosci in Poland, and Ceska Federal Petrinovich (food) bank in the Czech Republic (FoodCloud 2020). FoodCloud also operates three hubs that collect and organise surplus food from 107 manufacturers, growers, and distributors. They also manage a volunteer-run gleaning project to gather additional surplus food before the farm gate, and coordinate with another SFR initiative Falling Fruit to sell juice made from surplus.

FoodCloud annually surveys its community and charity partners to understand what social impact their work is having. Their 2019 findings show that the availability of surplus food has helped charities support more people, introduce more people to the other supports the community and charity partners offer, helped them engage with harder to reach people, helped them introduce new services and supports, and spend less money on food (FoodCloud 2020).

Interviews with food retailers, charities, and FoodCloud founders revealed FoodCloud's key game changing characteristics included (a) designing an ICT solution that allowed a large number of donor to recipient transactions to occur with relatively small staff team; (b) providing a large, trusted intermediary body between the food retailers and charities, overcoming the issue of charities operating at a local level while decisions about donations from food retailers were made higher up than an agreement with a local manager; and (c) creating, managing, and improving relationships between food retailers and charity partners by being a third party to intervene and address issues such as a charity's varying availability to collect donations and quality control concerns about the products donated (Weymes and Davies 2018).

FoodCloud wants to expand its impact reporting, to better estimate how their rescued food offsets carbon emissions and to move beyond data on quantities of food to more differentiated data on the type of food being donated. Once a better understanding of the food donations has been established, FoodCloud can begin to trace the food donations through the community and explore the downstream impacts and end use of donated food. A significant data gap exists about what happens to the donated food after it is donated. Additionally, such detailed data can be fed back upstream to the retailers to inform supply chain decisions.

RESOURCES

FoodCloud is funded by a mix of public and private bodies, as well as generating their own income from food retailers for their surplus redistribution service.

They are supported by the Department of Agriculture, Food and Marine, Enterprise Ireland, and Cork City Council. They have also secured funding from private sponsors, including Allied Irish Bank and Applegreen (Food-Cloud 2020).

FoodCloud has a well-developed volunteer programme and corporate volunteer partners to support the delivery of their service and gleaning projects. FoodCloud also benefits from pro bono services from IT companies, facilities management companies, security services, transport services, recycling services, and office supplies that support their logistics.

POLICY ENGAGEMENT

FoodCloud works primarily with the private and not for profit sectors, but has engaged opportunistically with national and international policy programmes. It is an official sustainability partner with Origin Green (Ireland's national food and drink sustainability programme, involving government, the private sector, and the full supply chain from farmers to food producers and right through to the foodservice and retail sector), offering opportunities for its members to redistribute their surplus food to local charity and community partners. In 2017 and 2018, FoodCloud participated in Ireland's Retail Action Group event to reduce food waste. In 2018 FoodCloud also participated in an EU Parliament event about the circular economy. In 2021, FoodCloud's gleaning project was featured as a case study of best practice for food waste reduction in the draft Agri-Food Strategy. FoodCloud is also an active member of the food donations sub-group of the EU FLW platform.

CHALLENGES

In the absence of a progressive policy environment around food in Ireland, FoodCloud has paved the way for many other initiatives to undertake SFR. Despite their obvious success as a first mover in this space in Ireland, they have also experienced challenges which are diverse in scope: from logistical and administrative to regulatory. For example, each relationship between community group and retailer needs to be managed for the unique circumstances each finds themselves in. Charities often lack resources, relying on a volunteer workforce, so FoodCloud had to respond to the practicalities of making surplus available when charities and their volunteers were able to collect it. Similarly, FoodCloud meets with each store to understand their processes and identify how best to embed surplus donations into workflows. FoodCloud must monitor and manage the relationships between food retailers and charities, intervening when collections are missed or the donations are of poor quality.

The lack of a strong regulatory framework around food waste reduction and SFR remains a key barrier. In Ireland, disposal of edible food to the general waste stream is a cheaper option than donation. Even so, while retailers make many of their donations for marketing and corporate social responsibility purposes, they do not cover the full costs of redistributing food, meaning FoodCloud has to source funds from elsewhere to maintain their operations. Additionally, as there are no Good Samaritan laws for food donation in Ireland, FoodCloud has to undertake significant administrative work to get waivers signed by charities to protect the food retailers from liability.

Despite FoodCloud being an exemplar rolled out in national policy documents, policy change has been slow to support such SFR, instead focusing on making donations easier for companies. The emphasis in Ireland is very much on voluntary agreements and commitments from Irish retailers (using mechanisms such as the Food Waste Charter discussed earlier) and the future policy direction will not change in the short term with national action plans in place until 2025 (DECC 2020, 25).

At a supra-national level, FoodCloud is a member of the EU Food Loss and Waste platform seeking to influence European policy. FoodCloud presented at the meeting of the sub-group on food donations in 2017, 2019, and 2021, on topics including the future of food donation and lessons from the Covid pandemic. However, while the sub groups have annual meetings and provide information materials and have carried out a review of the national policy contexts of food donations within the EU member states, progress on actual policy change driven by this platform has been slow to emerge.

London, the United Kingdom

National policy context

The United Kingdom has a national 'Food Waste Reduction Roadmap' managed by a government-funded charity, Waste Resources and Action Programme (WRAP), and the Institute of Grocery Distribution (IGD), launched in 2018. The Roadmap enables food companies to set targets, measure food waste, and identify actions to reduce it. SFR is one of the key actions of the roadmap (IGD and WRAP 2020). A voluntary agreement, called the Courtauld Commitment, established a public-private partnership between the UK government and food retailers in 2015, to reduce food waste by 20% by 2025. WRAP also has an SFR Working Group that aims to identify ways of increasing the beneficial use of surplus food, by working to remove barriers to SFR, investing in redistribution capacity and measuring and reporting changes. WRAP's latest report found that surplus redistribution in the United Kingdom has exceeded 320,000 tonnes (worth *c.* £1 billion) from 2015 to 2020, increasing by 65% from 2018 to 2020 (WRAP 2021b).

In 2020, the Department of Environment, Food and Rural Affairs (DEFRA) provided £12 million to fund SFR. This funding supported over 250 SFR projects, with 50% of the increase from 2019 to 2020 directly due to DEFRA's funding, and 38% due to finances flowing from the Government's pandemic response fund (WRAP 2021b). WRAP, DEFRA, and the UK Food Safety Authority have also collaborated to provide guidelines on labelling and redistribution. In January 2021, 'Xcess: The Independent Food Redistribution Network' was established, to work with DEFRA, WRAP, and IGD to unlock untapped surplus.

The main strength of the UK's policies for food redistribution is the centralised management and implementation under WRAP. Limitations include the absence of levies on disposal of edible food by large food businesses, the voluntary nature of commitments, and no obligations for public facing reporting.

City food sharing context

Embedded in the UK's comparatively stronger policy support for SFR, relative to Ireland, London has a dynamic SFR landscape. The form of SFR varies across initiatives, from gleaning seasonal gluts of local fruit trees and distributing it to food using community groups (e.g. Abundance Kingston). Beyond this, there are initiatives revalorising waste food by using it to prepare meals as part of a social dining experience (e.g. Beggars' Banquet, Dinner Exchange London), or processing surplus food into sellable condiments, dips, and juices (e.g. ChicP, JuiceCube, Rejuce), or social supermarkets that collect and sell edible waste food at reduced rates (e.g. Community shop) and models similar to Food-Cloud, such as FareShare, connecting supermarket surplus with local charities.

Case study: Be Enriched

Be Enriched was founded in 2013 and provides community meals and food made from donated surplus to five boroughs in South London. They cook meals with the surplus food and use these food services to build a sense of community and connection and develop skills in young people. They have developed a series of projects including their community canteens, a mobile food bus, summer camps with healthy food for youth, awareness campaigns about healthy eating, and cooking classes. Be Enriched receives surplus food donations from two large local supermarket chains (Be Enriched 2020).

SCALE AND IMPACT

Be Enriched is motivated by the scale of food waste in the United Kingdom, the jarring levels of food insecurity (8.4 million adults at risk), and the level of isolation experienced by residents in London. They have engaged with a preliminary assessment of their social, environmental, and economic impacts and identified their contribution to increasing access and consumption of fresh food, connecting and creating new support networks within communities, and increasing individuals' well-being through volunteering opportunities. They found that over 3,000 people have become more engaged with their community, that Be Enriched has distributed over 15,000 portions of fresh fruit and vegetables, and that all of their employees earn more than 10% above the minimum wage. By conducting a preliminary sustainability assessment, Be Enriched discovered impacts they were having that they had not previously considered important, for example in relation to reducing food waste by using donated edible surplus food instead of it being disposed of to landfill, and identified areas for future improvement to better meet their goals.

RESOURCES

Be Enriched relies on food donations, monetary donations, and sponsorship from the National Lottery Fund. They have nine staff members, many volunteers, and five members on their board of trustees. Be Enriched is a registered charity, and owns a company called the People's Kitchen, Brixton.

POLICY ENGAGEMENT

Be Enriched does not engage extensively in advocacy or policy. Its primary focus is community impact. However, the founder and CEO of Be Enriched is a Wandsworth Councillor and is deputy leader of the Wandsworth Labour party, and is highly engaged in local policy development and directions. The founder uses her platform to campaign to end food poverty and increase access to healthy food in her local area and throughout the United Kingdom. Be Enriched social media channels share information and evidence around how to end food insecurity and address food poverty in the United Kingdom.

CHALLENGES

Be Enriched have had to address a range of challenges for their operations, particularly in relation to organisational governance and funding. They had a very large paperwork load to get registered as a charity and were rejected three times before a lawyer worked with them pro bono over two years to support their application.

Being dependent on constant fundraising and grant applications is another challenge. They are developing alternative income sources, like a café, to reduce their dependency on once-off donations and ongoing grant applications. In addition, there are also the emotional challenges of working with volunteers and with vulnerable members of the community whose everyday lives can make regular attendance at events unpredictable. In particular, they face the challenge of raising awareness among those experiencing food poverty that there is free food available and communicating clearly what times and where the meals are happening. They use social media and posters, but mostly they rely on word of mouth to connect people with the community meals.

Barcelona, Spain

National policy context

Since 2013, Spain has had a national strategy to reduce food waste, called 'Más alimento, menos desperdicio' (more food, less waste), developed by the

Ministry of Agriculture, Food and the Environment. The strategy has used a combination of recommendations, voluntary agreements, self-regulation, and some new regulation proposals around food safety, liability, and fiscal incentives for donating food (Ministerio de agricultura pesca y alimentación 2013). In the most recent iteration, the 2017–2020 strategy, part of action area 3, 'Analysis and review of regulatory aspects', the committee specifically undertook a review of quality standard regulations that limit SFR. Additionally, the strategy commits to develop a national guide to facilitate the donation of food in the near future (Ministerio de agricultura pesca y alimentación 2018).

Spain allows corporations donating food to reclaim 35% of the food value in tax credits (European Commission 2017). In 2017, law changes clarified liability and responsibility around food donations. In June 2021, the Ministry of Agriculture, Food and Fisheries launched a public consultation prior to preparing a law on the prevention of food waste, which will include measures to facilitate the donation of food and contribute to meeting the food needs of the most vulnerable population.

City food sharing context

The SHARECITY 100 database (Davies et al. 2016) identified 16 SFR initiatives in Barcelona. Examples include apps where individuals can upload their surplus food and a neighbour can collect it for free (e.g. ComeYda), freegan communities that collect food from bins (e.g. Comida Basura), social cooking and dining experiences that use surplus food or 'ugly' foods that are rejected by food retail aesthetic standards (e.g. Plato De Gracia, DiscoSoupe), and many groups that provide education and awareness campaigns about uses for surplus food (e.g. Ifeed BCN, Plataforma Aprofitem Aliments).

Case study: Espigoladors

Founded in 2014, Espigoladors is a non-profit social enterprise that aims to fight food waste and loss while empowering those experiencing social exclusion, using transformative, participative, and inclusive sustainable activities. The three priority social needs that motivate Espigoladors are fighting for better food usage, guaranteeing the right to a healthy diet, and creating job opportunities for groups at risk of social exclusion. They employ four steps in their business model to reduce food waste and redistribute food:

1   Gleaning projects that gather surplus food and food not suitable for the market directly from the farm;
2   Donating gleaned food to other organisations who then distribute it to vulnerable groups;
3   Transforming gleaned food into preserves and other products to sell and help create employment opportunities for excluded groups;
4   Delivering awareness campaigns about how to minimise food waste.

Espigoladors are also motivated by wanting to restore the disappearing traditional practices of gleaning as a solution to modern food waste challenges. Espigoladors' values are social transformation, integrity, innovation, professionalism, and cooperation (Fundació Espigoladors 2021).

SCALE AND IMPACT

Espigoladors do not currently measure their social, environmental, and economic impacts in a consistent or comprehensive way. Annual impact reports are anecdotal and reflective, with some quantitative data included such as number of jobs, amount of food rescued, and number of volunteers. However, detailed analysis of the full range of well-being and environmental impacts such activities are having is not yet addressed in full. The 2018 annual report shows they donated food to over 75,000 families and created 26 training and job opportunities. They facilitate a network of producers allowing gleaning projects on their farms, and have a workshop to create preserve products from the 'unmarketable' food gleaned (Espigoladors 2019). By 2021, Espigoladors had rescued over 1,300 tonnes of food, working closely with 115 farms. This is equivalent to avoiding 875 tonnes of CO_2 being emitted and saving over 800 million litres of water. They highlight how their work directly contributes to six of the 17 United Nations SDGs. Further exploration of these impacts could include considering social metrics such as the well-being benefits of volunteers, economic variables such as whether their employees receive a fair, living wage, or additional environmental metrics such as reporting on their management of unavoidable food waste.

RESOURCES

In 2018, Espigoladors employed 20 people and worked with over 1,000 volunteers in their gleaning projects. They generate 39% of their income through sales of their branded products made from 'ugly' fruit and vegetables (brand name: 'És Im-perfect'), 57% from grants, and the remaining 4% from monetary donations (Espigoladors 2019).

POLICY ENGAGEMENT

Espigoladors engage with a variety of policy and advocacy networks around food waste. At a local level, they are members of 'platforma aprofitem els aliments', supported by Barcelona City Council, which offers legal advice, promotional materials, and advice to businesses about reducing food waste. Other city council networks they are members of 'Include a citizen agreement for an inclusive Barcelona' (Acord Ciutadá per una Barcelona Inclusiva) and Sustainable Barcelona (Barcelona +Sostenible).

At a national level, they participate in a city network for agroecology (red de Ciudades por la Agroecología), which includes over 1,000 organisations committed to environmental, social, and economic sustainability that collectively build a responsible city with people and the environment.

At a European level, they partnered with the EU research project 'ReFresh', which aims to identify solutions for food waste through public-private collaboration, the outputs of which included calls for the formulation of EU policy and support for national implementation of food waste policy frameworks.

CHALLENGES

Espigoladors started as an association and progressed to register as a 'non-profit organisation'. In Spain there is no formal legal mechanism to register as a social enterprise, which made it challenging for them to communicate their business model to private and public sectors. When seeking investment, they faced barriers because social enterprises are considered high-risk investments.

Espigoladors' ideal scenario is that the people receiving food donations from charities would also be volunteers gleaning on the farms. They have to overcome perceptions among their charity partners that beneficiaries are not volunteers, and engage with the people receiving food donations to invite them to volunteer and highlight the benefits of volunteering. Currently their volunteers are a mixture of people who receive the food donations and people motivated for other reasons such as environmental concerns about food waste. They also have to build trust with farmers who have expressed fears about having volunteers on their farms, potentially damaging their means of income.

When collaborating internationally, Espigoladors has found slow progress when working with groups in other countries that are primarily volunteer led with little staff capacity to maintain sufficient communication to build momentum.

Discussion

This chapter outlines the policy context of three European cities where SFR is taking place, and highlights the impacts and challenges of SFR initiatives active in these cities. Challenges experienced by SFR initiative case studies herein include a lack of data collection and reporting on their impacts, administrative demands restricting their capacity to deliver on their goals, poor resources and supports such as lack of favourable business models, and lack of strong local and national policy infrastructure to enable their work.

For the purposes of this discussion, we will focus on two of these barriers, which are interconnected:

1   A lack of data collecting and reporting practices among food redistribution initiatives, resulting in a dearth of evidence to inform strategic policies decisions

2   A lack of supportive policies and a persistence of unsupportive legacy policies

SFR initiatives, such as the case studies in this chapter, have significant sustainability potential (Davies 2019), but they often struggle to identify, demonstrate, and communicate the full extent of their impact and value (Mackenzie and Davies 2019). The reasons for this are multifaceted. It is sometimes due to a lack of reporting capacity internally and sometimes it is the high cost of purchasing external consultancy to undertake reporting, but most often it is because mainstream impact assessment tools have not been designed with SFR initiatives in mind. The SHARE IT toolkit is an example of an innovation designed to respond directly to these barriers (Mackenzie and Davies 2019). The cumulative impact of SFR currently has low visibility at multiple levels, from the initiatives, to public authorities and wider citizens. To move forward with evidence-based transitions to sustainable urban food systems, this impact needs to be made visible. SHARE IT was designed with this goal in mind.

SHARE IT offers a holistic multi-dimensional online platform that is free at point of use. It is organised into three features enabling sustainability impact assessment that is affordable, accessible, bespoke, and research-based. It achieves this through three innovative features conceptualised and developed in a co-design process with food sharing groups:

1   The Toolshed: with its comprehensive suite of easy-to-understand indicator questions, which allows non-experts to collect qualitative and quantitative data and auto-generate a visual, accessible Sustainability Impact Report;
2   The Talent Garden: which provides a virtual space to share alternative formats of impact evidence (e.g. audio, visual, narratives) that cannot be demonstrated in the Toolshed;
3   The Greenhouse: which provides a virtual networking hub for knowledge transfer and support.

Solutions such as SHARE IT are needed to enable data collection and reporting among SFR initiatives. However, the toolkit alone is insufficient, and further supporting services to embed data collection and reporting practices into SFR initiatives will be needed. SHARE IT offers part of the solution by being tailored and specific to the SFR context, but the challenge remains to sustainably enable and establish reporting practices among SFR initiatives to increase the internal and external awareness of their impacts and needs within the cities they operate in.

All three SFR case studies identified the need for more supportive policies around liability and traceability, fiscal incentives and levies, supportive structures for alternative business, and non-profit entities like social enterprises, increasing reporting capacity and visibility of the true value and impacts food redistribution initiatives can have in the fight against food waste.

Looking for good practices beyond the case studies above, France and Italy have piloted a new policy direction for managing surplus food from food retailers. It will be important to monitor and evaluate the impact of these policy decisions over time (also see Chapter 7 on France and Chapter 8 on Italy) to ascertain the impact on a range of issues, from environmental impacts from reduced disposal to landfill through to the scale and scope of surplus food redistribution intermediaries and ultimately the impacts it has overall on access to safe, sustainable, and healthy food.

One potential blind spot in the policy that is not being addressed by current SFR interventions is to not only focus on maximising recovering edible food from further down the waste hierarchy to redistribute within the community, but also look further up the waste hierarchy to prevent surplus from being generated in the first place. Food is highly commodified, and extensive fiscal subsidies and policy supports exist to maximise food production across the EU. For example, in Ireland where there is weak policy support for SFR, EU and national government interventions have enabled an export focused agricultural system that produces enough food for 50 million people, with a national population of just 4.7 million, with the majority of that food being environmentally unsustainable beef and dairy. Additionally, redistributing surplus to the community, away from waste streams, is a highly marketable activity from a CSR perspective for large retailers, but as a result it also brings with it a risk of social washing and greenwashing when the full costs of that redistribution are not covered. Policymakers and SFR initiatives need to keep their eye on such practices.

Conclusion

This chapter considers the policy context for three cities within which SFR initiatives are reducing food waste by redistributing surplus. There are a wide range of policy mechanisms that can enable SFR, and the impact of these can be seen in the varying extent of SFR case study activity in each city. Policy still favours the commercial wing of the redistribution food chain and does not demand full sustainability impact reporting of the activity. Additionally, the SFR initiatives themselves struggle to embed data collecting and impact reporting practices into their activities, which is consequential of and contributes to the problem of unsupportive policy. Some solutions have emerged, such as SHARE IT, but further work is needed to enable reporting among SFRs at scale and develop a more enabling policy environment. While the focus of this chapter has been on food waste reduction, in the context of SFR, it is important to also consider the other goals and impacts that these initiatives are working towards, from reducing food insecurity to reducing social exclusion. These co-benefits are often as important to initiatives as the food waste reduction element of their work; however, the development of policy for food waste reduction in the public sector rarely engages with other departments with responsibilities for these matters. Further joined-up decision-making is required to make policy decisions around food based on the full range of sustainability impacts activities create.

References

Be Enriched. 2020. https://www.be-enriched.org.

Communication from the Commission to the European Parliament, the Council, the European Economic and Social Committee and the Committee of the Regions: A Farm to Fork Strategy for a Fair, Healthy and Environmentally-Friendly Food System COM/2020/381 final (European Commission 2020a).

Communication from the Commission to the European Parliament, the Council, the European Economic and Social Committee and the Committee of the Regions: A New Circular Economy Action Plan For a Cleaner and More Competitive Europe COM/2020/98 (European Commission 2020b).

Davies, A. R. 2019. *Urban Food Sharing: Rules, Tools and Networks*. Bristol: Policy Press.

Davies, A. R., A. Cretella, and V. Franck. 2019. "Food Sharing Initiatives and Food Democracy: Practice and Policy in Three European Cities." *Politics and Governance* 7 (4): 8–20.

Davies, A. R., F. Edwards, B. Marovelli, O. Morrow, M. Rut, and M. Weymes. 2016. *Sharecity100 Database*. Dublin: Trinity College.

Davies, A. R., and D. Evans. 2019. "Urban Food Sharing: Emerging Geographies of Production, Consumption and Exchange. *Geoforum* 99: 154–59.

DECC. 2020. "Waste Action Plan for a Circular Economy." www.gov.ie/en/publication/4221c-waste-action-plan-for-a-circular-economy/. Government of Ireland, Dublin.

———. 2021a. *General Scheme of the Circular Economy Bill 2021*. Dublin: Government of Ireland.

Deloitte, Directorate-General for Health and Food Safety (European Commission), ECORYS. 2020. *Food Redistribution in the EU Mapping and Analysis of Existing Regulatory and Policy Measures Impacting Food Redistribution from EU Member States*. Brussels: European Commission.

Edwards, F. 2020. "Overcoming the Social Stigma of Consuming Food Waste by Dining at the Open Table." *Agriculture and Human Values*. https://doi.org/10.1007/s10460-020-10176-9.

Edwards, F., and D. Mercer. 2007. "Gleaning From Gluttony: An Australian Youth Subculture Confronts the Ethics of Waste. *Australian Geographer* 38 (3): 279–96.

———. 2012. "Food Waste in Australia: The Freegan Response." *The Sociological Review* 60: 174–91.

EPA. 2017. Accessed September 2021. www.foodwastecharter.ie.

Espigoladors. 2019. *Fundació Espigoladors Memoria de actividades 2018*. Barcelona: Espigoladors.

European Commission. 2017. *Financial Rules on Food Donation*. Brussels: European Commission.

FoodCloud. 2020. *FoodCloud 2019 Annual Report: Hungry for a Kinder World*. Dublin: FoodCloud.

FoodCloud. 2021. https://food.cloud/.

Fundació Espigoladors. 2021. https://espigoladors.cat/en/.

IGD and WRAP. 2020. The Food Waste Reduction Roadmap Progress Report 2020. Banbury: WRAP.

Mackenzie, S. G., and A. R. Davies. 2019. "SHARE IT: Co-Designing a Sustainability Impact Assessment Framework for Urban Food Sharing Initiatives." *Environmental Impact Assessment Review* 79: 106300. https://doi.org/10.1016/j.eiar.2019.106300.

Ministerio de agricultura pesca y alimentación. 2013. *Más alimento, menos desperdicio*.

———. 2018. *More Food, Less Waste Strategy 2017–2020*. Madrid, Spain: Ministerio de agricultura pesca y alimentación.

Papargyropoulou, E., R. Lozano, J. K. Steinberger, N. Wright, and Z. Bin Ujang. 2014. "The Food Waste Hierarchy as a Framework for the Management of Food Surplus and Food Waste." *Journal of Cleaner Production* 76: 106–15.

Vaqué, L. 2017. "French and Italian Food Waste Legislation: An Example for Other EU Member States to Follow?" *European Food and Feed Law Review* (3): 224–33. Accessed September 2, 2021. www.jstor.org/stable/90010366.

Weymes, M., and A. R. Davies. 2018. "Disruptive Technologies? Scaling Relational Geographies of ICT-Mediated Surplus Food Redistribution." SHARECITY Working Paper 3, Trinity College Dublin.

———. 2019. "[Re]Valuing Surplus: Transitions, Technologies and Tensions in Redistributing Prepared Food in San Francisco." *GeoForum* 99: 160–69. https://doi.org/10.1016/j.geoforum.2018.11.005.

WRAP. 2021b. *Surplus Food Redistribution in the UK 2015–2020*. Banbury: WRAP.

14 Mitigating barriers to surplus food donation in Italian retail and food service

Giulia Bartezzaghi, Claudia Colicchia, Paola Garrone, Marco Melacini, Alessandro Perego, and Andrea Rizzuni

Introduction

In the last decades, urban areas of developed countries have experienced increasing difficulties in guaranteeing food security and managing food waste (Zaman and Lehmann 2011; Sonnino, Marsden, and Moragues-Faus 2016; Fattibene et al. 2020). To tackle the 'food waste paradox'—people suffering from food insecurity in the face of large volumes of wasted food—local governments have developed policies towards more sustainable and inclusive food systems. Food recovery and redistribution (FR&R), namely the reuse of surplus food generated along the supply chain for human consumption, has been prioritised as a synergistic response to food insecurity and food waste (Alexander and Smaje 2008; Garrone, Melacini, and Perego 2014b; Papargyropoulou et al. 2014; Bilska et al. 2016; Albizzati et al. 2019), even though concerns are expressed about the implications of an exclusive reliance on FR&R for long-term food security (Tarasuk and Eakin 2003; Riches 2011; Mourad 2016; Arcuri 2019; Galli, Cavicchi, and Brunori 2019).

Urban FR&R relies on food donations from private donors and leverages the engagement of food banks and front-line organisations (e.g. food pantries) that serve vulnerable people. Canteens and retailers are important players of the city food system, but their involvement in FR&R is still limited by multiple barriers (see the section "Donation barriers for food service and retail").

This chapter illustrates a response to such barriers that has been developed and implemented in Milan in 2019, called Neighbourhood Hubs Against Food Waste (NHAFW), through a partnership involving the local government, business enterprises, non-profit organisations (NPOs), and a research advisory partner (i.e. the authors' university).

Milan is a large city in Lombardy (Northern Italy), with 1,398,000 residents in 2021 (ISTAT 2021). Like other urban areas of higher income countries, it faces the co-presence of food insecurity and food waste. In North-West Italy, absolute poverty is growing, because of the pandemic crisis, hitting 10.1% of residents in 2020 against 6.8% in 2019 (ISTAT 2020). Around 21,000 children were estimated to be at risk of poverty in the urban area of Milan in

DOI: 10.4324/9781003226932-19

2018 (Fondazione Cariplo 2018). Over 13,000 people, mostly foreign residents, used in 2019 the services of the charitable branch of Milan's Catholic diocese, with 42% of their assistance requests concerning food aids (Caritas Ambrosiana 2019). The largest food bank in Lombardy reports that it recovered almost 18,000 tonnes of surplus food (36 million equivalent meals) in 2020, and assisted over 230,000 people (Banco Alimentare della Lombardia 2021). Finally, Milan municipality produced in 2019 110 kilograms per inhabitant of organic solid waste (ISPRA 2020). Since the launch of the first pilot action in 2019, the practice NHAFW under study has been consolidated and replicated, and was awarded the first Edition of the Earth Shot Prize within the category 'Build a Waste-Free World', in October 2021, promoted by the Royal Foundation of the Duke and Duchess of Cambridge for its positive contribution to the society and the environment (Royal Foundation 2021).

We adopted multiple methods to analyse the initiative. First, we conducted an in-depth literature review of extant studies on corporate barriers to food donations, particularly for retail and food service operators. Second, to corroborate literature insights, eight semi-structured interviews were carried out. Finally, the analysis of collected information and the assessment of the pilot initiative allowed us to formulate conclusions on how the organisational and operational mechanisms of the policy may smoothen donation barriers.

The remainder of the chapter is organised as follows. The next section reviews barriers to donation in food service and food retail, illustrates the policy, and describes the interviews. After that, it analyses the results from interviews, integrates the literature insights, and puts forward recommendations for local policymakers. The last section illustrates the main conclusions and implications.

Analysis of the policy

Donation barriers for food service and retail

Enterprises are increasingly aware of the negative social, environmental, and economic effects of food waste. However, most of them still experience barriers to FR&R, the prioritised management option in the Food Waste Hierarchy (Papargyropoulou et al. 2014).

Several studies point out the presence of barriers to food donation when products are characterised by short shelf life and high perishability. Relevant efforts in terms of resources, procedures, and infrastructure are necessary for their FR&R (Garrone, Melacini, and Perego 2013, 2014a). In food processing and retail, a few product categories are traditionally donated to NPOs, such as ambient and canned food (Garrone, Melacini, and Perego 2013). In food service, the recoverability of cooked meals is low, inhibiting FR&R activities (Garrone, Melacini, and Perego 2013, 2014a). A reduced shelf life is likely to result in a large amount of waste (Buisman, Haijema, and Bloemhof-Ruwaard

2019), while some authors underline the effectiveness of policies aimed at the adoption of shelf life-based models (La Scalia et al. 2019; Gharehyakheh et al. 2019). A redefinition of existing norms regulating date marking—for instance allowing food donation after the Best Before Date (BBD)—might facilitate FR&R (FAO 2016; Baglioni et al. 2017). However, surplus food after BBD generated by retailers and upstream supply chain actors is little and food aid organisations might perceive it as of lower quality (Busetti 2019).

Difficulties in implementing food donation may arise due to the poor fit between FR&R activities and existing operational processes. Retail stores should pick up and store surplus food in ad hoc areas during daily activities (Garrone, Melacini, and Perego 2013; ECR 2015). Other additional activities must be carried out, such as the registration and repackaging of recovered products and the preparation of transportation and other fiscal documents (Sert et al. 2018; Busetti 2019). Similarly, FR&R from food service implies additional tasks and costs, such as putting surplus food in a special container, moving the filled container to a blast chiller, handling the blast chiller, and sealing and labelling the container (Sert et al. 2018). Donors must allocate human resources specifically to donation processes (Busetti 2019). Barriers are higher when donors do not have a systematic measurement system of surplus food and food waste, a clear definition of roles and responsibilities in charge of FR&R activities, and formalised agreements with NPOs (Sert et al. 2016). Lack of competency in handling surplus food may represent a public health threat (Milicevic et al. 2016). Moreover, small retail stores may not have the decision power to donate surplus food without corporate-level authorisations (Busetti 2019).

FR&R generally implies additional activities and costs for donors. When assessing possible options of surplus food management, the differential costs associated to operational, administrative, and managerial activities, and the costs of equipment and machinery necessary to FR&R, must be considered (Sert et al. 2018).

The Italian legislation provides for the deductibility of VAT on donated food products and allows municipalities to introduce fiscal incentives for food donors by reducing the waste tax proportionate to donations (Gazzetta Ufficiale della Repubblica Italiana 2016). Still, only a few cities in Italy have adopted such measures (EU Platform on Food Losses and Food Waste 2019). At the same time, companies tend to claim that fiscal incentives do not cover the additional costs incurred in FR&R activities (ECR 2015; Garrone et al. 2015; Baglioni et al. 2017). The actual economic advantage of food donations compared to recycling and disposal depends on the amount of surplus food generated and the rate of discounts adopted by the local municipality (Busetti 2019).

Another recurring barrier results from the uncertainty on norms regulating food donations as well as other possible destinations (Mithun Ali et al. 2019). Some companies have limited knowledge of the regulatory framework, preventing them from FR&R for human consumption (ECR 2015; Baglioni et al. 2017; Bharucha 2018). Moreover, companies perceive the administrative procedures for donating as burdensome (ECR 2015; Garrone et al. 2015).

Possible mismanagement of surplus food by NPOs creates a reputational risk for donors (ECR 2015; Martin-Rios et al. 2018). The redistribution of defective products may result in consequences on the health of final beneficiaries (Bharucha 2018) and in a reputational damage for the food donor (Mithun Ali et al. 2019). The suitability of NPOs should be assessed considering their logistics capabilities, transparency, and capillarity (Garrone et al. 2014b). Aside from reputation risks, donation may be hindered by operational constraints. NPOs may lack appropriate space and infrastructure to store, handle, and transport donated food, particularly for large quantities and perishable food, or may suffer the scarcity and inadequacy of staff and volunteer time allocated to FR&R (Hecht and Neff 2019). Moreover, food donors may not find available NPOs locally due to the weak capillarity of those associations (ECR 2015). Discontinuity of demand for surplus food in terms of quantity and variety required may occur (Gentilini 2013; De Boeck et al. 2017; Gharehyakheh et al. 2019). Unstructured FR&R processes and highly variable donations cause operational inefficiencies that discourage food donations (ECR 2015; Busetti 2019).

The context

As people increasingly migrate to urban settings, urban food systems are facing raising issues of lack of physical and financial access to food coupled with food waste generation (Zaman and Lehmann 2011; Sonnino, Marsden, and Moragues-Faus 2016; Fattibene et al. 2020). To respond to these challenges, municipalities have developed urban food policies (UFP) to provide access to healthy and affordable food for all (Raja et al. 2008), while preventing food waste (Treutwein and Langen 2021). FR&R is often carried out by private actors such as food banks and front-line NPOs that serve needy people. Those actors rely on food amounts and resources from private food donors, mainly restaurants and retail chains, with a marginal involvement of public welfare and policy (Treutwein and Langen 2021).

In this context, municipalities can be role models, enablers and facilitators, service providers or regulators, and planners (Bulkeley and Kern 2006; Bulkeley and Betsill 2005). The role of enablers refers to municipalities 'facilitating, co-ordinating and encouraging action through partnership with private and voluntary-sector agencies, and . . . various forms of community engagement' (Bulkeley and Kern 2006).

However, multi-stakeholder FR&R models are not yet well established (De Cunto et al. 2017). Local governments still face several challenges, such as the limited engagement of private stakeholders, other city departments, and levels of governance (De Cunto et al. 2017).

In this context, Milan has gained a prominent position for its innovative food policy, positioning food at the centre of the city's development. Together with the charitable branch of a large Italian bank, Milan has built a comprehensive food policy strategy to favour the transition to a more sustainable urban food system (FAO 2019). Since 2015, 211 cities have signed the international protocol of the Milan Urban Food Policy Pact and Framework for Action. In 2017, the Municipality established a Food Policy Office under the responsibility of the Deputy Mayor (Milano Food Policy 2018, 8).

The case

The initiative is 'Neighbourhood Hubs Against Food Waste' (NHAFW). Several actors (food service operators, retailers, NPOs, start-ups) have been long engaged in FR&R across the city. More recently, the Municipality has been reinforcing its policy efforts to build systemic platforms to integrate initiatives in collective action. The recommended actions to prevent food waste prescribe monitoring and collecting data, undertaking collaborations with the private sector and research centres, facilitating the involvement of stakeholders, mapping best practices, and favouring FR&R for human consumption (FAO 2019).

The guidelines of the Food Policy related to the strategic objective of reducing food waste include the promotion of FR&R and the promotion of partnerships with institutional, social, and economic entities. A favourable national regulatory environment aided the evolution of the local food redistribution policy (see Chapter 8). Legislative Decree 460/1997 and law 133/1999 grant VAT exemptions on donations. The Good Samaritan Law of 2003 (155/2003) limits the safety liability of donors to their internal processes until the donation occurs. Legislative Decree 35/2005 allows companies to deduct the value of donated items, up to 10% of taxable income or €70,000/year. Law 166/16 ('Gadda Law') simplifies donation processes paperwork and allows municipalities to provide further fiscal incentives. At the local level, in 2018, the Municipality established deductions of up to 50% on the variable municipal waste tax in proportion to the donated volumes.

NHAFW was conceived in 2016, when the Municipality of Milan, Politecnico di Milano (the authors' university), and a local business association signed an agreement protocol aimed at integrating actions, competences, and resources to reduce food insecurity and food waste in the urban area of Milan. Its objective is to design, implement, and monitor a surplus food redistribution system, highlighting and disseminating existing best practices and novel solutions, thanks to the cooperation of public agencies, business enterprises, and NPOs.

NHAFW leverages on consolidation hubs located in city neighbourhoods. The hubs overcome two issues of urban FR&R, namely centralised food banks' inefficiency in recovering small and heterogeneous volumes of surplus food generated by multiple donors (Garrone, Melacini, and Perego 2014b; Michalec et al. 2018), and the difficulty of food banks in delivering balanced and nutritious food mixes to beneficiaries, including fresh and prepared food (Tarasuk and Eakin 2003; Irwin et al. 2007; Sert et al. 2016).

The first hub was opened as a pilot in January 2019 in the Isola district, serving Milan's Municipality 9. The initiative relies on a large, differentiated set of participants and roles.[1]

NHAFW is managed by a *coordination domain*, the 'Signatory Board' (Municipality of Milan, Politecnico di Milano and the business association), with the role of network design, coordination, monitoring, and performance measurement. It takes strategic decisions and summons periodic plenary meetings between participants. The Municipality integrates the initiative within a broader local food redistribution policy and provides underused public spaces. It works synergistically with the philanthropic branch of a domestic bank, which facilitates the network creation, providing knowledge on poverty distribution across the city, and on possible beneficiary NPOs. Politecnico di Milano designs the logistic model and the measurement system. As an independent party, it monitors and reports individual and aggregate project performances and promotes collaboration mediating among participants. The business association facilitates the involvement of donor firms and supporters.

The activities needed to transfer surplus food from donors to recipients constitute the *operational domain*. Four retailers (nine points-of-sale) and one food service operator (five corporate canteens) donate surplus food and adopt a shared reporting system. Donors adapt their daily operations to perform project activities (deliver donations during the morning collection route, send data reports) but are not required to further standardise their internal processes. Donors are heterogeneous in their previous experience in donation activities. They are given the chance to participate in the network according to a flexible two-layer structure. *Informational* adhesion (sharing data on the volumes of donations, surplus food, and food waste generated in their operations and allowing enquiries on their processes, to highlight and disseminate best practices) is mandatory. Donors may participate also through *tangible* adhesion: their donations are conferred to the logistic intermediary and, in the case of retailers, collected and sorted in the hub and redistributed.

In the pilot hub, recipients are around 20 NPOs—mostly food pantries, while a few prepare food boxes. The regional branch of the main Italian food bank operates the hub, recovering, stocking, and sorting donated surplus food. Food banks have operational know-how and a comparative advantage in recovering and ensuring the quality of redistributed food (Riches 2002; Garrone, Melacini, and Perego 2014b). The space is made available by the Municipality and equipped with shelves for dry food and a refrigerated area for fresh products. Retailers' surplus food is collected each weekday with two trucks and consolidated in the hub by the end of the morning; it is then redistributed according to a predefined weekly schedule. Hub managers sort donations to NPOs, composing balanced mixes of fresh and dry food based on the number of beneficiaries served as well as specificities of the NPO (e.g. peculiar dietary needs due to age or other conditions of beneficiaries), to redistribute all the fresh food collected in the morning. Another truck collects prepared meals from canteens and directly redistributes them to front-line NPOs.

The model is designed to overcome limitations of traditional food banking (Tarasuk and Eakin 2003). Indeed, it is based on daily collections and on a fast redistribution network, which allows the recovery of fresh and perishable

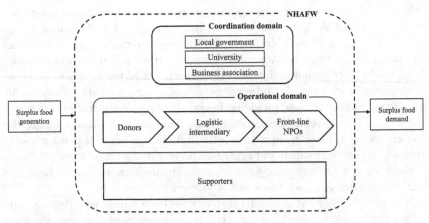

Figure 14.1 Summarises NHAFW functions and roles.

food. Coupled with the presence of a hub where multiple donations are consolidated, NHAFW allows the creation of balanced and nutritious mixes of products.

The operational domain relies on an array of actors (*supporting domain*) providing financial and material support for the development and operations of the hub.

During the first year of operations, the pilot hub recovered 77 tonnes of surplus food (corresponding to 154,000 meals and an economic value of €510,000), serving 1,300 households (2,500 adults and 1,500 children). Redistributed food includes fruit and vegetables, dry food, bread, pastry, dairy, and protein-based products, including meat and fish.

The network has further extended involving new donors, sponsors, and NPOs, leading to the launch of two additional hubs in Municipalities 3 and 8 in October 2020 and July 2021.

The replication comes with a continuous monitoring and optimisation activity of existing operational and coordination mechanisms. Indeed, NHAFW presents areas of improvement, including the coordination costs to manage the different actors, the difficulty of retrieving regularly data from food donors, the impact of external variables on the regular functioning of activities.[2] A series of actions has been designed to overcome these limitations, such as introducing paid personnel in charge of operational activities in the hubs, and having periodic alignment meetings among the coordinators and donors.

Interviews results

Multiple interviews were used to corroborate the literature review. Interviewed managers were chosen to cover the two supply chain stages, and to balance information from players participating in NHAFW with external insights.

Table 14.1 Interviews

Interview	Type	Job title	NHAFW role
A	Retailer	Supply chain manager	Operational (donor)
B	Retailer	CSR manager	
C	Food service	Food safety manager; Operational responsible	
D	Food service	CSR manager	None
E	Food service	CSR manager	
F	Food service	Specialist in collective food catering tenders	
G	Food bank	Managing director	Operational (intermediary)
H	Business association	Business relationships manager	Coordination

External players are chosen to be involved in surplus food redistribution, so to have a reasonable first-hand experience of barriers. Interviewees were contacted by e-mail, and interviews were conducted through Teams due to COVID-19 restrictions. Each interview took around one hour and was based on a semi-structured questionnaire, aimed at investigating the perception and the relevance of the six identified barriers and potentially find other ones. To facilitate respondents, the six barriers were anticipated by e-mail before the interview. The NHAFW interviewees were asked whether the perception of those barriers had changed after participation to NHAFW. At least two researchers were involved as interviewers, and interviews were recorded and subsequently manually transcribed.

Interviews are reported in Table 14.1. Information collected through interviews of retail and food service managers was complemented with two other interviews (G and H), carried out with two NHAFW participants, the food bank and the business association. Such interviews were further triangulated with audio and written notes collected throughout two years of the authors' direct participation to NHAFW, which involved multiple interactions with project participants.

When answering questions and discussing barriers, interviewees mostly agreed on their relevance, although perspectives of retailers and food service operators differ on important aspects. The analysis also reveals that some of the barriers recurrently experienced by food donors have been removed or alleviated through the operational and coordination mechanisms of NHAFW.

The *short residual shelf life of products* is confirmed to be a relevant barrier. Tensions emerge between economic, social, and environmental sustainability objectives. Indeed, retailers may try to sell products that are close to expiration through promotional discounts. While this ensures economic benefits, and sometimes allows avoiding waste, it may impede donations if the sale does not materialise. This is critical due to the very short time span left to NPOs to coordinate with the donor, recover, and redistribute surplus food before it expires.

'*Some categories are sold until the very last day, it is not only a moral decision but also an economic one*' (Interview B—Retailer).

Furthermore, retailers highlighted that a certain amount of surplus food is always going to be generated despite the efficiency efforts being made (Interview A—Retailer).

Food service operators equally highlight the difficulty in donating products with short residual life given the requirements in terms of redistribution infrastructure and cold chain (Interview D—Food service operator).

As a related operational barrier, the *discontinuity of demand for surplus food in terms of quantity and variety required* is highlighted as the main barrier for the donation of fresh (Interview B—Retailer) and prepared (Interview C—Food service operator) products.

Operationally, the project overcomes such barriers working on the frequency of collection stops and on coordination at the donor-intermediary interface, by agreeing daily collection routes from donors. Daily collection also allows fresh and prepared products to be donated and quickly redistributed, and provides donors stability in the size of downstream demand.

Additionally, creating a sizeable and geographically concentrated network allows the economic feasibility of recovery. Indeed, while recovery in urban areas is typically economically unsustainable due to the low volumes of individual collection points (Alexander and Smaje 2008), aggregating the volumes of multiple donors allows the saturation of transportation means and enhances the economics of recovery. Furthermore, this coordination avoids the risk of wasting resources when there is no surplus food to be retrieved (Alexander and Smaje 2008).

As a further consequence, aggregation of demand from multiple sources allows the composition of balanced healthy nutritional mixes of food and increases the capillarity of the network.

The food bank (Interview G) highlights that the model allows to provide recipient NPOs with a balanced mix of products, including fresh food and proteins, independently of their collection frequency.

At a coordination level, NHAFW represents a circularity broker filling the circularity hole between surplus food donors and recipients (Ciulli, Kolk, and Boe-Lillegraven 2020), timely matching the demand and supply of surplus food and recovering it before it becomes waste. The coordination domain performs brokerage functions (Ciulli, Kolk, and Boe-Lillegraven 2020) facilitating the informational exchange on features of demand and supply, allowing a better match (Interview B—Retailer). Furthermore, it allows negotiation and mediation to achieve an optimal trade-off between economic and social objectives. As anecdotal evidence of this, one donor agreed to adapt some of its last-minute discount policies to allow for more efficient recovery from the food bank.

Retailers emphasize the poor fit between recovery activities and existing operational activities especially due to additional administrative procedures, training and preparatory activities required for donation. In contrast, operational activities imply a negligible effort. Instead, food service operators also highlighted the burden of additional abatement, packaging and labelling activities.

'At the beginning, the activities are seen only as additional tasks to perform. [Kitchen workers] have to recover, label, abate, store in the fridge cells . . . some clients have noticed this, that it takes a relevant time to do this' (Interview C—Food service operator).

Consequently, the *cost of additional tasks* perceived by retailers is mostly the one of administrative and training procedures, while the cost of operational activities is deemed to be offset by costs savings (mainly waste management). This is consistent with some findings reported in literature (Holweg, Teller, and Kotzab 2016; Teller et al. 2018), although in general the economic efficiency of surplus food redistribution at the retail level is debated (Garrone, Melacini, and Perego 2014a; Holweg, Teller, and Kotzab 2016; Hermsdorf, Rombach, and Bitsch 2017).

'We did not do precise calculations, but costs are not barriers for us. Some tasks are not additional, and we can save on the cost of sorting and the variable part of the waste management tariff since we waste less kilograms' (Interview A—Retailer).

Food service operators instead highlight labour and equipment costs, as well as the activation and management of the relationship with the recipient NPO. Retailers (Interview B—Retailer) also highlighted the duplication of administrative and bureaucratic procedures when more recipients are present. Therefore, retailers may prefer to work with only one large, structured food bank.

The project works on these barriers through three levels: external standardisation, internal flexibility, sharing of best practices. External standardisation means that collection activities happen at pre-defined times, so that donor-recipient interface processes are standardised in the daily routine of the donor.

'When recovery takes place every day, the management of products is more efficient, and we also manage waste more efficiently. The planning of the activities is easier because we have set up in advance the routes. We have the guarantee that they come to collect five days a week . . . and that all stores have to give the same typologies of products' (Interview B—Retailer).

Internal flexibility means that, other than complying with the project interface processes, donors are not required to further standardize their internal processes. Finally, sharing best practices in the network allows participants to refine processes and activities thanks to the experience of researchers and operational actors active in surplus food redistribution. *'Exchanges and sharing in the network are tangible advantages for us'* (Interview B—Retailer).

The lack of knowledge about the regulatory environment and bureaucratic requirements is perceived as a barrier especially for those approaching donations for the first time. *'Gadda Law has made things simpler, but for someone who just starts donating it takes time to understand the legislation'* (Interview B—Retailer). One food service operator especially highlights the barrier of regulatory uncertainty in redistribution (Interview E—Food service operator).

The reputation risks related to possible mismanagement of surplus food by food aid organizations are relevant, especially with multiple, small recipient NPOs. This leads to the duplication of administrative procedures, and to

234 Giulia Bartezzaghi et al.

uncertainty about the proper handling of donations. For this reason, working with trustworthy, structured food banks and beneficiaries is considered fundamental by all interviewed donors.

'[The food bank we work with] gives us certainties on this. With smaller or less structured ones it may be a worry' (Interview C—Food service operator).

The project softens these barriers through the presence of a unique structured reference for donations to minimize administrative costs and the risk of mishandling of donations. Furthermore, especially for inexperienced donors, transaction costs due to information asymmetries when selecting recipients may be high. Their reliability in handling surplus food is scarcely observable ex-ante and may pose barriers to donation. Similarly, food aid organizations may be sceptical about accepting donations from untrusted sources. While the reputation of notable food banks or recipients may serve as a signal, this is not always enough. Interviews highlight that the direct involvement and monitoring of well-reputed institutions—the Municipality, the university and the business association—not only increases the visibility and reputational effects of participation, but also serves as a quality signal, certifying the correct management and monitoring of internal processes. Furthermore, it allows business firms to enter in an 'up and running' project. This is very clear in the words of the business association.

'[Being in a network] is a huge value . . . to approach firms . . . . . . and it will help us engaging realities which are not used to participating in this kind of projects nor to do this by themselves, because maybe they do not have the right structure internally or are not used to dealing with social responsibility . . . . The founders of the project are reputable and well-established . . . and so I enter a project where I trust that those actors have assessed its validity, usefulness, efficiency . . . . It is reassuring. . . . And I have already everything set up and studied, working by myself I may not be able to engage all the right partners, or it would take a lot of time and effort' (Interview H—Business Association).

Interestingly, interviewees participating in the project tend to perceive barriers as comparatively less important. Some confirm an enhancement in their donation processes when entering the project (even compared to donations made to the same food bank outside NHAFW). 'The donation has been optimized thanks to the scheduling. In other cities, sometimes we prepare surplus food and then they do not show up to collect it. This happens very rarely with NHAFW' (Interview C—Food service operator). On the opposite, sometimes non-participating actors express frustration with elements of the donation process which would be overcome through project participation. 'A barrier for us [related to how surplus food is handled by food aid organizations] is that for privacy reasons we are not able to know who are the beneficiaries' (Interview F—Food service operator).

Conclusions

FR&R has been since long part of the responses offered to food insecurity, but several facts concur to require an evolution of the traditional system, especially

Table 14.2 Interviews results and NHAFW mitigation mechanisms

Barrier	Perspective from interviews	NHAFW mitigation mechanisms
Short residual shelf life of products	Complex trade-offs between economic, social and environmental goals in handling products close to expiration	Increased frequency and regularity of collection stops; coordination at the donor-intermediary interface
Discontinuity of demand for surplus food in terms of quantity and variety	Retailers and food service operators highlight the difficulty in donating, respectively, fresh and prepared products	
Poor fit between recovery activities and the existing operational processes	Retailers emphasise the role of bureaucratic and administrative procedures. Food service operators also highlight abatement, labelling and packaging activities	External standardisation; internal flexibility; sharing of best practices
Costs of additional tasks	Retailers consider the additional costs of operational activities negligible, while perceiving costs related to administrative and bureaucratic procedures. Food service operators perceive the additional cost of labour and equipment	
Lack of knowledge about regulatory environment and administrative requirements	Particularly strong barrier for inexperienced donors	Unique, structured reference point for collection; certification role of the coordination mechanisms through reputation and monitoring
Reputation risks related to possible mismanagement of surplus food by food aid organisations	The barrier is strong when food aid organisations are multiple, small or unstructured	

in urban areas and for retailers and food service operators. Underprivileged residents of large cities are a rising number and exhibit a great fragmentation, a fact that multiplied the NPOs operating to serve the needy. Furthermore, increasing attention is given to the nutrition characteristics of redistributed food. To make available more fresh food and proteins, larger and more varied quantities of food should be recovered from canteens and retailers, and better transportation and storage capabilities should be deployed.

However, such goals would be hardly achievable without business enterprises (i.e. surplus food generators) on board of urban FR&R policies. To tackle this issue, we highlighted the most relevant barriers to FR&R at retail and food service level, and, leveraging on interviews with various actors in FR&R, has discussed the NHAFW policy of Milan and its impact on the main barriers for them.

Some implications for firms, NPOs, and municipalities that are willing to experiment with FR&R may be drawn from the analysis.

For firms willing to participate in FR&R, we have highlighted the main barriers and a solution to mitigate them. This may contribute to increasing business participation in donation activities as well as to the development of policies leveraging on mechanisms similar to those of NHAFW. At the very least, our results should help firms to focus on the barriers that are most relevant to them and to devise possible mitigating actions.

For NPOs working in FR&R activities, our contribution may help achieve a broader, more complete understanding of how to manage the donor-recipient interface. Indeed, the high frequency and predefined scheduling of recovery trips have been highlighted as crucial in reducing firm-level barriers and recovering higher quantities and more diverse mixes. Furthermore, a model to efficiently operate surplus food redistribution in a traditionally unfavourable context (retailers and food service operators in urban areas) has been proposed.

Finally, NHAFW, and its integration in a well-rounded UFP framework, may be of special interest for local governments, opening the way to similar policy interventions in their contexts. While our contribution focuses on reducing barriers for surplus food donors, necessary roles and competences to build a well-functioning FR&R network have also been illustrated. Given the proactive role of the municipality in the initiative, it may also rebalance the long-existing criticism of the passive role of public institutions in the delegation to food banks and other private NPOs of assistance to the food insecure (Riches 2011). This is especially true at a time in which food policy is occupying an increasingly central role in urban policies (Raja et al. 2008; Filippini, Mazzocchi, and Corsi 2019). Finally, interviews highlighted that the presence of partners that act as certifiers of the FR&R system and the sharing of best practices within the network are distinctive benefits brought by the initiative and should be taken into account when designing a new policy action.

Notes

1 For clarity, this chapter refers to operational and governance logics of the pilot hub.
2 Examples are emergency shocks like COVID-19, political elections, changes in internal organisations and priorities of donors, and the dependency on voluntary work.

References

Albizzati, Paola Federica, Davide Tonini, Charlotte Boyer Chammard, and Thomas Fruergaard. 2019. "Valorisation of Surplus Food in the French Retail Sector: Environmental and Economic Impacts." *Waste Management* 90: 141–51.

Alexander, Catherine, and Chris Smaje. 2008. "Surplus Retail Food Redistribution: An Analysis of a Third Sector Model." *Resources, Conservation and Recycling* 52 (11): 1290–98.

Ali, Syed Mithun, Md Abdul Moktadir, Golam Kabir, Jewel Chakma, Md Jalal Uddin Rumi, and Md Tawhidul Islam. 2019. "Framework for Evaluating Risks in Food Supply

Chain: Implications in Food Wastage Reduction." *Journal of Cleaner Production* 228: 786–800.

Arcuri, Sabrina. 2019. "Food Poverty, Food Waste and the Consensus Frame on Charitable Food Redistribution in Italy." *Agriculture and Human Values* 36 (2): 263–75.

Baglioni, Simone, Francesca Calò, Paola Garrone, and Mario Molteni, eds. 2017. *Foodsaving in Europe: At the Crossroad of Social Innovation.* Springer International Publishing. https://doi. org/10.1007/978-3.

Banco Alimentare della Lombardia. 2021. "Bilancio Sociale." https://cdn3.bancoalimentare. it/sites/bancoalimentare.it/files/bilancio_sociale_2020_banco_alimentare_lombardia_0. pdf.

Bharucha, Jehangir. 2018. "Tackling the Challenges of Reducing and Managing Food Waste in Mumbai Restaurants." *British Food Journal.* https://doi.org/10.1108/BFJ-06-2017-0324.

Bilska, Beata, Małgorzata Wrzosek, Danuta Kołożyn-Krajewska, and Karol Krajewski. 2016. "Risk of Food Losses and Potential of Food Recovery for Social Purposes." *Waste Management* 52: 269–77.

Buisman, M. E., R. Haijema, and J. M. Bloemhof-Ruwaard. 2019. "Discounting and Dynamic Shelf Life to Reduce Fresh Food Waste at Retailers." *International Journal of Production Economics.* https://doi.org/10.1016/j.ijpe.2017.07.016.

Bulkeley, Harriet, and Michele M. Betsill. 2005. "Rethinking Sustainable Cities: Multilevel Governance and the 'Urban' Politics of Climate Change." *Environmental Politics.* https://doi.org/10.1080/0964401042000310178.

Bulkeley, Harriet, and Kristine Kern. 2006. "Local Government and the Governing of Climate Change in Germany and the UK." *Urban Studies.* https://doi.org/10.1080/00420980600936491.

Busetti, S. 2019. "A Theory-Based Evaluation of Food Waste Policy: Evidence from Italy." *Food Policy* 88: 101749.

Caritas Ambrosiana. Osservatorio diocesano della povertà e delle risorse. 2019. "La povertà nella diocesi ambrosiana." www.caritasambrosiana.it/Public/userfiles/files/La%20 povert%C3%A0%20nella%20Diocesi%20ambrosiana-Dati%202019(1).pdf.

Ciulli, Francesca, Ans Kolk, and Siri Boe-Lillegraven. 2020. "Circularity Brokers: Digital Platform Organizations and Waste Recovery in Food Supply Chains." *Journal of Business Ethics.* https://doi.org/10.1007/s10551-019-04160-5.

De Boeck, Elien, Liesbeth Jacxsens, Helena Goubert, and Mieke Uyttendaele. 2017. "Ensuring Food Safety in Food Donations: Case Study of the Belgian Donation/Acceptation Chain." *Food Research International* 100: 137–49.

De Cunto, Arianna, Cinzia Tegoni, Roberta Sonnino, and Cécile Michel. 2017. *Food in Cities: Study on Innovation for a Sustainable and Healthy Production, Delivery, and Consumption of Food in Cities.* https://www.milanurbanfoodpolicypact.org/wp-content/uploads/2021/08/Eurocities-Food-in-Cities.pdf.

ECR. 2015. *La gestione dell'eccedenza alimentare: una guide per le aziende della filiera.* Milano: GS1 Italy.

EU Platform on Food Losses and Food Waste. 2019. *Redistribution of Surplus Food: Examples of Practices in the Member States,* 61–65. https://ec.europa.eu/food/safety/food-waste/eu-actions-against-food-waste/eu-platform-food-losses-and-food-waste_en.2.

FAO. 2016. "Food Recovery and Redistribution. A Practical Guide for Favourable Policies and Legal Frameworks in Europe and Central Asia." Working Paper.

———. 2019. *The Milan Urban Food Policy Pact Monitoring Framework.* Rome: FAO.

Fattibene, Daniele, Francesca Recanati, Katarzyna Dembska, and Marta Antonelli. 2020. "Urban Food Waste: A Framework to Analyse Policies and Initiatives." *Resources*. https://doi.org/10.3390/RESOURCES9090099.

Filippini, Rosalia, Chiara Mazzocchi, and Stefano Corsi. 2019. "The Contribution of Urban Food Policies Toward Food Security in Developing and Developed Countries: A Network Analysis Approach." *Sustainable Cities and Society*. https://doi.org/10.1016/j.scs.2019.101506.

Fondazione Cariplo. 2018. *Al Bando Le Povertà! Ricette Di Quartiere Per Contrastare La Povertà Minorile*.

Galli, Francesca, Alessio Cavicchi, and Gianluca Brunori. 2019. "Food Waste Reduction and Food Poverty Alleviation: A System Dynamics Conceptual Model." *Agriculture and Human Values* 36 (2): 289–300.

Garrone, Paola, Marco Melacini, and Alessandro Perego. 2013. *Feed the Hungry: The Potential of Surplus Food Recovery*. Milan: Fondazione per la Sussidiarieta`.

———. 2014a. "Opening the Black Box of Food Waste Reduction." *Food Policy*. https://doi.org/10.1016/j.foodpol.2014.03.014.

———. 2014b. "Surplus Food Recovery and Donation in Italy: The Upstream Process." *British Food Journal*. https://doi.org/10.1108/BFJ-02-2014-0076.

———. 2015. *Surplus food management against food waste. Il recupero delle eccedenze alimentari. Dalle parole ai fatti*. Milan: Fondazione Banco Alimentare; Politecnico di Milano.

Gazzetta ufficiale della Repubblica italiana. 2016. "Legge 19 Agosto 2016, n. 166." www.gazzettaufficiale.it.

Gentilini, Ugo. 2013. "Banking on Food: The State of Food Banks in High-Income Countries." *IDS Working Papers 2013* (415): 1–18.

Gharehyakheh, Amin, Caroline Krejci, Jaime Cantu, and Jamie Rogers. 2019. "Dynamic Shelf-Life Prediction System to Improve Sustainability in Food Banks." Proceedings of the 2019 IISE Annual Conference, Orlando, FL, pp. 18–21.

Hecht, Amelie A., and Roni A. Neff. 2019. "Food Rescue Intervention Evaluations: A Systematic Review." *Sustainability*. https://doi.org/10.3390/su11236718.

Hermsdorf, David, Meike Rombach, and Vera Bitsch. 2017. "Food Waste Reduction Practices in German Food Retail." *British Food Journal*. https://doi.org/10.1108/BFJ-06-2017-0338.

Holweg, Christina, Christoph Teller, and Herbert Kotzab. 2016. "Unsaleable Grocery Products, Their Residual Value and Instore Logistics." *International Journal of Physical Distribution and Logistics Management*. https://doi.org/10.1108/IJPDLM-11-2014-0285.

Irwin, Jennifer D., Victor K. Ng, Timothy J. Rush, Cuong Nguyen, and Meizi He. 2007. "Can Food Banks Sustain Nutrient Requirements? A Case Study in Southwestern Ontario." *Canadian Journal of Public Health*. https://doi.org/10.1007/bf03405378.

ISPRA. 2020. "Rapporto Rifiuti Urbani Edizione 2020." www.isprambiente.gov.it/files2020/pubblicazioni/rapporti/rapportorifiutiurbani_ed-2020_n-331-1.pdf.

ISTAT. 2020. *Le Statistiche Dell'ISTAT Sulla Povertà: Anno 2019*. Roma: Istituto Nazionale di Statistica.

———. 2021. "Popolazione residente al 1° gennaio." http://dati.istat.it/Index.aspx?QueryId=18460.

La Scalia, Giada, Rosa Micale, Pier Paolo Miglietta, and Pierluigi Toma. 2019. "Reducing Waste and Ecological Impacts Through a Sustainable and Efficient Management of Perishable Food Based on the Monte Carlo Simulation." *Ecological Indicators*. https://doi.org/10.1016/j.ecolind.2018.10.041.

Martin-Rios, Carlos, Christine Demen-Meier, Stefan Gössling, and Clémence Cornuz. 2018. "Food Waste Management Innovations in the Foodservice Industry." *Waste Management* 79: 196–206.

Michalec, Aleksandra, Martin Fodor, Enda Hayes, and James Longhurst. 2018. "Co-Designing Food Waste Services in the Catering Sector." *British Food Journal* 120 (12): 2762–77. https://doi.org/10.1108/BFJ-04-2018-0226.

Milano Food Policy. 2018. *Il sistema del cibo a Milano. Cinque priorità per uno sviluppo sostenibile.* Milan: Milano Food Policy.

Milicevic, Vesna, Giampaolo Colavita, Marta Castrica, Sabrina Ratti, Antonella Baldi, and Claudia M. Balzaretti. 2016. "Risk Assessment in the Recovery of Food for Social Solidarity Purposes: Preliminary Data." *Italian Journal of Food Safety.* https://doi.org/10.4081/ijfs.2016.6187.

Mourad, Marie. 2016. "Recycling, Recovering and Preventing 'Food Waste': Competing Solutions for Food Systems Sustainability in the United States and France." *Journal of Cleaner Production* 126: 461–77.

Papargyropoulou, Effie, Rodrigo Lozano, Julia K. Steinberger, Nigel Wright, and Zaini Bin Ujang. 2014. "The Food Waste Hierarchy as a Framework for the Management of Food Surplus and Food Waste." *Journal of Cleaner Production.* https://doi.org/10.1016/j.jclepro.2014.04.020.

Raja, Samina, Branden Born, Jessica Kozlowski Russell, David Adler, Majid Allan, Will Allen, Lauren Breen, et al. 2008. "A Planners Guide to Community and Regional Food Planning : Transforming Food Environments, Facilitating Healthy Eating." *American Planning Association*, Report Number 554.

Riches, Graham. 2002. "Food Banks and Food Security: Welfare Reform, Human Rights and Social Policy. Lessons From Canada?" *Social Policy and Administration.* https://doi.org/10.1111/1467-9515.00309.

———. 2011. "Thinking and Acting Outside the Charitable Food Box: Hunger and the Right to Food in Rich Societies." *Development in Practice.* https://doi.org/10.1080/0961 4524.2011.561295.

Royal Foundation. 2021. "Build a Waste-Free World Winner: Italy. The City of Milan Food Waste Hubs." https://earthshotprize.org/london-2021/the-earthshot-prize-winners-finalists/waste-free/.

Sert, Sedef, Paola Garrone, Marco Melacini, and Alessandro Perego. 2016. "Surplus Food Redistribution for Social Purposes: The Case of Coop Lombardia." In *Organizing Supply Chain Processes for Sustainable Innovation in the Agri-Food Industry*, 153–73. https://doi.org/10.1108/s2045-060520160000005025.

———. 2018. "Corporate Food Donations: Altruism, Strategy or Cost Saving?" *British Food Journal.* https://doi.org/10.1108/BFJ-08-2017-0435.

Sonnino, Roberta, Terry Marsden, and Ana Moragues-Faus. 2016. "Relationalities and Convergences in Food Security Narratives: Towards a Place-Based Approach." *Transactions of the Institute of British Geographers.* https://doi.org/10.1111/tran.12137.

Tarasuk, Valerie, and Joan M. Eakin. 2003. "Charitable Food Assistance as Symbolic Gesture: An Ethnographic Study of Food Banks in Ontario." *Social Science and Medicine.* https://doi.org/10.1016/S0277-9536(02)00152-1.

Teller, Christoph, Christina Holweg, Gerald Reiner, and Herbert Kotzab. 2018. "Retail Store Operations and Food Waste." *Journal of Cleaner Production.* https://doi.org/10.1016/j.jclepro.2018.02.280.

Treutwein, Regina, and Nina Langen. 2021. "Setting the Agenda for Food Waste Prevention—A Perspective on Local Government Policymaking." *Journal of Cleaner Production.* https://doi.org/10.1016/j.jclepro.2020.125337.

Zaman, Atiq Uz, and Steffen Lehmann. 2011. "Urban Growth and Waste Management Optimization Towards 'Zero Waste City'." *City, Culture and Society.* https://doi.org/10.1016/j.ccs.2011.11.007.

15 Food waste reduction through food re-distribution actions during COVID-19 in Brazil

Luciana Marques Vieira and Daniele Eckert Matzembacher

Introduction

Food redistribution in Brazil is an important activity related to nutrition and food security. In the country, it is more linked to social assistance policies than to the mitigation of the negative environmental impacts of food waste. According to a survey released by the Brazilian Network for Research on Food and Nutritional Sovereignty and Security (Rede PENSAN 2021), the country is experiencing an alarming situation of food insecurity and hunger. During the COVID-19 pandemic, 116.8 million Brazilians do not have full and permanent access to food. Specifically, 43.4 million (20.5% of the population) do not have enough food at home, while 19.1 million (9% of the population) are facing hunger (state of severe food insecurity). This problem extends to other countries, since, according to the report 'The State of Food Security and Nutrition in the World', around 30% of the world population did not have access to adequate food throughout the year 2020, indicating that the pandemic had consequences that will last for many years (FAO 2021).

Although hunger and food insecurity problems were aggravated during the pandemic, the problem is historical and structural in Brazil. Researchers are unanimous in the diagnosis that the problem of hunger in the country is related to the lack of income to eat properly. The lack of income is aggravated by high levels of unemployment and insufficient economic growth rates to incorporate people who each year want to enter the labour market, in addition to the lack of public policies in the field of food security (Belik, Silva, and Takagi 2001). In fact, until the COVID-19 pandemic, Brazil had no law or regulation dealing with both food redistribution and food waste issues. It was only during the pandemic that a new law was approved to exempt food donors from legal responsibility: Law 14.016/2020 (Brazil 2020), also known as the Law of the Good Samaritan. However, there is a lack of a regulatory framework on the subject, because this law does not regulate the donation processes. There is also no law or regulation related to food waste.

Recently, before the emergence of the Law of the Good Samaritan, there was an attempt to advance this public policy agenda through a multi-stakeholder

DOI: 10.4324/9781003226932-20

initiative. According to Matzembacher, Vieira, and de Barcellos (2021) this multi-stakeholder initiative was officially launched in October 2017 and engaged Brazilian universities, FAO, NGOs, business associations (such as ABRAS—Brazilian Association of Supermarkets), and others. It was led by the Inter-ministerial Committee for Food Security and Nutrition (CAISAN). A document setting out the inter-sectoral strategy for the reduction of FLW was prepared and publicly distributed, entitled Intersectoral Strategy for the Reduction of Food Loss and Waste in Brazil (CAISAN 2018). It proposed actions and measures for each value chain activity and the role that different stakeholders should play to reduce food losses and waste, as well as made an initial attempt to provide some guidance related to food redistribution and donation. It was believed that results from this initiative would be reflected in regulation schemes and voluntary standards (Matzembacher, Vieira, and de Barcellos 2021). However, in the new government, with Jair Bolsonaro as president (which started in January 2019), there was a setback and this committee ceased to exist.

This lack of action by the government can be understood as promoting institutional voids. Institutional voids are failures, caused mainly by the absence of the state and asymmetry in the market, intensified by society beliefs, rules, and culture. They intensify social inequalities because of the absence, weakness, or nonfulfillment of the role that is expected of the institutions (Agostini, Bitencourt, and Vieira 2020). Due to this institutional void, responses from society and companies to the problem of hunger and food insecurity began to emerge. Several organisations and initiatives have been working with food redistribution to address this problem for a long time, in which the Brazilian network of food banks is the most recognised, with more than 249 food banks identified. In addition to public and private food banks, organisations from the private sector and NGOs emerged more recently with the aim to redistribute food. Therefore, this chapter focuses on these last two and new configurations (private initiatives and NGOs).

The research developed sought to answer the following questions: How do different organisations promote food waste reduction through food redistribution actions during COVID-19 in Brazil? What are the barriers and facilitators faced by them? And what can be improved in terms of public policies related to food redistribution?

Two case studies were conducted aiming to answer these questions. The first case study is of a private organisation working with food redistribution in Brazil since 2018, before the pandemic. Primary data collection was based on two interviews with the founder and CEO. The first interview was in October 2018 (before the COVID-19 Pandemic) and the second interview was in August 2021 (at the end of the third wave of cases in Brazil). This longitudinal follow-up allowed a clearer understanding of how practices and policies aimed at food redistribution were affected in Brazil as a result of the social, political, and economic crisis caused by the pandemic. Secondary data were collected from the company website, social networks, and reports (in total four sources of information), 14 social media news, and a video showing an interview with the founder of the company. The second case study is of a multistakeholder initiative that emerged specifically during the pandemic to redistribute food to people in vulnerable situations. Primary data collection was based on an interview conducted in August 2021 with one of the project's founders. Secondary data were also collected from the project website, social networks, and reports (in total seven sources of information), seven social media news, and 15 videos containing, for example testimonials from participants. Moreover, for both cases, secondary data were also collected from public documents elaborated by the Brazilian government and news related to food waste, as well as food redistribution (24 sources of information). Data were analysed through a manual content analysis, and the results found were discussed among researchers.

In addition to this introduction, this chapter is structured as follows: The next section presents the details of each case studied. The subsequent section captures the discussion and conclusions, focusing on lessons for improving policies.

Analysis of the programmes

Many initiatives related to food waste reduction took place in Brazil during the Pandemic period; however, most of the initiatives were informal and with little dissemination of data, specifically allowing to understand the barriers, facilitators, and lessons learned in terms of public policies. Therefore, the selected cases were chosen following these criteria, especially considering the availability and quality of data, as well as access to participants within each initiative as they were connected to universities in Sao Paulo city. Therefore, this section presents two cases related to food waste reduction through food re-distribution actions during COVID-19 in Brazil.

Case 1—connecting food

Case 1 is from a social impact company that emerged in 2018 with the aim to redistribute surplus food from the supply chain, especially from retail, and donate it to social institutions that help people in need. The founder has been dedicated to studying food and its distribution processes for over 20 years. The company currently has nine employees and throughout 2021, it connected more than 160 new food retails to food redistribution, operating mainly in the region of São Paulo, the main financial centre of the country. The donor informs the company about the type, volume, and characteristics of the food waste, and the company is responsible for making a 'match' with social assistance entities, whether NGOs or food banks. This match is done using an ERP (Enterprise Resource Planning), a technology-based resource. The NGOs are responsible for collecting the food from the donors. This company profits from it since the donor pays for this service.

The company marketing position is that they are a complementary solution to those that already exist, such as food banks and urban crops, as well as any initiative that promotes food redistribution. This positioning, according to them, occurs because different logistical components demand different solutions for food waste. Therefore, they understand that there is no single solution to reduce food waste and to redistribute food. The company's value proposition includes mapping supply chain members with food waste and connecting them with social institutions that help people in need, mapping the profile of social institutions, providing training about food handling and collection process to these social institutions, managing information about food donations, managing the relationships in the food redistribution chain, and generating indicators about social, economic, and environmental impact.

With the COVID-19 pandemic, there was a need to restructure the food redistribution chain. There was a change in both the demand and supply sides. The pandemic has increased the number of people facing food insecurity and hunger due to loss of income or unemployment. This problem generated greater concern in society. Therefore, donations also increased, specifically of food that composes the 'basic food basket'. Another factor that positively influenced donations was a greater concern with ESG practices in the corporate environment (environmental, social, and corporate governance), which also occurred during the COVID-19 period. At the same time, many NGOs closed, for example those that serve food to children in public schools, while others increased the demand because, for example they became centres of food donation for groups of families. The company took about three weeks to make the adaptations needed, readjust the logistical processes, and map the new stakeholders involved in the food redistribution chain, as well as to adapt to the new volume of food donation.

Considering possible differences in relation to other private redistribution models, the company configuration is not new. There are some similar abroad. In Brazil that are private business (apps business models) aiming to commercialise food that would be wasted in secondary markets, selling food with a different appearance than it is valued in the market (sometimes called "imperfect foods") or products close to their expiration date. These are models that coexist and all of them are considered necessary by the company from this case. Compared to food banks, after the pandemic, there is a difference in the profile of who receives the donation. The company only donates to social institutions or to food banks. Food banks, in addition to redistributing to social institutions, also started to donate to family groups during the COVID-19 pandemic. These food banks are responsible for the transportation process, since donating companies do not make it. There are also cities in which food banks do not operate (usually small cities) and the company is able to reach these places. For these reasons, they position themselves as a complementary solution.

Another important difference the company has in comparison to other redistribution models is the focus on efficient and effective management. This is possible especially because it uses an ERP to connect donors to recipients.

In this way, the use of ERP helps to make more complex operational and logistical management, which improves the quality of their service and their capacity to respond to situations faster. Therefore, accountability and transparency differentiate this company from other redistribution models, mostly due to its ERP system. The company also audits the NGOs that receive the food donation, carrying out visits to see how they operate and whether the people in need are really being assisted.

Other redistribution activities, such as is the case of the company, should always be seen as complementary to food banks. Food banks are the main instrument to promote public policies regarding food redistribution. Therefore, the company is just another complementary component that helps to minimise the impact of hunger and food insecurity and, as a result, promotes the reduction of food waste in supply chains. In addition, the company contributes to filling institutional voids, helping civil society organisations to improve their performance in serving food to vulnerable people.

The approval of law 14.016/2020 during COVID-19 was an advance related to public policy and helped the company operation to be more reliable, since now food donors are protected from legal liability. However, there are still several barriers in terms of public policies faced by this company and others that they perceive as affecting the food redistribution activities more broadly. The first is that there is a lack of a regulatory framework on the subject in questions concerning the type of food donated and the integrity of the product or the nutritional value (as would be the case for ultra-processed products), for example. It is also important to take a 'step back' and promote public policies focused on food losses and waste, which precede redistribution activities.

Another barrier is that today the redistribution of food, in terms of public policies, is restricted to donating food or donating 'basic food baskets'. Food banks, for example focus excessively on the logistical process (receive and distribute food), but lack a stronger look at the social component, as food banks are instruments of public policy. It is necessary to look more closely at how the food reaches the final beneficiary, whether they actually consume it, and what the impact is—that is to see more of this social component and not just act as a logistical operator that redistributes the food. The strength of food banks must be in acting as food and nutrition security equipment, in the sense of providing more social assistance, helping to receive food, making preparation and recovery workshops, and this has been lost a lot over time. Neither NGOs nor food banks have strong actions to educate people in need about how to handle and prepare food to avoid food waste. There is also no monitoring of the structure that these people have at their home to use this food. There are cases of people, for example who received vegetables but do not have a stove at home to prepare this food. So this food ends up being thrown away. There are also cases of donations of soft drinks and chocolates, related to obesity and low nutritional value, which perhaps should not be part of food redistribution activities to malnourished children. Especially during COVID-19, in which obesity is a risk factor to the virus, this is an issue that needs to be discussed and regulated in terms of public policy. In addition, food banks have a component that is not technological, but human, as there are teams of social assistants and nutritionists to deal with education regarding food handling and social questions; this needs to be taken up more strongly according to the founder of Connecting Food. But this strengthening and reorganisation cannot be done individually by each food bank. It needs to start from the food bank network, as something institutional. If it is an individual action, it can affect their food donations negatively.

Another problem is that people in need receive food donations but remain without a job and without alternatives to improve their education. There is a lack of public policies that seek an effective solution to the broader social problem related to hunger and food insecurity. And food waste is a broader issue that has not yet reached the public policy agenda.

Case 2—Campo Favela

Case 2 is a food redistribution multistakeholder initiative that was carried out exclusively during the peak of COVID-19. The project team consisted of five people, all academic from the areas of management, operations and logistics, finance, economics, and marketing. However, the project had the voluntary help of more than 25 students and alumni of the university who organised the initiative. The initiative aimed to alleviate the economic and social effects of the COVID-19 pandemic on disadvantaged populations, specifically focusing on two activities in the food production and consumption value chain: family farmers and slum dwellers in Brazil.

The closure of commercial establishments and schools at the beginning of the COVID-19 pandemic reduced the distribution of products from family horticultural farmers. The surplus of fresh products would need to be disposed of quickly due to the perishability characteristic of the product. The alternative of selling these products through other channels did not prove to be feasible in the short term. Furthermore, because of the excess of supply, the prices paid by intermediaries would plummet in the short term, which also did not generate a satisfactory alternative for family producers. As a consequence, there would be a risk that a lot of quality fresh produce would be thrown away. This would imply an income reduction to family producers during the pandemics. This was already happening to producers in several places in Brazil. The disruption of marketing channels and, consequently food waste, would make small family farmers unable to support their families and would not have the money to restart planting when demand was re-established.

On the other hand, with closed public establishments and a drastic reduction in the circulation of people, there was a prospect of an abrupt drop in the income of families in the slums. The founders saw many news, reports, and surveys showing that many slum dwellers depended on informal jobs or jobs that depended on people's circulation in establishments such as shopping malls, bakeries, and restaurants. This information, combined with the founders' knowledge of supply chains and finance (they are university professors), generated concern and an expectation of a very difficult scenario for Brazil. They explained that surveys released at the time indicated that these people did not have money saved for emergencies and that in a few weeks they would start to face hunger. The problem was even more critical for children who had a large part of their meals done in public schools, which were closed. So, the demand for food in these people's homes would increase. Another aggravating factor was that at that time, the government had not yet announced any kind of help for these people.

Therefore, in the countryside, there would be food waste and no income for producers due to the lack of marketing channels. On the other hand, in the slums, there would be families with no or little income to buy food, and children without access to healthy food. Given this situation, the initiative was created in March 2020 by a group of academics from different areas, including operations, marketing, and finance. The initiative had two main objectives: (1) to help families in the rural areas and slums during the period of the pandemic, and also (2) to create a sustainable model that would allow a direct connection between producers and consumers in the slums. Reducing the number of intermediaries would also reduce food waste. As a result, fresh products (fruits and vegetables) could reach low-income families, slum dwellers, at a lower price, but at the same time pay a fair remuneration for farmers.

The initiative went through four distinct phases, each representing significant changes in the scope, form of financing and management of the operation. The first phase aimed at informal financing among groups of friends. The amount financed a delivery of fruits and vegetables made to the slum in the form of donation. In this process, it had the support of a start-up that bought food from small farmers, who had no sales channel at that time due to the pandemic. At the other side of the supply chain, the support of community leaders from the slums who assembled baskets with the food received and took charge of redistribution to vulnerable people. In the second phase, after formal financial support from an NGO, the operation began to redistribute food to more places, incorporating other slum, and increasing the operation's complexity. The food baskets also increased in size and started to have a greater variety of products with healthy nutritional content, consisting of eggs, fruits (bananas), and vegetables.

The third phase represents the incorporation of more donors, specifically NGOs and private companies. The operations model at the beginning of this phase followed a pattern similar to that of the previous stage. The initiative took on large proportions and reached 50 slums. At one point, the project's start-up partner, which was slowly recovering its customers as mainly restaurants were allowed to operate, gave space to another company to help with the operation. This company had no prospects of returning to supply the municipal schools, which remained closed for a long time. Other partners were also sought. Large donors began to invest their money in other initiatives, and there was also a substantial drop in donations to the project from individuals. Still, it had the support of a big Brazilian agribusiness company. Due to this company's requirement, donations began to take place in other regions as well, and the initiative expanded to four other Brazilian states.

Throughout the four phases, different models of food redistribution were tested, seeking to generate a sustainable system in the long-term considering logistic process (approximation between small family farmers and the slums) and marketing (which involved since the attempt to sell food with a price almost 70% lower comparing to a regular market and also the attempt to form a subscription club).

After 11 months of the operation, there were fewer restrictions due to the pandemics in Brazil, and it was difficult to obtain new donations. Therefore, the initiative ended in February 2021. In total, it raised almost R$3 million in donations, more than 873,000 kilograms of food were redistributed to 101,000 families in need in slums, directly or indirectly benefiting around 1,500 family farmers. The project helped Brazil face one of its most difficult times in terms of social and economic crisis.

The realisation of the project generated some learning and reflections. The first one concerns the points that facilitated the realisation of the food redistribution activities, with a prominent role for external financing and the media. Funding from various entities and companies allowed the project to have a much greater impact than originally intended. One of the points that favoured it was the dissemination by the media and also by 'influencers'. There was wide dissemination on television, in the news, and on the project's own social media, including testimonials from beneficiaries, whether producers, community leaders, and families from the favelas. The project sought to bring transparency, publishing reports informing the amounts collected, the volume of donations, collections from sales, among others. This created credibility and impacted the trust of the people involved.

Another lesson learned was that creating a sustainable model for the supply of fresh food requires in-depth knowledge of the different agents in the chain (producers, intermediaries, retailers, and consumers). The context in which this attempt to create a sustainable model takes place can affect its viability—the context of the pandemic gave to Campo Favela project a more emergency character than one of sustainability. Anyway, some of the communities tried to implement a more sustainable model, taking several lessons for future actions. In this sense, support and training in basic knowledge of management and agricultural techniques can help the links in the chain to overcome their most basic difficulties. The application of new technologies can also help control waste and reduce costs in this chain, but it is essential that these places, especially slums and rural areas, have access to a good quality network (Internet).

Specifically in relation to slums, creating a sustainable model may require changes in the mindset and habits of low-income families. There is a need to understand the consumption habits and tastes of *favela's* residents. Also, it should also be noted that each slum community is different and have different needs. Some slums could not be served due to the lack of formalised and minimally organised associations. Deliveries in smaller favelas are more difficult and costly, as they do not reach a minimum volume of delivery. There was a lack of trust in some members of favela's communities in relation to basket sales (where associations were implementing the sustainable model). This distrust arose because they were unaware of the Campo Favela project and believed that the baskets were donated to the communities. A direct communication with favela moderators through social media helped clarify issues such as these. Distribution points (usually associations) did not always have the best location and structure (refrigeration, space, and people) to store and distribute food. This is a very important problem. Many families have the habit of shopping for daily consumption, and they are unable to buy in advance due to uncertainty of income and lack of family budget planning, which makes it difficult to implement a planned purchase and sale of food loss and waste. Finally, the role of association leaders in the project brought confidence in the process of receiving and distributing donated products.

Among the difficulties encountered is the lack of knowledge of management practices and agricultural technologies, the issue that the producer does not account for and does not clearly know their input costs and this made it difficult at various times to define what would be considered a fair price; at the same time, the great volatility of prices paid to producers in Brazil ends up creating an enormous difficulty to reliably define a fair price. Other difficulties encountered throughout the project are related to the role of intermediaries that can, in some cases, generate a price increase and greater waste due to greater handling of the product; and the issue that deliveries to smaller slums are more difficult and costly, as they do not reach a minimum delivery volume. In addition, the redistribution model presented several challenges related to packaging costs, transportation costs, and sustainability issues, such as packaging waste. There was also difficulty in generating a sustainable business model in the long term, connecting production and consumption, and that did not depend on donations and who could go beyond the project.

In terms of public policies, the project generated the understanding that the creation of a sustainable model for the supply of fresh foods, which are important for food and nutrition security, requires in-depth knowledge of the various agents in the food supply chain. The promotion of collaboration and trust between the agents in the chain is essential for redistribution activities, one of these actions being related to transparency. In addition, these supply chain members need support and training in basic knowledge of food management and handling. Regarding technological aspects, the application of new technologies can help control waste and reduce costs in this chain, but it is essential that these places, especially slums and rural areas, have access to good quality Internet. Finally, the role of the media and digital influencers is also relevant, as there is a cycle where more media generates more donations, which generates greater impact.

Discussion and conclusions

The analysis of these two cases related to food redistribution indicates eight blind spots and lessons to improve public policies in Brazil: the need to create

Table 15.1 Blind spots and lessons to improve public policies in Brazil

Macro level	Meso level	Micro level
The need to create regulations	To focus on actions able to enhance the social impact of food redistribution	To make technology accessible to citizens;
The need to take a 'step back' and look at food losses and waste in addition to food redistribution	To incorporate technology to make redistribution processes more effective	The necessity to carry out complementary actions in relation to food redistribution that allow long-term solutions to the problem of hunger and food insecurity.
The need for the government to foster or to give tax incentives to businesses with social impact	The need to promote communication that generates more engagement	

regulations; to focus on actions able to enhance the social impact of food redistribution; to incorporate technology to make redistribution processes more effective; to make technology accessible to citizens; the need to promote communication that generates more engagement; the need to take a 'step back' and look at food losses and waste in addition to food redistribution; the need for the government to foster or to give tax incentives to businesses with social impact; and the necessity to carry out complementary actions in relation to food redistribution that allow long-term solutions to the problem of hunger and food insecurity. These eight blind spots can be considered according to three levels, as exposed in Table 15.1: macro (public policy), meso (supply and operations chain), and micro (focusing on citizens).

Regarding the macro level, it is possible to indicate three blind spots and lessons: the need to create better regulations, the need to take a 'step back' and look at food losses and waste in addition to food redistribution, and the need for the government to foster or to give tax incentives to businesses with social impact. Regarding the need to create regulations, the approval of the first law on food donation in Brazil during COVID-19 is a very positive step forward for actions aiming to improve social protection and to reduce food losses and waste. It solves the problem of legal security for the donor to some degree. On the basis of this law, new actions must be taken to regulate food redistribution activities and processes. Second, it is also important to take a 'step back' and promote public policies focused on food losses and waste, which precede redistribution activities. Reducing food losses and waste is part of the SDGs and must be pursued by every nation. The country was advancing through a multi-stakeholder group that formed a technical committee for an intersectoral strategy for the reduction of food losses and waste. It is important to resume these activities through a consistent and long-term public agenda. Third, activities aimed at redistributing food and, more broadly, reducing food losses and waste are also carried out by stakeholders from the private sector through social impact businesses that bring a series of benefits to society. Public policies can also encompass the solutions for private actors, whether fostering business with social impact or giving taxes reduction for them. Including these stakeholders in public policy helps to advance the social and environmental agenda in the country, it is another alternative that adds efforts with public policies.

Regarding the meso level, it is possible to indicate three blind spots and lessons: to focus on actions able to enhance the social impact of food redistribution, to incorporate technology to make redistribution processes more effective, and the need to promote communication that generates more engagement. First, through its actions, the government can also rescue the role of enhancing the social impact of food redistribution, mainly through food banks and NGOs. The social protection done needs, in addition to the logistical process, to develop NGOs 'capabilities and end beneficiaries on how to use the food received, as well as verifying if they have the conditions and physical infrastructure to prepare these foods. Today most of the organisations involved in this process already have the necessary team for this, with nutritionists and social assistants, which end up being underutilised. Therefore, an evaluation and restructuring of processes, mainly through a centralised network, can increase the potential of food redistribution to fight hunger and food insecurity. Second, a consistent agenda must also consider the role of technology in making redistribution processes more efficient. Redistribution centres, by incorporating technology, can improve their logistical and accountability processes. Third, the role of the media and influencers can also be considered on public agendas. In Brazil, very often, campaigns are carried out and publicised by the federal government. Investing in media and in the use of digital influencers is an alternative that may generate more impacts and even, in many situations, generate more credibility than communications coming from the government.

Regarding the micro-level, it is possible to indicate two blind spots and lessons: to make technology accessible to citizens; and the necessity to carry out complementary actions in relation to food redistribution that allow long-term solutions to the problem of hunger and food insecurity. First, technology can generate new models of redistribution; however, access to technology to the weakest links (family producers and the people who would benefit at the end of the chain) needs to be available, as well as the knowledge of how to make use of these tools. Second, food redistribution represents a lack of efficiency of food chains since this activity has as its input the food losses and waste. Although it has an important social component, which is to reduce hunger and food insecurity, it must be understood as a palliative measure in terms of public policies. Providing food to people in need, without focusing on other spheres related to hunger and food insecurity, does not solve the problem in the long run. Therefore, a lesson these two cases related to food redistribution bring it that public policies should also be attentive to the components of education and employment of the recipients of food donation to a long-term social protection be achieved. Food waste reduction through food re-distribution is a complex problem with a very great potential to generate social protection and impact through the improvement of public policies in Brazil.

Finally, in addition to these eight blind spots, it is necessary to consider that specific government actions to combat poverty should have the highest priority in the country and should essentially seek to increase the income of the poorest. COVID-19 shed light on social inequality such as food and nutrition insecurity. While some initiatives to tackle these problems are episodic, many can become permanent through an institutional support. The problem of food waste and redistribution is part of a broader context, in which all spheres of society, to some greater or lesser degree, end up connecting. Taking a more holistic and integrated view of this problem is essential in the discussion of public policies for food waste reduction and food re-distribution actions, whether in times of crisis, such as during COVID-19 in Brazil, or in more systemic situations. This is a lesson from Brazil.

References

Agostini, M. R., C. C. Bitencourt, and L. M. Vieira. 2020. "Social Innovation in Mexican Coffee Production: Filling 'Institutional Voids.'" *International Review of Applied Economics* 34 (5): 607–25.

Belik, W., J. G. D. Silva, and M. Takagi. 2001. "Políticas de combate à fome no Brasil." *São Paulo em perspectiva* 15: 119–29.

Brazil. 2020. "Lei 14.016 de 23 de junho de 2020." www.planalto.gov.br/ccivil_03/_ato 2019-2022/2020/lei/L14016.htm.

CAISAN—Câmara Interministerial de Segurança Alimentar e Nutricional. 2018. *Estratégia Intersetorial para a Redução de Perdas e Desperdício de Alimentos no Brasil.* Brasil: Ministério do Desenvolvimento Social (MDS)1–40. www.mds.gov.br/webarquivos/arquivo/ seguranca_alimentar/caisan/Publicacao/Caisan_Nacional/PDA_ingles.pdf.

FAO. 2021. *The State of Food Security and Nutrition in the World. Transforming Food Systems for Food Security, Improved Nutrition and Affordable Healthy Diets for All.* Rome: Food and Agriculture Organization of the United Nations.

Matzembacher, D. E., L. M. Vieira, and M. D. de Barcellos. 2021. "An Analysis of Multi-Stakeholder Initiatives to Reduce Food Loss and Waste in an Emerging Country—Brazil." *Industrial Marketing Management* 93: 591–604.

Rede PENSAN. 2021. *Brazilian Network for Research on Food and Nutritional Sovereignty and Security.* National Survey of Food Insecurity in the Context of the Covid-19 Pandemic in Brazil. https://pesquisassan.net.br/olheparaafome/.

What works in food loss and waste policy

Suggestions from the case studies

Simone Busetti

From *salvage parties* in Japan to the donation of seafood bycatch in Alaska, the book has crossed Asia, Africa, Europe, and South and North America. The world is innovating in the fight against food loss and waste (FLW), and the case studies report a wide variety of interventions, spanning from the local to the international scale. Notwithstanding obvious differences in design, implementation, and contexts, digging into the case studies reveals some common threads that are relevant to the practice and prospects of FLW policy.

This chapter is organised into eight sections, each labelled with one practical suggestion: (1) diversify the evidence base, (2) use existing data effectively, (3) stress the multiple goals of FLW policy, (4) calibrate tools and exploit synergies, (5) identify frictions and adverse interactive effects, (6) ensure effective implementation, (7) explore the non-programme features of success, and (8) recast food recovery and redistribution.

Notwithstanding these simple labels, the idea is neither to provide a checklist for designing the optimal policy, nor is it to give one-size-fits-all recommendations that are valid in all contexts. Rather, the goal is to discuss emerging topics, possible risks, and some advice that may help improve the decision, design, and implementation of FLW policy.

Diversify the evidence base

Measuring how much food is lost or wasted and identifying where this happens in the food chain are foundational for designing policy. Doing so allows interventions to be directed towards the greater sources of waste and provides a benchmark against which to evaluate effectiveness and progress. Importantly, measurements may also have a relevant political impact; data and indicators can highlight the existence of a problem, frame problems and solutions, and suggest specific views and approaches (Rottenburg et al. 2015). Data can make FLW a part of government and business agendas and increase the priority of formulating policy on it.

More data can certainly help improve interventions, and—as described in Chapter 1—several efforts are already being made to improve measurements,

DOI: 10.4324/9781003226932-21

especially on the path towards achieving the UN's SDGs. The chapters highlight two additional directions for improving our evidence base in a policy-relevant way.

A major avenue for further research concerns data on the motivations of actors in the food chain and the conditions that make them contribute to FLW. As pointed out in Chapter 2, several studies have been conducted on the causes of FLW, but better policy tailoring requires going from general causes and conditions to a more nuanced portrait of contexts and actors, with a focus on sectoral, geographic, and demographic differences. These data allow us to tackle FLW at its roots, concentrating on drivers (why FLW happens) in addition to symptoms (how much food is wasted or lost).

Some of these drivers have broad validity. Differences between young and elderly people, for instance—with the latter being more sensitive to frugal traditional values and less interested in environmental issues—are reported in cases as diverse as China and Italy. Other conditions will be context specific and highly idiosyncratic. In Chapter 9, for instance, Cristina Vasilescu mentions post-communist overbuying by Romanian consumers: passing from restricted access to food during the communist regime to high availability afterwards contributed to buying more without paying attention to quality, seasonality, or provenience. Chapter 8 shows how Italians waste comparatively more unopened and fresh food with respect to other Europeans—an important piece of knowledge for tailoring awareness and information campaigns. As the last example, in Chapter 5, Cavatassi, Delve, and Maggio report how fishers in Indonesia use overfishing as a strategy to anticipate potential loss from their catches—a behaviour dealt with thanks to the provision of refrigeration technology. Research on these specific drivers can add precision to policy design and significantly enhance the effectiveness of interventions.

A second avenue of development concerns information that can support policy implementation. This means designing information tools that produce, release, and use data to support food businesses, donors, food recovery organisations, and charities engaging with FLW interventions. Several examples are mentioned in the volume, including registers of food recovery organisations to increase matching the demand and supply of surplus food (Chapter 9), development of guidelines and FAQs for complying with legislation (Chapters 6, 11 and 12), and ICT solutions that expose data on overproduction (Chapter 8). In Chapter 13, Anna R. Davies and Alwynne McGeever present a tool for reporting the impact of food recovery organisations, which also includes virtual networking for sharing practices. Circulating these types of data, including the solutions implemented by administrations, businesses, and associations, is fundamental for capacity building in tackling FLW.

Use existing data effectively

Producing more data is always good, but it is costly and requires time and resources. In the meantime, an efficient way of improving policy is to work creatively with the data we already have. There is a huge untapped potential for existing data to help reduce FLW.

One of the most telling examples in the previous pages is the use of weather forecasts and big data to improve demand forecasting, as reported in the case of Japan by Chen Liu (Chapter 10). The Japan Weather Association provides accurate forecasts that are shared with actors in the food chain and can incorporate consumers' experiences of the day, hence improving the accuracy of demand and avoiding order overestimation. Chen Liu also describes how the use of artificial intelligence to analyse sales data can improve the prediction of quantities of goods. Interestingly, these kinds of strategies are usable on different scales, from industries to single shops. In fact, they are also reported in Chapter 6, in which it is described how chefs in EU Committee premises use weather forecasts for predicting how many people will show up in the canteen and hence how many meals to prepare (sunny days attract people outdoor).

In the case of Italy, it is suggested how accounting data on the payments to farmers for overproduction under the EU Common Agricultural Policy (CAP) could help distinguish recurrent overproduction from truly exceptional crises and possibly take preventive actions. Finally, in Chapter 4, Qiushi Yue, Daniella Salazar Herrera, and Omar Benammour propose that better integration with social protection data already present in national and local registries can help target food redistribution initiatives to the most food-insecure people and scale up food assistance.

In all these cases, the data already exist; they only need to be analysed, interpreted, and sometimes integrated with other existing databases. This is not an easy undertaking but one that is worth starting.

Stress the multiple goals of FLW policy

Like all complex problems, FLW lies at the intersection of several disciplines, policy domains, and government bodies. Tackling FLW may produce wider effects in terms of food security, sustainability, or nutrition. These kinds of interactions are part of the complexity of the FLW problem, but they may also provide consensus over tackling FLW.

Many examples in the book present positive effects in which FLW interventions contribute simultaneously to multiple goals. In Chapter 5, Cavatassi, Delve, and Maggio show how actions aimed at food security also increase sustainability and reduce food losses in fishery, crops, and livestock. They review several tools—new infrastructures, provision of facilities, technological updates, and training initiatives—all producing these multiple effects.

In Chapter 11, Xiaohua Yu describes how the interaction between reducing FLW and food security takes national importance in China. In a country characterised by low self-sufficiency, fighting FLW is a further way to enhance the food supply potential and is a matter of national security against the risk of weaponising food dependence.

Finally, all cases of food recovery in the book stress their social implications. After the COVID-19 pandemic, food recovery and redistribution to people in need spread from countries where it was consolidated (the United Kingdom, Ireland, France, and Italy) to new places worldwide (e.g. in this volume, Romania, Japan, and Brazil). The capacity of food surplus redistribution to produce a wide variety of social impacts is relevant in both affluent and less affluent countries. In Chapter 4, the recovery of seafood bycatch also plays a fundamental role in enhancing the nutritional value of meals, providing fragile people with quality proteins otherwise unavailable.

The fact that actions for fighting FLW contribute to multiple goals not only has value per se—solving multiple problems at once—but may also provide a political advantage, offering a lever of consensus and a flexible platform for political strategy. On the one hand, this means that policy change may be supported by large coalitions that unite advocates who are active in several fields and that cross the boundaries of traditional policy domains. These large coalitions may help limit counter-strategies, such as cherry-picking (Head 2008), according to which only the consensual and most manageable side of a complex problem is addressed, whereas more fundamental changes are left out of the government agenda. On the other hand, advocates for policy change may also use an apparently opposite strategy: going venue shopping and finding the decision arena—environmental, social, health, food, or else—that offers the best prospects for reaching their policy goals (Pralle 2003).

Calibrate tools and exploit synergies

As highlighted in country cases, FLW policy typically comprises a varied set of tools, such as incentives, regulations, capacity building, information, and public services. The setup of a calibrated mix that produces synergies—that is having reinforcing effects—is a typical ambition of sound policy design (Nilsson et al. 2012; May, Sapotichne, and Workman 2006). The chapters report several examples that are worth discussing, with the caveat of being realistic on the scope for synergies.

Several chapters discuss the vertical coherence of initiatives implemented at different territorial scales. In Chapter 13, Anna R. Davies and Alwynne McGeever show how local interventions in Dublin, London, and Barcelona can be eased or hindered by the presence or absence of a national policy clarifying the legal framework of food redistribution and donation. A similar comment is made in Chapter 4 about Costa Rica, where the absence of a national food donation law creates several barriers to local donation programmes, barriers that are related to liability protection, food safety, quality regulations, and date labels. Finally, the same potential for vertical integration is reported in Chapter 11, in which the Chinese national regulation mandating consumers to eat all ordered food in restaurants (the so-called Empty Plate Movement) is coupled with local guidelines issued by cities to instruct food facilities on new business models, the efficient use of ingredients, monitoring, and other actions that can change the food environment.

Horizontal coherence between different tools at the same geographic scale is also reported extensively across the book. Barriers related to the uncertainty of the legal framework, for instance, are dealt with in many ways, typically by complementing regulatory provisions with guidelines and information campaigns. In Chapter 9, Cristina Vasilescu describes the establishment of a national register of food banks and intermediaries as a way to match the demand and supply of food surplus—a potentially relevant innovation to complement regulations and incentives favouring donations. In describing the neighbourhood food hubs implemented in Milan, Bartezzaghi and colleagues stress how they integrate logistics support, networking, and information sharing. Finally, Chapter 8 presents two additional examples of horizontal coherence. One concerns integrated communication, in which nutritional messages for a healthy diet and sustainability messages regarding FLW are conveyed together, not only increasing efficiency but also embedding FLW in a network of initiatives (those related to health) that is already extensive and well developed. The second example focuses on the coupling of fiscal incentives and bureaucratic simplifications to donations, which, together, can favour donating food over product destruction—a cumulative effect that fiscal incentives alone could not have.

Although synergies are obviously good, it is important to keep in mind that these (sometimes) coherent policy mixes are rarely the products of rational and encompassing design efforts. Rather, they are the results of a progressive layering of subsequent reforms, the patching of different tools and much trial and error (Daugbjerg and Swinbank 2016; Capano 2019). What may look now like a consistent and synergic policy mix is often the product of long-term policy evolutions, as described in the cases of France, Italy, China, Japan, and the United States. This is to remind us that the optimal array of policy tools or the all-encompassing reform may be long-term achievements and not the only or the more practical paths to policy change. Incrementalism (Lindblom 1959; Bendor 2015) and apparently suboptimal strategies, such as segmenting the problem (Dente 2014), may sometimes offer more tractable decision-making processes and deliver radical change in the long run.

Identify frictions and adverse interactive effects

The obvious counterpart of synergy is friction, which occurs when the interaction between different tools or policies produces adverse effects. The chapters in the book show several cases of such negative interactions, especially concerning the clash between different policy domains.

One example is the intersection of FLW with overall waste management, particularly the comparative costs and benefits of different alternatives to managing surplus food. In Chapter 13, Anna R. Davies and Alwynne McGeever comment that the disposal of edible food is a cheaper option than donations in Ireland. In Chapter 10, Chen Liu shows how, given Japan's shortage of available landfill sites, recycling and incineration are very advanced and much more developed than food recovery, which is relatively new and regards only a small portion of surplus food. Both the relative costs and the consolidation of waste management alternatives in terms of practices, policies, and players can make it difficult to switch from one option to another and climb the food waste hierarchy towards the preferred options. Solutions to this kind of frictions are manifold, starting with a better calibration of incentives to the development of more innovative ways to make prevention and donations more appealing, such as logistics support (Chapter 8 and 14), innovative procurement (Chapter 4), or green labels (Chapter 7).

Another notable case of friction is the possible clash between food safety and FLW policy. In the case of Romania, while the Food Waste Law allows food donations at any time in the last ten days before the minimal validity date, the regulations implemented by food safety authorities seem to forbid the transfer of food close to expiry in the last five days before the minimal validity date. A similar case is described for Italy, where it was reported that local health authorities impeded donations of food after the best-before date before an explicit legal provision was passed in 2016, although it was already established that such food was edible and safe. In the two cases, there are both legal and administrative clashes—between sectoral regulations and different administrative bodies.

These kinds of frictions are to be expected with other sectoral legislation and agencies and can create barriers and uncertainties that reduce effectiveness. A possible solution entails building institutional arrangements that internalise points of friction, such as setting up inter-administrative task forces or other forms of collaborative joined-up governments (Pollitt 2003). The EU Platform on Food Losses and Waste presented in Chapter 6 is a case of institutions that can help reach greater inter-policy coherence. Another example is given in Chapter 8, which describes how the Italian National Table for Fighting Food Waste (a consultative forum representing all food actors and government bodies), although relatively weak, may have some potential for anticipating and fixing administrative frictions. Similarly, Chapter 4 reports how the management of the Fund for European Aid to the Most Deprived (FEAD) within national administrations in charge of social protections can internalise some of the needed integration between food aid initiatives at the local level and overall social protection programmes. Notice, finally, that as exemplified by the case of the Milan food hubs (Chapter 14), food policies implemented at the local level may offer a natural context for highly integrated actions.

Ensure effective implementation

The distance between what is decided and what is implemented is an old topic in the policy sciences (Sabatier and Mazmanian 1980; O'Toole 2000; Lipsky 2010; Pressman and Wildavsky 1973). Decisions can be met with formal compliance, tokenism, resistance, and limited enforcement. At a time when food waste is part of the mainstream political agenda, there is an actual risk that something needs to be done (Kingdon 1984), but decisions are followed by limited commitments and implementation gaps.

There certainly exist some *self-implementing* policies—interventions that need little control, money, or enforcement—but these are rare. A relevant example is described by Broad Leib and Ardura about the United States. Passed in 1996, the Bill Emerson Good Samaritan Food Donation Act provides comprehensive civil and criminal liability protection to food donors and non-profit organisations that distribute food donations to those in need, as long as they act without gross negligence or intentional misconduct. One of the main advantages of the law is precisely to have an automatic implementation: it does not require spending funds, reducing revenues or increasing enforcement; it only changes the structure of private rights, making legal claims difficult and decreasing donors' risks. However, even in such an easy case, together with the great results of the Emerson Act, the authors mention implementation problems, such as a lack of awareness and a lack of clarity, both related to the absence (at least until 2018) of a governmental office or agency maintaining awareness and issuing implementing regulations and guidance documents.

In most interventions, implementation is essential and can easily become problematic. In the case of France, Marie Mourad reports several examples of the distance between written regulations and their actual implementation. The 2016 French law mandates that all large food businesses must follow the food waste hierarchy, but the government has no capacity to monitor compliance. Similarly, the prohibition of destroying edible food clashes with a levy that is negligible and with the limited administrative capacity to control supermarkets. Even the most famous obligation in the law—the one involving the signing of contracts with food banks for donating surplus—is milder than it appears; in fact, no minimum quantity of food or regularity of donations is required.

Similar cases are reported across the whole volume. The Romanian Food Waste Law described in Chapter 9, for instance, had a tortuous political process: approved in 2016, suspended in 2017, substituted by a new law in 2018, and followed by the implementing regulation in 2019 and by further amendments in 2020. This journey watered down the law from a set of compulsory measures to a limited set of voluntary interventions. The sole obligation imposed on food businesses was to draft a yearly plan on food waste prevention and submit it to the Ministry of the Environment. Although apparently a tough intervention, the law established no control or transparency mechanism, and—at least until now—no plan has been published.

Finally, although we do not have data on implementation, the policy evolution in China helps illustrate the variable ability for implementing programmes. Fighting food waste started as an anti-corruption policy that prohibits extravagance in public administration. The hierarchical organisation of public bodies and the limitation of the prohibition to public officials may have ensured a widespread capacity to control and sanction behaviours. The extension of the policy through the recent Empty Plate Movement, with clients in restaurants being obliged to eat everything they order, brings implementation efforts to a whole new level.

In conclusion, the simple reminder is not to forget to factor in implementation when assessing the feasibility of decisions and their likely impacts. It is in their implementation that most policies fail, and the literature is rich not only with extraordinary cases of implementation gaps but also with methods of analysis and recommendations (for a review, see Hill and Hupe 2002).

Explore the non-programme features of success

The previous section provided classic examples of decisions followed by implementation gaps. A more general point is that policy designs work depending on a set of conditions—how target groups and beneficiaries react to the policy, contextual features, and so forth—that are not part of the design of the policy and may be found only in some contexts. This is a moment of frantic innovation in food loss and waste policy; tens of new solutions are promoted, but how and why they actually work is seldom examined. The possible risk of focusing on formal designs is promoting the diffusion of one-size-fits-all solutions that will necessarily deliver limited results across contexts.

One obvious example of a non-designed but fundamental element of success regards food recovery associations. They are key implementers of any programme favouring donations, but their resources are varied and often limited, magnifying or hampering the effects of public initiatives (be they regulations, incentives, or information campaigns). In Chapter 7, Marie Mourad recalls how the 2016 obligation to sign a contract for recovering food was softened in response to food bank representatives who feared receiving too much food and food of too low quality, having limited capacity for redistribution and fearing donation dumping. All the chapters on local initiatives describe several challenges that recovery organisations may face. In the case of London described in Chapter 13, for instance, it is described how Be Enriched copes with the typical problem of a lack of resources by developing alternative income streams, such as a café, which can reduce their dependency on once-off donations. Overall, the capacity of actors in food recovery and redistribution (e.g. whether they have access to logistics infrastructures and a cold-chain technology) and their presence across the country (e.g. whether they operate evenly in both urban and rural settings) are fundamental components of whether and how any donation policy will work in practice.

Another obvious example regards businesses, whose engagement or resistance to policy may sensibly change impacts. Some interesting examples of active engagement are reported in the case of Japan, in which Chen Liu presents the results of the reform of the one-third rule and best-before date. In the case of the EU Committee premises, Fabrizio D'Angelo describes how reducing food waste entailed exceptional commitment: developing a waste calculator in collaboration with an external consultant, setting up a monitoring system based on an analysis of weather forecasts and consumption data, acquiring new techniques for warming up and cooling food, investing in some small infrastructures and even organising a bike delivery service to help food recovery organisations. This kind of commitment is not to be expected by all food actors in all contexts but can make a major difference in how an intervention works. Chapter 8 shows how the legal permission to donate food after the best-before date is met with resistance by donors, who—notwithstanding they enjoy legal protection—fear food safety issues and the reputational consequences of food mismanagement. This can bring food businesses to make conservative choices notwithstanding favourable legislation (e.g. donating only certain categories of safe food, such as bread, pastries, and vegetables).

Here, the advice is to investigate in depth how interventions work, also by paying attention to all those factors that can magnify or neutralise the effect of the policy but are not part of its design. One way to do this is to work with theories of change, logic models, theory-based and realistic approaches to evaluation (Funnell and Rogers 2011; Chen and Rossi 1983; Pawson and Tilley 1997; Busetti 2019), all methods that can help avoid replication errors related to contextual fitness (Bardach 2004; Barzelay 2007; Busetti and Dente 2018).

Recast food recovery and redistribution

The use of surplus food for human consumption is ranked second in the food waste hierarchy and can be a fundamental tool for emergency assistance, increasing food security and income and providing opportunities for business and social innovation. The chapters highlight critical points and prospects for innovation that are worth discussing.

First, an evaluation of the impacts of food recovery should examine how much recovered food actually ends up being consumed by people in need. In the case of Sao Paulo (Chapter 15), Luciana Marques Vieira and Daniele Eckert Matzembacher mention that recipients of donated food may be unable to cook part of it because they lack stoves; this food will become household waste and would not provide aid to people in need. In Chapter 7, Marie Mourad raises a more general point about how donations may include second-class, junk or weird food, providing a disproportionate quantity of added fat, sugar, and salt. As mentioned in several chapters, only part of donations ends up being consumed by beneficiaries, and the risk of donation dumping is real. This means that the amount of food donated or the number of meals recovered when expressed in terms of calories are poor estimates of the value of food recovery. Having additional data on the downstream of redistribution—how much surplus food is actually consumed and what its nutritional value is—could allow for a more comprehensive evaluation of the impact of this option in terms of waste reduction.

Second, food recovery may cannibalise efforts at prevention, a danger mentioned in both chapters on Italy and France. FLW is a multifaceted phenomenon that can be tackled from many perspectives and with different interventions. As mentioned, a typical risk of complex policy problems is cherry-picking those interventions that are consensual and require the least change while avoiding more radical reforms of the food system. In this respect, although it is the only alternative to wasting food in many cases, food recovery may slow down more radical changes.

Finally, there is much scope for innovation in food recovery and redistribution. If food security is a public goal, intermediaries and charities cannot be substitutes for public programmes, nor can food surplus be the foundation of such aid. The Milan Neighbourhood Food Hubs are notable cases of the direct participation of public bodies in food recovery. The municipality of Milan and Politecnico di Milano, a public university, have partnered with private and social actors to create hubs that can enhance the logistics of food surpluses. The presence of both the municipality and the university worked as a quality signal certifying correct management and monitoring, hence increasing donors' trust and consequently favouring their participation.

The case studies also testify to the emergence of several examples of new models departing from the typical free redistribution from intermediaries to charities: direct donations to beneficiaries and provision of surplus food at discounted prices (Chapters 9 and 12), recovery by asking fees instead of doing it for free (Chapter 7), transforming surplus food into value-added products and creating community engagement (Chapter 13). As already mentioned, Chapter 4 describes the possible advantages of scaling up food aid interventions by embedding them into wider social protection programmes. In the case of Campo Favela, Luciana Marques Vieira and Daniele Eckert Matzembacker show how—in the disruption created by the COVID-19 pandemic—an innovative model connecting farmers with low-income families and slum dwellers could provide fresh products at lower prices and at the same time pay fair remuneration to farmers. In appraising the prospects for the development of such models, Emily M. Broad Leib and Ariel Ardura raise a general point worth reminding—how outdated regulations may hinder such innovations, potentially inhibiting solutions that are different from the ones protected by the law.

References

Bardach, Eugene. 2004. "Presidential Address? The Extrapolation Problem: How Can We Learn From the Experience of Others?" *Journal of Policy Analysis and Management* 23 (2): 205–20. https://doi.org/10.1002/pam.20000.

Barzelay, Michael. 2007. "Learning From Second-Hand Experience: Methodology for Extrapolation-Oriented Case Research." *Governance* 20 (3): 521–43. https://doi.org/10.1111/j.1468-0491.2007.00369.x.

Bendor, Jonathan. 2015. "Incrementalism: Dead yet Flourishing." *Public Administration Review* 75 (2): 194–205. https://doi.org/10.1111/PUAR.12333.

Busetti, Simone. 2019. "A Theory-Based Evaluation of Food Waste Policy: Evidence from Italy." *Food Policy* 88. https://doi.org/10.1016/j.foodpol.2019.101749.

Busetti, Simone, and Bruno Dente. 2018. "Designing Multi-Actor Implementation: A Mechanism-Based Approach." *Public Policy and Administration* 33 (1): 46–65. https://doi.org/10.1177/0952076716681207.

Capano, Giliberto. 2019. "Reconceptualizing Layering—From Mode of Institutional Change to Mode of Institutional Design: Types and Outputs." *Public Administration* 97 (3): 590–604. https://doi.org/10.1111/padm.12583.

Chen, Huey Tsyh, and Peter H. Rossi. 1983. "Evaluating With Sense: The Theory-Driven Approach." *Evaluation and Program Planning* 7 (3): 283–302. https://doi.org/10.1177/01 93841X8300700301.

Daugbjerg, Carsten, and Alan Swinbank. 2016. "Three Decades of Policy Layering and Politically Sustainable Reform in the European Union's Agricultural Policy." *Governance* 29 (2): 265–80. https://doi.org/10.1111/GOVE.12171.

Dente, Bruno. 2014. *Understanding Policy Decisions*. Cham: Springer. https://doi.org/10.1007/978-3-319-02520-9.

Funnell, Sue C., and Patricia J. Rogers. 2011. *Purposeful Program Theory*. San Francisco: Jossey-Bass.

Head, Brian W. 2008. "Wicked Problems in Public Policy." *Public Policy* 3 (2): 101–18.

Hill, Michael, and Peter Hupe. 2002. *Implementing Public Policy*. London: Sage.

Kingdon, John W. 1984. *Agendas, Alternatives and Public Policies*. Boston: Little, Brown and Company.

Lindblom, Charles. 1959. "The Science of 'Muddling Through'." *Public Administration Review* 19 (2): 79–88.

Lipsky, Michael. 2010. *Street-Level Bureaucracy: Dilemmas of the Individual in Public Service*. New York: Russell Sage Foundation.

May, Peter J., Joshua Sapotichne, and Samuel Workman. 2006. "Policy Coherence and Policy Domains." *Policy Studies Journal* 34 (3): 381–403. https://doi.org/10.1111/J.1541-0072.2006.00178.X.

Nilsson, Måns, Tony Zamparutti, Jan Erik Petersen, Björn Nykvist, Peter Rudberg, and Jennifer Mcguinn. 2012. "Understanding Policy Coherence: Analytical Framework and Examples of Sector—Environment Policy Interactions in the EU." *Environmental Policy and Governance* 22 (6): 395–423. https://doi.org/10.1002/EET.1589.

O'Toole, Laurence J. 2000. "Research on Policy Implementation: Assessment and Prospects." *Journal of Public Administration Research and Theory* 10 (2): 263–88. https://doi.org/10.1093/oxfordjournals.jpart.a024270.

Pawson, Ray, and Nick Tilley. 1997. *Realistic Evaluation*. London: Sage Publications.

Pollitt, Christopher. 2003. "Joined-up Government: A Survey." *Political Studies Review* 1 (1): 34–49. https://doi.org/10.1111/1478-9299.00004.

Pralle, Sarah B. 2003. "Venue Shopping, Political Strategy, and Policy Change: The Internationalization of Canadian Forest Advocacy." *Journal of Public Policy* 23 (3): 233–60. https://doi.org/10.1017/S0143814X03003118.

Pressman, Jeffrey L., and Aaron Wildavsky. 1973. *Implementation*. Berkeley: University of California Press.

Rottenburg, Richard, Sally E. Merry, Sung-Joon Park, and Johanna Mugler, eds. 2015. *The World of Indicators: The Making of Governmental Knowledge through Quantification*. Cambridge: Cambridge University Press.

Sabatier, Paul, and Daniel Mazmanian. 1980. "The Implementation of Public Policy: A Framework of Analysis." *Policy Studies Journal* 8 (4): 538–60. https://doi.org/10.1111/j.1541-0072.1980.tb01266.x.

Index

Note: Page numbers in *italics* indicate a figure and page numbers in **bold** indicate a table on the corresponding page.

Fukui Prefectural Federation of Women's Associations 163
Fund for European Aid to the Most Deprived (FEAD) 67–68, 72, 257

General Health Law (Costa Rica) 69
gleaning 48, 195
'*Good Food Strategy*' - Brussels 100
Good Samaritan Law (law 155/2003) 124, 126, 228
Good Samaritans Act 53, 126
Green Deal 99
greenhouse gas (GHG) emissions 1, 14, 31, 42, 86, 192
green water 31–32
grey water 31–32

High Level Panel of Experts 30
Hospitality and Food Service Agreement 50
hospitality sector 26, 28, 52, 113
households 1, 15, 19, 20, 21, 26, 29, 31, 32–33, 34, 35, 46, 49, 51, 52, 54, 64–65, 67, 68, 69, 70, 71, 72, 78, 79, 83, 84–87, 93, 98, 125–126, 132, 139, 141, 157, 158, 160, 161, 163, 164, 169–171, *172*, 179, 180–181, 188, 189, 192, 260

India 34
Indonesia 80–81, 89–90
information provision 51
information technology infrastructure 53, 135–136
infrastructure 25, 30, 47, 48, 53, 63, 65, 79, 80, 81, 83, 88, 89, 101, 102, 135–136, 148, 152, 153, 169, 177, 197, 219, 225, 227, 232, 250
innovation grants 47–48
Institute of Grocery Distribution (IGD) 214
Inter-ministerial Committee for Food Security and Nutrition (CAISAN) 241
International Fund for Agricultural Development (IFAD): action to reduce food loss 79–90; CCDP - Indonesia 80–81, 89–90; crop sector operations 83–86; fisheries sector operations 80–83; focus of operations 79; Food Loss Analysis methodology 79; livestock operations 86–88; mandate 79; PASP Project - Rwanda 83–84; PNAAFA-LGF Project - Lower Guinea and Faranah Expansion 85–86, 90; PROPESCA Project - Mozambique 81–83, 90; RDDP Rwanda 87–88;

SDCP - Kenya 86–87; Strategic Framework 79; Strategic Objectives 81; TLMSP Project - Timor-Leste 83–84
Ireland: Climate Action Plan 2019 211; 'Environmental Protection Agency Food Waste Charter' 210–211; FEAD 67–68, 72; FoodCloud 67, 73, 211–214; food donation 255, 256; food redistribution 211, 212, 213–214; Food Safety Authority of Ireland 211; 'Food waste prevention roadmap' 211; 'National Agri-Food Strategy' 211, 213; national policy 210–211; 'Waste Action Plan for a Circular Economy: Ireland's National Waste Policy 2020–2025, A' 210
Ireland Department of Employment Affairs and Social Protection (DEASP) 67, 73
Israel 202
Italy: best-before date regulation 133–135; brief history of policy 126–127; chronology of food waste policy **126**; deductibility of VAT 226; Emilia Romagna Region 135–136, 137; fiscal and bureaucratic incentives 127–130; food donation 124, 125, 126–131, 133–134, 137–138, 224–236; food loss and waste policy 124–138, 220–221, 253; food recovery 126–127, 130, 133–134, 224–236; Food Waste Law (law 166/2016) 124, 127, **128**, 129, 130–131, 133, 228; Good Samaritan Law (law 155/2003) 124, 126, 228; law 133/1999 127, 228; Legislative Decree 35/2005 228; Legislative Decree 460/1997 228; Legislative Decree 633/1972 127; liability protection 202; Milan 224–225, 227–236, 256, 261; Ministry of Agriculture 132; National Observatory on Food Surplus, Recovery and Waste 125, 132–133; National Table for Fighting Food Waste 131–132, 257; Neighbourhood Hubs Against Food Waste 224–225, 228–236, 256, 261; quantifying food waste 125–126; Research Council for Agricultural Research and Economics 132–133; waste tax 130–131

Japan: animal feed policy 53; 'Basic Act' 158–159; best-before date regulation 164, 165–168, 259; business practices 165–168; Cabinet Office, Ministry of Education, Culture, Sports, Science and Technology 160, 165; civil society practices 168–170; Consumer Affairs

Printed in the United States
by Baker & Taylor Publisher Services